TRACES OF THE PROPHETS

Advances in the Study of Islam

Series Editors: Abbas Aghdassi and Aaron W. Hughes

Advances in the Study of Islam publishes cutting-edge research that reflects the long history and geographic breadth of Islam. It seeks to rethink traditional literary canons while simultaneously offering innovative and alternative approaches to push beyond traditional understandings of Islam. The series provides a platform for creative studies spanning:

- Disciplines including religious studies, legal studies, archaeology and anthropology
- Theoretical questions including historical, philological, ethnographic, comparative and redescriptive
- Time periods from late antiquity to the present
- Geographical regions including the so-called Arab World, South Asia, Africa, Iran and the Persian World, Europe and North America

The series highlights both disciplinary and inter-disciplinary approaches to Islamic studies and challenges existing paradigms and norms by providing alternatives for the study of Islam. By doing this it pushes the study of Islam to the forefront of larger conversations in the Humanities and Social Sciences

Available Titles

New Methods in the Study of Islam
Abbas Aghdassi and Aaron W. Hughes

Traces of the Prophets: Relics and Sacred Spaces in Early Islam
Adam Bursi

edinburghuniversitypress.com/series/asi

TRACES OF THE PROPHETS

Relics and Sacred Spaces in Early Islam

Adam Bursi

EDINBURGH
University Press

Edinburgh University Press is one of the leading university presses in the UK. We publish academic books and journals in our selected subject areas across the humanities and social sciences, combining cutting-edge scholarship with high editorial and production values to produce academic works of lasting importance. For more information visit our website: edinburghuniversitypress.com

Edinburgh University Press Ltd
13 Infirmary Street
Edinburgh EH1 1LT

Typeset in 11/15 EB Garamond by
IDSUK (DataConnection) Ltd, and
printed and bound in Great Britain

A CIP record for this book is available from the British Library

ISBN 978 1 3995 2232 8 (hardback)
ISBN 978 1 3995 2234 2 (webready PDF)
ISBN 978 1 3995 2235 9 (epub)

CONTENTS

List of Abbreviations	vi
Acknowledgements	vii
Introduction	1
1 Grave Markers: Rhetoric and Materiality of Relic and Tomb Veneration in Early Islam	23
2 A Clear Sign: The Maqām Ibrāhīm and Early Islamic Continuity and Difference	47
3 Inverted Inventions: Finding and Hiding Holy Bodies in the First Islamic Century	80
4 Paradoxes and Problems of the Prophetic Body: Muḥammad's Corpse and Tomb	121
5 Places where the Prophet Prayed: Ritualising the Prophet's Traces	166
Epilogue	218
Bibliography	228
Index	269

ABBREVIATIONS

BSOAS	*Bulletin of the School of Oriental and African Studies*
CSCO	Corpus Scriptorum Christianorum Orientalium
DOP	*Dumbarton Oaks Papers*
EI[2]	*Encyclopaedia of Islam*, Second Edition
EI[3]	*Encyclopaedia of Islam*, Third Edition
EQ	*Encyclopaedia of the Qur'ān*
HTR	*Harvard Theological Review*
ILS	*Islamic Law and Society*
JAIS	*Journal of Arabic and Islamic Studies*
JAOS	*Journal of the American Oriental Society*
JNES	*Journal of Near Eastern Studies*
JSAI	*Jerusalem Studies in Arabic and Islam*
JSJ	*Journal for the Study of Judaism in the Persian, Hellenistic and Roman Period*
PG	*Patrologiae cursus completus, Series graeca* (ed. J.-P. Migne)
PO	*Patrologia Orientalis*
RMMM	*Revue des mondes musulmans et de la Méditerranée*

ACKNOWLEDGEMENTS

This book was assisted and influenced by a variety of people and places. Thanks to the itinerant nature of academic life – combined with the multifaceted complications of the ongoing pandemic since 2020 – it was researched, written, discussed and presented at several universities and other places, with the input of many colleagues and friends along the way.

The book's basic ideas emerged during my graduate work in the Department of Near Eastern Studies at Cornell University. Gestures towards what would wind up here appear in my dissertation, written under the guidance of Kim Haines-Eitzen, David Powers and Ross Brann. I'm extremely grateful for the support and expertise that they have each shared with me. I was also lucky to take classes at Cornell with Shawkat Toorawa, Lauren Monroe and Éric Rebillard, and to have many great colleagues and friends there, including Dustin Dash, Lorena Dremel Nash, Sarah J. Pearce, Hamza M. Zafer, Kristen Streahle, Rae Grabowski, Julie Balazs, Kyle Grove, Linda Ósp Heimisdóttir, Yael Wender and Rama Alhabian.

Post-doctoral positions provided the crucial time and resources necessary to pursue the research threads woven here, as well as colleagues who generously offered their insights and thought through questions with me. At the Marco Institute for Medieval and Renaissance Studies at the University of Tennessee, Knoxville, I greatly benefited from working and speaking with both faculty and graduate students, especially Tina Shepardson, Manuela Ceballos, Lauren

Whitnah, Alison Vacca, Gregor Kalas and Jacob Latham. At Utrecht University, I was very lucky to be part of a research group that included Christian Lange, Eyad Abuali, Simon Leese and Arash Ghajarjazi. Many other colleagues in the Department of Philosophy and Religious Studies at UU, and from other Dutch universities, were also kind and thoughtful interlocutors and friends, including Nina ter Laan, Nella van den Brandt, May Shaddel, Pieter Coppens, Cornelis van Lit, Hayat Ahlili, Melle Lyklema, Albertina Oegema, Katja Rakow, Birgit Meyer and Mehdi Sajid.

I've also been fortunate to be able to share this work-in-progress at various stages with audiences at conferences, seminars and invited talks. Richard McGregor invited me to present my work to a faculty seminar on material cultures at Vanderbilt University; Finbarr Barry Flood invited me to give a talk at the Silsila: Center for Material Histories at New York University; and Kevin Reinhart welcomed me to a workshop at Dartmouth College on concepts of ritual throughout Islamic history. Iman Abdulfattah, Abigail Balbale, Barry Flood and Usman Hamid graciously accepted my own invitation to participate in a panel on 'Historicizing Relic Practices in Islamic Pieties and Societies' for the 2020 online Annual Meeting of the Middle East Studies Association. The questions, suggestions and presentations offered by the participants at these venues were extremely helpful for many aspects of this book.

I'm especially grateful to everyone who read drafts of the book, chapters from it, and/or my book proposal, and provided me with their insightful feedback. This list includes: Eyad Abuali, Antonia Bosanquet, Manuela Ceballos, Arash Ghajarjazi, Kim Haines-Eitzen, Christian Lange, Simon Leese, Daisy Livingston, Ryan Lynch, Paula Manstetten, Michael Penn, David Powers, Arafat Razzaque and Ignacio Sanchez. Collectively and individually, they all helped make this a much better book. I'm grateful also for the book's inclusion in the EUP series 'Advances in the Study of Islam', edited by Abbas Aghdassi and Aaron Hughes. They, and the anonymous reviewers, likewise helped improve this book considerably. Any outstanding issues are, of course, solely my own responsibility.

Finally, I'm thankful for my family and friends, who have supported me in innumerable psychological, spiritual and material ways. My parents, Michael and Charlotte Bursi, and my in-laws, Mark Dahlager and Laura Melnick, have all been crucial supports. My friends, sprinkled over the world, have been sources of joy in these often-difficult times. Most importantly, the person who has been through this whole process with me, from Cornell to now, has been my wife, Elana Dahlager. I don't think I would have had the energy or will to finish this project without her emotional support, her critical reader's eye, and (maybe most importantly) her humour. I wouldn't have chosen anyone else to get trapped with in an apartment in the Netherlands during a plague. This book is dedicated to her.

INTRODUCTION

Sometime in the year 184 or 185 of the Hijrī calendar (i.e. 800 or 801 CE), a Muslim scholar named Wakīʿ b. al-Jarrāḥ was travelling in the city of Mecca. While there, Wakīʿ reported *ḥadīths* to some listeners: a well-known practice among many eighth- and ninth-century Muslims, who related oral reports about the Prophet Muḥammad and his Companions in order to learn about the practices and stories of the primordial Islamic community. One of Wakīʿ's traditions, though, did not invoke a witty saying of the Prophet, describe how he had performed a particular ritual, or narrate the past glories of battles fought by the early Muslims. Instead, Wakīʿ's narrated tradition described in graphic detail what had happened to the Prophet's body after his death: 'When the Messenger of God died, he was not buried until his belly swelled up and his little finger bent.'[1] According to this short tradition, the Prophet Muḥammad's corpse was not buried until signs of decay had already

[1] Yaʿqūb b. Sufyān al-Fasawī, *Kitāb al-Maʿrifa wa-l-taʾrīkh*, ed. Akram Ḍiyāʾ al-ʿUmarī, 4 vols (Medina: Maktabat al-Dār, 1989), 1:175–6; Ibn ʿAsākir, *Taʾrīkh Madīnat Dimashq*, ed. Muḥibb al-Dīn Abū Saʿīd ʿUmar b. Gharāma al-ʿAmrawī, 80 vols (Beirut: Dār al-Fikr: 1995–2001), 63:102–3; Shams al-Dīn Muḥammad b. Aḥmad al-Dhahabī, *Siyar aʿlām al-nubalāʾ*, ed. Shuʿayb al-Arnāʾūṭ et al., 25 vols (Beirut: Muʾassasat al-Risāla, 1981–8), 9:163; al-Dhahabī, *Taʾrīkh al-Islām wa-wafayāt al-mashāhīr wa-l-aʿlām*, ed. ʿUmar ʿAbd al-Salām al-Tadmurī, 53 vols (Beirut: Dār al-Kitāb al-ʿArabī, 1987–2000), 13 [191–200]:452–4. These

begun to appear on the body, with his belly swelling from collected fluids and his finger bent from rigor mortis.

The context for Wakīʿ's reporting of this particular *ḥadīth* goes unrecorded, and our sources differ on what happened next. But, whatever the case, Wakīʿ's report about the Prophet's corpse got him into a rather sticky situation. According to one version of these events, when the governor of Mecca heard what Wakīʿ had said about the Prophet, he imprisoned Wakīʿ and planned to kill him, going so far as to build a platform to carry out a public execution. With Wakīʿ in dire trouble, his colleague, the respected scholar Sufyān b. ʿUyayna, interceded with the Meccan governor, noting that Wakīʿ was a well-connected man whose family would complain to the caliph in Baghdad. Seeing the complications that this case might cause him, the governor relented and freed Wakīʿ, who promptly fled to Medina. However, Wakīʿ's words about the Prophet had preceded him to Medina, where a group planned to reverse the Meccan governor's leniency and stone Wakīʿ to death. Catching wind of this plot while on the road, Wakīʿ deviated from his planned route and retreated homewards to Kūfa in Iraq.

The Prophet's body was a contested subject in the early centuries of Islam.[2] The particular *ḥadīth* that brought so much scrutiny upon Wakīʿ was just one of the many narratives circulating throughout the early Islamic world that related drastically different details about the events surrounding the Prophet's death. The response that Wakīʿ received reflects the hostility that some early Muslims displayed towards the notion that the Prophet Muḥammad had simply died and decomposed like a normal human. In fact, in one version of the story, Wakīʿ defends his report about the Prophet's putrefaction by noting this social context surrounding the Prophet's death: 'Many of the Messenger of God's Companions said, "The Messenger of God did not die!"

narratives about Wakīʿ are discussed in Muhammad Qasim Zaman, *Religion and Politics Under the Early ʿAbbāsids: The Emergence of the Proto-Sunnī Elite* (Leiden: Brill, 1997), 142–3; Krisztina Szilágyi, 'After the Prophet's Death: Christian-Muslim Polemic and the Literary Images of Muhammad' (PhD diss., Princeton University, 2014), 121–32.

[2] For recent examinations of aspects of the Prophet's body and its interpretation by Muslim scholars, see Michael Muhammad Knight, *Muhammad's Body: Baraka Networks and the Prophetic Assemblage* (Chapel Hill: University of North Carolina Press, 2020); Denis Gril, 'Le corps du Prophète', *RMMM* 113–14 (2006): 37–57.

So, God wanted to show them a sign of his death.'[3] Pious disbelief in the Prophet's mortal death indeed caused several variant narratives about the nature of his corporeal afterlife. In some stories, rather than a mouldering corpse, Muḥammad's body remained redolent with sweet aroma and exhibited none of the decay usually found on the dead. According to these traditions, Muḥammad's was no ordinary body, but one that manifested his prophetic status even in death.

Wakīʿ's experience illustrates how these differing conceptions of the Prophet's body were not mere curiosities or obscure academic debates, but could be closely connected to vital issues of Islamic belief and identity. The crime that Wakīʿ had allegedly committed with his controversial *ḥadīth* is not specified in the extant narratives, but his words may have been understood as slandering the Prophet: a capital offence in this period, as speaking defamatory words about the Prophet was 'considered as an act of blasphemy and disbelief'.[4] Indeed, just a few years before Wakīʿ's misadventure, the chief judge of Fusṭāṭ reportedly encountered a Coptic Christian who said: 'Poor Muḥammad! He tells you that you will be in heaven, but is he there now? Poor man, his wealth did not help him when the dogs were eating his legs!'[5] Much as the Meccan governor planned to execute Wakīʿ for his *ḥadīth*, the Egyptian judge ruled that this Copt should be beheaded for his unkind words about the Prophet's

[3] Ibn ʿAsākir, *Ta'rīkh*, 63:100–1; al-Dhahabī, *Siyar*, 9:160; al-Dhahabī, *Ta'rīkh*, 13 [191–200]:451.

[4] *EI*[2], s.v. 'Shatm' (Lutz Wiederhold). For examples in early texts, see ʿAbd al-Razzāq b. Hammām al-Ṣanʿānī, *al-Muṣannaf*, ed. Ḥabīb al-Raḥmān al-Aʿẓamī. 11 vols (Beirut: al-Maktab al-Islāmī, 1983), 5:307–8; Abū Bakr Ibn Abī Shayba, *al-Muṣannaf*, ed. Ḥamad b. ʿAbd Allāh al-Jumʿa and Muḥammad b. Ibrāhīm al-Luḥaydān, 16 vols (Riyadh: Maktabat al-Rushd, 2004), 13: 136–7; Abū Bakr Aḥmad b. Muḥammad al-Khallāl, *Ahl al-milal wa-l-ridda wa-l-zanādiqa wa-tārik al-ṣalāt wa-l-farā'iḍ min Kitāb al-Jāmiʿ*, ed. Ibrāhīm b. Ḥamad b. Sulṭān, 2 vols (Riyadh: Maktabat al-Maʿārif, 1996), 1:339–42; ʿAbd Allāh b. Wahb b. Muslim al-Qurashī, *Kitāb al-Muḥāraba min al-Muwaṭṭa'*, ed. Miklos Muranyi (Beirut: Dār al-Gharb al-Islāmī, 2002), 76–7.

[5] Abū ʿUmar Muḥammad b. Yūsuf al-Kindī al-Miṣrī, *Kitāb al-Wulāt wa-kitāb al-quḍāt*, ed. Rhuvon Guest (Leiden: Brill, 1912), 382–3. The judge involved was al-Mufaḍḍal b. Faḍāla (d. 181/797), who held this position during the years 168–9/785–6 and again in 174–7/790–3. For his biography, see Matthew Tillier, 'Deux papyrus judiciaires de Fusṭāṭ (IIe/VIIIe siècle)', *Chronique d'Égypte* 89, fasc. 178 (2014): 426–8.

corpse.[6] Such a response suggests the affront of Wakīʿ's words: whatever the charge against him, his *ḥadīth* struck listeners as the kind of statement that no true Muslim would utter.[7]

The blasphemous or heretical implication of Wakīʿ's *ḥadīth* is further emphasised in another version of his story, in which Wakīʿ's fate is debated in Mecca before the ʿAbbāsid caliph Hārūn al-Rashīd (r. 170–93/786–809). On one side, Sufyān b. ʿUyayna defends Wakīʿ as simply having reported a *ḥadīth*: a perfectly normal act, with no reflection on his character. On the other side, the Meccan scholar ʿAbd al-Majīd b. ʿAbd al-ʿAzīz b. Rawwād (d. 206/821–2) argues that relating this *ḥadīth* reveals that 'in [Wakīʿ's] heart is deception (*ghishsh*) towards the Prophet'.[8] In ʿAbd al-Majīd's eyes, the belief in Wakīʿ's heart – and his identity as a Muslim – was called into question by his relating a narrative depicting the Prophet as a decaying body. Though Wakīʿ managed to escape execution, his *ḥadīth* placed him on the fault line between acceptable and unacceptable belief/behaviour and, in this case, between life and death.

Wakīʿ's story attests in particularly dramatic form to the importance of the issues that this book explores. As the hostile response to Wakīʿ's *ḥadīth* illustrates, the bodies of figures like the Prophet Muḥammad were powerful

[6] On this story and its connections to other texts, including the topos of wild dogs and the Prophet's corpse, see Szilágyi, 'After the Prophet's Death', 25–9; Szilágyi, 'A Prophet Like Jesus? Christians and Muslims Debating Muḥammad's Death', *JSAI* 36 (2009): 135–7.

[7] Szilágyi, 'After the Prophet's Death', 129. It is worth noting that the governor's planned punishment for Wakīʿ (execution, followed by public mortification) was used by the Umayyad and ʿAbbāsid dynasties to humiliate and discourage rebels and heretics. Sean W. Anthony, *Crucifixion and Death as Spectacle: Umayyad Crucifixion in its Late Antique Context* (New Haven: American Oriental Society, 2014), 51–64; Andrew Marsham, 'Public Execution in the Umayyad Period: Early Islamic Punitive Practice and Its Late Antique Contexts', *JAIS* 11 (2011): 101–36; Gerald Hawting, 'The Case of Jaʿd b. Dirham and the Punishment of "Heretics" in the Early Caliphate', in *Public Violence in Islamic Societies: Power, Discipline, and the Construction of the Public Sphere, 7th–19th Centuries* CE, ed. Christian Lange and Maribel Fierro (Edinburgh: Edinburgh University Press, 2009), 27–41; Steven Judd, 'Muslim Persecution of Heretics during the Marwānid Period (64–132/684–750)', *Al-Masāq* 23 (2011): 1–14.

[8] ʿAbd Allāh b. ʿAdī al-Jurjānī, *al-Kāmil fī ḍuʿafāʾ al-rijāl*, 7 vols (Beirut: Dār al-Fikr, 1984), 5:1983; Ibn ʿAsākir, *Taʾrīkh*, 63:101–2; al-Dhahabī, *Siyar*, 9:164; al-Dhahabī, *Taʾrīkh*, 13 [191–200]:454; al-Dhahabī, *Mīzān al-iʿtidāl fī naqd al-rijāl*, ed. Muḥammad Riḍwān ʿIrqsūsī, 5 vols (Beirut: Dār al-Risāla al-ʿĀlamiyya, 2009), 2:566.

symbols of religious identity for many early Muslims. In the stories that early Muslims told about Muḥammad's life, his body appeared as a fount of miraculous power: capable of healing the sick, feeding multitudes and supplying water from his fingertips, among many other feats. Like Muḥammad's body, those of other prophets, martyrs and imams likewise reflected these individuals' holiness by producing miracles during their lives and failing to decay after their deaths. Such figures even appear in the conclusion to the story of Wakīʿ and the Meccan governor. Praised for releasing Wakīʿ, the governor immediately regretted not punishing him: he had just remembered the story of how the corpses of the martyrs of the Battle of Uḥud (fought in the year 3/625) had been disinterred, totally undecayed, some forty years after their deaths.[9] Surely the Prophet's body would not have been any more susceptible to decay than these Muslims martyrs were.

The importance of holy bodies was reflected not only in the stories that Muslims related about them, but also in the rituals that they physically enacted with and around them. Contrary to the wholly iconoclastic image often drawn of Islam as a religious tradition, early Muslims visited and venerated many spaces and objects associated with the lives and remains of holy individuals throughout the Near East. Muḥammad's tomb and other spaces in Mecca and Medina became places of pilgrimage, prayed at and touched for their blessing; relics of his body, such as strands of his hair, emerged as devotional objects prized by their owners. Monuments associated with the Prophet Muḥammad were not the only sacred destinations, but Muslims also made pilgrimage to the burial places of other prophets and martyrs, among many further locations. The bodies of holy persons, as well as the spaces associated with their lives and deaths, functioned as important ideological and ritual sites for the formation and performance of early Islamic identity/-ies.

Yet the symbolic potency of these holy bodies and sacred spaces occasioned severe debates over the course of the seventh through ninth centuries, as individuals of varying ideological stripes from across the Islamic world offered differing and often competing ideas about the significances of holy persons and places within Islamic life. As in Wakīʿ's *ḥadīth*, some early Muslims presented

[9] On this and similar stories, see Adam Bursi, 'A Holy Heretical Body: Ṭalḥa b. 'Ubayd Allāh's Corpse and Early Islamic Sectarianism', *Studies in Late Antiquity* 2.2 (2018): 147–79.

viewpoints on the Prophet Muḥammad and other figures that were not particularly conducive to, or permissive of, their veneration. Similar to the variant representations of Muḥammad's corpse, different texts alternatively celebrated the bodies of Islamic martyrs as miraculously undecayed in their graves (like the martyrs of Uḥud), or instead lionised their fragmented corpses as 'skulls [lying] in the dust like rotten melons' after their virtuous deaths.[10] Commemorating and visiting the tombs of such figures were hotly debated topics that divided Muslim communities, with some seeing such activity as making the holy person's grave into an idol.[11]

This book sets out to explore the varied roles of holy bodies, their relics and the spaces associated with them within the emergence and formation of Islam over the first three centuries of the tradition's history. As Muslim scholars, caliphs and other authorities defined what beliefs and practices delineated the correct performance of Islam, sacred bodies and the spaces they occupied often stood at the contested boundaries of these formative Islamic identities. Holy bodies and spaces could draw boundaries internally within the larger Islamic community, as well as partition Muslim from non-Muslim. At the same time, the many similarities in beliefs, ritual practices and sacred spaces found among Muslims and other religious groups gesture towards the continuities and dialogues between these groups regarding conceptualisations and customs of sacred bodies and spaces. Muslim jurists were anxious to control such dialogues as they defined the boundaries between Muslim and non-Muslim, and marked Muslims' simultaneous continuity with, and difference from, other late antique religious communities. This book describes how early Muslims rhetorically and ritually deployed holy bodies and spaces as they defined what

[10] Adam Gaiser, *Shurāt Legends, Ibāḍī Identities: Martyrdom, Asceticism, and the Making of an Early Islamic Community* (Columbia: University of South Carolina Press, 2016), 75; Etan Kohlberg, 'Medieval Muslim Views on Martyrdom', *Mededelingen van de Afdeling Letterkunde* 60 (1997): 281–307.

[11] Thomas Leisten, 'Between Orthodoxy and Exegesis: Some Aspects of Attitudes in the Shari'a toward Funerary Architecture', *Muqarnas* 7 (1990): 12–22; Leor Halevi, *Muhammad's Grave: Death Rites and the Making of Islamic Society* (New York: Columbia University Press, 2007), 36–43, 187–91; Ondřej Beránek and Pavel Ťupek, *The Temptation of Graves in Salafi Islam: Iconoclasm, Destruction and Idolatry* (Edinburgh: Edinburgh University Press, 2018), 22–36.

it meant to be Muslim. The stories, rituals and debates surrounding holy bodies and sacred spaces – often called *āthār*, that is, 'traces' or 'relics' in Islamic texts – were interwoven with the formation and performance of early Islam.

Texts, Materials and Methodological Considerations

Modern scholars from different fields frequently depict Islam as a religious tradition characterised by strong opposition to tomb and relic veneration from the beginning of its history. Researchers in Christian history deploy Islam as an austere antithesis to the prevalence of saints' relics, shrines and stories within late antique and medieval Christianity.[12] Scholars of Islamic history suggest that the earliest period of Islam was largely or entirely devoid of relic and tomb veneration, and that such 'innovations' only developed in later centuries.[13] When they do address the appearance of relic and tomb veneration among early (and later) Muslims, scholars of Islamic law and religion frequently assign such activities to the domains of 'popular' or 'folk' practice, distinct from 'orthodox' or 'official' Islam.[14] Moreover, these practices are often attributed

[12] Peter Brown, *The Cult of the Saints: Its Rise and Function in Latin Christianity* (Chicago: University of Chicago Press, 1981), 9–10; Caroline Walker Bynum, *Christian Materiality: An Essay on Religion in Late Medieval Europe* (New York: Zone, 2011), 273–9.

[13] Daniella Talmon-Heller, *Islamic Piety in Medieval Syria: Mosques, Cemeteries and Sermons under the Zangids and Ayyūbids (1146–1260)* (Leiden: Brill, 2007), 55; Oleg Grabar, 'The Earliest Islamic Commemorative Structures, Notes and Documents', *Ars Orientalis* 6 (1966): 7–46; Robert Hillenbrand, *Islamic Architecture: Form, Function and Meaning* (New York: Columbia University Press, 1994), 253.

[14] Samuel M. Zwemer, 'Hairs of the Prophet', in *Ignace Goldziher Memorial Volume*, ed. Samuel Löwinger and Joseph Somogyi, 2 vols (Budapest: Globus, 1948), 1:48–54; Ignaz Goldziher, *Muslim Studies*, ed. S. M. Stern, trans. C. R. Barber and S. M. Stern, 2 vols (London: Allen & Unwin, 1967), 2:279–96, 322–32; Jacques Waardenburg, 'Official and Popular Religion in Islam', *Social Compass* 25 (1978): 315–41; Boaz Shoshan, 'High Culture and Popular Culture in Medieval Islam', *Studia Islamica* 73 (1991): 67–107; Jonathan P. Berkey, 'Tradition, Innovation and the Social Construction of Knowledge in the Medieval Islamic Near East', *Past & Present* 146 (1995): 38–65; Ahmet T. Karamustafa, 'Shi'is, Sufis, and Popular Saints', in *The Wiley Blackwell History of Islam*, ed. Armando Salvatore et al. (Oxford: Wiley Blackwell, 2018), 159–75; Daniella Talmon-Heller, *Sacred Place and Sacred Time in the Medieval Islamic Middle East: A Historical Perspective* (Edinburgh: Edinburgh University Press, 2020), 11, 17, 20, 182–3.

to Shīʿī communities, in contradistinction to the assumed Sunnī rejection of such objects and rituals.[15]

Using a diverse body of early texts, this book reconstructs a more complicated history of the attitudes and practices of early Muslims. Rather than accept an image of rigid early Islamic iconoclasm, or categorise Muslim relic and tomb veneration as exclusively 'popular' practice, I suggest we read Islamic texts and traditions about relics and tombs within the context of early Muslims' debates about ritual and the definition of distinctly Islamic identity/identities.[16] Moreover, when we read sources outside of the 'canonical' texts of Islamic *ḥadīth* and historiography, we find evidence of a plurality of views and activities that complicate prevailing understandings of the place of sacred objects and spaces in emergent forms of Islam.

My approach to these sources is informed by the insights of the cultural, linguistic and material 'turns' in the study of late antique texts. Utilising a 'wide diversity of theories and methods borrowed from poststructuralism', scholars of late antiquity have argued that historians are 'always dealing with language, not directly with "the thing itself"'.[17] As a result, we now acknowledge that late antique Christian texts 'lie in a largely unknown and dubious relation to the "reality" of the ancient Church, and should often be approached with a hermeneutic of suspicion and by reading against the grain'.[18] Likewise, rabbinic texts 'did not simply reflect reality but constituted attempts to construct

[15] Grabar, 'Earliest Islamic Commemorative Structures', 39. Pushing back against such assumptions, see Karamustafa, 'Shi'is, Sufis, and Popular Saints', 171; Christopher S. Taylor, 'Reevaluating the Shi'i Role in the Development of Monumental Islamic Funerary Architecture: The Case of Egypt', *Muqarnas* 9 (1992): 1–10. See also Harry Munt, *The Holy City of Medina: Sacred Space in Early Islamic Arabia* (Cambridge: Cambridge University Press, 2014), 136.

[16] My usage of 'iconoclasm' and 'iconoclastic' follows a more expansive meaning of these terms, beyond specific reference to the destruction of religious images. See Beránek and Ťupek, *Temptation of Graves*, 14.

[17] Dale B. Martin, 'Introduction', in *The Cultural Turn in Late Antique Studies: Gender, Asceticism, and Historiography*, ed. Dale B. Martin and Patricia Cox Miller (Durham, NC: Duke University Press, 2005), 8–9.

[18] Elizabeth A. Clark, *History, Theory, Text: Historians and the Linguistic Turn* (Cambridge, MA: Harvard University Press, 2004), 170.

it, that is, they are statements of ideology'.[19] Such texts were not simple statements or stories for these communities: they participated in wider discourses, and were operative in the 'production of reality' of communal identity, thought and practice.[20]

These interpretive methods and considerations offer useful tools for approaching Islamic sources, as early Islam has increasingly been understood as a religious tradition that emerged in dialogue with the surrounding cultures and traditions of the late antique Near East.[21] Like the texts composed within other communities, those produced by early Muslims are 'texts of a highly literary, rhetorical, and ideological nature'.[22] The diverse literature available for studying early Islam – including *ḥadīth* compilations, narrative histories, biographical collections and juristic responsa – transmitted, drew upon and adapted stories of early and paradigmatic Muslim figures in a variety of ways, often 'in bids for political or spiritual legitimation'.[23] Using diverse literary techniques, Muslim authors 'utilized rhetoric to persuade their audiences of a particular reading of history'.[24]

Such insights are particularly important due to the issues with dating texts from, and about, the first centuries of Islamic history. As researchers have long acknowledged, using Islamic texts to reconstruct the historical events and developments of the first centuries AH is a methodologically fraught

[19] Seth Schwartz, *Imperialism and Jewish Society from 200 B.C.E. to 650 C.E.* (Princeton: Princeton University Press, 2001), 8. Quoted in Daniel Boyarin, *Border Lines: The Partition of Judaeo-Christianity* (Philadelphia: University of Pennsylvania Press, 2004), 49. Schwartz is here describing the approach of Jacob Neusner. Cf. also ibid., 7, 50, 158.

[20] Andrew Jacobs, *Remains of the Jews: The Holy Land and Christian Empire in Late Antiquity* (Stanford: Stanford University Press, 2004), 207.

[21] Robert Hoyland, 'Early Islam as a Late Antique Religion', in *The Oxford Handbook of Late Antiquity*, ed. Scott Fitzgerald Johnson (Oxford: Oxford University Press, 2012), 1,053–77.

[22] Clark, *History, Theory, Text*, 159.

[23] Nancy Khalek, '"He Was Tall and Slender, and His Virtues Were Numerous": Byzantine and Hagiographical Topoi and the Companions of Muḥammad in al-Azdī's *Futūḥ al-Shām*', *Writing 'True Stories': Historians and Hagiographers in the Late Antique and Early Medieval Near East*, ed. Arietta Papaconstantinou, Muriel Debié and Hugh Kennedy (Turnhout: Brepols, 2010), 107.

[24] Najam Haider, *The Rebel and the Imām in Early Islam: Explorations in Muslim Historiography* (Cambridge: Cambridge University Press, 2019), 12.

project. The problem emerges in large part from the fact that the majority of extant Arabic literary testimonies to the first Islamic centuries were composed (at least in their current forms) in the ninth century CE or later. In the last decades, scholars have developed useful methods of source criticism for reading these texts, such that earlier layers within the compilations can be identified and plausibly dated.[25] Yet, as Sean Anthony has recently noted, even with these crucial tools, in many cases 'the chasm between source and event is never really eliminated; it is only narrowed'.[26] We thus depend upon chronologically late texts for the reconstruction of early Islamic history, despite the fact that these sources arguably 'often tell us more about their date of composition than they do about the events they purport to relate'.[27]

Acknowledging the rhetorical and chronological positioning of our sources, we must likewise keep in mind the ways that many of these texts were themselves operative in the 'production of reality' for early Muslims. Like other late antique groups, Muslim communities used texts – and especially stories of exemplary figures – to reinforce, indeed to create, their senses of themselves.[28] Historical narratives were key components in the creation and maintenance of early Muslim sectarian identities, with differing communal conceptions often turning on divergent readings of the events of the early Islamic *umma*.[29]

[25] This '*isnād*-cum-*matn*' methodology was pioneered by Gregor Schoeler and Harald Motzki. Some of their most important contributions are now available in English translations: Gregor Schoeler, *The Biography of Muḥammad: Nature and Authenticity*, trans. Uwe Vagelpohl, ed. James E. Montgomery (New York: Routledge, 2011); Harald Motzki, Nicolet Boekhoff-van der Voort and Sean W. Anthony, *Analysing Muslim Traditions: Studies in Legal, Exegetical and Maghāzī Ḥadīth* (Leiden: Brill, 2010); Harald Motzki, *The Origins of Islamic Jurisprudence: Meccan Fiqh before the Classical Schools*, trans. Marion H. Katz (Leiden: Brill, 2002). Also important is the critical work of G. H. A. Juynboll, whose methodology is outlined in his *Encyclopedia of Canonical Ḥadīth* (Leiden: Brill, 2007), xvii–xxx.

[26] Sean W. Anthony, *Muhammad and the Empires of Faith: The Making of the Prophet of Islam* (Oakland: University of California Press, 2020), 7.

[27] Chase Robinson, *Islamic Historiography* (Cambridge: Cambridge University Press, 2003), 51.

[28] Thomas Sizgorich, *Violence and Belief in Late Antiquity: Militant Devotion in Christianity and Islam* (Philadelphia: University of Pennsylvania Press, 2009).

[29] Scott C. Lucas, *Constructive Critics,* Ḥadīth *Literature, and the Articulation of Sunnī Islam: The Legacy of the Generation of Ibn Saʿd, Ibn Maʿīn, and Ibn Ḥanbal* (Leiden: Brill, 2004), 221; Adam Gaiser, 'A Narrative Identity Approach to Islamic Sectarianism', in *Sectarianization: Mapping the New Politics of the Middle East*, ed. Nader Hashemi and Danny Postel (New York: Oxford University Press, 2017), 61–75.

The stories told about figures like the Prophet, the early caliphs and the Shīʿī imams 'influenced how people felt about that history' and 'helped erect sectarian boundaries'.[30] One textual form – *ḥadīth*s, that is, stories and statements orally transmitted from (or attributed to) the Prophet Muḥammad and other early figures – 'functioned over centuries as a common intersectarian discourse among different groups of the Islamic society', and served as 'an important vehicle for expressing ideas'.[31] Narratives and reports reified and 'produced' the early Islamic community, in part by narratively and ideologically defining the difference between Muslims and non-Muslims.

Of course, texts were far from the only means by which such differentiation occurred. Stories and statements operated alongside – and often rhetorically justified – other, much more material means of erecting and naturalising communal boundaries. While this book points to the importance of relics and tombs as rhetorical devices in the formation of early Islamic identities, I am also well aware that relics and tombs were (in many cases) physical, material things. By paying attention to bodies, relics and the spaces they occupied, this book takes part in the recent 'material turn' in the study of the humanities and social sciences, and in the study of religion more specifically.[32]

The material turn can be summarised as 'the claim of material things and phenomena – objects, practices, spaces, bodies, sensations, affects, and so on – to a place at the center of scholarly inquiry'.[33] In contradistinction to the common focus in Religious Studies on beliefs and dogma (and the prime repository for these, texts), the material turn instead considers that 'religion must be understood as deriving from rudimentary human experiences, from lived embodied practices'.[34] Such work involves not only considerations of the individual, but also of the 'things' that the individual experiences: the material world of objects

[30] Matthew Pierce, *Twelve Infallible Men: The Imams and the Making of Shiʿism* (Cambridge, MA: Harvard University Press, 2016), 41, 65.

[31] Pamela Klasova, 'Ḥadīth as Common Discourse: Reflections on the Intersectarian Dissemination of the Creation of the Intellect Tradition', *Al-ʿUṣūr al-Wusṭā* 28 (2020): 299, 315.

[32] For useful overviews of recent work, see Sonia Hazard, 'The Material Turn in the Study of Religion', *Religion and Society: Advances in Research* 4 (2013): 58–78; Peter J. Bräunlein, 'Thinking Religion Through Things: Reflections on the Material Turn in the Scientific Study of Religion\s', *Method and Theory in the Study of Religion* 28 (2016): 365–99.

[33] Hazard, 'Material Turn', 58.

[34] S. Brent Plate, *A History of Religion in 5½ Objects: Bringing the Spiritual to Its Senses* (Boston: Beacon Press, 2014), 15.

and spaces. An acknowledgement of the power of such 'things' is thus a component of the material turn, as scholars 'insist that the materiality of material things themselves must be carefully considered, not merely interpreted for their implications on human concerns'.[35] This 'new materialism' asks scholars 'to approach agency as something distributed across assemblages of subjects and objects, human and nonhuman actors'.[36]

Many researchers of late antique religions have adopted these insights, perhaps because late antique religious forms seem to have undergone a 'material turn' of their own between the fourth and seventh centuries. As Patricia Cox Miller argues, this '"material turn" indicates a shift in the late ancient Christian sensibility regarding the signifying potential of the material world (including especially the human body), a shift that reconfigured the relation between materiality and meaning in a positive direction'.[37] This 'increasing materiality inherent in late antique notions of sanctity' was embodied in a 'new tactile piety', exemplified in the proliferation of the Christian cults of relics and icons, and pilgrimages to visit them.[38] Late antique Jews also appear to have been part of this 'material turn', as they 'came to share with their Christian contemporaries a set of common presuppositions regarding how certain objects mediated the divine or spiritual realm precisely through their participation in materiality'.[39]

35 Hazard, 'Material Turn', 64.

36 Sonia Hazard, 'Thing', *Early American Studies* 16.4 (2018): 794.

37 Patricia Cox Miller, *The Corporeal Imagination: Signifying the Holy in Late Ancient Christianity* (Philadelphia: University of Pennsylvania Press, 2009), 3.

38 Georgia Frank, *The Memory of the Eyes: Pilgrims to Living Saints in Christian Late Antiquity* (Berkeley: University of California Press, 2000), 120–1. Miller writes that 'matter became central to Christian identity in late antiquity, first in the form of relics, and then in the form of icons'. Miller, *Corporeal Imagination*, 142.

39 Ra'anan Boustan, 'Jewish Veneration of the "Special Dead" in Late Antiquity and Beyond', in *Saints and Sacred Matter: The Cult of Relics in Byzantium and Beyond*, ed. Cynthia Hahn and Holger A. Klein (Washington, DC: Dumbarton Oaks Research Library and Collection, 2015), 62. Rafael Neis, for example, has argued that 'the "visual turn" ascribed to late-antique piety [. . .] is a hitherto overlooked but crucial component of later (that is, Amoraic and later) rabbinic piety', with rabbis figured as '"icons" of the sacred' and 'objects of sacred visuality'. Rafael Rachel Neis, *The Sense of Sight in Rabbinic Culture: Jewish Ways of Seeing in Late Antiquity* (Cambridge: Cambridge University Press, 2013), 10, 17, 181, 203–4, 230.

The material turn has only recently begun to impact research in Islamic Studies, a discipline that historically has not highly prioritised questions of embodiment and materiality.[40] The study of early Islam has often been characterised by an 'overwhelmingly logo-centric approach', which presents this dynamic period as 'distinguished by primarily conceptual or for that matter textual transformation'.[41] Utilising the innovations and questions of the material turn, scholars have begun to draw attention to 'how physical materials [. . .] were also part of these evolving discourses' of emergent Islam.[42] As Elizabeth Key Fowden states, 'Muḥammad's world and that of his rival heirs was alive with objects and images as well as words'.[43]

Among those objects were relics and tombs. While relic and tomb veneration has been marginalised within the academic study of Islam, recent scholars have taken a materially-focused turn to examine 'the historical reality of relics in Islam'.[44] Much of the work on relics in Islam has concentrated on the medieval and early modern periods, with their varied textual and material evidence of the place of relics and associated ritual practices among Muslim groups.[45]

[40] Anna Bigelow, 'Introduction: Thinking with Islamic Things', in *Islam Through Objects*, ed. Anna Bigelow (London: Bloomsbury, 2021), 1–13; James Grehan, *Twilight of the Saints: Everyday Religion in Ottoman Syria and Palestine* (Oxford: Oxford University Press, 2014), 4. On the predominance of 'intellectual-historical' and 'doctrinal' analysis in the study of early Shīʿism, see Edmund Hayes, 'The Institutions of the Shīʿī Imāmate: Towards a Social History of Early Imāmī Shiʿism', *Al-Masāq* 33.2 (2021): 188–204.

[41] Elizabeth Key Fowden, 'Shrines and Banners: Paleo-Muslims and their Material Inheritance', in *Encompassing the Sacred in Islamic Art*, ed. Lorenz Korn and Çiğdem İvren (Wiesbaden: Reichert Verlag, 2020), 5–23.

[42] Fowden, 'Shrines and Banners', 8.

[43] Fowden, 'Shrines and Banners', 20.

[44] Josef W. Meri, 'Relics of Piety and Power in Islam', in *Relics and Remains*, ed. Alexandra Walsham, *Past & Present* Supplement 5 (Oxford: Oxford University Press, 2010), 98. A recent article comments that 'it is worth noting that the question of relics in Islam has not received much attention from researchers to date'. Annabelle Collinet, Sepideh Parsapajouh and Michel Boivin, 'Bodies & Artefacts. Relics and Other Devotional Supports in Shiʿa Societies in the Indic and Iranian World: An Introduction', *Journal of Material Cultures in the Muslim World* 1 (2020): 191–8.

[45] Meri, 'Relics of Piety', 97. Cf. Brannon M. Wheeler, *Mecca and Eden: Ritual, Relics, and Territory in Islam* (Chicago: University of Chicago Press, 2006), 71–98; Josef W. Meri, *The*

But researchers have begun to use textual and archaeological evidence to demonstrate the presence and significance of relic and tomb veneration from early in Islamic history.[46] As Nancy Khalek argues, '[t]he encounter with Byzantine Christian praxis had a strong impact on Muslim worship in the arena of relic veneration' and 'the veneration of relics and the visitation of tombs became part of an Islamic repertoire of values that took on a life of its own in an Islamized landscape'.[47] My own previous work has examined stories about relics in early Islamic texts to argue that Muslims participated in the pervasive late antique discourses related to holy bodies and tombs.[48]

Uncovering Prophetic Traces: Finding Material Religion in Early Islamic Texts

Because the material world of the first Islamic centuries has not, by and large, survived for investigation, we are generally reliant upon texts to reconstruct early Muslims' material practices.[49] An important feature of the Islamic tex-

Cult of Saints among Muslims and Jews in Medieval Syria (Oxford: Oxford University Press, 2002); Talmon-Heller, *Islamic Piety*; Taylor, *In the Vicinity*; Grehan, *Twilight of the Saints*; Christine Gruber, *The Praiseworthy One: The Prophet Muhammad in Islamic Texts and Images* (Bloomington: Indiana University Press, 2019); Richard J. A. McGregor, *Islam and the Devotional Object: Seeing Religion in Egypt and Syria* (Cambridge: Cambridge University Press, 2020); Finbarr Barry Flood, 'Bodies and Becoming: Mimesis, Mediation, and the Ingestion of the Sacred in Christianity and Islam', in *Sensational Religion: Sensory Cultures in Material Practice*, ed. Sally M. Promey (New Haven: Yale University Press, 2014) 459–93; Finbarr Barry Flood, *Technologies de dévotion dans les arts de l'Islam* (Paris: Hazan, 2019); Karen G. Ruffle, 'Presence in Absence: The Formation of Reliquary Shi'ism in Qutb Shahi Hyderabad', *Material Religion* 13.3 (2017): 329–53.

[46] Sarah Z. Mirza, 'The Peoples' Hadith: Evidence for Popular Tradition on Hadith as Physical Object in the First Centuries of Islam', *Arabica* 63 (2016): 30–63.

[47] Nancy Khalek, *Damascus after the Muslim Conquest: Text and Image in Early Islam* (Oxford: Oxford University Press, 2011), 86.

[48] Bursi, 'Holy Heretical Body'; Adam Bursi, 'A Hair's Breadth: The Prophet Muhammad's Hair as Relic in Early Islamic Texts', in *Religious Competition in the Greco-Roman World*, ed. Nathaniel P. DesRosiers and Lily C. Vuong (Atlanta: SBL Press, 2016), 219–31; Adam Bursi, 'Fluid Boundaries: Christian Sacred Space and Islamic Relics in an Early *Ḥadīth*', *Medieval Encounters* 27.6 (2021): 478–510.

[49] For examples of the destruction or suppression of early Islamic material culture, see Shahab Ahmed, *What is Islam? The Importance of Being Islamic* (Princeton: Princeton University

tual discourses surrounding relics and tombs is the vocabulary used, and especially one word that provides this book's title: *āthār*. Essentially meaning 'trace, sign, or vestige', *āthār* (and its singular form, *athar*) is commonly understood as the word for physical 'relics' within Islamic texts.[50] '*Āthār*' is semantically similar to the vocabulary for relics found in Christian contexts in various languages.[51] In fact, it appears as one of the words used in reference to relics of Jesus, biblical prophets and saintly martyrs in Christian Arabic texts.[52]

At the same time, 'the semantic range of the term *athar* itself is rather broader' in Islamic texts than just bodily remains.[53] *Āthār* is used in reference to objects associated with a holy person, as well as places associated with a holy person's presence. Similar phenomena are found in Christian contexts, in which a wide variety of objects, materials and places – extending far beyond the saintly body itself – were treated as 'relics' of holy persons. More particular to Islamic contexts, though, is the fact that the term *āthār* 'was also regularly treated as a synonym for *ḥadīth*, in the sense of the accounts of the words and

Press, 2016), 532–7; McGregor, *Islam and the Devotional Object*, 135–8. Many relics, of indeterminate date, were collected by the Ottomans and are held now in the Topkapı Palace. See Hilmi Aydın, *The Sacred Trusts: Pavilion of the Sacred Relics, Topkapı Palace Museum, Istanbul* (Somerset, NJ: The Light, 2004); Wendy M. K. Shaw, 'Between the Secular and the Sacred: A New Face for the Department of the Holy Relics at the Topkapı Palace Museum', *Material Religion* 6.1 (2010): 129–31.

50 *EI*², s.v. 'Athar' (Ignaz Goldziher and T. J. de Boer); Meri, 'Relics of Piety', 100; Meri, *Cult of Saints*, 317.

51 Robert Wiśniewski, *The Beginnings of the Cult of Relics* (Oxford: Oxford University Press, 2019), 2–3.

52 *The Life of Timothy of Kākhushtā: Two Arabic Texts*, ed. and trans. John C. Lamoreaux and Cyril Cairala, *PO* 48.4 (Turnhout: Brepols, 2000), 534–5; Eutychius of Alexandria, *The Book of the Demonstration (Kitāb al-Burhān)*, ed. Pierre Cachia and trans. W. Montgomery Watt, 4 vols, CSCO 192–3 and 209–10 (Louvain: Secrétariat du CorpusSCO, 1960–1), I:165 (no. 310), 197 (no. 364), 205–7 (nos 382–4); Agapius of Manbij, *Kitāb al-ʿUnwān*, ed. Louis Cheikho, CSCO 65 (Beirut: Typographeo Catholico, 1912), 45, 51.

53 McGregor, *Islam and the Devotional Object*, 120. Collinet, Parsapajouh and Boivin, 'Bodies & Artefacts', 191 note that 'The term relic [. . .] has no literal translation in neither [*sic*] Arabic, Turkish, Persian, nor Urdu' and that 'The equivalent term used for relic in Islam is *āthār* [. . .], covering a much more general meaning than relic'. For the words used in an early modern South Asian context, see Ruffle, 'Presence in Absence', 350 n.5.

deeds of the Prophet'.[54] The words and stories of the Prophet Muḥammad were thus also conceptualised as his 'relics'. In effect, both material and immaterial meanings could be conveyed with the word '*āthār*', and its meaning is highly dependent on the context of usage.

Modern historians have frequently assumed that Muslims in the first centuries AH (and, indeed, thereafter) were primarily interested in collecting and transmitting the Prophet's *ḥadīth*s (i.e. oral and textualised reports), but paid relatively little attention to his material *āthār*. Tayeb El-Hibri, for example, writes that an 'orthodoxy' developed by the ninth century CE, in which '[t]he authority of the Prophet becomes limited to *ḥadīth* texts' as the *'ulamā'* 'became determined to limit discussions of Prophetic objects to a minimum level'.[55]

While the Prophet's physical relics are mentioned in the major *ḥadīth* collections, El-Hibri suggests that these textual compendiums 'deployed the minimal mention of these items to outline what is legally permissible or culturally aesthetic in lifestyle'.[56] To illustrate this argument, El-Hibri notes a set of reports found in the canonical Sunnī *Ṣaḥīḥ* collection of the revered *ḥadīth* scholar Muḥammad b. Ismā'īl al-Bukhārī (d. 256/870). In his book, al-Bukhārī includes several reports that mention strands of the Prophet's hair that were retained by the Prophet's wife Umm Salama (d. *c.* 59/679–80). Importantly, these reports describe the Prophet's hairs as having been dyed red: thus, al-Bukhārī places the reports in his chapter on clothing (*libās*), in a section on

[54] Eerik Dickinson, 'Ibn al-Ṣalāḥ al-Shahrazūrī and the Isnād', *JAOS* 122.3 (2002): 484; G. H. A. Juynboll, *Muslim Tradition: Studies in Chronology, Provenance and Authorship of Early* Ḥadīth (Cambridge: Cambridge University Press, 1983), 33–4. Cf. also Adam Gaiser, '*Ballaghanā 'an an-Nabī*: Early Basran and Omani Ibāḍī Understandings of *Sunna* and *Siyar*, *Āthār* and *Nasab*', *BSOAS* 83.3 (2020): 437–48.

[55] Tayeb El-Hibri, 'The Abbasids and the Relics of the Prophet', *Journal of Abbasid Studies* 4 (2017): 84–8. El-Hibri argues that 'the genesis of interest in prophetic relics was rooted in the early Abbasid period', and specifically during the reigns of the caliphs al-Ṣaffāḥ (r. 132–6/749–54), al-Manṣūr (r. 136–58/754–75) and, especially, al-Mutawakkil (r. 232–47/847–61). He interprets mentions of earlier relic veneration as 'back projection[s]', though 'some Prophetic objects may have lingered after his death'. This re-dating of developments to the 'Abbāsid period is characteristic of El-Hibri's wider approach to the Arabic historiographical tradition. For a critique, see Anthony, *Muhammad and the Empires*, 144 n.78.

[56] El-Hibri, 'Abbasids and the Relics', 86.

cosmetic treatments for hair that has turned white with age (*shayb*).[57] In this literary context, the reports about the Prophet's hair appear as evidence 'on the permissibility, even encouragement, of dyeing the hair', itself a contested subject in the early centuries of Islam.[58] Rather than holiness or power associated with these fragments of the Prophet's body, their placement amid discussions of hair dyeing textualises these physical artifacts and turns them into literary evidence for reconstructing the Prophet's *sunna*.

The 'distribution and collection of the Prophet's remains *as text*' was undeniably an important development of this early period.[59] This is reflected in the increasing emphasis, over the eighth and ninth centuries, on *ḥadīth*s as documentation of the Prophet's behaviour.[60] Indeed, the very creation of works like al-Bukhārī's *Ṣaḥīḥ* testifies to the growing emphasis on the Prophet's textual relics and the 'mimetic image of Muhammad' as a primary model for Muslim ritual behaviour.[61] Yet, as Michael Muhammad Knight argues, 'observable patterns in [the *ḥadīth* canon] do not amount to a discursive unity or a sweeping and absolute transformation in the corpus's treatment of Muhammad's body'.[62] Throughout *ḥadīth* compendia, we see a 'diversity of ways they imagine the prophetic body' and 'multiple logics of the body coexist alongside each other'.[63] Even as the 'principal of emulating the Prophet underlay scholars' efforts to define how rituals should be performed', nonetheless, evoking the

[57] Muḥammad b. Ismāʿīl al-Bukhārī, *Ṣaḥīḥ al-Bukhārī* (Damascus: Dār Ibn Kathīr, 2002), 1,487 (kitāb al-libās, bāb 66).

[58] El-Hibri, 'Abbasids and the Relics', 86. On this early legal discussion, see G. H. A. Juynboll, 'Dyeing the Hair and Beard in Early Islam: A Ḥadīth-Analytical Study', *Arabica* 33.1 (1986): 49–75; Ahmed El Shamsy, 'The Curious Case of Early Muslim Hair Dyeing', in *Islam at 250: Studies in Memory of G. H. A. Juynboll*, ed. Petra M. Sijpesteijn and Camilla Adang (Leiden: Brill, 2020), 187–206.

[59] Wheeler, *Mecca and Eden*, 75, emphasis added.

[60] Joseph E. Lowry, 'The Prophet as Lawgiver and Legal Authority', in *The Cambridge Companion to Muḥammad*, ed. Jonathan E. Brockopp (New York: Cambridge University Press, 2010), 83–102.

[61] Gordon D. Newby, 'Imitating Muhammad in Two Genres: Mimesis and Problems of Genre in Sîrah and Sunnah', *Medieval Encounters* 3.3 (1997): 266–83.

[62] Knight, *Muhammad's Body*, 23.

[63] Ibid., 99.

'symbolic or literal *presence* of the Prophet' – including with his relics – was also a component of many *ḥadīth* reports.[64]

The Prophet's hair usefully illustrates the 'multiple logics' of the Prophet's body found in early texts. In the *ḥadīth* in al-Bukhārī's section on hair dyeing, the Prophet's hair colour is sighted within the narrative context of a healing ritual using this powerful matter. According to the narrator, ʿUthmān b. ʿAbd Allāh b. Mawhab (d. 160/776–7), 'My people sent me to Umm Salama with a cup of water [. . .] for the lock of the Prophet's hair. Whenever a person was struck by an evil eye or something, he would send a vessel [of water] to her. I looked into the small bell (*al-juljul*) and saw little red hairs.'[65] The description here is terse, but parallel versions in other *ḥadīth* collections clarify things: 'Umm Salama had a small silver bell containing hairs of the Prophet. Whenever someone was sick or had been struck by an evil eye, he would bring a vessel of water [to Umm Salama] and put the [Prophet's] hair in it, then drink from it and perform ablutions with it.'[66] The report's location in al-Bukhārī's section on 'clothing' certainly allows a reader to use the colour of the Prophet's hair as evidence for reconstructing the Prophet's usage of hair dyes. At the same time, the narrative context of how and why ʿUthmān saw the hair demonstrates a very different way of reading and using the Prophet's body. In this *ḥadīth*, the Prophet's hair is a cherished object and a physical source of healing power.

[64] Marion H. Katz, 'The Prophet Muḥammad in Ritual', in Brockopp, *Cambridge Companion to Muḥammad*, 139–57, emphasis added.

[65] On ʿUthmān b. ʿAbd Allāh b. Mawhab, see Muḥammad b. Saʿd b. Manīʿ al-Zuhrī, *Kitāb al-Ṭabaqāt al-kabīr*, ed. ʿAlī Muḥammad ʿUmar, 11 vols (Cairo: Maktabat al-Khānjī, 2001), 7:568; Khalīfa b. Khayyāṭ, *Kitāb al-Ṭabaqāt*, ed. Akram Ḍiyāʾ al-ʿUmarī (Baghdad: Maṭbaʿat al-ʿĀnī, 1967), 273.

[66] Isḥāq b. Ibrāhīm b. Makhlad al-Ḥanẓalī al-Marwazī, *Musnad Isḥāq ibn Rāhwayh*, ed. ʿAbd al-Ghafūr ʿAbd al-Ḥaqq Ḥusayn Burr al-Balūshī, 5 vols (Medina: Maktabat Dār al-Īmān: 1991–5), 4:141–2 (no. 1,913), 172–3 (no. 1,958); ʿUmar b. Shabba, *Taʾrīkh al-Madīna al-munawwara*, ed. Fahīm Muḥammad Shaltūt, 4 vols (Beirut: Dār al-Turāth, 1990), 618; al-Bayhaqī, *Dalāʾil al-nubuwwa wa-maʿrifat aḥwāl ṣāḥib al-sharīʿa*, ed. ʿAbd al-Muʿṭī Qalʿajī, 7 vols (Beirut: Dār al-Kutub al-ʿIlmiyya, 1985), 1:236; Meri, 'Relics of Piety', 105; Bursi, 'Hair's Breadth', 223–4. The Kūfan Isrāʾīl b. Yūnus b. Abī Isḥāq (d. *c.* 162/778–9) seems to be the common link for the versions of this report in which the Prophet's hair is used for healing.

Indeed, the power of the Prophet's hair appears, by many accounts, to have extended beyond textualised evocations into material usages among Muslims of the first centuries AH. Veneration and ritual manipulation of the Prophet's hairs appears among seventh- and eighth-century figures, who cherished these objects and used them in various ritual contexts. Scholars and caliphs wore, healed with and were buried alongside strands of the Prophet's hair.[67]

Ninth-century figures, such as the revered scholar Aḥmad b. Ḥanbal (d. 241/855), did much the same. For example, Ibn Ḥanbal's son reports: 'I saw my father take a strand of the Prophet's hair and place it upon his mouth and kiss it. I believe I saw him place it upon his head or eyes, then plunge it into water and drink, seeking a cure through it.'[68] Ibn Ḥanbal is also said to have to worn some of the Prophet's hair tucked inside his clothes, and to have said that this Prophetic amulet had protected him from torture during the Miḥna.[69] According to reports attributed to his copyist Abū Jaʿfar Muḥammad b. Abī Ḥātim al-Warrāq, al-Bukhārī likewise wore hairs of the Prophet, sewn into the lining of his clothing.[70] Early Muslims – up to and including figures of the *ḥadīth* movement, such as Ibn Ḥanbal and al-Bukhārī – were not only interested in the normative precedents embodied in stories of the Prophet's hair, but used and experienced the strands themselves as powerful material objects.

Reports about the Prophet Muḥammad and other Muslim figures did not circulate in an ideological or material vacuum in the first centuries of Islamic history. These oral and written texts were transmitted (as Elizabeth Key

[67] Bursi, 'Hair's Breadth', 224–30.

[68] ʿAbd Allāh b. Aḥmad, *Masāʾil al-Imām Aḥmad ibn Ḥanbāl*, ed. Zuhayr al-Shāwīsh (Beirut: al-Maktab al-Islāmī, 1981), 447; al-Dhahabī, *Siyar*, 11:212; Ibn al-Jawzī, *Virtues of the Imām Aḥmad ibn Ḥanbal*, ed. and trans. Michael Cooperson, 2 vols (New York: New York University Press, 2013–15), 1:346–7.

[69] al-Dhahabī, *Siyar*, 11:250; Ibn al-Jawzī, *Virtues of the Imām*, 2:108–9.

[70] al-Dhahabī, *Siyar*, 12:453; al-Dhahabī, *Taʾrīkh*, 19 [251–60]: 263; Ibn Ḥajar al-ʿAsqalānī, *Hady al-sārī muqaddimat Fatḥ al-bārī*, ed. Abū Qutayba Naẓar Muḥammad al-Fāryābī, 2 vols (Riyadh: Dār al-Ṭayba, 2006), 1294. These traditions seem to come from Muḥammad b. Abī Ḥātim's biographical collection *Shamāʾil al-Bukhārī* (The Good Qualities of al-Bukhārī), on which see al-Dhahabī, *Siyar*, 12:392; Christopher Melchert, 'Bukhārī and his *Ṣaḥīḥ*', *Le Muséon* 123.3–4 (2010): 427 n.8. On what being a scholar's *warrāq* entailed, see Beatrice Gruendler, *The Rise of the Arabic Book* (Cambridge, MA: Harvard University Press, 2020), 119–21.

Fowden phrases it) in a physical world 'alive with objects and images as well as words'. It is largely texts that have survived for our analysis of the early Islamic centuries. But, when we read those texts with a materially-inclined eye, we see evidence of an embodied world of venerated objects and places: or, as Islamic sources often call them, 'traces' of prophets and other holy people. In the chapters that follow, I attempt to recover some of this world, and use it to explore the material context of emergent Islamic practice and identity.

Organisation of Materials

Chapter 1 uses a set of *ḥadīth*s that narrate the Prophet Muḥammad's final words as an entry point for the themes discussed throughout this book. On his deathbed in the city of Medina, the Prophet reportedly cursed Jews and Christians and barred them from the Arabian Peninsula, citing their use of the graves of their prophets as places of worship (or, literally, mosques). While modern scholarship has tended to read these *ḥadīth*s as representative of the sum of early Islamic attitudes towards the veneration of relics and tombs, I suggest that these narratives were part of a much larger debate on such subjects among early Muslims. Literary and archaeological evidence attests both to the existence of such venerational practices among early Muslims and to the discomfort that these activities might provoke. Situating the book's arguments within the context of research on religious identity in late antiquity, and the role therein of relics and sacred spaces, this chapter provides a historical and theoretical framework for the chapters that follow.

Chapter 2 examines the variant discourses and rituals surrounding one particular prophetic relic: the Maqām Ibrāhīm, a stone in Mecca believed to contain the miraculously-inscribed footprints of the prophet and patriarch Abraham. In early Muslims' rhetorical deployments of this relic of a scriptural figure, the Maqām Ibrāhīm displays both Islamic connections to, and deviations from, other late antique communities. Connecting the Muslim community to the ancient biblical past, the Maqām was also used to assert Islamic superiority over contemporary Jews and Christians. Yet even as Muslims used the Maqām to situate their claims to interreligious ascendency, discussions about how Muslims should (and should not) physically engage with the Maqām also point to ideological and ritual concerns about this sacred object. This literal 'trace' of a prophet – a landmark at the centre of Islam's emergent sacred geography – illustrates that relics functioned as important rhetorical and ritual markers of identity within the emerging Islamic community.

Broadening the vista beyond Mecca and Medina to the wider Near East, Chapter 3 argues that early Muslim storytellers and historians creatively utilised the late antique discourse of corporeal relics to illustrate and justify the status of early Muslims as the new divinely-ordained rulers of the Near East. In stories found within *ḥadīth*s and historical texts, Muslims discover the remains of many different holy persons (including scriptural prophets and patriarchs) at different sites during and after the Islamic conquests. With inscriptions announcing their pious beliefs, these relics testify that the Jewish, Christian and Arab pasts prepared the way for, and anticipated, the coming of Islam. In these stories, the Muslim discoverers acknowledge the sacrality of the bodies, while also effacing them: once uncovered, the corpses are reburied and hidden from any potential prying eyes or grasping hands. Rather than enshrining these sacred witnesses, their new caretakers bury them underground, with the result that only the conquering Muslims know where the relics reside. Simultaneously embracing and rejecting prophetic bodies, such stories reflect early Muslims' ambivalences about corporeal relics and their veneration, and the complicated early Islamic inheritances from, and repudiations of, earlier religious communities.

Chapter 4 focuses on early discussions of one such hidden prophetic body that was particularly significant for early Muslims: that of the Prophet Muḥammad. Seemingly from the moment of his death, the status of Muḥammad's body was hotly debated among early Muslims. These debates covered not only whether or not the Prophet's corpse had decayed, as we saw in Wakīʿ's story, but also where his corpse was physically located. Was the Prophet interred in his tomb in Medina, or had he been raised to heaven in body and/or spirit? The answers to these questions impacted (and were impacted by) one of the Prophet's principal functions in early Islamic thought: as the Muslim community's intercessor before God. Conceptions of the Prophet's corporeal status and location were tied to the question of how his intercession could be guaranteed. The answers to these doctrinal queries, in turn, affected early Islamic rituals, including prayers offered for the Prophet and pilgrimage to his grave.

Chapter 5 examines the ritualisation of several 'sites of memory' (to borrow Pierre Nora's phrase) associated with the Prophet Muḥammad's life in and around the cities of Mecca and Medina. The memorialisation of 'places where the Prophet prayed' began quite early, as we find them textually recorded in early texts and architecturally materialised by Umayyad and 'Abbāsid authorities. In early reports, Muslims visit and pray at these locations: thus, not only objects or texts, but also places were conceptualised as sacred 'traces' through their association with the Prophet Muhammad. Utilising early *ḥadīth*s and historical texts, I outline how these sites were ritually and materially sanctified – and debated – in the seventh, eighth and early ninth centuries.

1

GRAVE MARKERS: RHETORIC AND MATERIALITY OF RELIC AND TOMB VENERATION IN EARLY ISLAM

Scholarship has argued that the formation of Islamic identity/-ies in the first centuries after the Hijra was closely connected to the differentiation of Muslims from surrounding religious groups, especially Jews and Christians. As M. J. Kister writes, 'The main concern of the religious leaders of the Muslim society was to establish some barrier between the Muslim community and the communities of the Jews, Christians and Magians. This separation was to be upheld in the various spheres of social relations, as well as in rites and customs.'[1] In a variety of social arenas, Muslim religious authorities attempted to clarify (or create) the distinction between Muslims and non-Muslims by prescribing differences in dress, places of worship and forms of ritual performance.[2]

[1] M. J. Kister, '"Do Not Assimilate Yourselves . . ." *Lā tashabbuhū* . . .', *JSAI* 12 (1989): 324.

[2] Albrecht Noth, 'Problems of Differentiation between Muslims and Non-Muslims: Re-Reading the "Ordinances of 'Umar" (*al-Shurūṭ al-'Umariyya*)', trans. Mark Muelhaeusler, in *Muslims and Others in Early Islamic Society*, ed. Robert Hoyland (Aldershot: Ashgate, 2004), 103–24; Mark R. Cohen, 'What Was the Pact of 'Umar? A Literary-Historical Study', *JSAI* 23 (1999): 100–57; Milka Levy-Rubin, *Non-Muslims in the Early Islamic Empire: From Surrender to Coexistence* (Cambridge: Cambridge University Press, 2011); Luke Yarbrough, 'Origins of the *Ghiyār*', *JAOS* 134.1 (2014): 113–21; Suliman Bashear, 'Qibla Musharriqa and Early Muslim Prayer in Churches', *Muslim World* 81.3–4 (1991): 267–82; Youshaa Patel, *The Muslim Difference: Defining the Line between Believers and Unbelievers from Early Islam to the Present* (New Haven: Yale University Press, 2022).

Among these zones of differentiation, sacred spaces were simultaneously physical and ideological sites, where Muslims both materialised and idealised the distinctions between Muslims and non-Muslims. The Arabian Peninsula – specifically its north-western region, the Ḥijāz, the location of the holy cities of Mecca and Medina – offered a notable site for such early Islamic boundary formation. Drawing in part on the prohibition at Qurʾān 9:28 against non-believers approaching al-Masjid al-Ḥarām ('the Holy Mosque', interpreted to mean the site of the Kaʿba in Mecca), Muslim thinkers pronounced that Jews and Christians should be barred from entering this Islamic holy land.[3] Even more explicitly than in the Qurʾān, this geographic and sectarian demarcation was enshrined in statements ascribed to the Prophet Muḥammad's final days.[4] 'If I survive', the Prophet states in one account, 'I will expel the Jews and the Christians from the Arabian Peninsula, in order to leave only Muslims in it.'[5] With these words, Muḥammad literally maps out the difference between

[3] Christopher Melchert, 'Whether to Keep Unbelievers Out of Sacred Zones: A Survey of Medieval Islamic Law', *JSAI* 40 (2013): 177–94; Harry Munt, '"No Two Religions": Non-Muslims in the Early Islamic Ḥijāz', *BSOAS* 78 (2015): 249–69. On the emergence of the prohibition against non-believers entering Muslim worship spaces, and its connection to issues of ritual purity, see Marion H. Katz, *Body of Text: The Emergence of the Sunnī Law of Ritual Purity* (Albany: State University of New York Press, 2002), 160–4.

[4] ʿAbd al-Malik b. Hishām, *Kitāb Sīrat Rasūl Allāh: Das Leben Muhammed's nach Muhammed Ibn Isḥāk bearbeitet von Abd el-Malik Ibn Hischām*, ed. Ferdinand Wüstenfeld, 2 vols (Göttingen: Dieterichsche Universitäts-Buchhandlung, 1858–60), 1,021; Ibn Saʿd, *Ṭabaqāt*, 2:223; Aḥmad b. Ḥanbal, *Musnad al-Imām Aḥmad ibn Ḥanbal*, ed. Shuʿayb al-Arnaʾūṭ et al., 50 vols (Beirut: Muʾassasat al-Risālah, 1993–2001), 43:371 (no. 26,352); ʿAbd al-Razzāq, *Muṣannaf*, 6:53, 56 (nos 9,984, 9,990), 10:359 (nos 19,367, 19,369); Abū Bakr Aḥmad b. ʿAmr b. ʿAbd al-Khāliq al-ʿAtakī al-Bazzār, *al-Baḥr al-zakhkhār al-maʿrūf bi-Musnad al-Bazzār*, ed. Maḥfūẓ al-Raḥmān Zayn Allāh et al., 20 vols (Medina: Maktabat al-ʿUlūm wa-l-Ḥikam, 1988–2009), 1:349 (no. 230). Many of these traditions are associated with the important Medinan traditionist and historian Ibn Shihāb al-Zuhrī (d. 124/742). See Stephen J. Shoemaker, *The Death of a Prophet: The End of Muhammad's Life and the Beginnings of Islam* (Philadelphia: University of Pennsylvania Press, 2012), 92, 94. An interesting, seemingly early version is associated with Ibn Jurayj (d. 150/767–8): ʿAbd al-Razzāq, *Muṣannaf*, 6:57–8 (no. 9,993), 10:361 (no. 19,372).

[5] ʿAbd al-Razzāq, *Muṣannaf*, 6:54 (no. 9,985), 10:359 (no. 19,365); Muslim b. al-Ḥajjāj al-Qushayrī, *Ṣaḥīḥ Muslim*, ed. Muḥammad Fuʾād ʿAbd al-Bāqī, 5 vols (Cairo: Dār Iḥyāʾ al-Kutub al-ʿArabiyya, 1955), 3:1388 (no. 1,767); Abū Dāwūd Sulaymān b. al-Ashʿath

Muslims and their others, and the Islamic holy land is imagined as purely Muslim from (ideally) the time of the Prophet Muḥammad onwards.

In several versions of his deathbed statements, Muḥammad connects the expulsion of Jews and Christians with condemnation of a specific practice and type of sacred space: the veneration of the tombs of prophets. According to a report attributed to the Umayyad caliph ʿUmar b. ʿAbd al-ʿAzīz (r. 99–101/717–20), 'the last thing that the Prophet said was, "God fight the Jews and the Christians, who took the tombs of their prophets as places of worship! Let there not remain two religions in the land of the Arabs!"'[6] In a *ḥadīth* related from the Companion Abū ʿUbayda b. al-Jarrāḥ (d. 18/639), the Prophet's final words were, 'Expel the Jews of the Ḥijāz and the people of Najrān [that is, Christians] from the Arabian Peninsula! Know that the worst of people are those who take the tombs of their prophets as places of

al-Sijistānī, *Kitāb al-Sunan*, ed. Muḥammad ʿAwwāma, 5 vols (Jedda: Dār al-Qibla li-l-Thaqāfa al-Islāmiyya, 1998), 3:485 (no. 3,024); Muḥammad b. ʿĪsā al-Tirmidhī, *al-Jāmiʿ al-kabīr*, ed. Bashshār ʿAwwād Maʿrūf, 6 vols (Beirut: Dār al-Gharb al-Islāmī, 1996), 4:253–4 (nos 1,606–7); Aḥmad b. Shuʿayb al-Nasāʾī, *Kitāb al-Sunan al-Kubrā*, ed. Ḥasan ʿAbd al-Munʿim Shalbī, 12 vols (Beirut: Muʾassasat al-Risāla, 2001), 8:58 (no. 8,633); Ibn Ḥanbal, *Musnad*, 1:329, 341, 343 (nos 201, 215, 219); al-Khallāl, *Ahl al-milal*, 1:126 (no. 138); Abū ʿUbayd al-Qāsim b. Sallām, *Kitāb al-Amwāl*, ed. Muḥammad ʿImāra (Beirut: Dār al-Shurūq, 1989), 180 (no. 271); al-Bazzār, *Musnad*, 1:348, 351 (nos 229, 234); Abū Bakr Aḥmad b. al-Ḥusayn al-Bayhaqī, *al-Sunan al-kubrā*, ed. Muḥammad ʿAbd al-Qādir ʿAṭā, 11 vols (Beirut: Dār al-Kutub al-ʿIlmiyya, 2003), 9:349 (no. 18,748); Juynboll, *Encyclopedia*, 223; Melchert, 'Whether to Keep', 184. These are many variants, including ones saying that the Prophet will expel 'the polytheists' (*al-mushrikīn*). Ibn Abī Shayba, *Muṣannaf*, 11:347 (no. 33,539). See further below.

[6] ʿAbd al-Razzāq, *Muṣannaf*, 6:54 (no. 9,987), 10:359–60 (no. 19,368); Mālik b. Anas, *al-Muwaṭṭaʾ* [recension of Yaḥyā b. Yaḥyā al-Laythī al-Andalusī], ed. Bashshār ʿAwwād Maʿrūf, 2 vols (Beirut: Dār al-Gharb al-Islāmī, 1997), 2:470 (no. 2,606); idem, *al-Muwaṭṭaʾ* [recension of Suwayd b. Saʿīd al-Hadathānī], ed. ʿAbd al-Majīd Turkī (Beirut: Dār al-Gharb al-Islāmī, 1994), 159 (no. 184), 469 (no. 641); idem, *al-Muwaṭṭaʾ* [recension of Abū Muṣʿab al-Zuhrī al-Madanī], ed. Bashshār ʿAwwād Maʿrūf and Maḥmūd Muḥammad Khalīl, 2 vols (Beirut: Muʾassasat al-Risāla, 1998), 1:223 (no. 571), 2:62–3 (no. 1,861); idem, *al-Muwaṭṭaʾ* [recension of ʿAbd Allāh b. Maslama al-Qaʿnabī], ed. ʿAbd al-Majīd Turkī (Beirut: Dār al-Gharb al-Islāmī, 1999), 256 (no. 328); Muḥammad b. al-Ḥasan al-Shaybānī, *Muwaṭṭaʾ al-imām Mālik*, ed. ʿAbd al-Wahhāb ʿAbd al-Laṭīf (Cairo: Wizārat al-Awqāf, 1994), 285 (no. 874); Ibn Saʿd, *Ṭabaqāt*, 2:212, 223; al-Bayhaqī, *Sunan*, 9:350 (no. 18,750); al-Bayhaqī, *Dalāʾil al-nubuwwa*, 7:204; Melchert, 'Whether to Keep', 184.

worship!'[7] These reports link Jewish and Christian worship at the sites of their prophets' graves with the need for their expulsion from 'the land of the Arabs'. They are cursed and called 'the worst of people' for their construction and visitation of worship spaces – literally *masājid*, 'mosques' – atop their holy persons' remains. This behaviour is cited as a crucial point of differentiation between Muslims and non-Muslims. Islamic practice is explicitly contrasted with that of Jews and Christians, whose religions (*adyān*) are equated with the veneration of tombs.

These textual traditions indicate that the rejection of relic and tomb veneration was a powerful current within early Islamic discourse. Such practices are cited as a crucial point of distinction between Muslims and their near others, Christians and Jews. The question becomes: how should we read these early Islamic sources? Should we interpret them as reflections of historical reality, or as the kind of rhetorical fashioning and interreligious polemic characteristic of so many early Islamic interactions with Jews and Christians? I suggest that we keep these latter issues in mind, and analyse these iconoclastic reports as part of the gradual formation of Muslim identity and practice over the course of

[7] Ibn Ḥanbal, *Musnad*, 3:221, 223, 227 (nos 1,691, 1,694, 1,699); Abū Yaʿlā Aḥmad b. ʿAlī al-Muthannā al-Taymī, *Musnad Abī Yaʿlā al-Mawṣilī*, ed. Ḥusayn Salīm Asad al-Dārānī, 16 vols (Beirut: Dār al-Maʾmūn li-l-Turāth, 1984–90), 2:177 (no. 872); Ḥumayd b. Zanjawayh, *Kitāb al-Amwāl*, ed. Shākir Dhīb Fayyāḍ (Riyadh: Markaz al-Malik Fayṣal li-l-Buḥūth wa-l-Dirāsāt al-Islāmiyya, 1986), 277–9 (nos 421–2); ʿAlī b. ʿUmar al-Dāraquṭnī, *al-ʿIlal*, ed. Muḥammad b. Ṣāliḥ b. Muḥammad al-Dabbāsī, 10 vols (Muʾassasat al-Rayyān, 2011), 2:260 (no. 679); Abū Bakr Aḥmad b. ʿAmr b. Abī ʿĀṣim, *al-Āḥād wa-l-mathānī*, ed. Bāsim Fayṣal Aḥmad al-Jawābira, 6 vols (Riyadh: Dār al-Rāya, 1991), 1:185 (nos 235–7); al-Bayhaqī, *Sunan*, 9:349–50 (no. 18,749). Variant versions appear in al-Bazzār, *Musnad*, 4:105 (no. 1,278); Ibn Abī Shayba, *Muṣannaf*, 11:346–7 (no. 33,535); al-Khallāl, *Ahl al-milal*, 1:126–7 (no. 139); ʿAbd Allāh b. ʿAbd al-Raḥmān al-Dārimī, *Musnad al-Dārimī al-maʿrūf bi-Sunan al-Dārimī*, ed. Ḥusayn Salīm Asad al-Dārānī, 4 vols (Riyadh: Dār al-Mughnī, 2000), 1,622–3 (no. 2,540); Abū Bakr ʿAbd Allāh b. al-Zubayr al-Qurashī al-Ḥumaydī, *Musnad al-Ḥumaydī*, ed. Ḥusayn Salīm Asad al-Dārānī, 2 vols (Damascus: Dār al-Saqā, 1996), 1:198 (no. 85); Abū ʿUbayd, *Kitāb al-Amwāl*, 181 (no. 276); Abū Dāwūd Sulaymān b. Dāwūd al-Jārūd, *Musnad Abī Dāwūd al-Ṭayālisī*, ed. Muḥammad b. ʿAbd al-Muḥsin al-Turkī, 4 vols (Cairo: Ḥajar, 1999), 1:185 (no. 226); Muḥammad b. Ismāʿīl al-Bukhārī, *Kitāb al-Taʾrīkh al-kabīr*, 4 vols in 8 (Hyderabad: Dāʾirat al-Maʿārif al-ʿUthmāniyya, 1941–64), 2/2:57 (no. 1,950); Ibn Abī ʿĀṣim, *Āḥād*, 184 (no. 234); Melchert, 'Whether to Keep', 184.

the seventh, eighth and ninth centuries CE. In fact, when read within the wider corpus of early Islamic texts, we see that these traditions occupied one side of a continuum of early Muslim perspectives related to issues of venerating material objects and places. Indeed, beyond these rhetorical formulations, textual and archaeological evidence provides glimpses of different usages of tombs and relics among early Muslims.

Situating Early Islamic Criticisms of Christian and Jewish Tomb and Relic Veneration

Polemic against the adoration of holy persons appears throughout many early Islamic texts, often functioning as a strong rhetorical dividing line between Muslims and non-Muslims. Already in the Qur'ān, Jews and Christians are accused of having 'taken their rabbis and their monks, as well as the Messiah son of Mary, as lords beside God' (Q 9:31).[8] Immediately preceding this verse is the statement that 'The Jews said "Ezra is the son of God", and the Christians said, "The Messiah is the son of God",' 'deluded' claims that repeat 'what earlier disbelievers had said' (Q 9:30). While this is the sole qur'ānic mention of Jews' semi-divine conception of Ezra, criticisms of Christians' 'exaggerated' (Q 4:171, 5:77) ideas about Jesus are a more common polemical theme in the text.[9] These verses represent one instance of the much wider qur'ānic criticism of Jews' and (particularly) Christians' inappropriate veneration of certain figures and, thereby, participation in a cardinal qur'ānic sin: *shirk*, the association of other beings as 'partners' with God. In Q 9:31, this censure is explicitly extended to Jewish and Christian attitudes towards rabbis and monks.

[8] Holger M. Zellentin, '*Aḥbār* and *Ruhbān*: Religious Leaders in the Qur'ān in Dialogue with Christian and Rabbinic Literature', in *Qur'ānic Studies Today*, ed. Angelika Neuwirth and Michael A. Sells (London: Routledge, 2016), 262–93; Matthew Dal Santo, *Debating the Saints' Cult in the Age of Gregory the Great* (Oxford: Oxford University Press, 2012), 334. See also Gerald R. Hawting, *The Idea of Idolatry and the Emergence of Islam: From Polemic to History* (Cambridge: Cambridge University Press, 1999), 51, 74 n.20.

[9] Alternative readings have suggested that the qur'ānic mention of 'Uzayr may instead be in reference to Jewish angel veneration. See Patricia Crone, 'The *Book of Watchers* in the Qur'ān', in *The Qur'ānic Pagans and Related Matters: Collected Studies in Three Volumes*, ed. Hanna Siurua, 3 vols (Leiden: Brill, 2016), 1:183–218.

As for tomb and relic veneration, the Qur'ān gives almost no attention to these issues either positively or negatively. Tombs, and what rituals to perform at them, are not thoroughly discussed in the Qur'ān.[10] Arguably the only clear mention of relics occurs at Q 2:248, where 'remnants of the families of Moses and Aaron' (*baqiyyatun mimmā taraka āl Mūsā wa-āl Hārūn*) are said to have been carried inside the Israelites' Ark of the Covenant. It is not specified what exactly these Mosaic and Aaronite items were, but their possession is associated with the authority of the Israelite king Saul, and the Ark as a whole is called a divine sign (*āya*).[11] Notably, the word used for 'remnants' (or, perhaps, 'relics') in this verse is *baqiyya*, not *āthār* as would become much more common in subsequent Islamic literature. While *āthār* does appear in several qur'ānic verses, nowhere is the word used with reference to relics.

Polemic against Jewish and Christian veneration of holy persons – and, specifically, of their relics, tombs and icons – becomes much more detailed in post-qur'ānic sources, such as *ḥadīth*s and historical reports. In a report set during the Prophet's final illness, two of his wives describe a beautiful church that they had seen in Ethiopia. Hearing this, the Prophet fulminates: 'When a righteous man dies among these people, they build a place of worship (*masjid*) upon his grave and decorate it with icons. They are the worst of God's creation!'[12] In reports set during the conquest of Syria, the caliph 'Umar b. al-Khaṭṭāb

[10] *EQ*, s.v. 'Burial' (Juan Eduardo Campo).

[11] McGregor, *Islam and the Devotional Object*, 149. On the Ark of the Covenant as an 'ur-reliquary' in Christian and Jewish tradition, see Cynthia Hahn, *The Reliquary Effect: Enshrining the Sacred Object* (London: Reaktion, 2017), 40–4.

[12] Ibn Abī Shayba, *Muṣannaf*, 3:367 (no. 7,622), 4:565 (no. 11,926); Muslim, *Ṣaḥīḥ*, 1:375–6 (no. 528); al-Bukhārī, *Ṣaḥīḥ*, 116–18 (kitāb al-ṣalāt, bāb 48, 54), 323 (kitāb al-janā'iz, bāb 70); Aḥmad b. Shu'ayb al-Nasā'ī, *Sunan al-Nasā'ī*, ed. Muḥammad Nāṣir al-Dīn al-Albānī and Abū 'Ubayda Mashhūr b. Ḥasan Āl Salmān (Riyadh: Maktabat al-Ma'ārif li-l-Nashr wa-l-Tawzī', 1988), 118 (no. 704); Ibn Sa'd, *Ṭabaqāt*, 2:211; Abū 'Awāna Ya'qūb b. Isḥāq, *Musnad Abī 'Awāna*, ed. Ayman b. 'Ārif al-Dimashqī, 5 vols (Beirut: Dār al-Ma'rifa, 1998), 1:334 (nos 1,189–91); Ibn Ḥanbal, *Musnad*, 40:296 (no. 24,252); Ibn Rāhwayh, *Musnad*, 2:264–5 (nos 768–9); Juynboll, *Encyclopedia*, 203. This tradition is of course also connected to issues of 'iconophobia' in early Islam: Bashear, 'Qibla Musharriqa', 273; Christian C. Sahner, 'The First Iconoclasm in Islam: A New History of the Edict of Yazīd II (AH 104/AD 723)', *Der Islam* 94.1 (2017): 51–3; Daan van Reenen, 'The *Bilderverbot*, a new survey', *Der Islam* 67.1 (1990): 50.

(r. 13–23/634–44) refuses to enter churches there due to the icons (presumably of Jesus, Mary and/or saints) displayed in them.[13] In a *ḥadīth* found in early Shīʿī texts, the Prophet praises his cousin ʿAlī b. Abī Ṭālib (d. 40/661, the third caliph and first Shīʿī imam), but stops himself from saying too much, 'lest a group from my community say about you what the Christians said about Jesus son of Mary [. . .] and none of the people would pass without taking the dust from under your feet, seeking blessing from it.'[14]

Such polemic was also found in other genres. An anonymous, likely ʿAbbāsid-period Islamic text polemicises against Christian relic practices, saying: 'You entomb your dead in your worship places – which God commanded you to keep pure – and heal your sick [in them].'[15] The writer alleges that the prophet Isaiah predicted that 'Those who take their worship spaces as graves and cleanse them with the bones of the dead [. . .] will be burned in a fire that does not go out until the Day of Resurrection.' The author interprets this pseudo-Isaianic citation as a rebuke to Christians specifically, since 'You know that no community does that but yours!'.

While these texts largely target Christians, some traditions condemn Jews' participation in these kinds of practices. In one, the Prophet states, 'God fight the Jews (*al-Yahūd*), for they have taken the graves of their prophets as places of worship!'[16] In another, it is the Children of Israel (*banū Isrāʾīl*) who are said

[13] ʿAbd al-Razzāq, *Muṣannaf*, 1:411–12 (nos 1,610–11), 10:398 (no. 19,486); Ibn Abī Shayba, *Muṣannaf*, 11:577 (no. 34,420); al-Bukhārī, *Ṣaḥīḥ*, 117 (kitāb al-ṣalāt, bāb 54); Bashear, 'Qibla Musharriqa', 274–5; van Reenen, '*Bilderverbot*', 51, 52.

[14] Muḥammad b. Yaʿqūb b. Isḥāq al-Kulaynī al-Rāzī, *al-Kāfī*, ed. ʿAlī Akbar al-Ghaffārī, 8 vols (Tehran: Dār al-Kutub al-Islāmiyya, 1388–1389 AH [1968]), 8:57 (no. 18); Ibn Bābawayh al-Qummī, *Amālī al-Ṣadūq*, intro. Muḥammad Mahdī al-Mūsawī al-Kharsān (Najaf: al-Maṭbaʿa al-Ḥaydariyya, 1970), 85 (*majlis* 21); Furāt b. Ibrāhīm b. Furāt al-Kūfī, *Tafsīr Furāt al-Kūfī*, ed. Muḥammad al-Kāẓim, 2 vols (Beirut: Muʾassasat al-Tārīkh al-ʿArabī, 2011), 2:407; *Kitāb Sulaym b. Qays al-Hilālī*, ed. Muḥammad Bāqir al-Anṣārī al-Zanjānī (Qom: Nashr al-Hādī, 1420 AH [1999–2000]), 413 (no. 58); Muḥammad b. ʿAlī b. Shahrāshūb, *Manāqib Āl Abī Ṭālib*, ed. Muḥammad Kāẓim al-Kutubī, 3 vols (Najaf: al-Maṭbaʿa al-Ḥaydariyya, 1956), 2:166. While the explicit reference here is to Jesus, collecting dust from footprints as a material blessing is a recurrent motif in late antique saints' lives.

[15] Dominique Sourdel, 'Un pamphlet musulman anonyme d'époque ʿAbbāside contre les Chrétiens', *Revue des études islamiques* 34 (1966): 17 (French) and 29 (Arabic).

[16] ʿAbd al-Razzāq, *Muṣannaf*, 1:406 (no. 1,589); al-Bukhārī, *Ṣaḥīḥ*, 118 (kitāb al-ṣalāt, bāb 55); Ibn Ḥanbal, *Musnad*, 13:226 (no. 7,826); Ibn Saʿd, *Ṭabaqāt*, 2:211.

to have done this.[17] Thus both Christians and Jews were the targets of early Islamic ridicule for their treatment of holy persons' graves and bodies.

This polemic did not emerge out of nowhere. In no small part, these Islamic traditions reflect the actual prominence of relic and tomb veneration among late antique communities. As Peter Brown writes, 'late-antique Christianity, as it impinged on the outside world, *was* shrines and relics'.[18] The 'religion of relics' of late antique and early medieval Christianity was a widespread 'system of interrelated practices with respect to holy people and places, together with popular theories and theological reflection that explained and justified those practices'.[19] The Islamic criticisms of Jews may appear more misplaced, since relic and tomb veneration has often been understood as 'marginal and indeed foreign to Judaism'.[20] But, contrary to this conventional wisdom, recent research has pointed to evidence of a 'historical shift [. . .] toward the end of late antiquity in Jewish attitudes toward the bodies of the special dead', which 'delineated new modes of piety that would enable and even encourage the formation in the medieval period of networks of holy tombs'.[21] Indeed, rabbinic texts reference several holy bodies and sacred places that some late antique Jews visited and venerated.[22]

[17] 'Abd al-Razzāq, *Muṣannaf*, 1:406 (no. 1,591).

[18] Brown, *The Cult of the Saints*, 12.

[19] Derek Krueger, 'The Religion of Relics in Late Antiquity and Byzantium', in *Treasures of Heaven: Saints, Relics, and Devotion in Medieval Europe*, ed. Martina Bagnoli, Holger A. Klein, C. Griffith Mann and James Robinson (Baltimore: Walters Art Museum, 2010), 5–17.

[20] Boustan, 'Jewish Veneration', 61–81, with discussion of previous scholarship at 63–5.

[21] Ibid., 62, 81.

[22] Ibid., 'Jewish Veneration', 67–81; Joshua Levinson, 'There Is No Place Like Home: Rabbinic Responses to the Christianization of Palestine', in *Jews, Christians, and the Roman Empire: The Poetics of Power in Late Antiquity*, ed. N. Dohrmann and Annette Yoshiko Reed (Philadelphia: University of Pennsylvania Press, 2013), 99–120; Rafael Rachel Neis, 'Religious Lives of Image-Things, *Avodah Zarah*, and Rabbis in Late Antique Palestine', *Archiv für Religionsgeschichte* 17 (2016): 91–121; Jeffrey Rubenstein, 'Hero, Saint, and Sage: The Life of R. Elazar b. R. Shimon in Pesiqta de Rab Kahana 11', in *The Faces of Torah: Studies in the Texts and Contexts of Ancient Judaism in Honor of Steven Fraade*, ed. Michal Bar-Asher Siegal, Tzvi Novick and Christine Hayes (Göttingen: Vandenhoeck & Ruprecht, 2017), 509–28; Jeffrey Rubenstein, 'A Rabbinic Translation of Relics', in *Crossing Boundaries in Early Judaism and Christianity. Ambiguities, Complexities,*

Given the significance of saint, relic and tomb cult within late antique Christianities and – to a much lesser extent – Judaisms, one can easily see how avoidance of such practices and ideas could be useful in differentiating Islamic praxis and identity from those of the surrounding communities. A few non-Islamic texts from the first centuries AH indeed indicate that this was the case. For example, the Chalcedonian monk Anastasius of Sinai, writing in the late seventh century, says that Muslims (or 'Saracens', as he calls them) 'trample under their feet, mock, set fire to, and destroy' materials such as 'the cross, the saints, relics, holy oils, and many other things'.[23] In the *Chronicle* of the Christian monk Theophanes the Confessor (d. *c.* 818 CE), the author condemns the Byzantine emperor Leo III for, among other things, the fact that 'he made loathsome [the saints'] relics like his mentors, the Arabs, did'.[24] The Syriac *Disputation between a Muslim and a Monk of Bēt Ḥālē* (composed perhaps in the late eighth or early ninth century) finds a Muslim character stating to a Christian, 'We are vigilant concerning the commandments of Muḥammad [. . .] we do not worship the cross, or the bones of martyrs, or images as you do.'[25] In these texts, rejection of relics is presented as characteristic of early Muslims, and a point of differentiation from late antique Christians. These texts seem to corroborate the iconoclastic Islamic traditions, and provide witness to early Muslims' rejection of relic veneration.

and Half-Forgotten Adversaries: Essays in Honor of Alan F. Segal, ed. Kimberly B. Stratton and Andrea Lieber (Leiden: Brill, 2016), 314–32; Eyal Ben-Eliyahu, '"On That Day, His Feet Will Stand on the Mount of Olives": The Mount of Olives and Its Hero between Jews, Christians, and Muslims', *Jewish History* 30 (2016): 29–42.

[23] MS Vaticanus gr. 2592, 124r. Translation adapted from Robert Hoyland, *Seeing Islam as Others Saw It: A Survey and Evaluation of Christian, Jewish, and Zoroastrian Writings on Early Islam* (Princeton: Darwin Press, 1997), 100–1; Jessica Lee Ehinger, 'Revolutionizing the Status Quo: Appeals to Pre-Islamic Christianity in the Writings of Anastasius of Sinai', *Studies in Late Antiquity* 3 (2019): 28–9.

[24] *Theophanis Chronographia*, ed. Carolus de Boor, 2 vols (Leipzig: 1883–5), 1:406; *The Chronicle of Theophanes Confessor: Byzantine and Near Eastern History AD 284–813*, trans. Cyril Mango and Roger Scott (Oxford: Clarendon Press, 1997), 561 (adapted).

[25] David G. K. Taylor, 'The Disputation between a Muslim and a Monk of Bēt Ḥālē: Syriac Text and Annotated English Translation', in *Christsein in der islamischen Welt: Festschrift für Martin Tamcke zum 60. Geburtstag*, ed. Sidney H. Griffith and Sven Grebenstein (Wiesbaden: Harrassowitz, 2015), 208 (section 9).

Yet we must keep in mind that these Christian texts are themselves rhetorically inflected literary productions, whose authors were interested in articulating Christian boundaries and identity in the face of the emergent religious 'Other' of Islam. In his story collection, Anastasius presents a polemical image of Muslims, whom he frequently compares to, and associates with, demons.[26] Rather than testimony to actual destruction of relics, Anastasius' mention of Muslims trampling on sacred items is a depiction of stereotyped 'wrong belief'.[27] Similarly, Theophanes' *Chronicle* deploys an image of Arab disrespect for saints' relics and – especially – icons in order to criticise the iconoclast Christian emperor Leo III (r. 717–41). Yet while Theophanes calls Leo 'Saracen-headed' for his removal and destruction of icons, actual connections between the Byzantine and Islamic iconoclasms are debated.[28] Moreover, there is little evidence (outside Theophanes' brief and unspecific mention) of relics being drawn into Leo's iconoclastic actions.[29] Finally, the *Disputation* offers a highly orchestrated literary exchange that addresses commonly debated points of Church doctrine, including the veneration of relics and icons. By the text's formulaic ending, the Muslim interlocutor comes round to the Christian monk's position on these issues, admitting that 'your way of thinking is better than ours'.[30]

These texts certainly depict Muslims as offering little respect for Christian relics. But Anastasius, Theophanes and the *Disputation*'s author all present

[26] Ehinger, 'Revolutionizing the Status Quo', 26–30; Bernard Flusin, 'Démons et Sarrasins: l'auteur et le propos des *Diègèmata stèriktika* d'Anastase le Sinaïte', *Travaux et Mémoires* 11 (1991): 381–409.

[27] Ehinger, 'Revolutionizing the Status Quo', 23.

[28] Sahner, 'First Iconoclasm', 6, 10, and the sources cited therein.

[29] John Wortley, 'Iconoclasm and Leipsanoclasm: Leo III, Constantine V and the Relics', *Byzantinische Forschungen* 8 (1982): 253–79; Stephen Gero, *Byzantine Iconoclasm during the Reign of Leo III, with Particular Attention to the Oriental Sources*, CSCO 346, Subsidia 41 (Louvain: Secrétariat du CorpusSCO, 1973), 97–102.

[30] The Muslim character even admits that, in the case of the image of Jesus sent to King Abgar of Edessa, 'it is right that that all who believe in Christ should honour his image'. See Sidney H. Griffith, 'Crosses, Icons and the Image of Christ in Edessa: The Place of Iconophobia in the Christian–Muslim Controversies of Early Islamic Times', in *Transformations of Late Antiquity: Essays for Peter Brown*, ed. Philip Rousseau and Manolis Papoutsakis (Burlington: Aldershot, 2009), 63–84.

these images of Muslims in the process of making theological and doctrinal arguments for their Christian audiences. To the extent that these texts provide evidence of early Muslims' rejection of relics, we must remain aware of these authors' rhetorical aims in emphasising (if not creating) potential differences between Christians and Muslims.

On the other hand, other Christian texts from the first centuries AH instead depict Muslims as friendly towards, and even solicitous of, Christians' relics. Christian hagiographies feature Muslim characters who seek out saints' relics, and related materials, for healing and blessing.[31] In one case, a Muslim emir himself wields a piece of the True Cross to heal a demoniac of his illness.[32] Meanwhile, in the responsa of the Syrian Orthodox bishop Jacob of Edessa (d. 708 CE), Jacob is asked if it is acceptable to provide Muslims with *ḥnānā*: that is, oil and water mixed with dust from relics of the saints.[33] Jacob gives his enthusiastic approval, saying that 'None should at all hinder anything like this'.[34] With this brief mention of Christians distributing relics to Muslims, we perhaps catch a glimpse of a tangible form of interreligious mixing at the turn of the eighth century CE.[35] Rather than rejecting or destroying relics, Muslims in these texts seek out such materials from Christian saints and leaders.

[31] Michael Philip Penn, *Envisioning Islam: Syriac Christians and the Early Muslim World* (Philadelphia: University of Pennsylvania Press, 2015), 134–8, 156–8; Jack Tannous, *The Making of the Medieval Middle East: Religion, Society, and Simple Believers* (Princeton: Princeton University Press, 2018), 364–71; *Life of Timothy of Kākhushtā*, 508–9, 584–5.

[32] Michael Penn, 'Demons Gone Wild: An Introduction and Translation of the Syriac *Qenneshre Fragment*', *Orientalia Christiana Periodica* 27 (2013): 367–99. Cf. Hoyland, *Seeing Islam*, 142–7.

[33] On *ḥnānā*, see Christelle Jullien and Florence Jullien, 'Du *ḥnana* ou la bénédiction contestée', in *Sur les pas des Araméens chrétiens: Mélanges offerts à Alain Desreumaux*, ed. Françoise Briquel Chatonnet and Muriel Debié (Paris: Geuthner, 2010), 333–49.

[34] Arthur Vööbus (ed. and trans.), *The Synodicon in the West Syrian Tradition*, 4 vols (Louvain: Secrétariat du CorpusSCO, 1975–6), 1:249.

[35] For analysis of this passage, see Penn, *Envisioning Islam*, 159–60; Tannous, *Making of the Medieval Middle East*, 154, 370–1; David G. K. Taylor, 'The Syriac Baptism of St John: A Christian Ritual of Protection for Muslim Children', in *The Late Antique World of Early Islam: Muslims among Christians and Jews in the East Mediterranean*, ed. Robert G. Hoyland (Princeton: Darwin Press, 2015), 452–3.

Of course, as with the Christian writers mentioned before, here too we must be wary of the rhetorical strategies of these texts' authors, who had their own reasons for presenting Muslims as desirous of Christian holy men and their relics. Muslim characters seeking out Christian saints and relics would affirm to Christian audiences the power and authenticity of these holy people and objects. While Jacob of Edessa's text appears to be less literarily constructed than the hagiographies, his willingness to distribute *ḥnānā* to Muslims could likewise be seen as a 'demonstration of Christian power' to provide healing through this blessed material.[36] In short, whether they depict Muslims decrying or desiring relics, late antique Christian texts likely provide only opaque access to any historical reality of early Muslims' views on or activities with relics. Instead, these texts display Christians' efforts to define themselves, in part, through comparison with Muslims.

I would argue that similar rhetorical efforts to define boundaries and identity are at play in the Islamic traditions that criticise Jews and Christians for their relic and tomb worship. And – like the Christian texts' presentations of Muslims as either relic defilers or desirers – the reliability of these Islamic traditions is quite questionable. For example, the enactment of sectarian boundaries clearly colours the traditions about the Prophet's call to expel Jews and Christians from the Arabian Peninsula, the emergent Islamic holy land. This early Islamic narrative place-making is reminiscent of the biblical stories about the Israelites' destruction of the Canaanites and their idols during the conquest of the Land of Israel. There, too, the expulsion of 'foreign' elements from a sacred terrain was presented as a necessary component of the creation of a new, pure community.[37] Yet, like the continued Canaanite presence in Israel even after the 'conquest' of the Israelite Holy Land, there is considerable evidence of ongoing Jewish and Christian habitation in Arabia long after their alleged expulsion.[38]

[36] Penn, *Envisioning Islam*, 160. For a different perspective, see Tannous, *Making of the Medieval Middle East*, 370.

[37] Lawrence M. Wills, *Not God's People: Insiders and Outsiders in the Biblical World* (Lanham: Rowman & Littlefield, 2008).

[38] Munt, 'No Two Religions', 259–64.

While the historicity of an expulsion of Christians and Jews from Arabia is dubious, there was a clear significance in the rhetorical enactment of this geographic and sectarian boundary.[39] These expulsion traditions seem to have taken shape in the eighth and ninth centuries, as Muslim authorities drew increasingly sharper communal boundaries between Muslims and others.[40] By the late eighth or early ninth century, a version of Muḥammad's final wishes circulated in which he commands the Muslim community to expel not Jews and Christians, but 'the associaters' or 'the polytheists', the *mushrikīn*.[41] Likely uncoincidentally, it is in this same period that 'the term *mushrikūn* was in the process of becoming a common synonym for "People of the Book" (Jews and Christians) within Islamic jurisprudential and exegetical circles'.[42]

The *ḥadīth*s and other Islamic texts that criticise the veneration of tombs and relics – and closely associate these practices with Jews and Christians – are highly charged pieces of polemic. The Prophet calls Jews and Christians 'the worst of God's creation' because of such practices, strongly discouraging Muslim participation in them. Indeed, grave veneration functions in several of the expulsion traditions as a – if not the – primary rationale for the alleged banishment of Jews and Christians from the Arabian Peninsula. These traditions articulated, and thus helped to create, an important distinction between Muslims and non-Muslims, and between Islamic and non-Islamic practice.

39 Aaron W. Hughes, *An Anxious Inheritance: Religious Others and the Shaping of Sunnī Orthodoxy* (New York: Oxford University Press, 2022), 45–8.

40 Melchert, 'Whether to Keep', 184; Munt, 'No Two Religions', 266, 269; Juynboll, *Encyclopedia*, 223; Peter Webb, *Imagining the Arabs: Arab Identity and the Rise of Islam* (Edinburgh: Edinburgh University Press, 2016), 136–7, 166–7.

41 'Abd al-Razzāq, *Muṣannaf*, 6:57 (no. 9,992), 10:361 (no. 19,371); Ibn Abī Shayba, *Muṣannaf*, 11:346 (no. 33,534); Abū Dāwūd, *Sunan*, 3:484 (no. 3,023); al-Bayhaqī, *Sunan*, 9:349 (no. 18,747). My dating here is based on the analysis and attribution to Sufyān b. 'Uyayna (d. *c.* 198/814) provided in Nicolet Boekhoff-van der Voort, 'Untangling the "Unwritten Documents" of the Prophet Muḥammad. An *Isnād-cum-Matn* Analysis of Interwoven Traditions', *Religions* 12.8 (2021), https://doi.org/10.3390/rel12080579 (last accessed 7 June 2023). This attribution is noted also in Melchert, 'Whether to Keep', 184.

42 Anna Chrysostomides, '"There Is No Harm in It": Muslim Participation in Levantine Christian Religious Festivals (750–1000)', *Al-Masāq* 33.2 (2021): 131. For some examples, see Hawting, *Idea of Idolatry*, 82.

Such Prophetic statements were clearly components of arguments made against Muslim participation in tomb and relic rituals, and they certainly helped to authorise, and likely create, opposition to these practices among many early Muslims. In later centuries, these reports would be deployed by many Muslim writers and thinkers as important evidence in their own polemics against tomb and relic veneration.[43]

'What they Made': Glimpses of Early Islamic Tomb and Relic Veneration

What do such rhetorical claims and polemical accusations tell us about Muslims' lived practices and beliefs regarding tomb and relic veneration in the seventh, eighth and ninth centuries? Historians of medieval Islamic law note that '[a]s witnesses to cultural and religious life, the ulama cannot be treated as straightforward, disinterested bystanders', since they had their own ideological agendas to pursue.[44] This was just as true (if not truer) of the *ḥadīth* scholars in the first Islamic centuries, whose authority was generally rather limited.[45] Simultaneously, from the non-'scholarly' side, there was often 'thin' knowledge of the specifics of prescribed Islamic ritual and practice among converts to the new faith.[46] If some early Muslims incorporated a rejection of relic and tomb veneration into their emerging orthodoxies, were other Muslims aware of, and concerned with, this dogma?

43 Daniella Talmon-Heller, 'Historiography in the Service of the *Muftī*: Ibn Taymiyya on the Origins and Fallacies of *Ziyāra*', *ILS* 26 (2019): 234, 247–8; Talmon-Heller, *Sacred Place*, 112; Christopher S. Taylor, *In the Vicinity of the Righteous:* Ziyāra *and the Veneration of Muslim Saints in Late Medieval Egypt* (Leiden: Brill, 1999), 180–3.

44 Grehan, *Twilight of the Saints*, 5. On the methodological issues involved with using Islamic legal sources for reconstructing social history, see David S. Powers, *Law, Society, and Culture in the Maghrib, 1300–1500* (Cambridge: Cambridge University Press, 2002), 21–2; Amalia Zomeño, 'The Stories in the Fatwas and the Fatwas in History', in *Narratives of Truth in Islamic Law*, ed. Baudouin Dupret, Barbara Drieskens and Annelies Moors (London: I. B. Tauris, 2008), 25–49.

45 Jonathan E. Brockopp, *Muhammad's Heirs: The Rise of Muslim Scholarly Communities, 622–950* (Cambridge: Cambridge University Press, 2017), 57. On the usage of legal sources in reconstructing early Islamic social history, see Halevi, *Muhammad's Grave*, 5–13.

46 Tannous, *Making of the Medieval Middle East*, 276; Harry Munt, 'What Did Conversion to Islam Mean in Seventh-Century Arabia?' in *Islamisation: Comparative Perspectives from History*, ed. A. C. S. Peacock (Edinburgh: Edinburgh University Press, 2017), 83–101.

A variety of sources illustrate a tension between the iconoclastic rhetoric of the Prophet's deathbed wishes and the apparent reality of early Muslim veneration of prophets' and holy persons' tombs and relics. Indeed, as Yusuf Ragheb noted in an article published fifty years ago regarding Islamic prohibitions against building shrines upon tombs, 'These prescriptions were violated from the earliest times of Islam'.[47] While Ragheb's article largely relied on relatively late literary evidence, I will show here that early texts already witness Muslim rituals involving sacred tombs, objects and spaces. In addition to literary material, archaeological evidence provides further signs of Muslim veneration of sites associated with sacred figures.

A distinct site of tension in the early Islamic centuries was found at the Prophet Muḥammad's tomb. Early texts suggest that the Prophet himself foresaw, and feared, the practices that might come to surround it. In biographies of the Prophet, his wife 'Āʾisha bt. Abī Bakr (d. 58/678) reports that, during his final illness, the Prophet placed a cloak over his face, which he would occasionally lift from his mouth and shout: 'God's curse be on the Christians and the Jews, for they have taken the graves of their prophets as places of worship!'[48] In many versions of this narrative, 'Āʾisha glosses Muḥammad's words, explaining that he was 'warning against the like of what they [Jews and Christians] did'. Elsewhere, she comments: 'His grave would have been made prominent, if not for the fear that it be taken as a worship space.'[49]

[47] Yūsuf Rāġib, 'Les premiers monuments funéraires de l'Islam', *Annales Islamologiques* 9 (1970): 22.

[48] Ibn Hishām, *Sīra*, 1,021; 'Abd al-Razzāq, *Muṣannaf*, 1:406 (no. 1,588), 5:431–2, 8:464–5 (no. 15,917); Ibn Sa'd, *Ṭabaqāt*, 2:211, 226; al-Bukhārī, *Ṣaḥīḥ*, 118 (kitāb al-ṣalāt, bāb 55), 855 (kitāb aḥādīth al-anbīyāʾ, bāb 50), 1,089 (kitāb al-maghāzī, bāb 83), 1,471 (kitāb al-libās, bāb 19); Muslim, *Ṣaḥīḥ*, 1:377 (no. 531); al-Nasāʾī, *Sunan*, 118 (no. 703); Abū 'Awāna, *Musnad*, 1:333 (no. 1,183); al-Dārimī, *Sunan*, 881 (no. 1,443); Ibn Ḥanbal, *Musnad*, 40:66 (no. 24060), 43:87–8, 370, 373 (nos 25,916, 26,350, 26,353); Sulaymān b. Aḥmad al-Ṭabarānī, *Musnad al-Shāmiyyīn*, ed. Ḥamdī 'Abd al-Majīd al-Salafī, 4 vols (Beirut: Muʾassasat al-Risāla, 1989), 4:216 (no. 3,131); al-Bayhaqī, *Dalāʾil al-nubuwwa*, 7:203. This tradition is connected with the teaching of Ibn Shihāb al-Zuhrī: Juynboll, *Encyclopedia*, 705; Shoemaker, *Death of a Prophet*, 94.

[49] Ibn Abī Shayba, *Muṣannaf*, 3:367 (no. 7,621); Ibn Sa'd, *Ṭabaqāt*, 2:212; al-Bukhārī, *Ṣaḥīḥ*, 320–1, 336 (kitāb al-janāʾiz, bāb 61, 96), 1,088 (kitāb al-maghāzī, bāb 83); Muslim, *Ṣaḥīḥ*, 1:376 (no. 529); Abū 'Awāna, *Musnad*, 1:332–3 (nos 1,181–2); Ibn Ḥanbal, *Musnad*, 41:58, 383 (nos 24,513, 24,895), 43:254 (no. 26,178); Ibn Rāhwayh, *Musnad*, 2:263 (no. 767); Aḥmad b. Yaḥyā al-Balādhurī, *Ansāb al-ashrāf*, vol. 1, ed. Muḥammad Ḥamīdullāh (Cairo:

Similar Prophetic commands about his grave are recorded elsewhere in *ḥadīths*. The Companion Jundab b. ʿAbd Allāh (d. 64/683–4) reports that, five days before his death, the Prophet said: 'Those before you took the tombs of their prophets and their saints as places of worship. Do not take tombs as places of worship, I forbid you from that!'[50] In another *ḥadīth*, the Prophet pleads, 'Oh God, do not make my grave into an idol (*wathan*) to be prayed towards [or, worshipped]! God's anger is strong against those who take the graves of their prophets as places of worship!'[51]

Despite these warnings and prohibitions, the Prophet Muḥammad's grave did, in fact, become a prominent place of Muslim worship. As part of the grand reconstruction of the Prophet's Mosque in Medina under the caliph al-Walīd b. ʿAbd al-Malik (r. 86–96/705–15) and his governor over the Ḥijāz, ʿUmar b. ʿAbd al-ʿAzīz, the Prophet's tomb was incorporated, inside an enclosed chamber in the building's south-eastern corner, into the mosque structure itself. With this construction of an 'imperial monument' in the Medina Mosque, 'the caliphate proceeded to transform Muḥammad's low grave into an official shrine'.[52] As Harry Munt has put it, 'it seems as though al-Walīd and ʿUmar b. ʿAbd al-ʿAzīz

Dār al-Maʿārif, 1959), 551 (no. 1,119). The apparent common link for this version is the somewhat obscure Kūfan transmitter Hilāl b. Miqlāṣ [or b. Abī Ḥumayd] al-Wazzān, active in the early eighth century: Ibn Saʿd, *Ṭabaqāt*, 8:444.

[50] Ibn Abī Shayba, *Muṣannaf*, 3:366–7 (no. 7,620); Ibn Saʿd, *Ṭabaqāt*, 2:211; Muslim, *Ṣaḥīḥ*, 1:377–8 (no. 532); Abū ʿAwāna, *Musnad*, 1:334–5 (no. 1,192); Ibn ʿAsākir, *Taʾrīkh*, 30:252. The common link is ʿUbayd Allāh b. ʿAmr (d. 180/796–7, Raqqa), who narrates it from Zayd b. Abī Unaysa (d. *c.* 124/742–3, al-Rahā) > ʿAmr b. Murra (d. *c.* 110/728–9, Kūfa) > ʿAbd Allāh b. al-Ḥārith al-Najrānī (d. *c.* 85/704, Kūfa) > Jundab.

[51] ʿAbd al-Razzāq, *Muṣannaf*, 1:406 (no. 1,587); Ibn Abī Shayba, *Muṣannaf*, 3:366 (no. 7,618), 4:566 (no. 11,930); Ibn Saʿd, *Ṭabaqāt*, 2:212; Mālik, *Muwaṭṭaʾ* [recension of Yaḥyā al-Laythī], 1:243 (no. 475); Mālik, *Muwaṭṭaʾ* [recension of Abū Muṣʿab], 1:223 (no. 570); Mālik, *Muwaṭṭaʾ* [recension of Suwayd], 159 (no. 184); Mālik, *Muwaṭṭaʾ* [recension of al-Qaʿnabī], 255–6 (no. 328). The common link for this tradition appears to be either Zayd b. Aslam (d. 136/753–4 or 143/760–1) or ʿAṭāʾ b. Yasār (d. 103/721–2), a Medinan legal authority and a Medinan *qāṣṣ* respectively. On them, see Juynboll, *Encyclopedia*, 689; Lyall R. Armstrong, *The* Quṣṣāṣ *of Early Islam* (Leiden: Brill, 2017), 123–4, 161, 177, 299. A slightly different version of this report is transmitted through a different set of *isnāds*, clustering around the Medinan transmitter Suhayl b. Abī Ṣāliḥ (d. 138/755): Ibn Saʿd, *Ṭabaqāt*, 2:213; Ibn Ḥanbal, *Musnad*, 12:314 (no. 7,358); al-Ḥumaydī, *Musnad*, 2:224 (no. 1,055); Abū Yaʿlā, *Musnad*, 12:33–4 (no. 6,681); al-Bukhārī, *Taʾrīkh*, 2/1:47 (no. 177).

[52] Halevi, *Muhammad's Grave*, 195; Munt, *Holy City of Medina*, 106.

were, right at the end of the first century AH, the first to provide a shrine for the Prophet Muḥammad in Medina'.[53]

Of course, in the eighth century and thereafter, the Muslims who related stories about the Prophet's deathbed pronouncements knew all about these architectural developments that had occurred in the years since his death. In some cases, the story transmitters were themselves directly involved with the Umayyad construction efforts.[54] Scholars have argued that the traditions about the Prophet's warnings to future Muslims were likely produced to critique the Umayyad building project in Medina and Muslims' worship practices there.[55] Indeed, the conflict between the Prophet's rhetoric and the reality of his tomb's commemoration would have been difficult to ignore.

'Āʾisha's glosses of the Prophet's words also seem to critique the Umayyad building project. In most versions, her comment that the Prophet was 'warning against the like of what they did' seemingly interprets the Prophet as cautioning the Muslim community regarding what the Jews and Christians had done with the graves of their prophets. In one version, however, the wording attributed to her – 'he was warning them [the Muslims] against the like of what they made' (*yuḥadhdhiru-hum mithla ma ṣanaʿū*) – can plausibly be read as referencing what the Muslim community itself did with Muḥammad's tomb.[56] Notably, this version is transmitted by Ṣāliḥ b. Kaysān (d. *c.* 140/757–8): a Medinan scholar, involved in the Umayyad construction of the Prophet's Mosque, who appears in the *isnād*s for some traditions criticising the veneration of the tombs of prophets.[57] Here, Ṣāliḥ perhaps endows 'Āʾisha with foreknowledge of what the Muslim community would do with their Prophet's tomb.

[53] Munt, *Holy City of Medina*, 111.

[54] This included the Umayyad governor (and later caliph) 'Umar b. 'Abd al-ʿAzīz, who we encountered above transmitting a tradition on the Prophet's wish to expel Jews and Christians from Arabia because of their tomb veneration. Cf. Munt, 'No Two Religions', 265; Munt, *Holy City of Medina*, 108 n.51; Essam S. Ayyad, *The Making of the Mosque: A Survey of Religious Imperatives* (Piscataway, NJ: Gorgias, 2019), 353–4, 402–3.

[55] Munt, *Holy City of Medina*, 108; Shoemaker, *Death of a Prophet*, 259; Halevi, *Muhammad's Grave*, 193.

[56] Ibn Saʿd, *Ṭabaqāt*, 2:211; Ibn Ḥanbal, *Musnad*, 43:373 (no. 26,353). Ṣāliḥ b. Kaysān also appears in the *isnād*s of other, slightly variant versions of this *ḥadīth*: Ibn Hishām, *Sīra*, 1021; Ibn Ḥanbal, *Musnad*, 43:370 (no. 26,350).

[57] Munt, *Holy City of Medina*, 108 n.51.

In addition to these *ḥadīths*, Islamic historical texts about the city of Medina also offer traces of evidence suggesting that Muslims used the Prophet's grave as a site of worship from an early date. According to a report attributed to the important Medinan scholar ʿUrwa b. al-Zubayr (d. *c.* 93–4/711–13), prior to its Umayyad-era reconstruction, the wall around Prophet's burial spot had grown thin and weak because 'the people had eaten it' (*qad akala-hu al-nās*) by scraping pieces of it off.[58] This report suggests that seventh- and early eighth-century visitors were collecting (and perhaps consuming) pieces of the Prophet's tomb structure as contact relics, much like Christians did at their own saints' shrines. Later histories indicate that this wall had itself been erected because people were

[58] *Kitāb al-Manāsik wa-amākin ṭuruq al-ḥajj wa-maʿālim al-jazīra*, ed. Ḥamad al-Jāsir (Riyadh: Manshūrāt Dār al-Yamāma li-l-Baḥth wa-l-Tarjama wa-l-Nashr, 1969), 375–6. The *isnād* for the report is: Ṣāliḥ b. Muḥammad (active early ninth century, Baghdad) > Sulaymān b. ʿAbd al-ʿAzīz [al-Zuhrī] (active early ninth century) > his father [ʿAbd al-ʿAzīz b. ʿImrān b. ʿAbd al-ʿAzīz, known as Ibn Abī Thābit al-Aʿraj] (d. 197/812–13, Medina/Baghdad) > [ʿAbd al-Raḥmān b. ʿAbd Allāh b. Dhakwān] Ibn Abī al-Zinād (d. *c.* 174–5/790–2, Medina/Baghdad) > Hishām b. ʿUrwa (d. 146/763–4, Medina/Baghdad) > his father [ʿUrwa b. al-Zubayr]. The association of the report with ʿUrwa b. al-Zubayr is plausible, as he lived in Medina in this period and was allegedly in contact there with both the governor ʿUmar b. ʿAbd al-ʿAzīz and the caliph al-Walīd. Ibn Abī al-Zinād's transmission of material from Hishām b. ʿUrwa is attested elsewhere. Cf. Anthony, *Muhammad and the Empires*, 106–9. The *isnād* is otherwise weak, with Sulaymān b. ʿAbd al-ʿAzīz as the weakest link. This son of the Medinan ʿAbd al-ʿAzīz b. ʿImrān is not well-known as a transmitter, but he is a frequently cited source in the *Kitāb al-Manāsik*, especially for reports on the Prophet's Mosque. ʿAbd al-ʿAzīz b. ʿImrān was himself considered untrustworthy as a *ḥadīth* transmitter, but his historical *akhbār* (especially about Medina) were accepted. The two of them (ʿAbd al-ʿAzīz and his son) were descendants of the Prophetic Companion ʿAbd al-Raḥmān b. ʿAwf (d. *c.* 32/652–3), and their family were well-connected elites in Medina. On these transmitters, see Abū Bakr Aḥmad b. ʿAlī al-Khaṭīb al-Baghdādī, *Taʾrīkh Madīnat al-Salām*, ed. Bashshār ʿAwwād Maʿrūf, 16 vols (Beirut: Dār al-Gharb al-Islāmī, 2001), 10:435 (no. 4,810), 11:494–8 (no. 5,312), 12:200–3 (no. 5,556); Essam S. Ayyad, 'An Historiographical Analysis of the Arabic Accounts of Early Mosques: With Special Reference to those at Madina, Baṣra and Kūfa', *Journal of Islamic Studies* 30.1 (2019): 12; Munt, *Holy City of Medina*, 108 n.48, 159; Asad Q. Ahmed, *The Religious Elite of the Early Islamic Ḥijāz: Five Prosopographical Case Studies* (Oxford: Prosopographica et Genealogica, 2011), 59; Tobias Andersson, *Early Sunnī Historiography: A Study of the* Tārīkh *of Khalīfa b. Khayyāṭ* (Leiden: Brill, 2019), 129; *EI*[3], s.v. 'Ibn Abī l-Zinād' (Christopher Melchert).

taking 'dust from the Prophet's grave', leading 'Ā'isha to request that a wall be built around it.[59] When people then began taking dust from a small opening (*kūwa*) in this new wall, 'Ā'isha ordered that the opening be plugged up.

Collecting contact relics was not all that was allegedly done at the Prophet's tomb: prayer was too. Further on in the same report cited above, 'Urwa b. al-Zubayr says that the Umayyad builders structured the new enclosure around the tomb in an unusually angled way, 'such that it would not be prayed towards'. A report transmitted from the Medinan historian Abū Ghassān Muḥammad b. Yaḥyā al-Kinānī (d. *c.* 210/825–6) states that the builders constructed the enclosure in its distinctive pentagonal shape 'out of dislike that it resemble the square Ka'ba and be taken as a *qibla* to be prayed towards'.[60] In another report attributed to 'Urwa b. al-Zubayr, it is explicitly affirmed that 'the people (*al-nās*) would pray towards the [Prophet's] tomb, so 'Umar b. 'Abd al-'Azīz ordered that it [the wall?] be elevated such that the people would not pray towards it'.[61] These traditions suggest that Muslims visited and prayed at the Prophet's tomb even before the Umayyad reconstruction.

[59] Ibn al-Najjār, *al-Durra al-Thamīna fī ta'rīkh al-Madīna*, ed. Muḥammad Zaynahum Muḥammad 'Azab (Cairo: Maktabat al-Thaqāfa al-Dīniyya, 1995), 211; Abū Bakr b. al-Ḥusayn b. 'Umar al-Marāghī, *Taḥqīq al-nuṣra bi-talkhīṣ ma'ālim dār al-hijra*, ed. Muḥammad 'Abd al-Jawwād al-Aṣma'ī (Medina: al-Maktaba al-'Ilmiyya, 1955), 105–6; 'Alī b. 'Abd Allāh al-Samhūdī, *Wafā' al-wafā bi-akhbār Dār al-Muṣṭafā*, ed. Qāsim al-Sāmarrā'ī, 5 vols (London: Mu'assasat al-Furqān li-l-Turāth al-Islāmī, 2001), 2:301.

[60] al-Samhūdī, *Wafā' al-wafā*, 2:302; Halevi, *Muhammad's Grave*, 194; Munt, *Holy City of Medina*, 108. A similar comment appears in Ibn Abī Zayd al-Qayrawānī, *Kitāb al-Jāmi' fī al-sunan wa-l-ādāb wa-l-māghāzī wa-l-tārīkh*, ed. Muḥammad Abū al-Ajfān and 'Uthmān Baṭṭīkh (Beirut: Mu'assasat al-Risāla, 1983), 141.

[61] Abū Bakr Muḥammad b. al-Ḥasan al-Ājurrī, *Kitāb al-Sharī'a*, ed. 'Abd Allāh b. 'Umar b. Sulaymān al-Dumayjī, 6 vols (Riyadh: Dār al-Waṭan, 1997), 5:2,389–90 (no. 1,871); al-Samhūdī, *Wafā' al-wafā*, 2:305; Ibn Ḥajar al-'Asqalānī, *Fatḥ al-bārī bi-sharḥ Ṣaḥīḥ al-Bukhārī*, ed. Abū Qutayba Naẓar Muḥammad al-Fāryābī, 17 vols (Riyadh: Dār al-Ṭayba, 2005), 4:195. The *isnād* for the report in al-Ājurrī (d. 360/970–1) is: Muḥammad b. Makhlad al-Dūrī (d. 331/942–3, Baghdad) > Rawḥ b. al-Farj b. Zakariyyā (d. 288/900–1, Baghdad) > Abū Ṭālib 'Abd al-Jabbār b. 'Āṣim (d. *c.* 230/844–5, Baghdad) > Shu'ayb b. Isḥāq (d. 189/804–5, Baṣra/Damascus) > Hishām b. 'Urwa > his father ['Urwa]. On these transmitters, see al-Khaṭīb al-Baghdādī, *Ta'rīkh*, 4:499–501 (no. 1,673), 9:395 (no. 4,463), 11:411–12 (no. 5,757); al-Dhahabī, *Siyar*, 9:103; Ibn Sa'd, *Ṭabaqāt*, 9:353, 476.

In fact, according to one apologetic tradition, the Umayyad project in Medina was an attempt to discipline 'the people' away from these rituals at the tomb. Transmitted from the Medinan historian Muḥammad b. al-Ḥasan b. Zabāla (d. after 199/814–15), this report directly connects 'Umar b. 'Abd al-'Azīz's construction to the Prophet's iconoclastic deathbed wishes. According to this report, 'Umar tucked the tomb structure away in the corner of the mosque 'so that the people would not take it as a special *qibla* for prayer inside the mosque. That was because the Messenger of God said, "God fight the Jews who took the tombs of their prophets as places of worship", and he said, "Oh God, do not make my grave into an idol!"'[62]

While these reports offer evidence of early Muslim veneration of the Prophet's tomb, they generally place such activity among 'the people', in what could plausibly (if polemically) be described as 'popular practice'. Yet, as we will see in chapters below, veneration of the Prophet Muḥammad's tomb and relics is evidenced not only in the criticisms that such practices receive in early texts, but also in positive descriptions of them. Visiting the Prophet's grave, touching his *minbar* for blessing, and praying at sites associated with his life are all condemned by various early Muslim voices, who reprimand the individuals and groups whom they encounter performing such rituals. But in addition to these criticisms – sometimes immediately preceding or following them – we find reports of prominent Muslims performing such rituals. Reports of Companions visiting and praying at the Prophet's tomb appear in several cases, with a positive valence given to them. *Ḥadīth*s attributed to the Prophet encourage visitation of this grave, and associate this ritual with his intercession on the Day of Judgement. Looking at sources beyond the canonical *ḥadīth* compilations (and even within them), we find challenged terrain regarding devotion to the Prophet.[63]

These sources about the Prophet Muḥammad's tomb are far from the only evidence of early Muslims visiting and venerating spaces associated with prophets and other holy persons. Beyond the literary evidence for the visitation of many other sites – several of which will be explored in the following chapters – archaeological evidence provides intriguing glimpses of early

[62] al-Samhūdī, *Wafā' al-wafā*, 2:306. Ibn Zabāla transmits this from Muḥammad b. Hilāl (d. 162/778–9, Medina). On the latter, see Ayyad, 'Historiographical Analysis', 15.

[63] These reports will be discussed at greater length in Chapters 4 and 5.

Muslims' possible ritual practices at sacred locations. I close this chapter by examining two such sites: the Kathisma shrine outside Jerusalem, and the mosque at Ruṣāfa in northern Syria.

Originally built in the fifth century CE, the Church of the Kathisma was located south of Jerusalem, on the route towards Bethlehem.[64] Its name came from a stone found at the church's centre that local tradition identified as the 'seat' (in Greek, *kathisma*) where the Virgin Mary had rested while she was pregnant with Jesus and journeying to Bethlehem. This stone was 'the focus and the *raison d'être* of the church', which was constructed in an octagonal shape with an ambulatory surrounding the stone, guiding visitors around the sacred site/relic at the building's centre.[65] Visitors took blessings from the stone: a pipe flowed water over it and into a collection area, supplying pilgrims with a consumable contact relic 'hallowed by its contact with the holy "seat" of the Virgin'.[66] Indeed, archaeologists have uncovered a glass vessel at the Kathisma site similar to those that were used to collect such fluids from other sacred sites around Jerusalem.[67]

Though the Kathisma site began its life as a Christian sacred space, archaeological evidence suggests that Muslims adopted it too in the late seventh and eighth centuries. At the stratigraphic level of this period, two notable architectural additions to the building have been uncovered: a floor niche pointing southward, identified by researchers as a *miḥrāb* directing prayer towards Mecca; and a floor mosaic depicting three palm trees, with notable similarities to iconography found at the Dome of the Rock.[68] It appears that Muslims adopted (and adapted) the site for its associations with Jesus and Mary, and perhaps identified it as the site of Jesus' birth.[69]

[64] Rina Avner, 'The Kathisma: A Christian and Muslim Pilgrimage Site', *ARAM* 18–19 (2006–7): 541–57.

[65] Avner, 'Kathisma', 544; Rina Avner, 'The Dome of the Rock in Light of the Development of Concentric Martyria in Jerusalem: Architecture and Architectural Iconography', *Muqarnas* 27 (2010): 31–49.

[66] Avner, 'Kathisma', 547. On the site's association with sacred waters, see Stephen Shoemaker, 'Christmas in the Qur'ān: The Qur'ānic Account of Jesus' Nativity and Palestinian Local Tradition', *JSAI* 28 (2003): 11–39.

[67] Avner, 'Kathisma', 547.

[68] Avner, 'Kathisma', 550; Avner, 'Dome of the Rock', 42–4; Shoemaker, 'Christmas in the Qur'ān', 36–7.

[69] Shoemaker, 'Christmas in the Qur'ān', 34–5; Avner, 'Dome of the Rock', 42.

A site with a similar Christian and Islamic connection was located in the city of Ruṣāfa in northern Syria. The monumental church there held a shrine containing the remains of the famed Christian saint Sergius, allowing this site to emerge as a prominent pilgrimage destination by the fifth and sixth centuries.[70] Like the Kathisma church and its stone, archaeological evidence from Ruṣāfa points to pilgrims' collection of contact relics from Sergius' remains: flask fragments and a basin in Sergius' sarcophagus at the site 'suggest that oil, or water, was poured over the bones, collected, and then distributed among the pilgrims' for blessing and healing.[71]

During the caliphate of Hishām b. ʿAbd al-Malik (r. 105–25/724–43), a mosque was constructed directly adjacent to the church-shrine in Ruṣāfa. This new mosque shared with the church basilica a courtyard, accessible through a door in the mosque's *qibla* wall. Notably, this courtyard was the avenue through which pilgrims entered the shrine containing Sergius' relics. Researchers have argued that this architectural intervention 'suggests an effort to benefit from the saint's miracle-working presence and to provide Muslims with a place nearby to worship – and even to participate in the cult of St. Sergius'.[72]

Thus, at both the Kathisma and Ruṣāfa, we find evidence of early Muslims venerating sacred relics, here in the form of a holy woman's stone and a holy man's bones. While the archaeological record here permits only interpretations and not definitive statements, the flask fragments and other materials uncovered at these sites suggest the possibility that Muslims took contact relics from these objects just as Christian pilgrims did, and as some Muslims were said to do at the Prophet Muḥammad's tomb.[73] Moreover, the resources put into these buildings indicate that these were not simply sites of 'popular piety', but the

[70] Elizabeth Key Fowden, *The Barbarian Plain: Saint Sergius between Rome and Iran* (Berkeley: University of California Press, 1999); Fowden, 'Sharing Holy Places', *Common Knowledge* 8.1 (2002): 124–46.

[71] Fowden, *Barbarian Plain*, 85–6.

[72] Fowden, 'Sharing Holy Places', 135; Dorothea Weltecke, 'Multireligiöse Loca Sancta und die mächtigen Heiligen der Christen', *Der Islam* 88.1 (2012): 81–2; Mattia Guidetti, *In the Shadow of the Church: The Building of Mosques in Early Medieval Syria* (Leiden: Brill, 2017), 52–5, 85.

[73] Flood, 'Bodies and Becoming', 466.

recipients of elite Muslim patronage, including (in the case of Ruṣāfa) from the caliph himself.

The textual and material sources examined here point to the veneration of tombs and other sites and objects from early in Islamic history. Instead of a complete rejection of relic and tomb veneration, varied sources indicate that such practices were likely well-known, if sometimes hotly debated, rituals among early Muslims.[74] Like so many other areas of Islamic ritual practice, questions about tomb and relic veneration were not closed from argument in the early period.[75] Instead, these various sources appear to reflect, as Stephen Shoemaker argues, 'a diversity of opinion within the early Islamic community'.[76] Strongly iconoclastic perspectives clearly circulated among early Islamic communities. But these were not the only voices in the debate around how (and whether) to engage with material embodiments of the sacred, such as relics and tombs.

Conclusion

With this brief discussion, we see that there is a more complicated picture than early Muslims' complete rejection of relic and tomb veneration. As I have mentioned (and will explore at greater length in the following chapters) some early Muslims did venerate the tombs and relics of prophets and other individuals, and in some cases took such practices as significant elements of their performance of Islam. The sacredness of Islamic lands was often enhanced by the 'discovery' therein of the tombs of ancient prophets and other holy persons. The tombs of new, specifically Islamic figures became venerated places of commemoration; pilgrimages to these locations, and rituals

[74] A similar argument appears in Nancy Khalek, 'Medieval Muslim Martyrs to the Plague: Venerating the Companions of Muhammad in the Jordan Valley', in Hahn and Klein, *Saints and Sacred Matter*, 92–3.

[75] 'It is obvious that these diverse traditions reflect differences in the opinions of various circles of Muslim scholars and indicate that in the early period of Islam many ritual prescriptions were not yet firmly established.' M. J. Kister, 'On "Concessions" and Conduct: A Study in Early *Ḥadīth*', in *Studies on the First Century of Islamic Society*, ed. G. H. A. Juynboll (Carbondale and Edwardsville: Southern Illinois University Press, 1982), 89–107.

[76] Shoemaker, *Death of a Prophet*, 259–60.

involving these holy people's relics, became signs of piety and identity. At the same time, situating relic and tomb veneration as characteristic of Jews and Christians offered a useful polemical device for distinguishing Islamic from non-Islamic identity and practice. Tombs, relics and early Islamic identity were thus bound together in important and sometimes conflicting ways that are lost when we solely focus on – and accept as exclusively 'Islamic' – the evidence of rejection and iconoclasm.

2

A CLEAR SIGN: THE MAQĀM IBRĀHĪM AND EARLY ISLAMIC CONTINUITY AND DIFFERENCE

In his *Akhbār Makka* (Reports of Mecca), the ninth-century historian Muḥammad b. Isḥāq al-Fākihī includes a short report about a man named George (in Arabic, Jurayj), 'who was either a Jew or a Christian and became a Muslim while he was in Mecca'.[1] The very night of George's conversion, a particularly sacred Meccan landmark went missing. The Maqām Ibrāhīm, or 'Station of Abraham', was a stone believed to contain traces of the prophet Abraham's footprints, miraculously impressed there during the period when Abraham built the Kaʿba – the House of God in Mecca – with the help of his son Ishmael.[2] After the Maqām's disappearance from its seat near the Kaʿba was discovered, a search found the stone in George's possession, as George

[1] Abū ʿAbd Allāh Muḥammad b. Isḥāq b. al-ʿAbbās al-Fākihī, *Akhbār Makka fī qadīm al-dahr wa-ḥadīthihi*, ed. ʿAbd al-Malik b. ʿAbd Allāh b. Duhaysh, 2nd ed., 6 vols (Beirut: Dār Khiḍr, 1994), 1:452 (no. 991). On this historian and his work, see *EI*[2], s.v. 'al-Fākihī' (Franz Rosenthal).

[2] On stories of the Maqām Ibrāhīm and its creation, see M. J. Kister, 'Maqām Ibrāhīm: A Stone with an Inscription', *Le Muséon* 84 (1971): 477–91; Harald Motzi, 'Abraham, Hagar and Ishmael at Mecca: A Contribution to the Problem of Dating Muslim Traditions', in *Books and Written Culture of the Islamic World: Studies Presented to Claude Gilliot on the Occasion of His 75th Birthday*, ed. Andrew Rippin and Roberto Tottoli (Leiden: Brill, 2015), 361–84.

'wanted to take it to the king of Rome', the Byzantine emperor.[3] Caught red-handed, George was stripped of his stolen treasure and beheaded.

A Jewish/Christian man becomes a Muslim in Mecca, steals an ancient stone to bring it to a Christian ruler, and is subsequently executed for this theft. Since we have no additional sources to corroborate this story, it is difficult to know how to read this terse report. Anonymously cited by al-Fākihī from what 'some people say', there is a gossipy or folkloristic air to the short story of this man George and his unusual scheme – otherwise unknown to Islamic history – to bring the Maqām Ibrāhīm to the Byzantine emperor. However, rather than an isolated record of an obscure figure and a strange incident in local Meccan history, this brief report illustrates a cultural dialogue that extended throughout a wide temporal and geographical milieu: namely, the conceptions of (and conflicts over) relic veneration among communities of the late antique and early medieval Mediterranean and Near Eastern world.

Referenced in the Qur'ān as one of God's 'clear signs' in this world, the Maqām Ibrāhīm was believed to mark the very spot where Abraham had called humanity to perform the ḥajj to Mecca.[4] Another tradition in al-Fākihī's *Akhbār Makka* describes this momentous historical occasion in wondrous terms. When someone asks about the footprints that can be seen in the Maqām, an early Jewish convert to Islam named 'Abd Allāh b. Salām (d. 43/663–4) responds:

> What is present in the stone would not be there today without God's wish to make it one of His signs. When Abraham was commanded [by God] to call the people to the ḥajj, he stood upon the Maqām. The Maqām grew bigger, until it was higher than the mountains and loftier than everything beneath it. He said, 'O people, answer your Lord's call!' The people answered, 'We are here, God, we are here!' Abraham's footprint was there in the stone, as God wished.[5]

[3] Regarding the connotations of *malik al-Rūm* as a term for the Byzantine emperor, see Nadia Maria El Cheikh, *Byzantium Viewed by the Arabs* (Cambridge, MA: Harvard University Press, 2004), 86–8.

[4] For alternative early Islamic interpretations of the phrase 'Maqām Ibrāhīm' in the Qur'ān and *ḥadīth*, see Gerald R. Hawting, 'The Origins of the Muslim Sanctuary at Mecca', in Juynboll, *Studies on the First Century of Islamic Society*, 23–47.

[5] al-Fākihī, *Akhbār Makka*, 1:442–3 (no. 966); Abū al-Walīd Muḥammad b. 'Abd Allāh b. Aḥmad al-Azraqī, *Akhbār Makka wa-mā jā' fīhā min al-āthār*, ed. 'Abd al-Malik b. 'Abd Allāh b. Duhaysh (Mecca: Maktabat al-Asadī, 2003), 533–4 (no. 639); Uri Rubin, 'Between

According to this story, the Maqām both enabled the beginning of the ḥajj – by temporarily growing gigantic in size, allowing Abraham to call out to the whole world – and commemorated that moment in stone by absorbing the imprints of Abraham's feet. Abraham is further said to have used the stone to mark his *qibla*, that is, to direct prayer in the correct direction towards the Kaʿba.[6] Much more than a stone, the Maqām thus represented a tangible fragment of the prophetic past, manifesting Islamic sacred history in material form. Miraculously inscribed with the impressions of Abraham's feet where he stood, the stone displayed the patriarch's *āthār*: literally his 'footsteps' or 'traces' and, by extension, his 'remains' or 'relics'. This stone – housed next to (or sometimes directly attached to) the Kaʿba, the most sacred location on earth for Muslims – was a relic of the prophet Abraham.

Indeed, rather than a simple theft, George's attempt to remove the Maqām Ibrāhīm from Mecca resembles a relic translation (or *translatio*) of the sort found throughout late antique and medieval texts in a variety of literary contexts and languages.[7] In such stories, believers elaborately transfer – or covertly abscond with – a saint's body or a similar holy object in order to install it in a new location, where this sacred treasure might be (according to its movers, at least) more 'properly' venerated. Like the tales of saints' corpses stolen in the dead of night by jealous worshippers or rival sects, George's nighttime looting of a scriptural patriarch's stone footprints highlights the significance

Arabia and the Holy Land: A Mecca–Jerusalem Axis of Sanctity', *JSAI* 34 (2008): 353. Similar traditions are reported from the early jurist Mujāhid b. Jabr (d. *c.* 100–4/718–22): al-Fākihī, *Akhbār Makka*, 1:447–8 (nos 979, 981); ʿAbd al-Razzāq, *Muṣannaf*, 5:97 (no. 9,101). See also al-Azraqī, *Akhbār Makka*, 817.

[6] al-Azraqī, *Akhbār Makka*, 534 (no. 639); al-Fākihī, *Akhbār Makka*, 1:443 (no. 966); Rubin, 'Between Arabia and the Holy Land', 353–4.

[7] Martin Heinzelmann, *Translationsberichte und andere Quellen des Reliquienkultes* (Turnhout: Brepols, 1979); René Aigrain, *L'hagiographie: ses sources, ses méthodes, son histoire* (Paris: Bloud et Gay, 1953), 186–92; Pierre Maraval, *Lieux saints et pèlerinages d'Orient: histoire et géographie des origines à la conquête arabe* (Paris: Cerf, 1985), 48–50; Patrick Geary, *Furta Sacra: Theft of Relics in the Central Middle Ages*, rev. ed. (Princeton: Princeton University Press, 1990); Jeanne-Nicole Mellon Saint-Laurent, 'Bones in Bags: Relics in Syriac Hagiography', in *Syriac Encounters*, ed. Maria Doerfler, Emanuel Fiano and Kyle Smith (Leuven: Peeters, 2015), 439–54; Rubenstein, 'Rabbinic Translation'.

and power that individuals and communities saw in the possession of physical embodiments of holy persons and, thereby, sacred history. George's plan to move the Maqām Ibrāhīm from Mecca to the Byzantine emperor places the stone within the ranks of the many remnants of biblical and post-biblical Christian history – including the remains of Hebrew prophets and Christian martyrs, as well as objects such as the wood of the True Cross – that Byzantine emperors had 'translated' to churches in Constantinople from the fourth century onwards.[8] George (and, implicitly, his narrator al-Fākihī) thus treat this piece of Islamic sacred history as a relic, the same kind of object that Christians had long used to accrue spiritual power for their Christian capital.

As much as George's actions illustrate the sacrality of the Maqām, his failed *translatio* also evokes another late antique and early medieval topos: criticism of the veneration of holy persons and their relics. As discussed in the previous chapter, relic and tomb worship was a target of early Islamic polemic against Jews and Christians. However, the critiques that early Muslims directed at Jews and Christians echo anxieties and debates that plagued and divided those same communities. Due to concerns over associating human beings with divine power, the cults of saints and relics prompted controversies from the time of their genesis.[9] These debates continued through the centuries and, as Matthew

[8] Bernard Flusin, 'Construire une nouvelle Jérusalem: Constantinople et les reliques', in *L'Orient dans l'histoire religieuse de l'Europe: L'invention des origines*, ed. Mohammad Ali Amir-Moezzi and John Scheid (Turnhout: Brepols, 2000), 51–70; Liz James, 'Bearing Gifts from the East: Imperial Relic Hunters Abroad', in *Eastern Approaches to Byzantium*, ed. Antony Eastmond (London: Routledge, 2001), 119–31; Holger A. Klein, 'Sacred Relics and Imperial Ceremonies at the Great Palace of Constantinople', in *Visualisierungen von Herrschaft: Frühmittelalterliche Residenzen – Gestalt und Zeremoniell*, ed. Franz Alto Bauer (Istanbul: Ege Yayınları, 2006), 79–99; Ra'anan Boustan, 'The Spoils of the Jerusalem Temple at Rome and Constantinople: Jewish Counter-Geography in a Christianizing Empire', in *Antiquity in Antiquity: Jewish and Christian Pasts in the Greco-Roman World*, ed. Gregg Gardner and Kevin L. Osterloh (Tübingen: Mohr Siebeck, 2008), 357.

[9] David G. Hunter, 'Vigilantius of Calagurris and Victricius of Rouen: Ascetics, Relics, and Clerics in Late Roman Gaul', *JECS* 7.3 (1999) 401–30; Gillian Clark, 'Victricius of Rouen: Praising the Saints', *JECS* 7.3 (1999): 365–99; Nicholas Constas, 'An Apology for the Cult of Saints in Late Antiquity: Eustratius Presbyter of Constantinople, *On the State of Souls after Death* (CPG 7522)', *JECS* 10 (2002): 267–85; Miller, *Corporeal Imagination*, 51, 60–1, 65, 110–15; Wortley, 'Iconoclasm and Leipsanoclasm', 253–79.

Dal Santo writes, 'however conventionally late antiquity is presented as an "age of saints", the status of that cult and its propriety as an authentic expression of Christian monotheism was clearly contested and disputed'.[10]

Connecting these threads, Dal Santo suggests that 'the early Muslim "Believers" did not perhaps so much invent as absorb and channel existing critiques of the cult of the saints'.[11] Yet such critiques were levelled at Muslim believers too: for the Maqām Ibrāhīm was an object of physical veneration not just for George, but for many early Muslims. Muslim pilgrims, scholars and rulers piously touched the stone and drank fluids that had come into contact with it. George was clearly presented as over-zealous in his pursuit of the Maqām, but the stone itself long provoked debate about the proper way of engaging with such a material piece of sacred history.

The ambiguous tale of George and the Maqām Ibrāhīm illustrates the engagement of early Islamic literature – and the participation of early Muslims – in ongoing discussions about the veneration of relics in the Mediterranean and Near Eastern world. While Islam is often understood as an iconoclastic religious tradition bereft of relic veneration, objects like the Maqām Ibrāhīm complicate such simple categorisations. In this chapter, I will use several texts about the Maqām Ibrāhīm to illustrate some overarching issues regarding the contested place of material relics within early Islam. George's story – as well as other texts involving the Maqām Ibrāhīm studied here – evoke a set of themes: early Muslims' complex and often ambiguous literary and physical engagements with relics; the roles of Jews and Christians, both real and imagined, in these discussions; and the ways that these ideological and ritual concerns were involved in the production and enactment of early Islamic identities.

'Never a Foot More Like It': The Maqām Ibrāhīm as Witness to Islamic Past and Present

Whatever the historical veracity of George's alleged encounter with the Maqām Ibrāhīm might be, the story fits perfectly within the literary world of the late antique and early medieval Near East. In texts from this period, the relics of holy persons are frequently drawn upon as embodiments of sanctity and/or

[10] Dal Santo, *Debating the Saints' Cult*, 319.

[11] Ibid., 334.

authority, materialising claims about the present in the form of objects from the past. Early Islamic texts likewise utilise the Maqām Ibrāhīm to make claims about the Muslim community's present authority, by virtue of their connection to the scriptural (and non-scriptural) sacred past. In many texts, the Maqām appears as an illustration of the Muslim community's simultaneous connection to – but usurpation of – earlier groups, including Jews, Christians and pre-Islamic Arabs. The Maqām functions in these texts as a material witness to Islam's antiquity and inheritance from these earlier traditions, while also standing as proof of the Muslim *umma*'s present, divinely-guided authority over these other communities.

As mentioned above, the general outlines of the story of George and the Maqām Ibrāhīm resemble a relic *translatio*, of the sort found throughout a wide variety of late antique literatures. Beyond this literary form, several narrative features of this story highlight the ideological entanglement of the emergent Muslim *umma* with the Jewish and Christian past. George is ambiguously identified in the story as Jewish or Christian – as well as a Muslim convert – and his complicated identity echoes the Jewish figures who frequently feature in late antique Christian stories about the 'discovery' (or *inventio*) of biblical relics. Within such stories, Jewish guides often function as repositories of scriptural wisdom, who reveal to Christian relic-seekers (either willingly or by force) the locations of material from the biblical past buried in the Holy Land, such as the bones of Old Testament prophets and the wood of the True Cross. In this role, these Jewish characters not only physically locate the relics themselves, but authenticate the identity of the sacred remains for their new Christian owners.

Moreover, as they frequently embrace Christian faith in the narrative process of the relics' uncovering, these Christianised Jews also ideologically corroborate imperial Christian supersessionistic ideas of Christianity's inheritance of the Jewish past.[12] Functioning as 'doubly inscribed figures [who] face two ways without being two-faced', these Jewish guides 'can represent at once the Jewish past that has been mastered, as well as the Jewish past that has graciously ceded place and been absorbed into the Christian present'.[13]

[12] Jacobs, *Remains of the Jews*, 174–91.

[13] Jacobs, *Remains of the Jews*, 182; Andrew Jacobs, 'The Remains of the Jew: Imperial Christian Identity in the Late Antique Holy Land', *Journal of Medieval and Early Modern Studies* 22 (2003): 29, 31–2, quoting Homi K. Bhabha, *Location of Culture* (London: Routledge, 1991), 97.

George personifies a similarly forward- and backward-looking affirmation of Islamic claims to present authority, rooted in an engagement with the Judaeo-Christian past. With his effort to steal the Maqām Ibrāhīm for the Byzantine emperor, George identifies this stone as a piece of sacred matter, an Abrahamic relic worthy of veneration. Alongside his conversion to Islam, George's recognition of the Maqām as a genuine relic narratively legitimises the new Abrahamic community that displays this object in their sacred centre, and that in this period held control over a significant portion of the Mediterranean and Near Eastern world. Yet rather than guiding Muslims to some buried piece of scriptural history, George authenticates what the Muslims already possess within their own midst. Rather than uncovering a long-buried secret, George testifies to the manifest fact before everyone's eyes: the supremacy of the new religious polity in the Near Eastern world. Like ʿAbd Allāh b. Salām – the Jewish convert to Islam whom we encountered above explaining the footprints in the Maqām Ibrāhīm, and who appears elsewhere as a 'native informant' on biblical material for Muslim audiences – George embodies a Judaeo-Christian past that has been superseded and fully absorbed into an Islamic present.[14]

While George's story testifies to a period in which this Islamic present already exists, the Maqām is also used to prophesy the coming of an Islamic future. In hagiographic narratives recorded in biographies of the Prophet Muḥammad, the Maqām Ibrāhīm attests to Islam's connection to past scriptural communities by physically confirming Muḥammad's Abrahamic ancestry. In a story situated during Muḥammad's childhood, his grandfather ʿAbd al-Muṭṭālib is approached by a group of the Banū Mudlij. They were a tribe renowned for their skill in the ancient Arabian craft of *qiyāfa*: the interpretation of footprints and other bodily features for the purposes both of tracking wild animals, and of establishing human beings' paternity.[15] The Banū Mudlij

[14] On ʿAbd Allāh b. Salām, see *EI* [2], s.v. "Abd Allāh b. Salām' (Joseph Horovitz); *EI* [3], s.v. "Abdallāh b. Salām' (Michael Lecker); Samuel A. Stafford, 'Constructing Muḥammad's Legitimacy: Arabic Literary Biography and the Jewish Pedigree of the Companion ʿAbd Allāh b. Salām (d. 43/633)', *JSAI* 47 (2019): 133–86; Stafford, 'The Conversions of ʿAbdallāh ibn Salām (d. 43/633): A Legendary Moment in the Biography of Muḥammad's Jewish Companion', *BSOAS* 84.2 (2021): 237–61; Hughes, *Anxious Inheritance*, 107–9.

[15] *EI* [2], s.v. 'Ḳiyāfa' (T. Fahd); Toufic Fahd, *La divination Arabe. Études religieuses, sociologiques et folkloriques sur la milieu natif de l'Islam* (Leiden: Brill, 1966), 370–8; Robert Hoyland, 'Physiognomy in Islam', *JSAI* 30 (2005): 361–402. For citations of the Banū Mudlij's reputed

advise 'Abd al-Muṭṭālib to 'protect him [Muḥammad], for we have never seen a foot more like the one in the Maqām than his'.[16] A similar event occurs years later, after Muḥammad's prophetic mission had begun and he had been forced to flee from Mecca due to the Quraysh's persecution of him and his followers. Wanting to catch the Prophet as he hides in the desert, the Quraysh employ the expertise of a *qāyif*. When this tracker-cum-physiognomist is asked to follow Muḥammad's trail, he looks at the Prophet's tracks and marvels, 'How similar this is to that footprint in the Maqām!'[17]

Within these stories, the Maqām mutely testifies to Muḥammad's parentage from the ancient prophet Abraham and (by extension) Islam's proximity to earlier Judaism and Christianity. Through his footprint's similarity to the Maqām Ibrāhīm, Muḥammad is shown to be a descendant of Abraham, and indeed one 'more similar' to him than any of his other offspring. In the emphasis on Muḥammad's body revealing his prophetic identity, these stories resemble other *sīra* narratives where Christian monks and Jewish rabbis comprehend Muḥammad's status as a prophet. When these Christian and Jewish figures see certain physical marks on Muḥammad's shoulders and elsewhere on his body, they recognise the 'signs of prophecy' that they have read about in their scriptures.[18] Like his other corporeal features, here Muḥammad's feet exhibit his

skill in this area, see Abū 'Uthmān 'Amr b. Baḥr al-Jāḥiẓ, *Kitāb al-Tarbīʿ wa-l-tadwīr*, ed. Charles Pellat (Damascus: Institut Français de Damas, 1955), 91–2 (no. 176); Ibn Qutayba, *The Excellence of the Arabs*, ed. James Montgomery and Peter Webb, trans. Sarah Bowen Savant and Peter Webb (New York: New York University Press, 2017), 132–3; 'Alī b. al-Ḥusayn al-Masʿūdī, *Murūj al-dhahab wa-maʿādin al-jawhar*, ed. and trans. C. Barbier de Meynard and J.-B. Pavet de Courteille, 9 vols (Paris: Imprimerie impériale, 1861–77), 3:341–2; Abū Manṣūr 'Abd al-Malik b. Muḥammad b. Ismāʿīl al-Thaʿālibī, *Thimār al-qulūb fī-l-muḍāf wa-l-mansūb*, ed. Muḥammad Abū al-Faḍl Ibrāhīm (Sidon: al-Maktaba al-ʿAṣriyya, 2003), 104 (no. 170).

16 Ibn Saʿd, *Ṭabaqāt*, 1:96–7; Kister, 'Maqām Ibrāhīm', 483.

17 R. G. Khoury, *Wahb b. Munabbih. Der Heidelberger Papyrus PSR Heid Arab 23*, 2 vols (Wiesbaden: Otto Harrassowitz, 1972), 1:144 (line 17). Textual corrections to Khoury's edition are noted in M. J. Kister, 'On the Papyrus of Wahb b. Munabbih', *BSOAS* 37.3 (1974): 551. On this early text, see Brockopp, *Muhammad's Heirs*, 86–93, 145–7.

18 On Muḥammad's body reflecting his prophetic status to observers, see Uri Rubin, *The Eye of the Beholder: The Life of Muḥammad As Viewed by the Early Muslims* (Princeton: Darwin Press, 1995), 21–43; Knight, *Muhammad's Body*, 29–50.

status as prophet. Notably, however, the Maqām Ibrāhīm is mirrored not by Muḥammad's body itself, but by his *āthār*, or 'traces'. The resemblance between the traces of Muḥammad and Abraham evokes a connection between the Muslim prophet and his Abrahamic predecessor, ready to be seen by willing eyes.

Yet the recognitions spurred by the Prophet's body and its traces are suffused with conflict. The acknowledgement of Muḥammad's prophecy leads not to confirmation by Muḥammad's contemporaries, but more often to denial or rejection due to worries about what he spells for their future. Even as the Banū Mudlij recognise young Muḥammad's special status through his bodily characteristics, this good news is mixed with their warning that 'Abd al-Muṭṭālib must protect him. While the Banū Mudlij do not specify what dangers Muḥammad faces, their anxieties prove to be well-founded. Over the course of his childhood, an Arab diviner (*'arrāf*) and soothsayer (*kāhin*) each attempts to kill the young Muḥammad on the basis of auguries they read upon his body, forecasting to pagan Arab audiences that 'his gods will kill the people of your religion (*dīn*) and destroy your gods!'.[19]

The Banū Mudlij's forebodings are echoed in the warnings of Christian monks, who similarly caution Muḥammad's relatives about the dangers that 'the Jews' will pose to his life due to their 'jealousy' of his prophethood.[20] Indeed, several *sīra* stories present Jewish figures as themselves aware of Muḥammad's coming prophecy – having recognised the same scripturally-based marks on his body that the Christian monks see – yet dismissive of these signs. In one such story, al-Zabīr b. Bāṭā, 'the most learned of the Jews' in Medina, admits that he had effaced scriptural passages that had 'described the prophet Aḥmad's attributes' and then denied that such passages had ever existed.[21] In another story, Muḥammad explicitly asks a learned Jewish scholar of Medina if he recognises him as a prophet. The scholar responds, 'By God, yes! And the people know what I know, for indeed your attributes and description are clear in the Torah. But they are jealous of you.'[22] A similar rejection of prophetic evidence

[19] Ibn Sa'd, *Ṭabaqāt*, 1:126, 140; Rubin, *Eye of the Beholder*, 53–4.

[20] Ibn Sa'd, *Ṭabaqāt*, 1:99, 129–30; Rubin, *Eye of the Beholder*, 50.

[21] Ibn Sa'd, *Ṭabaqāt*, 1:133; Reuven Firestone, 'The Problematic of Prophecy: 2015 IQSA Presidential Address', *JIQSA* 1 (2016): 14.

[22] Ibn Sa'd, *Ṭabaqāt*, 1:138.

occurs when the pagan *qāyif* identifies the resemblance between Muḥammad's footprint and the Maqām Ibrāhīm. Some versions of the story record the villainous Qurashī leader Abū Sufyān erasing Muḥammad's footprints with his sleeve and dismissing the tracker's prescient words, saying contemptuously, 'The old man has gone senile.'[23]

In these stories of rejected annunciation, the Prophet's body is melded with biblical scriptural fulfilment, making the two corpora (body and text) into mutually reinforcing proofs of Muḥammad's prophetic status. While they do not cite biblical scripture, the stories of the Maqām Ibrāhīm clearly fit into this larger theme. The proximity of Muḥammad's footprint to that of Abraham testifies to his Abrahamic lineage, just as the signs on his body demonstrate his biblically-mandated prophetic identity.

At the same time, the role of *qiyāfa* in demonstrating Muḥammad's consanguinity with Abraham places these events within the realm of ancient Arabian wisdom. Physiognomy was categorised as one of the 'sciences of the Arabs' (*ʿulūm al-ʿarab*) by early Islamic thinkers,[24] and Muḥammad's identification by these Arab ritual experts is key to the stories.[25] Indeed, *sīra* stories attribute a corroborative role to the Arabian soothsayers (*kuhhān*) directly alongside (and seemingly in comparable authority to) Jewish rabbis and Christian monks in attesting to Muḥammad's status as a true prophet.[26]

[23] al-Thaʿālibī, *Thimār al-qulūb*, 104 (no. 170); Abū Saʿd Manṣūr b. al-Ḥusayn al-Ābī, *Nathr al-durr*, ed. Khālid ʿAbd al-Ghanī Maḥfūẓ, 7 vols (Beirut: Dār al-Kutub al-ʿIlmiyya, 2004), 7:122–3.

[24] Ibn Qutayba, *Excellence of the Arabs*, 132–3; al-Jāḥiẓ, *al-Bayān wa-l-tabyīn*, ed. ʿAbd al-Salām Muḥammad Hārūn, 4 vols (Cairo: Maktabat al-Khānijī, 1968), 4:32; al-Jāḥiẓ, *Manāqib al-Turk*, in *Rasāʾil al-Jāḥiẓ*, ed. ʿAbd al-Salām Muḥammad Hārūn, 4 vols (Cairo: Maktabat al-Khānjī, 1964–79), 1:70; al-Zubayr b. Bakkār, *Akhbār al-Muwaffaqiyyāt*, ed. Sāmī Makkī al-ʿĀnī, 2nd ed. (Beirut: ʿĀlam al-Kutub, 1996), 300 (no. 213); Ibn ʿAbd Rabbihi al-Andalusī, *al-ʿIqd al-farīd*, ed. Mufīd Muḥammad Qumayḥa et al., 9 vols (Beirut: Dār al-Kutub al-ʿIlmiyyah, 1983), 3:278; al-Masʿūdī, *Murūj al-dhahab*, 3:333–43; al-Thaʿālibī, *Thimār al-qulūb*, 104 (no. 170).

[25] There is likely also an emphasis here on Muḥammad's Arab identity as a descendant through Abraham of the Arab progenitor, Ishmael. Webb, *Imagining the Arabs*, 211–22; Mohsen Goudarzi, 'The Ascent of Ishmael: Genealogy, Covenant, and Identity in Early Islam', *Arabica* 66 (2019): 415–84.

[26] Ibn Hishām, *Sīra*, 130–4; Muḥammad b. Isḥāq, *Kitāb al-Siyar wa-l-maghāzī*, ed. Suhayl Zakkār (Damascus: Dār al-Fikr, 1978), 111–12. Tales of soothsayers in ancient Arabian

The correspondences that the *qāyif* draws between Muḥammad's and Abraham's feet are likewise an acknowledgement of Muḥammad's prophecy among such non-monotheist Arabian ritual experts. They read different signs from those the Jews and Christians read, but nonetheless come to the same conclusions about Muḥammad's prophetic future.

While these *sīra* stories highlight the Arabian valence of the Maqām Ibrāhīm, the Maqām appears as a decidedly Judaeo-Christian proof of Muḥammad's prophecy, and Islam's victory, in the *Kitāb al-Dīn wa-l-Dawla* (Book of Religion and Empire) of ʿAlī b. Rabban al-Ṭabarī.[27] A Nestorian convert to Islam active in the mid-ninth century, ʿAlī al-Ṭabarī compiled in this book a long list of Jewish and Christian scriptural prooftexts to demonstrate that the prophethood of Muḥammad, and the reign of the Islamic empire, were both fore-ordained by God and were clearly predicted in the pre-qurʾānic scriptures.

ʿAlī al-Ṭabarī likewise interprets the Maqām Ibrāhīm as an Islamic fulfilment of biblical prophecy. Discussing a mention of God having 'stirred up the pious one from the east and called him to the place of his foot' (Is 41:2), he glosses: 'the one who is called to the place of the foot of the "friend of God" is the Prophet.'[28] Identifying Muḥammad as the messianic 'pious one from the east', ʿAlī al-Ṭabarī interprets the Isaiaic description of his being called to God's

kingdoms predicting Muḥammad's coming appear in Ibn Hishām, *Sīra*, 9–11, 28; Muḥammad b. Jarīr al-Ṭabarī, *Taʾrīkh al-rusul wa-l-mulūk*, ed. M. J. de Goeje, 3 series in 15 vols (Leiden: Brill, 1879–1901), 1/2:909; *The History of al-Ṭabarī. Volume V: The Sāsānids, the Byzantines, the Lakmids, and Yemen*, trans. C. E. Bosworth (Albany: State University of New York Press, 1999), 175 (with an *isnād* from Ibn Isḥāq). On soothsayers, see Rubin, *Eye of the Beholder*, 53–5; *EQ*, s.v. 'Soothsayer' (Devin Stewart); Marilyn Waldman, *Prophecy and Power: Muhammad and the Qur'an in the Light of Comparison* (Sheffield: Equinox, 2012), 59–61; Webb, *Imagining the Arabs*, 125. The continuing relevance of 'soothsayers' after the advent of Islam is suggested by commands not to visit them or believe what they say: ʿAbd al-Razzāq, *Muṣannaf*, 11:209–11 (nos 20,346–51); Ibn Abī Shayba, *Muṣannaf*, 8:28 (nos 23,872, 28,375); ʿAbd Allāh b. Wahb b. Muslim al-Qurashī al-Miṣrī, *al-Jāmiʿ fī-l-ḥadīth*, ed. Muṣṭafā Ḥasan Ḥusayn Muḥammad Abū al-Khayr, 2 vols (Riyadh: Dār Ibn al-Jawzī, 1996), 2:764–7 (nos 683–7).

27 David Thomas, "Alī l-Ṭabarī', in *Christian–Muslim Relations: A Bibliographic History. Volume 1 (600–900)*, ed. David Thomas and Barbara Roggema (Leiden: Brill, 2009), 669–74.

28 *The Polemical Works of ʿAlī al-Ṭabarī*, ed. and trans. Rifaat Ebied and David Thomas (Leiden: Brill, 2016), 364–5.

'foot' as a reference to the 'place of the foot of the "friend of God"'. 'Friend of God' (*khalīl Allāh*) is a qur'ānic name for Abraham, and 'Alī al-Ṭabarī clearly intends here the Maqām Ibrāhīm. He does similar exegetical work on a description of the eschatological restoration of the Israelite Temple, in which God says that He will 'beautify the place of my sanctuary, and I will glorify where my feet rest' (Is 60:13). 'Alī asks his reader, 'Do you know of the foot of the "friend of God"?' and wonders what place could be meant by Isaiah's extended description of a frequently visited house of God 'other than Mecca'.[29] In these mentions of God's 'foot', 'Alī finds references to the Maqām Ibrāhīm, further situating Islamic history as a fulfilment of biblical prophecy.

More allusions to the Maqām Ibrāhīm are discovered in biblical mentions of the worship to be thrown at the 'feet' of God and/or His messiah. After their defeat, God's humbled opponents will display their subordination in deferential acts of servitude: 'his enemies [will] lick the dust' (Ps 72:9), 'lick the dust at your feet' (Is 49:23), and 'bow down at your feet' (Is 60:14). Unsurprisingly, 'Alī al-Ṭabarī equates these biblical mentions of eschatological victory with the emergence of Islam. For, such acts of capitulation have been shown to none 'except the Prophet (may God bless him and give him peace) and his community, and except Mecca and the trace there of Abraham's foot (*athar qadam Ibrāhīm*)'.[30] Imagining the Maqām Ibrāhīm nearly as a physical embodiment of Islamic victory, 'Alī situates the stone as the focal point of non-Muslims' resignation to Muslim rule:

> In Mecca the nations bowed down on their faces in prostration to God, and tyrants licked the places of Abraham's foot and the Prophet's feet (may God bless them and give them peace) humbling themselves, seeking blessing, and bringing themselves low.[31]

It is unclear if 'Alī al-Ṭabarī here means to equate 'Abraham's foot and the Prophet's feet' in the literal manner that we saw in the stories of the *qāyif* above, or if he is simply referencing Mecca as the location where both prophets had physically trod. In either case, the implication is clear: in their humble veneration of these places of Abraham's and Muḥammad's feet, the conquered

[29] *Polemical Works of 'Alī al-Ṭabarī*, 380–3.

[30] Ibid., 346–7.

[31] Ibid., 388–9.

peoples of the world physically and symbolically perform their submission to God and to Islam.

The nations' defeat is all the more comprehensive for ʿAlī al-Ṭabarī's clothing it in the language of biblical scripture, thus appropriating a central component of Jewish and Christian identities. ʿAlī was himself a convert from Christianity to Islam, and his Islamic exegesis of scripture booms with triumphalist themes. In his retelling of sacred history, an ascendant Islamic community has achieved God-given dominance over the lands, peoples and religious traditions of Judaism and Christianity. In this respect, he could scarcely have asked for a better illustration of his reading of prophecy than George, who not only converted to Islam while in Mecca, but was so entranced by the Maqām Ibrāhīm that he tried to steal it. Yet, as we will see in the next section, subjugated peoples would not be alone in their veneration of the Maqām Ibrāhīm.

'You Were Not Commanded to Stroke It': Ambiguities of Touching the Maqām Ibrāhīm

While various forms of reverence for living and dead holy persons were important and (at times) central components of the communal rituals and identities of many Jewish and Christian groups, these practices occupied an ambivalent and often controversial position within – and between – different communities. Discussing the literary 'justifications' for relic theft in medieval Europe, Patrick J. Geary notes that '*translationes* exhibit a certain tension' as Christians authors questioned whether stolen relics were 'true thefts, morally reprehensible and hence sinful' or 'but one more acceptable way of acquiring a saint'.[32] The legality and morality of George's theft are not debated by the narrator of George's tale, but a similar tension weaves through his engagement with the Maqām Ibrāhīm. While George's theft testifies to the sacred status of the Maqām, it simultaneously exposes him as unable to temper his zeal for a material manifestation of the sacred. As this Jewish-Christian convert reveals the supremacy of Islam through his desire for the Maqām Ibrāhīm, he likewise models how not to engage with the object: dramatically illustrated by his execution for stealing it.

George's story thus makes a claim not only about community and history, as manifested in relics, but also about the (im)proper engagement with such

[32] Geary, *Furta Sacra*, 108.

material embodiments of the sacred. A Jewish/Christian convert kidnaps a relic from its Muslim caretakers to bring it to the Byzantine emperor. This might be read as an instance of a late antique and early medieval topos: the censure and mockery of venerators of holy persons and relics, and the characterisation of such adherents as fools who would resort even to thievery from their desire for these objects.

But, given Islamic accusations against Jews and Christians about their proclivities towards relics and tombs, it is noteworthy that George had reportedly converted to Islam by the time he stole the Maqām Ibrāhīm. Indeed, while George's theft was an unusual case, his actions would not have been incomprehensible among early Muslims in Mecca. We saw ʿAlī al-Ṭabarī describing defeated nations slavishly licking the Maqām and 'seeking blessing' from it. While al-Ṭabarī's polemic makes his descriptions difficult to use for reconstructing actual ritual practice, other texts indicate that people in Mecca venerated the Maqām in ways endemic to late antique relic cult. In multiple texts, we find mentions of perfuming, circumambulating, stroking and kissing the stone.[33] Indeed, Christian apologists draw attention to such practices in some of their earliest polemics against Islam. Protesting Muslim criticisms of Christian venerations of icons and relics, Christian writers pointed to Muslims' own worship practices at both the Maqām Ibrāhīm and the Black Stone (al-Ḥajar al-Aswad) set in the Kaʿba. They claimed that Muslims kissed and rubbed themselves against these sacred objects.[34] It seems that early Muslims did, on occasion, have some quite physical interactions with the Maqām.

Some of the principal evidence of these rituals at the Maqām Ibrāhīm appears not in Christian criticisms, but in the misgivings expressed about them by several early Muslim authorities.[35] The Meccan scholar Mujāhid b. Jabr (d. *c.* 100–4/718–22), for example, reportedly adjured Muslims, 'Do not touch

[33] On such practices among late antique Christians, see Wiśniewski, *Beginnings of the Cult of Relics*, 122–43.

[34] Barbara Roggema, 'Muslims as Crypto-Idolaters – A Theme in the Christian Portrayal of Islam in the Near East', in *Christians at the Heart of Islamic Rule: Church Life and Scholarship in ʿAbbasid Iraq*, ed. David Thomas (Leiden: Brill, 2003), 3–11; Peter Schadler, *John of Damascus and Islam: Christian Heresiology and the Intellectual Background to Earliest Christian–Muslim Relations* (Leiden: Brill, 2018), 150–1, 226–7.

[35] Adam Bursi, '"You Were Not Commanded to Stroke It, But to Pray Nearby It": Debating Touch within Early Islamic Pilgrimage', *Senses and Society* 17.1 (2022): 8–21.

the Maqām, for it is among the signs of God', citing the qur'ānic mention of the Maqām Ibrāhīm as among God's 'clear signs' (*āyāt bayyināt*) (Q 3:96–7).[36] Elsewhere, Mujāhid is said to have simply commanded, 'Do not kiss the Maqām and do not touch it!'[37] Another prominent Meccan ritual expert, 'Aṭā' b. Abī Rabāḥ (d. 115/733), reportedly 'disapproved' of touching and kissing the Maqām.[38] Mujāhid, 'Aṭā' and Ṭāwūs b. Kaysān (d. *c.* 101/719–20) are said to have all chastised Layth b. Abī Sulaym (d. *c.* 143/760–1) when they saw him circumambulating the Maqām in the manner of the Kaʿba.[39]

Despite this scholarly disapproval, Muslims' recurrent participation in such activities is clear in a report from the Baṣran scholar Qatāda b. Diʿāma (d. *c.* 117/735–6). Glossing the qur'ānic call to 'Take the Maqām Ibrāhīm as a place of prayer' (Q. 2:125), Qatāda argues:

> They were commanded to pray nearby it, not to stroke it! But this community took upon itself something that those communities before it had not. It has been reported to us from someone who saw [Abraham's] heel and his toes [in the Maqām]: but this community did not stop stroking [the Maqām] until those were worn away and obliterated.[40]

[36] al-Azraqī, *Akhbār Makka*, 531 (nos 634–5); al-Fākihī, *Akhbār Makka*, 1:451 (no. 989); *Tafsīr al-imām Mujāhid ibn Jabr*, ed. Muḥammad 'Abd al-Salām Abū al-Nīl (Cairo: Dār al-Fikr al-Islāmī al-Ḥadītha, 1989), 256. On Mujāhid, see *EI*², s.v. 'Mudjāhid b. Djabr al-Makkī' (Andrew Rippin).

[37] Ibn Abī Shayba, *Muṣannaf*, 5:624 (no. 15,737).

[38] al-Fākihī, *Akhbār Makka*, 1:458 (nos 1,005–6); 'Abd al-Razzāq, *Muṣannaf*, 5:49 (no. 8,957). When asked about this issue, Aḥmad b. Ḥanbal (d. 241/855) replied, 'Do not stroke it': *Masā'il al-imām Aḥmad ibn Ḥanbal wa-Isḥāq ibn Rāhwayh bi-riwāyat Isḥāq ibn Manṣūr al-Marwazī*, ed. Muḥammad b. 'Abd Allāh al-Zāḥim et al. (Medina: al-Jāmiʿa al-Islāmiyya, 2004), 5:2258 (no. 1,541).

[39] Ibn Abī Shayba, *Muṣannaf*, 5:640 (no. 16,092).

[40] Abū al-Naḍr Saʿīd b. Abī 'Arūba al-'Adawī, *Kitāb al-Manāsik*, ed. 'Āmir Ḥasan Ṣabrī (Beirut: Dār al-Bashā'ir al-Islāmiyya, 2000), 68–9 (no. 23); al-Azraqī, *Akhbār Makka*, 532 (no. 637); Abū Jaʿfar Muḥammad b. Jarīr al-Ṭabarī, *Tafsīr al-Ṭabarī: Jāmiʿ al-Bayān 'an ta'wīl āy al-Qur'ān*, ed. 'Abd Allāh b. 'Abd al-Muḥsin al-Turkī et al., 26 vols (Cairo: Dār Hajar, 2001), 2:527–9; Abū Bakr al-Ṭurṭūshī, *Kitāb al-Ḥawādith wa-l-bidaʿ*, ed. 'Abd al-Majīd Turkī (Beirut: Dār al-Gharb al-Islāmī, 1990), 268 (no. 239); Hūd b. Muḥakkam al-Hawwārī, *Tafsīr Kitāb Allāh al-'azīz*, ed. Bālḥāj b. Saʿīd al-Sharīfī, 4 vols (Beirut: Dār al-Gharb al-Islāmī, 1990), 1:145. On Qatāda, see *EI*², s.v. 'Ḳatāda b. Diʿāma' (Charles Pellat); Abdulrahman al-Salimi, *Early Islamic Law in Basra in the 2nd/8th Century:* Aqwāl Qatāda b. Diʿāma as-Sadūsī (Leiden: Brill, 2018), 3–19.

According to Qatāda, the qur'ānic instruction to take the Maqām Ibrāhīm as a 'place of prayer' (*muṣallā*) meant simply praying near the stone, without any need to touch it.[41] Others, however, clearly felt differently, and Qatāda laments how their continual stroking had worn away the imprints of Abraham's feet that had once been distinctly visible in the Maqām.

Notably, Qatāda specifies that 'this community' – that is, the Muslim community – had caused this loss by '[taking] upon itself something that those communities before it had not'. Qatāda cites an eyewitness to this effect, saying that it was 'reported to us from someone who saw' the footprints more clearly in the past. He may be referencing a report attributed to the Companion Anas b. Mālik (d. 93/712): 'I saw in the Maqām his toes, the soles of his feet and his heels. The trace changed, as the stroke of the people's hands effaced it.'[42] Thus, the degradation of the Maqām Ibrāhīm was believed to have occurred quickly, being observable even within the lifetime of a Companion of the Prophet Muḥammad. Though they had not stolen the Maqām itself, as George had done, the early Muslim *umma* had committed a collective act of pious larceny by robbing the Maqām of its visible traces of Abraham.[43] These reports accuse the *umma* of exceeding its qur'ānic mandate through its worship of the Maqām Ibrāhīm, with the effects forever visible upon the stone itself.

These differing conceptions and treatments of the Maqām Ibrāhīm might be interpreted as manifestations of a distinction between 'elite' and 'popular' religion among early Muslims. On the one hand are the jurists and authorities,

[41] For other examples of this interpretive formulation in early texts, see *Tafsīr Muqātil b. Sulaymān*, ed. 'Abd Allāh Maḥmūd Shiḥāta, 5 vols (Beirut: Mu'assasat al-Tārīkh al-'Arabī, 2002), 1:137–8; *Masā'il al-imām Aḥmad ibn Ḥanbal wa-Isḥāq ibn Rāhwayh*, 5:2258 (no. 1,541).

[42] al-Fākihī, *Akhbār Makka*, 1:450 (nos 986–7). Elsewhere, the centre of the Maqām (between the two footprints) is described as 'worn thin from the touching it received in the past': al-Azraqī, *Akhbār Makka*, 544; al-Fākihī, *Akhbār Makka*, 1:481; Ibn Rusta, *Kitāb al-A'lāk al-nafīsa*, ed. M. J. de Goeje (Leiden: Brill, 1892), 40; Ibn al-Faqīh al-Hamadhānī, *Kitāb al-Buldān*, ed. Yūsuf al-Hādī (Beirut: 'Ālam al-Kutub, 1996), 77; Yāqūt al-Ḥamawī, *Mu'jam al-buldān*, 5 vols (Beirut: Dār Ṣādir, 1977), 5:164.

[43] Another report attributes the Maqām's loss of miraculous healing ability to polytheists' touch: al-Azraqī, *Akhbār Makka*, 443, 531 (nos 410, 633); al-Fākihī, *Akhbār Makka*, 1:443 (no. 968). A change in the Maqām's colour is also mentioned: al-Azraqī, *Akhbār Makka*, 533 (no. 638); al-Fākihī, *Akhbār Makka*, 1:442 (no. 965).

such as Mujāhid and Qatāda, who urge Muslims to pursue a chaste engagement with sacred spaces and objects like the Maqām, often framing their assertions about proper ritual around the textual authority of the Qur'ān and other scriptural sources.[44] On the other hand are those chastised for their excessively physical interactions with the Maqām, the effects of which were etched into the stone itself. The opposition between these groups is concisely sketched in a report where the early authority ʿAbd Allāh b. al-Zubayr (d. 73/692) sees a group of people – or, in an alternative version, sees 'the people' (*al-nās*) as a whole – stroking the Maqām. Correcting them, Ibn al-Zubayr says, 'You were not commanded to stroke it, but only to pray nearby it!'[45] The preferred juristic method of engagement with the Maqām is embodied in the practice of ʿAbd Allāh b. ʿUmar (d. 73/692–3), the pious son of the caliph ʿUmar b. al-Khaṭṭāb. When Ibn ʿUmar wanted to pray near the Maqām, he placed enough space for one or two men between himself and it.[46]

While many early Muslim thinkers – and indeed many modern scholars – might agree with this distinction between 'elite' and 'popular' relic practices, such a 'two-tiered' understanding fails to convey accurately the complex usages of relics like the Maqām Ibrāhīm.[47] Recall that Layth b. Abī Sulaym – who was remembered within the Islamic scholarly tradition as a significant authority on the rituals of the ḥajj – was himself criticised by several authorities for his ritual actions around the Maqām. Moreover, not only did the Maqām serve as a useful symbol of authority and identity for Muslim elites, but the latter themselves participated at times in similar (or identical) relic practices to those that are often attributed to 'the people'.

[44] Bernard Weiss, *The Spirit of Islamic Law* (Athens: University of Georgia Press, 1998).

[45] ʿAbd al-Razzāq, *Muṣannaf*, 5:49 (no. 8,958); Ibn Abī Shayba, *Muṣannaf*, 5:624 (no. 15,736); al-Fākihī, *Akhbār Makka*, 1:457 (no. 1,004); *Masāʾil al-imām Aḥmad riwāyat Abī Dāwūd Sulaymān ibn al-Ashʿath al-Sijistānī*, ed. Ṭāriq b. ʿAwaḍ Allāh b. Muḥammad (Cairo: Maktabat Ibn Taymiyya, 1999), 160–1 (no. 760).

[46] ʿAbd al-Razzāq, *Muṣannaf*, 5:49 (no. 8,960). For more on Ibn ʿUmar, see below and Chapter 5.

[47] This has been articulated regarding late antique and medieval Christian practice: Brown, *Cult of the Saints*, 17–22; Patrick Geary, 'Sacred Commodities: The Circulation of Medieval Relics', in *The Social Life of Things: Commodities in Cultural Perspective*, ed. Arjan Appadurai (Cambridge: Cambridge University Press, 1986), 181. The point has also been made about early and medieval Islamic rituals: Munt, *Holy City of Medina*, 143 n.88; Beránek and Ťupek, *Temptation of Graves*, 36–7.

We find early Muslim leaders deploying the Maqām Ibrāhīm as an embodiment of both group identity and individual authority. Early historical texts indicate that the Maqām was housed in a box that was only unlocked by the Kaʿba's attendants during times of ritual prayer (*ṣalāt*) in Mecca, and – for some period of time – only when the prayer was led by either the caliph or the governor of Mecca.[48] In this context, the visual presence of the Maqām itself would have been prominently associated with a ritual that drew together the Muslim community in Mecca, and with those authorities who themselves led the prayer there.[49] Moreover, later texts report that, at the conclusion of prayer, the imam would 'touch' or 'salute' (*istalama*) the Maqām before it was again covered.[50] The prayer leader would not only be visually associated with the Maqām during the prayer itself, but would be seen having a tactile engagement with it as part of the conclusion to the rite. While the extant sources are fairly taciturn on the specifics of the Maqām's involvement in the ritual prayer, it appears that the stone was actively utilised by Muslim figures in structuring this communal ritual at Mecca and in articulating their own authoritative place within it.

Furthermore, Muslim authorities not only drew upon the Maqām as a unifying symbol, but also utilised it as a physical font of sacred power. When the ʿAbbāsid caliph al-Mahdī (r. 158/775–169/785) went on ḥajj to Mecca in 160/777, one of the Kaʿba's attendants (known as the *ḥajaba*) carried the Maqām to the caliph's quarters, where the ruler 'stroked [the Maqām], then poured water into it and drank it', before he sent the stone to members of his family so that they could do the same.[51] Similar elite participation in such rituals is attested a century later, during the renovation of the Maqām and its resting place in 256/870. On more than one occasion, the governor

[48] al-Fākihī, *Akhbār Makka*, 1:482; Kister, 'Maqām Ibrāhīm', 483–4. Ibn ʿAbd Rabbihi, *al-ʿIqd al-farīd*, 7:286 reports: 'during the ḥajj season [*al-mawsim*] a pierced iron box is placed on it, so that hands may not reach it'.

[49] On the significance of leading the prayer for political allegiance, see Patricia Crone, *God's Rule: Government and Islam* (New York: Columbia University Press, 2004), 289–90.

[50] Shams al-Dīn al-Muqaddasī, *Aḥsān al-taqāsīm fī maʿrifat al-aqālīm*, ed. M. J. de Goeje, 2nd ed. (Leiden: Brill, 1906), 72–3; Yāqūt al-Ḥamawī, *Muʿjam al-buldān*, 5:165.

[51] al-Azraqī, *Akhbār Makka*, 542–3 (no. 652); al-Fākihī, *Akhbār Makka*, 1:475 (no. 1,045); Kister, 'Maqām Ibrāhīm', 484.

ʿAlī b. al-Ḥasan ordered the *ḥajaba* to bring the Maqām to the city's administrative quarters (*dār al-imāra*), where audiences stroked the Maqām, invoked God's blessings and recited praise of the prophet Abraham. These audiences are said to have included the governor, scholars (*jamāʿat min al-nās man ḥamlat al-ʿilm*), and the author al-Fākihī himself.[52] At one such event, a group stroked the Maqām and poured water from the Zamzam well into it, drinking this powerful fluid and collecting it in bottles for later usage.[53]

Though some jurists may have disapproved of these activities, we see that Muslim scholars and political elites in the eighth and ninth centuries, including the caliph and his family, went far beyond 'praying near' the Maqām Ibrāhīm. Not only might they touch it as they led the communal prayers: they could be found piously caressing it and imbibing contact fluids from it, much like Christians did with their own saintly relics.[54] Rather than a distinction between popular and elite practice – defined by the former group's willingness to touch the stone, while the latter holds off – any difference in practice turns here on accessibility, with the elite being the ones most able to approach this powerful object. Veneration of the Maqām was a delicate matter, but was often positively valenced as a marker of piety, power and Islamic identity. Indeed, it was not the only such sacred footprint in the early Islamic world: a point to which the next section turns.

'How Pagan They Are!': Marking Muslim Difference with Footprints

The Qur'ān commentary of the Shīʿī scholar ʿAlī b. Ibrāhīm al-Qummī (d. after 307/919) contains a version of the story, mentioned above, about a *qāyif* tracking the Prophet Muḥammad as he flees from persecution in

[52] This governor is elsewhere identified as ʿAlī b. al-Ḥusayn b. Ismāʿīl b. al-ʿAbbās b. Muḥammad. *The History of al-Ṭabarī. Volume XXXIV: Incipient Decline*, trans. Joel L. Kraemer (Albany: State University of New York Press, 1989), 223. There, 'b. al-Ḥasan' appears as a variant.

[53] al-Fākihī, *Akhbār Makka*, 1:478–9 (no. 1,045); Kister, 'Maqām Ibrāhīm', 484–5. In his travelogue, the Andalusian scholar Ibn Jubayr (d. 614/1217) narrates his participation in very similar rituals at the Maqām, including drinking Zamzam water from the footprints. Abū al-Ḥusayn Muḥammad b. Aḥmad b. Jubayr, *Riḥla*, ed. William Wright, 2nd rev. ed. by M. J. de Goeje (Leiden: Brill, 1907), 84–5.

[54] Bursi, 'Fluid Boundaries', 492–5 and the bibliography cited there.

Mecca.[55] When the *qāyif* – who is identified here as Abū Kurz of the tribe of Khuzāʿa – is shown the Prophet's footprint in the dirt outside his empty house in Mecca, he exclaims: 'This is the foot of Muḥammad? By God, it is a sister of the foot in the Maqām!'[56] Abū Kurz then follows the tracks of the Prophet and the Prophet's travelling companion, the later caliph Abū Bakr, through the desert. The two refugees' prints suddenly end at a cave's mouth, covered in a thick, unbroken spider's web, which would have been cleared away by anyone recently entering the cave. Dumbfounded as to where Muḥammad and Abū Bakr could be, Abū Kurz marvels, 'The two of them have not traveled past this spot: either they ascended into the sky or descended under the earth!' The story's narrator quickly explains that, in fact, 'God had dispatched a spider that weaved a web over the mouth of the cave' in order to mask the hiding spot of the two fleeing Muslims. Once their pursuers had left, Muḥammad and Abū Bakr were then able to leave the cave and continue on their journey to Medina.

While God's divine intervention in the form of the spider's web is the narrative crux of this story, the footprints play a role here as well.[57] Abū Kurz wonders at the appearance of Muḥammad's foot and its similarity to Abraham's in the Maqām Ibrāhīm: an annunciatory topos encountered in stories discussed above. He likewise marvels at the sudden disappearance of the Prophet's (and Abū Bakr's) tracks, and speculates that the two 'ascended into the sky or descended under the earth'. In the tracker's eyes, only a miracle could explain the traces in the dirt that make it appear that the two men had disappeared into thin air.

[55] 'Alī b. Ibrāhīm al-Qummī, *Tafsīr al-Qummī*, ed. Sayyid Muḥammad Bāqir al-Muwaḥḥid al-Abṭaḥī et al., 3 vols (Qum: Mu'assasat al-Imām al-Mahdī, 2014), 1:394. On this author and his *tafsīr*, see *EI*[3], s.v. "Alī b. Ibrāhīm al-Qummī' (Mohammad Ali Amir-Moezzi); Meir M. Bar-Asher, *Scripture and Exegesis in Early Imāmī-Shiism* (Leiden: Brill, 1999), 33–56.

[56] The *qāyif* is identified as Kurz b. ʿAlqama from the tribe of Khuzāʿa in Ibn Saʿd, *Ṭabaqāt*, 6:282, 8:19–20; Hishām b. Muḥammad al-Kalbī, *Nasab Maʿadd wa-l-Yaman al-kabīr*, ed. Nājī Ḥasan, 2 vols (Beirut: ʿĀlam al-Kutub, 1988), 2:444. Ibn al-Kalbī does not include the story about the Maqām Ibrāhīm.

[57] On the story of the spider and the cave's mouth, see Uri Rubin, 'The Life of Muḥammad and the Qur'ān: The Case of Muḥammad's Hijra', *JSAI* 28 (2003): 40–64. The story appears already in the early *sīra* text on papyrus attributed to Wahb b. Munabbih: Khoury, *Wahb b. Munabbih*, 1:144 (lines 23–4). Corrections to Khoury's edition appear in Kister, 'On the Papyrus of Wahb', 552; R. G. Khoury, 'Quelques remarques supplementaires concernant la papyrus de Wahb b. Munabbih', *BSOAS* 40.1 (1977): 21.

Though Abū Kurz's speculation that Muḥammad and Abū Bakr 'ascended into the sky' was incorrect, this idea is perhaps a gesture towards the close association between footprints and heavenly ascensions at several Near Eastern spaces venerated in late antiquity. In this period, a number of stones were believed to contain different sacred figures' footprints, and were cherished and visited by different groups. In such cases, the footprints were often said to have been moulded into stone by a figure at the moment of his ascension into the sky: for example, Jesus was raised from the (later) location of the Church of the Ascension on the Mount of Olives, and Abraham rose into the sky atop the Maqām to call the world to ḥajj.[58] Abū Kurz's confused guess about the disappeared Muḥammad and Abū Bakr hints, perhaps satirically, towards this larger context of sacred footprints associated with heavenly ascensions.

Such footprints emerged as sites of both worship and contestation, as Muslims and non-Muslims disputed the appropriateness of venerating these stones and the implications imbedded in such acts. For example, a conflict about one such location is described in a tradition from the famous Companion ʿAbd Allāh b. Masʿūd (d. *c.* 32/652–3). Here, the Foundation Stone on the Temple Mount in Jerusalem evokes a theological discussion:

> Ibn Masʿūd passed by an elderly man who was relating stories from the Torah – but when the man saw Ibn Masʿūd, he fell silent. Ibn Masʿūd asked [the group that had been listening], 'What was your companion relating to you?' They said, 'He reported that, after God created the skies and the earth, He ascended to the sky from the Temple Mount [Bayt al-Maqdis], and placed His foot upon the Stone on the Temple Mount.' [. . .] Ibn Masʿūd said, 'Why do you not refute him? Say what the faithful servant Abraham said, "I do not like those [gods] that disappear" (Q. 6:76), meaning [a god that] leaves or is removed. For the Jews doubt your religion!'[59]

[58] For mentions of Jesus' footprints in the Church of the Ascension, see Sulpicius Severus, *Chronica* 2.33; *Itinerarium Antonini Placentini* 23; Adomnán, *De locis sanctis* 1.23. For translations and discussion, see John Wilkinson, *Jerusalem Pilgrims before the Crusades* (Jerusalem: Ariel, 1977), 100–1, 166, 194; Erik Inglis, 'Inventing Apostolic Impression Relics in Medieval Rome', *Speculum* 96 (2021): 311.

[59] Abū Yaʿqūb Yūsuf b. Ibrāhīm al-Warjlānī, *Kitāb al-Tartīb fī-l-ṣaḥīḥ min ḥadīth al-rasūl*, ed. Nūr al-Dīn ʿAbd Allāh b. Ḥumayd al-Sālimī (Muscat: Maktabat Masqaṭ, 2003), 404–5. This tradition is recorded in the *Musnad* attributed to the Ibāḍī imam al-Rabīʿ b. Ḥabīb (d. between 180/796 and 190/806), a text which exists today only in the rearrangement produced by al-Warjlānī (d. 570/1174). On this text and its issues, see John C. Wilkinson, 'Ibāḍī

Here, an apparently Jewish figure teaches from the Torah that God had ascended to heaven from the Temple Mount, placing His divine foot on the Foundation Stone – and, implicitly, creating the indentation found there – in the process. In retaliation, Ibn Masʿūd cites a qur'ānic verse in which Abraham distinguishes the true God from false ones, such as stars and other celestial bodies that 'disappear' from the sky during the day. Going further, Ibn Masʿūd then asserts that such 'attribution to God of bounds and disappearance' (*waṣafū-hu bi-l-ḥudūd wa-l-zawāl*) is a form of polytheism or *shirk*, though a pernicious form 'more invisible than ants crawling on a black stone in the dark of night'.[60]

The Foundation Stone thus gives rise to a discussion of divine anthropomorphism, a charge that Ibn Masʿūd levels at the (purportedly) Jewish assertion that God had planted His foot on the Temple Mount on His way up to heaven.[61] This polemical topos reappears in a report about the response of ʿAbd Allāh b. ʿUmar b. al-Khaṭṭāb – whom we saw above praying near, but not touching, the Maqām Ibrāhīm – when he is asked about the Stone on the Temple Mount:

> He trembled with fear and anxiety that they were attributing bounds and movement to God and said, 'He is too exalted and too sublime for the characteristics of created beings to be ascribed to him! These are the words of the Jews, the enemies of God!'[62]

Again the idea of God physically moving from earth to heaven, and the attribution to Him of a foot to plant on the Stone, is framed as a Jewish conception. It is 'the Jews, the enemies of God' that ascribe such 'bounds and movement' to God

Ḥadīth: An Essay on Normalization', *Der Islam* 62.2 (1985): 231–59; Ersilia Francesca, 'The Formation and Early Development of the Ibāḍī Madhhab', *JSAI* 28 (2003): 260–77; Josef van Ess, *Theology and Society in the Second and Third Centuries of the Hijra: A History of Religious Thought in Early Islam*, trans. John O'Kane and Gwendolin Goldbloom, 4 vols (Leiden: Brill, 2017–19), 2:228–31.

[60] See discussion of these passages in Josef van Ess, "Abd al-Malik and the Dome of the Rock: An Analysis of Some Texts', in *Bayt al-Maqdis: ʿAbd al-Malik's Jerusalem*, ed. Julian Raby and Jeremy Johns (Oxford: Oxford University Press, 1992), 94ff.

[61] On these issues, see Wesley Williams, 'A Body Unlike Bodies: Transcendent Anthropomorphism in Ancient Semitic Tradition and Early Islam', *JAOS* 129 (2009): 19–44; Livnat Holtzman, *Anthropomorphism in Islam: The Challenge of Traditionalism (700–1350)* (Edinburgh: Edinburgh University Press, 2018).

[62] al-Warjlānī, *Kitāb al-Tartīb*, 398.

in their heretical misunderstanding of the divine nature. While the divine foot is not explicitly referenced, mention of the Foundation Stone – which allegedly contained His footprint – leads to a discussion of the correct conception of God and his (lack of) corporeal form.

As Josef van Ess has noted of these passages, 'We are indeed close to Jewish ideas'.[63] Within rabbinic sources and Jewish mystical texts, God's body is discussed in terms that are often far from allegorical.[64] Moreover, the Foundation Stone's role as the site of the beginning of creation, and of God's direct presence, appears in several rabbinic texts.[65] Combining these elements together, a story in the *Pirke de Rabbi Eliezer* (a late antique rabbinic midrash of the book of Genesis) describes God's foot physically meeting the Foundation Stone.[66] In a commentary on the story of Jacob's ladder at Gen 28, we read:

> And Jacob returned to gather the stones, and found that all of them had become one stone, and he set it as a pillar (Gen 28:18) [. . .] What did the Holy One, blessed be He, do? He stretched out his right foot, and sank the stone

[63] Van Ess, ''Abd al-Malik and the Dome', 95. See also Josef van Ess, 'The Youthful God: Anthropomorphism in Early Islam', in *Kleine Schriften*, ed. Hinrich Biesterfeldt, 3 vols (Leiden: Brill, 2018), 2: 628–9.

[64] José Costa, 'The Body of God in Ancient Rabbinic Judaism: Problems of Interpretation', *Revue de l'histoire des religions* 227.3 (2010): 283–316; Daniel Boyarin, 'The Eye in the Torah: Ocular Desire in Midrashic Hermeneutic', in *Sparks of the Logos: Essays in Rabbinic Hermeneutics* (Leiden: Brill, 2003), 3–23; Eliot R. Wolfson, 'Images of God's Feet: Some Observations on the Divine Body in Judaism', in *People of the Body: Jews and Judaism from an Embodied Perspective*, ed. Howard Eilberg-Schwartz (Albany: State University of New York Press, 1992), 143–81; Howard Eilberg-Schwartz, 'The Problem of the Body for the People of the Book', in Eilberg-Schwartz, *People of the Body*, 17–46; Meir Bar-Ilan, 'The Hand of God: A Chapter in Rabbinic Anthropomorphism', in *Rashi 1040–1990: Hommage à Ephraïm E. Urbach. Congrès européen des études juives*, ed. Gabrielle Sed-Rajna (Paris: Éditions du CERF, 1993), 321–35.

[65] Philip S. Alexander, 'Jerusalem as the *Omphalos* of the World: On the History of a Geographical Concept', *Judaism* 46 (1997): 155–7; Jeffrey L. Rubenstein, 'From Mythic Motifs to Sustained Myth: The Revision of Rabbinic Traditions in Medieval Midrashim', *HTR* 89.2 (1996): 135–7; Naomi Koltun-Fromm, 'Jerusalem Sacred Stones from Creation to Eschaton', *Journal of Late Antiquity* 10.2 (2018): 408–9; Emmanouela Grypeou and Helen Spurling, *The Book of Genesis in Late Antiquity: Encounters between Jewish and Christian Exegesis* (Brill: Leiden, 2013), 291–2; Shoemaker, *Death of a Prophet*, 235.

[66] H. L. Strack and Günter Stemberger, *Introduction to the Talmud and Midrash*, ed. and trans. Markus Bockmuehl, 2nd ed. (Minneapolis: Fortress Press, 1996), 328–30; Katharina E. Keim, *Pirqei deRabbi Eliezer: Structure, Coherence, Intertextuality* (Leiden: Brill, 2017).

> to the depths of the depths, and He made it the keystone of the earth [. . .] Therefore, it is called the Foundation Stone, because from there is the navel of the earth, and from there all the earth was extended, and the Temple of the Lord stands upon it.[67]

Amalgamating the sites of Joseph's pillar in Bethel, the Temple in Jerusalem and the 'navel of the earth' from which creation began, this rabbinic story explicitly connects God's foot stepping upon the Foundation Stone with several crucial moments of sacred history. We can see, therefore, that a dialogue with actual Jewish traditions is likely embedded in these polemical early Islamic traditions that reference Jewish beliefs about the sacred status of the Foundation Stone and its connection to God's foot.[68]

Yet stories of God's ascending to heaven from the Foundation Stone are recorded not in Jewish sources, but in Islamic traditions in praise of Jerusalem and its environs. Notably, these traditions are attributed to Jewish authorities in several cases, such as one said to have come from the mouth of the early, semi-legendary Jewish convert to Islam, Kaʿb al-Aḥbār:

> In the Torah, God says to the Foundation Stone of the Temple Mount, 'You are my lower throne, and from you I rose to the sky. From beneath you I

[67] *PRE*, ch. 35. *Pirke de-Rabbi Elieser: Nach der Edition Venedig 1544 unter Berücksichtigung der Edition Warschau 1852*, ed. Dagmer Börner-Klein (Berlin: de Gruyter, 2004), 437. This passage is translated (slightly adapted here) in Grypeou and Spurling, *Book of Genesis in Late Antiquity*, 292. This and related passages are discussed in Rachel Adelman, 'Midrash, Myth, and Bakhtin's Chronotope: The Itinerant Well and the Foundation Stone in *Pirqe de-Rabbi Eliezer*', *Journal of Jewish Thought and Philosophy* 17.2 (2009): 143–76.

[68] In the case of *Pirke de Rabbi Elieser*, its likely date of composition around the eighth century CE allows the possibility of familiarity with, or influence from, Islamic traditions throughout the text. Keim, *Pirqei deRabbi Eliezer*, 190–5. Regarding the Pirke's traditions on the Foundation Stone, Adelman suggests that the 'the author of *PRE* adopts the earlier Jewish tradition identifying the Temple Mount with the navel of the earth, and merges it with the Islamic legend about the al-Aksa mosque', referencing stories of the Prophet's ascension during his *miʿrāj*. Adelman, 'Midrash, Myth, and Bakhtin's Chronotope', 163–6. However, Adelman does not engage with the Islamic traditions about God's ascension from the Stone, which almost certainly pre-date those that associate the Foundation Stone with the Prophet. Furthermore, it is not clear if the Prophet's ascension was yet located at this space by the period of *PRE*'s composition. See further discussion below.

extended the earth, and all the water that streams from the peaks of mountains [originates] from beneath you.'[69]

There is clearly a connection to Jewish traditions about the significance of the Foundation Stone here, but with an added emphasis on the Stone as the spot from which God ascended to the heavens. This appears also in a tradition that 'We find in the written book [the Torah] that when God had created the earth and wanted to ascend to the sky [. . .] His ascension occurred from the Foundation Stone'.[70] It is possible that there are reflections here of Palestinian Jewish beliefs that were current in the early Islamic period: Muslims incorporated many late antique Jewish traditions – both biblical and not – into their own texts in praise of Jerusalem.[71]

These early Islamic traditions about the Foundation Stone do not only testify to controversy between early Muslims and Jews: they connect also to intra-Muslim disputes on theological issues and related religious matters. One tradition, recorded in Shīʿī and Ibāḍī texts, is reported from Muḥammad b. ʿAlī (d. 81/700–1): the caliph ʿAlī b. Abī Ṭālib's third-born son, who was often called Ibn al-Ḥanafiyya ('the son of the Ḥanafī woman'). Ibn al-Ḥanafiyya says:

God fight the people of Syria: how pagan they are! They say that God placed His foot upon the Foundation Stone on the Temple Mount. One of His

[69] Abū Bakr Muḥammad b. Aḥmad al-Wāsiṭī, *Faḍā'il al-Bayt al-Muqaddas*, ed. Isaac Hasson (Jerusalem: Magness Press, 1979), 69–71 (nos 111, 116); Abū al-Maʿālī al-Musharraf b. al-Murajjā b. Ibrāhīm al-Maqdisī, *Faḍā'il Bayt al-Maqdis wa-l-Khalīl wa-faḍā'il al-Shām*, ed. Ofer Livne-Kafri (Shafā ʿAmr: Dār al-Mashriq, 1995), 106–9 (nos 113, 122); Ibn al-Faqīh, *Kitāb al-Buldān*, 148. Kaʿb al-Aḥbār frequently functions in early Islamic texts as a symbolic repository of Jewish and Christian knowledge turned to Islamic purposes. See Hughes, *Anxious Inheritance*, 109–11. On the cosmogenic significance of water originating from the Foundation Stone, see Koltun-Fromm, 'Jerusalem Sacred Stones', 410; Adelman, 'Midrash, Myth, and Bakhtin's Chronotope', 167–72.

[70] al-Wāsiṭī, *Faḍā'il*, 70 (no. 114); Ibn al-Murajjā, *Faḍā'il*, 108–9 (no. 120). The report is attributed to Sawāda b. ʿAṭā' al-Ḥaḍramī, an otherwise unknown figure.

[71] Van Ess, ''Abd al-Malik and the Dome', 89, 95; Moshe Sharon, 'The "Praises of Jerusalem" as a Source for the Early History of Jerusalem', *Bibliotheca Orientalis* 49 (1992): 56–67; Izhak Hasson, 'The Muslim View of Jerusalem: The Qur'ān and Ḥadīth', in *The History of Jerusalem: The Early Muslim Period, 638–1099*, ed. Joshua Prawer and Haggai Ben-Shammai (Jerusalem: Yad Izhak Ben-Zvi, 1996), 349–85; Shoemaker, *Death of a Prophet*, 231–45.

servants, Abraham, placed his own foot upon a stone, and he made it a *qibla* for the people![72]

Like Ibn Mas'ūd's accusation of idolatry against Jews who assert that God had stepped on the Foundation Stone, Ibn al-Ḥanafiyya here mocks such an idea as 'pagan'. A Shīʿī version of the report makes this theological point even clearer when Ibn al-Ḥanafiyya adds that God 'has no equal and no like [. . .] He is hidden from looking eyes, but He does not leave nor disappear like transitory things do. There is nothing like Him.'[73] We again see an accusation of bad theology rooted in an overly anthropomorphic conception of God's foot and its resting place.

Beyond the charge of anthropomorphism, Ibn al-Ḥanafiyya's statement connects also to differing ideas about sacred space. Ibn al-Ḥanafiyya levels his criticism here not at Jews, as Ibn Mas'ūd and Ibn 'Umar had done, but instead at the 'people of Syria' (*ahl al-Shām*). Rather than a condemnation of the whole of the people of Syria, his phrasing here likely references the Umayyad dynasty, whose political and religious power and interests were centred there.[74] The Umayyads emphasised the sacred status of Palestine, and especially the city of Jerusalem, where the Temple Mount stood. It was there that the caliph 'Abd al-Malik b. Marwān (r. 65–86/685–705) constructed the Dome of the Rock: the 'Rock' was the Foundation Stone upon which God had supposedly stepped. 'Abd al-Malik and his caliphal successor, his son al-Walīd (r. 86–96/705–15), not only patronised the construction of the Dome, but also furnished an elaborate ritual programme for venerating the space. Attendants twice-weekly covered the Foundation Stone in perfume and filled the building with incense, eventually releasing a cloud of fragrant smoke into the sky as a sign that the Dome of the Rock was ready to receive visitors.[75]

[72] al-Warjlānī, *Kitāb al-Tartīb*, 398–9.

[73] Abū al-Naṣr Muḥammad b. Mas'ūd al-'Ayyāshī, *Tafsīr al-'Ayyāshī*, ed. Hāshim al-Rasūlī al-Maḥallātī, 2 vols (Beirut: Mu'assasat al-A'lamī, 1991), 1:78 (no. 94); Kister, 'Maqām Ibrāhīm', 481 n.19. The vocabulary here echoes Q 6:76, like Ibn Mas'ūd's argument cited above.

[74] Gerald R. Hawting, *The First Dynasty of Islam: The Umayyad Caliphate AD 661–750*, 2nd ed. (London: Routledge, 2000).

[75] Amikam Elad, 'Why Did 'Abd al-Malik Build the Dome of the Rock? A Re-Examination of the Muslim Sources', in Raby and Johns, *Bayt al-Maqdis*, 33–58; Julian Raby, 'In Vitro Veritas: Glass Pilgrim Vessels from 7th-Century Jerusalem', in *Bayt al-Maqdis: Jerusalem and*

The Umayyads' association of the Foundation Stone with God's foot appears in a few historical reports, where their reverence for the Stone is further criticised. In one case, the caliph ʿAbd al-Malik gushes to an audience, 'This is the Foundation Stone of the Merciful One, upon which He placed His foot.' Exasperated, the scholar ʿUrwa b. al-Zubayr replies:

> God the Most Blessed and Most High says, 'His throne extends over the heavens and the earth' (Q 2:255), and you say, 'He placed His foot on this'?! No, this is simply a mountain, of the sort that God told us He 'will blast them into dust and leave a flat plain'. (Q 20:105–6)[76]

Deploying qurʾānic citations, ʿUrwa criticises not only the idea of God's foot resting upon a stone, but also the ascription of any significance to the Temple Mount. ʿUrwa asserts that this place is merely a mountain, like the many others that God will destroy at the end of time.

In a similar report, ʿAbd al-Malik and ʿUrwa are both present when Kaʿb al-Aḥbār (a Jewish convert to Islam, whom we met above) states, 'The Foundation Stone will be the resting place of the Merciful One's foot on the Day of Judgment.' Here, an association between the Stone and God's foot is again attributed to a Jewish authority. In this case, though, Kaʿb locates God's foot on the Foundation Stone in the eschatological future, rather than the primordial past.[77] As with ʿAbd al-Malik's claims about the Stone, ʿUrwa protests:

> Kaʿb lies! No, the Foundation Stone is merely one of the mountains of which God says, 'They ask you about the mountains: say, "My Lord will blast them into dust".' (Q 20:105)[78]

Early Islam, ed. Jeremy Johns (Oxford: Oxford University Press, 1999), 113–90; Shoemaker, *Death of a Prophet*, 235–6; Adam Bursi, 'Scents of Space: Early Islamic Pilgrimage, Perfume, and Paradise', *Arabica* 67 (2020): 200–34.

76 Muḥammad b. Isḥāq b. Khuzayma, *Kitāb al-Tawḥīd wa-ithbāt ṣifāt al-rabb ʿazza wa-jalla*, ed. ʿAbd al-ʿAzīz b. Ibrāhīm al-Shahwān (Riyadh: Dār al-Rushd, 1988), 250; Van Ess, "Abd al-Malik and the Dome', 98. On ʿUrwa's relationship with ʿAbd al-Malik and Umayyads, including their patronage of him, see Josef Horovitz, *The Earliest Biographies of the Prophet and their Authors*, ed. Lawrence I. Conrad (Princeton: Darwin Press, 2002), 18–26.

77 The Foundation Stone's association with eschatology also occurs in other traditions. Cf. Ofer Livne-Kafri, 'Jerusalem in Early Islam: The Eschatological Aspect', *Arabica* 53.3 (2006): 382–403.

78 Ibn Jarīr al-Ṭabarī, *Tafsīr*, 16:164.

According to the report, "Abd al-Malik was silent' after ʿUrwa's words, leaving ambiguous his opinion on the conflicting interpretations of the Foundation Stone's eschatological significance.[79] While these reports are certainly 'not facts, but literature', they communicate something of what 'people *believed* ʿAbd al-Malik believed' regarding the Foundation Stone and the reasoning behind the Dome of the Rock's construction.[80]

As has been discussed extensively by scholars both ancient and modern, the Umayyad promotion of the Dome of the Rock as a sacred space and locus of pilgrimage likely stood in tension with the patronage and visitation (especially during the ḥajj) of the Kaʿba in Mecca.[81] Often cited in this discussion is a passage from the *Taʾrīkh* (History) of Ibn Wāḍiḥ al-Yaʿqūbī (fl. ninth century):

> ʿAbd al-Malik forbade the people of Syria from performing the ḥajj. This was because Ibn al-Zubayr would compel the pilgrims to give him the oath of allegiance [while they were in Mecca for ḥajj]. Seeing this, ʿAbd al-Malik forbade the people of Syria to leave for Mecca. But the people became agitated, saying 'You keep us from performing the ḥajj to God's Sacred House, even though God has made it obligatory for us!' ʿAbd al-Malik said to them [. . .] 'The mosque of Jerusalem will take the place for you of the Sacred Mosque [in Mecca]. This stone – upon which, it is related, the Messenger of God set his foot when he ascended to heaven – shall take the place of the Kaʿba for you.' He built a dome over the stone, hung brocade curtains upon it, and appointed keepers to look after it. He enjoined people to circumambulate around it, just as they circumambulate around the Kaʿba.[82]

According to al-Yaʿqūbī, the political conflict between the Umayyads in Syria and Ibn al-Zubayr in the Ḥijāz led to a rivalry also between the two sacred spaces of the Temple Mount and the Kaʿba. Historians have questioned the

[79] Livne-Kafri, 'Jerusalem in Early Islam', 388 suggests that "Abd al-Malik's silence seems to signify support of Kaʿb's view'.

[80] Van Ess, "Abd al-Malik and the Dome', 98.

[81] For an overview of scholarship, see Milka Levy-Rubin, 'Why Was the Dome of the Rock Built? A New Perspective on a Long-Discussed Question', *BSOAS* 80.3 (2017): 441–64.

[82] Aḥmad b. Abī Yaʿqūb b. Jaʿfar b. Wahb b. Wāḍiḥ, *Taʾrīkh*, ed. Martijn T. Houtsma, 2 vols (Leiden: Brill, 1883), 2:311; *The Works of Ibn Wāḍiḥ al-Yaʿqūbī: An English Translation*, ed. Matthew S. Gordon et al., 3 vols (Leiden: Brill, 2018), 3:958–9 (adapted here). On this author, see Sean Anthony, 'Was Ibn Wāḍiḥ al-Yaʿqūbī a Shiʿite Historian? The State of the Question', *Al-ʿUṣūr al-Wusṭā* 24 (2016): 15–41.

reliability of this and similar historical traditions, which clearly reflect anti-Umayyad points of view in their ascription of ulterior, political motives to the Umayyads' patronage of the Dome of the Rock.[83] There is likewise debate on the extent to which the Umayyads' efforts would actually have been diverting pilgrimage from the Kaʿba, as 'there is no clear evidence that pilgrimage to the Kaʿba had become a fixed feature of Muslim belief and practice at the end of the seventh century'.[84]

What we can see, though, are the ways that these conflicts were framed in the religious and historical texts that emerged over the course of the eighth and ninth centuries. Strikingly, several texts anchor the competing Islamic sacred geographies in the different footprints that the sites claimed to possess. In Ibn al-Ḥanafiyya's report, the tension between Syrian and Arabian sacred spaces is manifested as a comparison between the stones exhibiting God's and Abraham's feet. Explicitly juxtaposing the Foundation Stone in Jerusalem with the Maqām Ibrāhīm in Mecca, Ibn al-Ḥanafiyya mocks the theological impossibility of God's leaving a footprint on a stone. He further notes that Abraham – a mere servant of God – had imprinted such a stone, and that God had commanded that this stone become the people's *qibla*, that is, the direction towards which they direct their prayer. Perhaps subtly referencing the early Muslims' movement of their *qibla* away from Jerusalem and towards Mecca,[85] Ibn al-Ḥanafiyya implicitly asks how God's footprint could exist in Jerusalem if a mere man's footprint in Mecca is the spot towards which prayer is directed. The existence of the Maqām Ibrāhīm, and its exalted status, are thus deployed to trump claims of the Foundation Stone's holiness.

While the Maqām Ibrāhīm is not explicitly mentioned in al-Yaʿqūbī's report about the competing Syrian and Arabian sacred places, another prophet's footprint is: the Prophet Muḥammad's. In al-Yaʿqūbī's text, the caliph ʿAbd al-Malik announces that the Foundation Stone 'shall take the place of the Kaʿba' for the people of Syria, and notes that 'the Messenger of God set his foot [upon this Stone] when he ascended to heaven'. Rather than God stepping on the Stone, here mention is made of the Prophet's foot, which ʿAbd al-Malik connects to the story of the Prophet's ascension to heaven, the Miʿrāj. The sacredness of the

[83] Shoemaker, *Death of a Prophet*, 241–57.

[84] Chase F. Robinson, *ʿAbd al-Malik* (Oxford: OneWorld, 2005), 96.

[85] Shoemaker, *Death of a Prophet*, 223–4.

Stone in Jerusalem is thus connected to this pivotal moment in Islamic sacred history, when the Prophet ascended to heaven and directly interacted with other prophets and with God.[86]

Reading the context underlying al-Yaʿqūbī's report is difficult, since early Muslims expressed both polemical and laudatory rhetoric surrounding Jerusalem's holiness. Does al-Yaʿqūbī mean to diminish the Foundation Stone's sacredness by associating it with Muḥammad's ascension, rather than with God's? Or is he simply reporting contemporary lore associated with the Stone's sacredness that he knew? The tradition of God's ascending from the Stone is certainly the earlier tradition, perhaps influenced by pre-existing Jewish ideas, and it likely directed the Umayyads' earliest patronage of the space.[87] The association of the Stone instead with Muḥammad's ascension, and thus with his footprint, is a later, secondary development, stemming from efforts to provide specifically Islamic connotations to Jerusalemite sacred spaces.[88] Indeed, al-Yaʿqūbī's identification of the Stone with Muḥammad's place of ascension is notably earlier than others writers' mentions of this association.[89] In fact, later writers are often dismissive of the traditions about the Prophet's footprint on the Foundation Stone. It is possible that Yaʿqūbī's mention may also have such a polemical intent, perhaps to discredit ʿAbd al-Malik's alleged attempt to replace the Kaʿba.

Conclusion: Footprints, Stones and Relics in Early Islam

A Muslim convert stealing the Maqām Ibrāhīm to bring it to Constantinople; a Qurʾān scholar lamenting his community's frequent touching of the stone; a caliph and his retinue drinking water out of its ancient footprints; a comparison between the Maqām and God's imprint in the Foundation Stone in Jerusalem: these brief stories and reports offer snapshots of the different and often discordant perspectives on relic veneration found throughout the first centuries of

86 *EQ*, s.v. 'Ascension' (Michael Sells).

87 Heribert Busse, 'Jerusalem in the Story of Muhammad's Night Journey and Ascension', *JSAI* 14 (1991): 35–8; Van Ess, ''Abd al-Malik and the Dome', 99–100; Shoemaker, *Death of a Prophet*, 236–7, 256.

88 Shoemaker, *Death of a Prophet*, 349; Hasson, 'Muslim View of Jerusalem', 358–9.

89 Amikam Elad, *Medieval Jerusalem and Islamic Worship: Holy Places, Ceremonies, Pilgrimage* (Leiden: Brill, 1995), 49–50, 57–8, 72–6; Elad, 'Why ʿAbd al-Malik Build the Dome of the Rock', 43–4.

Islam. Like other late antique and medieval groups, early Muslims used relics in a plethora of ways in defining themselves as a community, drawing distinctions (as well as connections) between themselves and others. Taking part in the late antique and early medieval conversation about relics and their veneration, early Muslims debated among themselves how exactly these relics might be used: what was appropriate, what was beneficial, and what was beyond the pale of acceptable practice.

That the Maqām Ibrāhīm displays Abraham's footprints in stone provides an interesting example for the study of relics within early Islam. A footprint is, by its nature, 'an image of absence; it is a space, an empty space, whose emptiness is constituted precisely by a presence that no longer is'.[90] Footprints are able to represent a presence that is not there, and thus – for a viewer with the prerequisite knowledge and cultural context – can point towards a person, but without iconographically representing them. This 'indexical' quality has sometimes been called upon to explain the veneration of footprints in particular religious traditions, such as Islam, that are commonly understood to be averse to visual representations of holy persons.[91] Brannon Wheeler has drawn upon such ideas in order to suggest that, in Islam, '[r]ituals and relics are about absence'.[92] Commenting on

[90] Jacob N. Kinnard, *Places in Motion: The Fluid Identities of Temples, Images, and Pilgrims* (Oxford: Oxford University Press, 2014), 34.

[91] I draw here on Charles Sanders Peirce's concept of the 'indexical' quality of symbols. On footprints as indices, see Albert Atkin, 'Peirce on the Index and Indexical Reference', *Transactions of the Charles S. Peirce Society* 41 (2005): 166. See also Ruffle, 'Presence in Absence', 334–6. In Buddhist Studies, the Buddha's footprints have often been interpreted as 'a central means of representing the Buddha's presence through his absence', related to hesitations about iconographically depicting the Buddha. Kinnard, *Places in Motion*, 61. Such thinking has been extended to other objects as well, including the Buddha's corporeal relics, which Buddhologists have read as 'denot[ing] the presence of the Buddha in his very absence'. Robert H. Sharf, 'On the Allure of Buddhist Relics', *Representations* 66 (1999): 77. These arguments have also been incisively critiqued: Sharf, 'On the Allure of Buddhist Relics', 78; Gregory Schopen, 'Burial "Ad Sanctos" and the Physical Presence of the Buddha in Early Indian Buddhism: A Study in the Archeology of Religions', *Religion* 17 (1987): 210; Schopen, 'Relic', in *Critical Terms for Religious Studies*, ed. Mark C. Taylor (Chicago: University of Chicago Press, 1998), 259–62.

[92] Wheeler, *Mecca and Eden*, 131, and his comparison between Islam and Buddhism at 96–7. For a similar comparison of footprint relics in Buddhism, Islam and Christianity, see Luca Patrizi, 'Impronte, ritratti e reliquie di profeti nell'Islam', in *Sacre impronte e oggetti «non fatti da mano d'uomo» nelle religioni*, ed. Adele Monaci Castagno (Alessandria: Edizioni dell'Orso, 2011), 81–94.

the Prophet Muḥammad's footprints and corporeal relics venerated by medieval and modern Muslims, Wheeler writes that these objects 'do not appear to be understood as a means to venerate the prophet Muhammad's physical body', but rather 'the prophet Muhammad's relics and their distribution seem to reflect and stress his physical absence'.[93]

Does the Maqām Ibrāhīm – the footprint of the prophet Abraham – testify to such an attitude among early Muslims? Did this stone offer a way for early Muslims to commemorate Abraham's absence? There was certainly an ambivalence about the Maqām Ibrāhīm, represented most clearly in the tensions surrounding the act of touching it. Yet the belief that the stone endured in the world as Abraham's literal, physical traces – his *āthār* – is likely what led to such pious actions in the first place. Rather than commemorating Abraham's absence, the stone's physical presence was a 'clear sign' in the world, created by God so that people might look upon it and believe. Indeed, according to some traditions, the Maqām stood as the *qibla* itself, the physical marker towards which prayer should be directed. The stone did not primarily demarcate Abraham's absence, but rather his traces' continued presence.[94]

Commenting on the stones that late antique Christian pilgrims visited in the Holy Land and elsewhere – stones that moved, spoke, displayed the impressions of Christ's body, and spontaneously produced sacred fluids – Glenn Peers writes, 'One can say that not all late antique stones were alive, in other words, but special ones were and could be so again.'[95] We can profitably speak of the Maqām Ibrāhīm as a similarly 'animate' presence in late antique Mecca. During Abraham's life, the Maqām had miraculously grown to the size of a mountain and absorbed the shapes of Abraham's footprints. According to

[93] Wheeler, *Mecca and Eden*, 80. For examples of relics that have been understood to produce Islamic figures' 'presence in absence' in modern contexts, see Ruffle, 'Presence in Absence', 333–6; Frank J. Korom, 'The Presence of Absence: Using Stuff in a South Asian Sufi Movement', *AAS Working Papers in Anthropology* 23 (2012): 1–19; Mikkel Rytter, 'The Hair of the Prophet: Relics and Affective Presence of the Absent Beloved among Sufis in Denmark', *Contemporary Islam* 13 (2019): 49–65.

[94] Cf. Caroline Walker Bynum, 'Footprints: The Xenophilia of a European Medievalist'. *Common Knowledge* 24.2 (2018): 291–311, esp. 303–6.

[95] Glenn Peers, 'Object Relations: Theorizing the Late Antique Viewer', in Johnson, *Oxford Handbook of Late Antiquity*, 985.

some traditions, it would grow again in the future, and also speak. A tradition attributed to Mujāhid b. Jabr states that the Maqām and the Black Stone set in the Kaʿba 'will both come forward on the Day of Judgment, bigger than [the mountain of] Abū Qubays. Each will have eyes, a tongue, and lips, and they will testify for those that visited them.'[96] Instead of a marker of Abraham's absence, the Maqām Ibrāhīm was itself a significant, animate presence, quite central to the early Islamic sacred landscape. And as the next chapters will demonstrate, it was far from the only one.

[96] ʿAbd al-Razzāq, *Muṣannaf*, 5:30–2 (nos 8,882, 8,883, 8,890); al-Azraqī, *Akhbār Makka*, 445–50 (nos 415, 419, 426, 427); al-Fākihī, *Akhbār Makka*, 1:93 (no. 28); al-Ḥasan al-Baṣrī (attrib.), *Faḍāʾil Makka wa-l-sakan fīhā*, ed. Sāmī Makkī al-ʿĀnī (Kuwait: Maktabat al-Falāḥ, 1980), 30; Kister, 'Maqām Ibrāhīm', 482. Abū Qubays is a mountain to the east of the Sacred Mosque in Mecca.

3

INVERTED INVENTIONS: FINDING AND HIDING HOLY BODIES IN THE FIRST ISLAMIC CENTURY

The previous chapter began with the story of a dubiously Jewish, Christian and/or Muslim man's attempted theft of the Maqām Ibrāhīm. As we saw, the Maqām Ibrāhīm represented Islamic claims to both continuity with and difference from earlier Near Eastern religious communities. This chapter begins with another relic story, but one which largely inverts the scheme of George stealing the Maqām Ibrāhīm. Instead of an (ambiguously) non-Muslim man failing to abduct an Islamic relic, this story narrates a group of Muslims successfully moving a relic of the Jewish and Christian past: the corpse of the prophet Daniel. But rather than displaying this prophetic relic as a symbol of victory or monotheistic supremacy, the conquering Muslim army hides Daniel's corpse, seemingly to get rid of it forever.

The story of Daniel's corpse is set in the 640s CE during the siege of al-Sūs, a city in the Persian province of Khūzistān, amid the Muslim conquest of the Sassanian Empire. An early account appears in an anonymous East Syrian (i.e. Nestorian) record – now conventionally called the *Khūzistān Chronicle* – of late Sasanian and early Islamic history:

> The Arabs assailed and besieged Shūsh [al-Sūs]. In a few days they had conquered it and killed all the nobles there. They seized the house in it called the House of Mār Daniel, and took the treasure that – in accord with the commandment of kings – had been kept there since the days of Darius and

> Cyrus. They broke open and took the silver coffin, in which was laid an embalmed body, which many said was Daniel's body, and others said was King Darius'.[1]

According to this Syriac Christian text, the Muslim army took as spoil a biblical prophet's body, allegedly preserved since the days of the ancient Persian kings. In this very early account of the conquest of Khūzistān, we see Muslims quite interested in a prophet's body.[2] Taking the corpse away as a prize alongside other treasure, the Muslims here arguably participate in a form of relic translation: just the sort of activity that led to George's beheading when he tried to steal the Maqām Ibrāhīm from Mecca.

There is no further mention of Daniel's body in the *Khūzistān Chronicle* – but Islamic traditions have much to say about what happened next, which was quite unlike what usually occurred in Christian relic translations. Rather than publicly install the corpse for worship, the Muslims hid Daniel's body. Sources record different methods of hiding the body, including digging and filling in empty graves to conceal which one held Daniel; damming a nearby river and burying him underneath the river bed; or simply burying the body in an anonymous location. Though the specifics vary, texts agree that Daniel was removed from the Persian treasury and placed in a much less august location. Inverting the standard late antique relic narratives, the Muslims' discovery of Daniel leads to the obscuring of this ancient corpse, rather than its celebration.

The discovery and translation of Daniel's body thus provides an interesting picture of early Muslims' interactions with one holy person's relics. Both Christian and Islamic sources agree that the Muslim army did *something* with Daniel. Yet exactly *what* happened to the body is not clear. While the *Khūzistān Chronicle* provides early testimony to the corpse's removal, the Islamic sources

[1] Nasir al-Ka'bi, *A Short Chronicle on the End of the Sasanian Empire and Early Islam 590–660 A.D.* (Piscataway, NJ: Gorgias Press, 2016), 102–3; Ignazio Guidi (ed.), *Chronica Minora, pars prior*, 2 vols (Paris: Typographeo Reipublicae, 1903), 1:36–7. I have slightly adapted the translation of this passage found in Michael Philip Penn, *When Christians First Met Muslims: A Sourcebook of the Earliest Syriac Writings on Islam* (Oakland: University of California Press, 2015), 51.

[2] On the date of the *Khūzistān Chronicle*, see Chase F. Robinson, 'The Conquest of Khūzistān: A Historiographical Reassessment', *BSOAS* 67.1 (2004):14–39; Hoyland, *Seeing Islam*, 185; Shoemaker, *Death of a Prophet*, 34.

provide information about how that act was interpreted by the Muslims who retold the history of their conquests. The historical event itself – the Muslims' discovery of Daniel's body during the conquest of Khūzistān – was narrated and elaborated upon in various ways by subsequent generations of historians and storytellers.

Discussing the Islamic narrations of the conquest of Khūzistān, Chase Robinson suggests that '[t]he Daniel tradition seems to have been informed by iconoclastic concerns', as the Islamic sources 'are drawn together by a shared concern to make the site inaccessible to those determined to locate – and perhaps translate – relics'.[3] Robinson is not alone in such a reading: medieval Muslim authors like Ibn Taymiyya (d. 728/1328) and his student Ibn Qayyim al-Jawziyya (d. 751/1350) cite the story of the Muslim army hiding Daniel's body as evidence of the early Muslim generations' avoidance of tomb veneration.[4] In comparison to the *Khūzistān Chronicle* – in which the prophet's corpse was carried away, seemingly as treasure – the early Islamic sources' quick burial of the corpse suggests a specific desire to hide Daniel from view.

While hiding a prophet's body certainly could paint an iconoclastic picture, I suggest that these early Islamic texts display a more complex deployment of Daniel than simply the rejection or erasure of his corpse. This chapter illustrates how these Islamic stories about Daniel reflect Muslims' engagement with the Christian and Jewish pasts and the newly Islamic present. Drawing upon the pervasive late antique discourse of sacred relics, these stories rhetorically utilise prophetic remains in justifying the Muslims' position as the new, divinely-ordained rulers of the Near East. Placing the Islamic conquests within a Jewish and Christian idiom, Daniel and his relics testify that the monotheistic past has prepared the way for – and in fact anticipated – the coming of Islam. The apocalyptic prophet Daniel becomes both a material and a textual witness to the emergence of Islam.

Moreover, Daniel's was only one of several sacred corpses that Muslims reportedly encountered at sites throughout the Near East during, and in the

[3] Robinson, 'Conquest of Khūzistān', 29.

[4] Muhammad Umar Memon, *Ibn Taimīya's Struggle Against Popular Religion: With an Annotated Translation of his Kitāb al-Iqtiḍā' aṣ-ṣirāt al-mustaqīm mukhālafat aṣḥāb al-jaḥīm* (The Hague: Mouton, 1976), 17, 268–9; Taylor, *In the Vicinity*, 182–3; Meri, *Cult of Saints*, 127; Beránek and Ťupek, *Temptation of Graves*, 55; Talmon-Heller, 'Historiography in the Service', 234.

decades after, the Islamic conquests. These stories highlight the holiness of such bodies, lying as silent witnesses to the divinely-inspired monotheistic past. Loud echoes of the late antique pattern of relic *inventio* reverberate in these stories, in which holy persons' relics are discovered and testify to their martyrdoms for their monotheistic faith. Yet rather than enshrining these saintly bodies, the Muslim discoverers most often rebury them underground, such that no one might know where the relics reside. In other cases, the locations of the bodies – including Daniel's – are in fact remembered and used in making space sacred. Yet, in these latter cases, too, the bodies are usually not enshrined, but are often simply gestured towards by stories and communal memory.

The stories examined in this chapter are characterised by a desire to remember sacred bodies, without allowing them to be physically present: a sort of narrative *damnatio memoriae* of holy persons' remains. Simultaneously embracing and rejecting prophetic bodies, these stories reflect early Islamic ambivalences about corporeal relics, and the complicated early Islamic inheritances from earlier monotheistic communities. These stories utilise the late antique discourse of holy relics, but adapt that discourse's topoi for emergent Islamic conceptions of history and community, and for early Muslims' sentiments on how to engage with bodies and sacred space. We will see that these stories offer evidence of important dialogues with earlier late antique traditions regarding holy persons and their relics, while making space for developing Islamic ideas and practices.

'What Will Come in the Future': Finding Daniel in the Islamic Conquests

Unlike the obscure story of George's misadventure in Mecca, the events surrounding the Islamic discovery of the prophet Daniel's corpse in Khūzistān are relatively well-attested within the late antique textual record. To begin with, traditions of Daniel's burial place in Persia are witnessed in several Christian texts from the centuries before (and after) the advent of Islam.[5] The body's

[5] Reference to Daniel's burial among the Persian royalty – though without specification of the tomb's location – appears in the Christian apocryphon *Lives of the Prophets*. This text's dating is unclear: it is attested in a sixth-century Greek manuscript, but is likely far older in origin. D. R. A. Hare, 'The Lives of the Prophets', in *The Old Testament Pseudepigrapha*, ed. James H. Charlesworth, 2 vols (Garden City, NY: Doubleday, 1983–5), 2:379–99; Sebastian Brock, 'The *Lives of the Prophets* in Syriac: Some Soundings', in *Biblical Traditions in Transmission:*

famed location in al-Sūs is mentioned in a sixth-century Latin Christian pilgrimage guide to the holy sites of the East, for example.[6] Another mention appears in the seventh-century Armenian history ascribed to Sebēos, which includes a story where the Christian emperor Maurice (r. 582–602) attempts to transport to Byzantium 'the body of that dead man which was kept in the city of Shawsh, in the royal treasury, placed in a bronze container. The Persians called it [the body of] Kay Khosrov [a legendary Persian king], and the Christians said it was that of the prophet Daniel.'[7] When a series of miracles makes clear that the corpse did not wish to leave al-Sūs, Maurice acquiesces and instead sends gifts to Daniel's body in Persia.[8]

Unlike Maurice, the Muslim army appears to have been quite successful in moving this prophetic corpse. Stories of their discovery and transfer of Daniel's body feature not only in the nearly contemporaneous Syriac account found in the *Khūzistān Chronicle*, but are 'positively ubiquitous' throughout Islamic

Essays in Honour Michael A. Knibb, ed. Charlotte Hempel and Judith M. Lieu (Leiden: Brill, 2006), 21–37. Later recensions of the Syriac version of *Lives of the Prophets* do mention al-Sūs: for example, an abbreviated version in Sinai Syr. 10 (a ninth-century Melkite manuscript) states, 'Daniel was from the tribe of Judah; he died and was buried in a castle in Shūshan.' Agnes Smith Lewis, *Catalogue of the Syriac Manuscripts in the Convent of S. Catharine on Mount Sinai* (London: C. J. Clay & Sons, 1894), 6. See also: Isaac H. Hall, 'The Lives of the Prophets', *Journal of the Society of Biblical Literature and Exegesis* 7.1 (1887): 35–6. Arabic historical texts say that the Sasanian ruler Shāpūr II (r. 310–79) rebuilt al-Sūs, after it was ravaged by war, 'beside the fortress that has within it a sarcophagus containing the corpse of the prophet Daniel'. al-Ṭabarī, *Ta'rīkh*, 1/2:840; *History of al-Ṭabarī*, 5:57; Abū Ḥanīfa Aḥmad b. Dāwūd al-Dīnawarī, *Kitāb al-Akhbār al-Ṭiwāl*, ed. Vladimir Guirgass (Leiden: Brill, 1888), 51. Interestingly, 'the tomb of the prophet Daniel in the church in al-Sūs' is named among 'the holy relics and objects of veneration which Christ gave us in this world' in Eutychius of Alexandria, *Book of the Demonstration*, I:205–6 (no. 382). It is unclear what mention of Daniel's burial in a church (*kanīsa*) indicates about the corpse's location by the time of this ninth- or tenth-century text's composition.

[6] Theodosius, *De situ terrae sanctae* 30, ed. Paul Geyer, in *Itineraria et alia geographica*, CCSL 175 (Turnhout: Brepols, 1965), 124. The text reads: 'In Persia, the body of Saint Daniel lies in a place called Susa, which is thirty miles from Babylon.'

[7] *The Armenian History attributed to Sebeos*, trans. and commentary by R. W. Thomson, James Howard-Johnston and Tim Greenwood (Liverpool: Liverpool University Press, 1999), 30–1 (ch. 14).

[8] On this hagiographic trope, see Wiśniewski, *Beginnings of the Cult of Relics*, 111.

reports on the conquest of Khūzistān.[9] In the years following the conquest, Muslim storytellers and historians narrated and re-narrated these events, braiding them with imagery from strands of late antique hagiography. In this process, not only did the raconteurs make the prophet Daniel into a late antique saint – or, more precisely, a late antique saintly relic – but the Muslim conquest was also made into a fulfilment of biblical prophecy. The discovery of Daniel's body provided a narrative opportunity to connect the Islamic conquests with the scriptural and apocalyptic history of the wider Near Eastern world.

The individuals who told stories about the discovery of Daniel's body – and about the conquest of Khūzistān more generally – were largely from the Iraqi garrison towns of Baṣra and Kūfa, where many of the Muslim conquerors of Khūzistān settled.[10] One account is recorded in Yūnus b. Bukayr's (d. 199/815) recension of the biography of the Prophet Muḥammad compiled by Muḥammad b. Isḥāq (d. 150/767).[11] According to the report's *isnād*, the account was transmitted by the Baṣran scholar Abū Khalda Khālid b. Dīnār (d. mid-eighth century) from another Baṣran, Abū al-ʿĀliya Rufayʿ b. Mihrān (d. *c.* 93/712), who narrates the events in the first person.[12] The dialogue between Abū Khalda and Abū al-ʿĀliya is reported thus:

> Abū al-ʿĀliya said, 'When we conquered Tustar, we found in the treasury of [the Sasanian commander] al-Hurmuzān a bier with a dead man lying upon it. Next to his head was a book. We brought the book to ʿUmar b. al-Khaṭṭāb, who called for Kaʿb. Kaʿb transcribed it into Arabic. I was the first Arab to read it, reading as I would the Qur'ān.' I [Abū Khalda] then asked Abū al-ʿĀliya, 'What was in [the book]?' He [Abū al-ʿĀliya] said, 'Your lives, your affairs, the intent of your words, and what will come in the future.' I asked, 'What did you do with the man?' He said, 'We dug thirteen separate graves during the day and buried him that night. We levelled all the graves so the people would not know

[9] Robinson suggests that these scenes represent examples of the 'survival of authentic material' within the early Islamic historiographical tradition. Robinson, 'Conquest of Khūzistān', 28, 37.

[10] On the 'post-conquest politics' involved in the claimants to ownership of this history, see Robinson, 'Conquest of Khūzistān', 23–5, 36.

[11] On the recension of Ibn Isḥāq transmitted by Yūnus b. Bukayr, see Schoeler, *Biography of Muḥammad*, 28, 32–3; Miklos Muranyi, 'Ibn Isḥāq's *Kitāb al-Maġāzī* in der *riwāya* von Yūnus b. Bukair. Bemerkungen zur frühen Überlieferungsgeschichte', *JSAI* 14 (1991): 214–75.

[12] *EI*[3], s.v. 'Abū l-ʿĀliya al-Riyāḥī' (G. H. A. Juynboll).

> where he was and dig him up.' I asked, 'What would they want with him?' He said, 'When the sky withheld [rain] from them, they would bring out his bier in order to make it rain.' I asked, 'Who do you think the man was?' He said, 'A man called Daniel.' I asked, 'How long ago had he died before you found him?' He said, 'Three hundred years before.' I asked, 'Had he changed at all [in that time]?' He said, 'No, except for some little hairs on the back of his neck. Indeed, the earth does not decay the flesh of the prophets, nor do wild beasts eat them.'[13]

A variety of issues are evoked by this text, including the fact that Daniel is discovered in Tustar (another city in Khūzistān) instead of al-Sūs, as well as the allegation that the corpse's previous caretakers had used it to bring rain during seasons of drought. Before considering those issues, I will start here with the objects themselves that Abū al-ʿĀliya and the other Muslim conquerors uncovered in the treasury: Daniel's body, and the book beside it.

Abū al-ʿĀliya's testimony indicates that Daniel, despite being dead for 300 years, showed no decay on his body, the only visible change being 'some little hairs [lost or grown?] on the back of his neck'. The ancient prophet's miraculously preserved corpse thus manifests physical qualities common to late antique holy men and women in several religious traditions.[14] The incorruptibility of saints' bodies is a prominent theme in late antique Christian hagiographical literature, in which the non-decaying corpse 'signal[s] the sanctity of the body'.[15] Rabbinic sources also make note of several imputrescible holy

[13] Ibn Isḥāq, *Kitāb al-Siyar*, 66–7; al-Bayhaqī, *Dalāʾil al-nubuwwa*, 1:381–2; Ibn Kathīr, *al-Bidāya wa-l-nihāya*, 14 vols (Beirut: Maktabat al-Maʿārif, 1990), 2:40; Ibn Taymiyya, *Iqtiḍāʾ al-ṣirāṭ al-mustaqīm li-mukhālafat aṣḥāb al-jaḥīm*, ed. Nāṣir b. ʿAbd al-Karīm al-ʿAql, 2 vols (Riyadh: Dār Ishbīliyyā, 1998), 2:199; Ibn Taymiyya, *Majmūʿ al-fatāwā*, ed. ʿAbd al-Raḥmān b. Muḥammad b. Qāsim and Muḥammad b. ʿAbd al-Raḥmān b. Muḥammad, 37 vols (Medina: Mujammaʿ al-Malik Fahd li-Ṭibāʿat al-Muṣḥaf al-Sharīf, 2004), 27:270–1; Ibn Qayyim al-Jawziyya, *Ighāthat al-lahfān fī maṣāʾid al-shayṭān*, ed. Muḥammad ʿUzayr Shams et al. (Mecca: Dār ʿĀlam al-Fawāʾid, 2010), 368–9. A translation of this passage appears in Brannon M. Wheeler, *Prophets in the Quran: An Introduction to the Quran and Muslim Exegesis* (London: Continuum, 2002), 281–2.

[14] For an extended discussion of this theme in late antique Christian, Jewish and Islamic texts, see Bursi, 'Holy Heretical Body'.

[15] Wiśniewski, *Beginnings of the Cult of Relics*, 110. For examples, see Bursi, 'Holy Heretical Body', 153.

persons, such as in the Talmudic statement: 'Our rabbis taught that there were seven over whom the maggots and worms [of the grave] had no power, and they were Abraham, Isaac, Jacob, Moses, Aaron, Miriam, and Benjamin son of Jacob' (b. Bat. 17a).[16]

Early Islamic sources canonised this idea in a Prophetic *ḥadīth* that closely parallels Abū al-ʿĀliya's explanation for Daniel's uncorrupted state. Asked how believers' prayers will reach him after he has died and decayed in the ground, the Prophet Muḥammad responds, 'God has forbidden the earth to consume the bodies of the prophets.'[17] A rarer version has the Prophet say, 'The earth does not consume the body of anyone to whom the Holy Spirit (*al-rūḥ al-qudus*) has

[16] MS Paris, Bibliothèque nationale de France, Suppl. Heb. 1337, fol. 19r. Slightly variant versions of this passage appear in MS Vatican, Bibliotheca Apostolica, Ebr. 115, fol. 72v; MS Munich, Cod. Hebr. 95, fol. 316v. For other examples found in rabbinic literature, see Bursi, 'Holy Heretical Body', 154; Rubenstein, 'Rabbinic Translation'.

[17] Ibn Abī Shayba, *Muṣannaf*, 3:602 (no. 8,781); Ismāʿīl b. Isḥāq al-Azdī, *Faḍl al-ṣalāt ʿalā al-nabī*, ed. Ḥusayn Muḥammad ʿAlī Shukrī (Beirut: Dār al-Kutub al-ʿIlmiyya, 2008), 38–9 (no. 22); al-Nasāʾī, *Sunan*, 225 (no. 1,374); Abū Dāwūd, *Sunan*, 2:84–5 (no. 1,040), 2:299–300 (no. 1,526); Ibn Mājah, *Sunan Ibn Mājah*, ed. Muḥammad Fuʾād ʿAbd al-Bāqī, 2 vols (Cairo: ʿĪsā al-Bābī al-Ḥalabī, 1972), 1:345 (no. 1,085), 1:524 (nos 1,636–7); Ibn Ḥanbal, *Musnad*, 26:84 (no. 16,162); al-Dārimī, *Sunan*, 2:981 (no. 1,613); Muḥammad b. Isḥāq b. Khuzayma, *Ṣaḥīḥ Ibn Khuzayma*, ed. Muḥammad Muṣṭafā al-Aʿẓamī (Beirut: al-Maktab al-Islāmī, 2003), 838–9 (nos 1,733–4); Ibn Abī ʿĀṣim, *Kitāb al-Ṣalāt ʿalā al-nabī*, ed. Ḥamdī ʿAbd al-Majīd al-Salafī (Damascus: Dār al-Maʾmūn li-l-Turāth, 1995), 49–50 (no. 63); Sulaymān b. Aḥmad al-Ṭabarānī, *al-Muʿjam al-kabīr*, ed. Ḥamdī ʿAbd al-Majīd al-Salafī, 25 vols (Cairo: Maktabat Ibn Taymiyya, 1983), 1:216–17 (no. 589); ʿAlāʾ al-Dīn ʿAlī b. Balbān al-Fārisī, *al-Iḥsān fī taqrīb Ṣaḥīḥ Ibn Ḥibbān*, ed. Shuʿayb al-Arnaʾūṭ, 18 vols (Beirut: Muʾassasat al-Risāla, 1988), 3:191 (no. 910); al-Bayhaqī, *Ḥayāt al-anbiyāʾ baʿda wafāti-him*, ed. Aḥmad b. ʿAṭiyya al-Ghāʾirī (Medina: Maktabat al-ʿUlūm wa-l-Ḥikm, 1993), 88–90; Abū Nuʿaym al-Isbahānī, *Kitāb Dalāʾil al-nubuwwa* (Hyderabad: Dāʾirat al-Maʿārif al-ʿUthmāniyya, 1977), 496. The *isnād* is: al-Ḥusayn b. ʿAlī al-Juʿfī (d. 203/819, Kūfa) > ʿAbd al-Raḥmān b. Yazīd b. Jābir (d. *c.* 153/770, Syria) > Abū al-Ashʿath Sharāḥīl b. Āda al-Ṣanʿānī (d. *c.* 60/680, Damascus) > Aws b. Aws al-Thaqafī (d. mid-1st/7th cent., Syria). Szilágyi, 'Prophet Like Jesus', 157 n.95 notes that this tradition '[p]robably [. . .] developed under the influence of Christian saints' lives'. Indeed, the tradition appears to have originated in Syria, an important early site of theological and prophetological debate with Christians: Steven C. Judd, *'Abd al-Rahman b. 'Amr al-Awza'i* (London: Oneworld, 2019), 64–8; Anthony, *Muhammad and the Empires*, 223–4.

spoken.'[18] In a Shīʿī version, imam Jaʿfar al-Ṣādiq (d. 148/765) reports that the Prophet had said, 'God has forbidden the earth to consume any of our flesh.'[19] The 'our' of Jaʿfar's statement appears to refer not just to the prophets, but also to the Shīʿī imams such as Jaʿfar himself.

The holy body's imperviousness to wild animals, and its ability to bring rain, are also topoi familiar from stories of late antique saints and relics. Miraculous protection from wild animals is a common theme within stories of living Christian saints and their relics, and is found in rabbinic texts as well.[20] A particularly close parallel to the description of Daniel's uneaten body appears in the seventh-century Greek *Acts of Anastasios the Persian*:

[18] Ismāʿīl b. Isḥāq, *Faḍl al-ṣalāt*, 39 (no. 23). This is a *mursal* tradition with an Iraqi *isnād*: Abū al-Qāsim Ismāʿīl b. Yaʿqūb [Ibn al-Jirāb] (d. 345/956, Baghdad) > Ismāʿīl b. Isḥāq al-Qāḍī (d. 282/896, Baghdad) > Sulaymān b. Ḥarb (d. *c.* 224/839, Baṣra) > Jarīr b. Ḥāzim (d. 175/791, Baṣra) > al-Ḥasan al-Baṣrī (d. 110/728, Baṣra) > Prophet. A similar tradition is cited from al-Zubayr b. Bakkār's (d. 256/870) *Akhbār al-Madīna* on the authority of al-Ḥasan in Jalāl al-Dīn al-Suyūṭī, *al-Khaṣāʾiṣ al-kubrā*, ed. Muḥammad Khalīl Harrās, 3 vols (Cairo: Dār al-Kutub al-Ḥadītha, 1967) 3:403.

[19] Abū Jaʿfar Muḥammad b. al-Ḥasan b. Farrūkh al-Ṣaffār, *Baṣāʾir al-Darajāt fī faḍāʾil āl Muḥammad*, ed. al-Sayyid Muḥammad al-Sayyid al-Ḥasan al-Muʿallim, 2 vols (Qum: Maktabat al-Ḥaydariyya, 2005), 2:346–7; Douglas Karim Crow, 'The Death of al-Ḥusayn b. ʿAlī and Early Shīʿī Views of the Imamate', in *Shīʿism: Origins and Early Development*, ed. Etan Kohlberg (Aldershot: Ashgate Variorum, 2003), 61. Crow notes the connection of this description of the imams to the 'incorruptibility of the bodies of the saints' within medieval Christian traditions.

[20] Alison Goddard Elliott, *Roads to Paradise: Reading the Lives of the Early Saints* (Hanover: University Press of New England, 1987), 145–51; Patricia Cox Miller, *In the Eye of the Animal: Zoological Imagination in Ancient Christianity* (Philadelphia: University of Pennsylvania Press, 2018), 119–54; Eliezer Diamond, 'Lions, Snakes and Asses: Palestinian Jewish Holy Men as Masters of the Animal Kingdom', in *Jewish Culture and Society under the Christian Roman Empire*, ed. Richard Kalmin and Seth Schwartz (Leuven: Peeters, 2003), 251–83; Rubenstein, 'Rabbinic Translation', 328. There is almost undoubtedly also a reference intended here to the biblical story of Daniel in the lions' den (Dan. 6), which itself served as a model for the stories of late antique holy persons' interactions with animals: Elliott, *Roads to Paradise*, 151–3. Similar animal tales appear in Islamic tales about monks: Bradley Bowman, 'Refuge in the Bosoms of the Mountains: A Ninth-Century Muslim Appraisal of Monastic Piety', *Islam and Christian-Muslim Relations* 30.4 (2019): 459–82.

when this saint's martyred corpse is thrown to wild dogs, they 'did not touch it, but looked like they were guarding it'.[21] Miraculous rain production is another common motif in stories of Christian and Jewish holy men of late antiquity.[22] In the Syriac *Life of Peter the Iberian*, as soon as the saint enters the drought-ridden region of Madaba, a downpour appears and 'all the water reservoirs [. . .] were filled from the blessing'.[23] Relics also performed such feats. In the Latin *Revelatio Sancti Stephani*, the translation of the bones of the martyr Stephen to Jerusalem is followed by a rainfall, ending a drought that had plagued the land.[24] The Syriac *Cave of Treasures* reports that after Jesus' crucifixion, 'whenever there was a lack of rain, they would bring [Jesus'] tunic outside: and as soon as they raised it towards the face of the sky, a great rain would fall'.[25]

Similarly hagiographic themes are evoked in another account of the discovery of Daniel's body, this one recorded in the *Muṣannaf* of Ibn Abī Shayba (d. 235/849). Transmitted through another Iraqi *isnād*, this text is attributed to Anas b. Mālik (d. 93/712), a Companion who took part in the

[21] *Acts of Anastasios the Persian* (*BHG* 84), 41; ed. and trans. in Bernard Flusin, *Saint Anastase le Perse et l'histoire de la Palestine au début du VIIe siècle*, 2 vols (Paris: Centre National de la Recherche Scientifique, 1992), 1:86–7.

[22] Peter Brown, 'The Rise and Function of the Holy Man in Late Antiquity', *Journal of Roman Studies* 61 (1971): 95, 97; Michal Bar-Asher Siegal, *Early Christian Monastic Literature and the Babylonian Talmud* (New York: Cambridge University Press, 2013), 112–19; Richard Kalmin, 'Holy Men, Rabbis, and Demonic Sages in Late Antiquity', in *Jewish Culture and Society under the Christian Roman Empire*, ed. Richard Kalmin and Seth Schwartz (Leuven: Peeters, 2003), 213–49; Hayim Lapin, 'Rabbis and Public Prayers for Rain in Later Roman Palestine', in *Religion and Politics in the Ancient Near East*, ed. Adele Berlin (Bethesda: University Press of Maryland, 1996), 105–29.

[23] John Rufus, *Vita Petri Iberii* 122; *The Lives of Peter the Iberian, Theodosius of Jerusalem, and the Monk Romanus*, ed. and trans. Cornelia B. Horn and Robert R. Phenix Jr. (Atlanta: Society of Biblical Literature, 2008), 180–1.

[24] *Revelatio Sancti Stephani* (A) 9.50; ed. in S. Vanderlinden, '*Revelatio Sancti Stephani* (BHG 7850–6)', *Revue des études byzantines* 4 (1946): 216. This detail does not appear in Version B of the text.

[25] *La Caverne des Trésors: les deux recensions syriaques*, ed. Su-Min Ri, CSCO 486, Scriptores Syri 207 (Louvain: Peeters, 1987), 416.

conquest of Khūzistān before settling in Baṣra. Anas narrates that, during the conquest of the city of Tustar:

> We found a man in a coffin whose nose was a cubit [in size]. They used to seek aid and seek rain through him. Abū Mūsā [al-Ashʿarī (d. *c.* 42–53/662–73), the leader of the Muslim army in Khūzistān][26] wrote to ʿUmar b. al-Khaṭṭāb about this. ʿUmar wrote back: 'This is one of the prophets. Fire does not consume the prophets, nor does the earth.' He also wrote: 'You and one of your companions (meaning a companion of Abū Mūsā) should bury him in a place that no one knows except for the two of you.' So Abū Mūsā and I went and buried him.[27]

While the body is not explicitly identified in this tradition, it is clear from the context that it is meant to be Daniel.[28] As in Abū al-ʿĀliya's report, we again find mention of people using the body to seek rain, as well as more general forms of divine aid. In response to the Muslim commander Abū Mūsā's request for guidance, ʿUmar identifies the corpse as belonging to a prophet, noting their bodies' incorruptibility, much as Abū al-ʿĀliya does in his version of the story.[29] ʿUmar commands that the corpse should be buried in an anonymous spot, an order which Anas claims to have carried out alongside Abū Mūsā.

While much of Anas's report echoes Abū al-ʿĀliya's version, a novel feature is the mention of the size of Daniel's nose. At the size of a cubit (i.e. over two feet), Daniel's nose suggests that the prophet possesses a gigantic body, as such a nose would likely reside upon a proportionately enormous frame.[30] The notion of ancient figures being gigantic in size is again a motif with hagiographic

[26] *EI*³, s.v. 'al-Ashʿarī, Abū Mūsā' (Michael Lecker).

[27] Ibn Abī Shayba, *Muṣannaf*, 11:564 (no. 34,393). The *isnād* runs: Shādhān [al-Aswad b. ʿĀmir] (d. 208/823–4, Baghdad) > Ḥammād b. Salama (d. 167/783–4, Baṣra) > Abū ʿImrān al-Jawnī (d. 128/745–6, Baṣra) > Anas.

[28] Robinson, 'Conquest of Khūzistān', 33 seems mistaken in stating that this report refers to 'another (now unidentified) prophet in Tustar' alongside Daniel's in al-Sūs. However, he is correct that the identification of which city in Khūzistān had possessed Daniel's body is seemingly at issue here. See further below.

[29] The mention of invulnerability to fire may be a reference to the story of Shadrach, Meshach and Abednego's protection from the burning furnace in Dan. 3.

[30] *EI*², s.v. 'Dhirāʿ' (W. Hinz). An abbreviated version of Anas's report without full *isnād* is cited in Ibn Kathīr, *al-Bidāya*, 2:41, where Ibn Kathīr also cites a description (attributed to Abū al-ʿĀliya but without further *isnād*) of the nose as the length of a hand (*shibr*). Mention of

precedents. In a letter describing the discovery of the bodies of the Christian martyrs Gervasius and Protasius in 386 CE, the bishop Ambrose of Milan describes them as 'two men of marvelous stature, such as those of ancient days'.[31] Rabbinic texts record the gigantic bodies of various biblical figures, such as when a rabbi is able to stand straight up within the eye socket of the half-buried skull of King David's son, Absalom (b. Nid. 24b).[32]

Given these parallels, it is worthwhile to read these early Islamic representations of Daniel within the wider frame of late antique holy men and woman. The biblical prophet's body has been accorded the qualities of holiness that we often find in the stories of saints, patriarchs and rabbis, such as corporeal incorruptibility, protection from animals, the ability to produce miracles like rain, and (more rarely) great bodily size. As David Satran writes of the late antique holy man, 'telling is the pervasive effect which his model of behavior exerted on the portrayal of revered figures of the past – patriarchs, philosophers, and apostles. [. . .] The outcome is nothing less than the emergence of the prophet as holy man.'[33] The attribution of these qualities to Daniel illustrates early Muslims' awareness of the ideas and characterisations of sacred figures that circulated among other late antique religious communities. Daniel is here a late antique holy man, whose relics physically demonstrate his status as a prophet.

Daniel's great height and *shibr*-length nose also appears in Aḥmad b. Muḥammad b. Ibrāhīm al-Thaʿlabī, *Kitāb al-Qiṣaṣ al-anbiyāʾ al-musammā bi-l-ʿArāʾis* (Cairo: al-Maṭbaʿa al-ʿĀmira al-Sharafiyya, 1906), 202; *ʿArāʾis al-Majālis fī Qiṣaṣ al-Anbiyāʾ or 'Lives of the Prophets'*, trans. William M. Brinner (Leiden: Brill, 2002), 571. This description is, however, absent in the earlier, parallel text: Aḥmad b. Aʿtham al-Kūfī, *Kitāb al-Futūḥ*, ed. Muḥammad ʿAbd al-Muʿīd Khān et al., 8 vols (Hyderabad: Maṭbaʿat Jamʿiyyat Dāʾirat al-Maʿārif al-ʿUthmāniyya, 1968–75), 2:7–8. It is unclear if the line has been added to al-Thaʿlabī's text, or was originally present in and subsequently excised from Ibn Aʿtham's.

31 Ambrose, *Epistula* 22.2; *A Select Library of the Nicene and Post-Nicene Fathers of the Christian Church*, series 2, ed. and trans. Philip Schaff et al. (Grand Rapids: Eerdmans, 1952–6), 10:437. See Wiśniewski, *Beginnings of the Cult of Relics*, 120.

32 Samuel Krauss, 'Jewish Giants in the Gentile Folklore', *Jewish Quarterly Review* 38.2 (1947): 144–5. For traditions on the gigantic bodies of biblical patriarchs, see Louis Ginzberg, *The Legends of the Jews*, trans. Henrietta Szold et al., 7 vols (Philadelphia: Jewish Publication Society of America, 1909–38), 1:232, 304, 332, 336; 5:225 n.97, 267 n.317, 283 n.88, 285 n.98.

33 David Satran, *Biblical Prophets in Byzantine Palestine: Reassessing the* Lives of the Prophets (Leiden: Brill, 1995), 100–1.

Beyond these typological elements, the stories about the discovery in Khūzistān also draw upon a motif more specific to Daniel: his role as a prophetic prognosticator. In these narratives, Daniel's prophetic gifts fit into a specifically Islamic sacred history. For example, in another report from Ibn Abī Shayba's *Muṣannaf*, when the Muslim commander Abū Mūsā al-Ashʿarī writes to ʿUmar b. al-Khaṭṭāb asking what to do with Daniel's body, the caliph answers that he should 'wash Daniel with lote-tree (*sidr*) leaves and the water of aromatic flowers, and pray over him. Indeed, he is a prophet, who asked his Lord that no one inherit from him except the Muslims.'[34] ʿUmar suggests that Daniel – with prophetic foresight – had presaged the arrival of the Muslims and had asked God that only they would 'inherit from him' (*yarith-hu*). Rather than Jews or Christians, Muslims are the true inheritors of Daniel, and thus the ones who lay his body to rest properly: embalmed with 'lote-tree leaves and the water of aromatic flowers', plants recalling the paradisiacal scents described in the Qurʾān.[35] ʿUmar's words are partially paralleled in a *ḥadīth* reported from the Baghdadī ascetic and scholar Ibn Abī al-Dunyā (d. 281/894), in which the Prophet Muḥammad asserts, 'Daniel asked his Lord that the community of Muḥammad would bury him'.[36] The Muslims' burial of Daniel thus fulfils the prophet's pious wishes, as well as his predictions for the future.[37]

[34] Ibn Abī Shayba, *Muṣannaf*, 11:564 (no. 34,392). The *isnād* is: Hammām b. Yaḥyā b. Dīnār (d. 164/790, Baṣra) > Farqad b. Yaʿqūb al-Sabakhī (d. 131/748–9, Baṣra) > Abū Tamīma Ṭarīf b. Mujālid (d. *c.* 95/713, Baṣra). This report also appears in Ibn ʿAsākir, *Taʾrīkh*, 58:344, 67:160. Similar advice from ʿUmar about perfuming the corpse appears at: Ibn Kathīr, *al-Bidāya*, 2:41.

[35] Cf. Q. 53:14–16, 55:12, 56:28, 56:89; Ailin Qian, 'Delights in Paradise: A Comparative Survey of Heavenly Food and Drink in the Quran', in *Roads to Paradise: Eschatology and Concepts of the Hereafter in Islam*, ed. Sebastian Günther and Todd Lawson, 2 vols (Leiden: Brill, 2017), 1: 252, 256; *EI*[3], s.v. 'Lote Tree' (Christian Lange). On usage of these plants in embalming, see Anya H. King, *Scent from the Garden: Musk and the Medieval Islamic World* (Leiden: Brill, 2017), 275, 353; Halevi, *Muhammad's Grave*, 53–4; Wheeler, *Mecca and Eden*, 105.

[36] Ibn Kathīr, *al-Bidāya*, 2:41; Wheeler, *Prophets in the Quran*, 282. This tradition does not appear in the published versions of Ibn Abī al-Dunyā's *Kitāb al-Qubūr*. However, some of the same Daniel traditions cited in Ibn Kathīr's text are attributed to Ibn Abī al-Dunyā also in Ibn Rajab al-Ḥanbalī, *Kitāb Aḥkām al-khawātīm wa-mā yataʿallaq bi-hā*, ed. Abū al-Fidāʾ ʿAbd Allāh al-Qāḍī (Beirut: Dār al-Kutub al-ʿIlmiyya, 1985), 109–10; Muḥammad b. Mūsā al-Damīrī, *Ḥayāt al-ḥayawān al-kubrā*, 2 vols (Cairo: Sharikat Maktabat wa-Maṭbaʿa Muṣṭafā al-Bābī al-Ḥalabī wa-Awlāduhu, 1978), 1:9–10.

[37] Note that in Christian relic inventions, 'the finding of relics is usually presented as resulting from the desire of the saint himself'. Wiśniewski, *Beginnings of the Cult of Relics*, 110.

Similarly prophetic predictions of the Muslims' arrival appear in other stories of the conquest of Khūzistān, where the eschatological overtones associated with the Book of Daniel are repurposed for Islamic usage. In his description of the uncovering of Daniel's body in Tustar, Abū al-ʿĀliya mentions the discovery of a book lying next to Daniel's head.[38] While this book is never explicitly identified, its physical connection with Daniel's corpse suggests that it was authored by him, or at least associated with his prophetic gifts. When the book is brought to the caliph ʿUmar, he sends for Kaʿb al-Aḥbār – a Jewish scholar and Muslim convert whom we have encountered before – who 'transcribes' the book into Arabic from its original language. Abū al-ʿĀliya claims to have been the 'first Arab' to read this Danielic book, doing so, in fact, 'as I would the Qurʾān'. Asked what the book contained, Abū al-ʿĀliya responds: 'Your lives, your affairs, the intent of your words, and what will come in the future.'

In this book found alongside the corpse of the prophet Daniel, the arrival of the Muslim conquerors is thus predicted. Abū al-ʿĀliya's description of the book containing 'your lives [and] your affairs' is certainly meant to apply to the Muslim community. Placing Islamic history within a prophetic timeline, Daniel's book intimates a pre-qurʾānic awareness of the future arrival of the Muslim *umma*. The book's original language is not identified, but the Jewish sage Kaʿb al-Aḥbār's ability to 'transcribe' the text implies that it may have been Hebrew. Thus, the Book of Daniel – or another, apocryphal book attributed to him – is said to have prophesied the coming of Islam.[39]

This was not an entirely novel idea. Christian and Jewish writers of the seventh and later centuries interpreted the Islamic conquests through the lens of the Book of Daniel, surmising that the Islamic caliphate was the predicted 'fourth beast' and/or 'fourth kingdom' that presaged the end of time.[40]

[38] Discovery of an ancient text (sometimes alongside other relics) is another hagiographic trope. Paul C. Dilley, 'The Invention of Christian Tradition: "Apocrypha", Imperial Policy, and Anti-Jewish Propaganda', *Greek, Roman, and Byzantine Studies* 50 (2010): 586–615; Dilley, 'Christian Icon Practice in Apocryphal Literature: Consecration and the Conversion of Synagogues into Churches', *Journal of Roman Archaeology* 23 (2010): 285–302.

[39] Lorenzo DiTommaso, *The Book of Daniel and the Apocryphal Daniel Literature* (Brill: Leiden, 2005).

[40] Walter Emil Kaegi, Jr., 'Initial Byzantine Reactions to the Arab Conquest', *Church History* 38.2 (1969): 139–49; H. J. W. Drijvers, 'The Gospel of the Twelve Apostles: A Syriac Apocalypse from the Early Islamic Period, in *The Byzantine and Early Islamic Near East. I. Problems in the Literary Source Material*, ed. Averil Cameron and Lawrence I. Conrad (Princeton:

However, the Islamic traditions' interpretations of Daniel are instead coloured by a distinctly Islamic interpretation of history. In this view, Daniel had indeed foretold 'what will come in the future', but that future would see the Muslims triumphantly on God's side. This reading also appears in the *Kitāb al-Dīn wa-l-Dawla*, where 'Alī b. Rabban al-Ṭabarī argues that 'the fourth [beast] is therefore the empire of the Arabs, without doubt about it, and this is the everlasting empire which God said would not come to an end or yield empire or authority to any other'.[41] Daniel's prophecy is turned to decisively Islamic purposes in 'Alī al-Ṭabarī's assertion that the Islamic empire 'is the last of the empires', which will rule without end.

But did Abū al-'Āliya – or the transmitters of his tradition – understand Daniel's prophecy as fulfilled at the time of the conquests, or as yet-to-be fulfilled, further in the future? An alternative version of Abū al-'Āliya's report appears in Nu'aym b. Ḥammād's (d. 229/844) *Kitāb al-Fitan* (Book of Tribulations), a collection of apocalyptic Islamic traditions of the eighth and early ninth centuries.[42] In this shortened account, when Ka'b al-Aḥbār transcribes Daniel's book into Arabic, the book is reported to contain 'what will happen, meaning the tribulations' (*al-fitan*).[43] In this reading, Daniel's prophecies seem to pertain less triumphantly to the Islamic conquests, but instead to the

Darwin Press, 1992), 189–213; Bernd Witte, 'The Apocalypse of Pseudo-Athanasius', in Thomas and Roggema, *Christian–Muslim Relations*, 275–80; Wout Jacques van Bekkum, 'Four Kingdoms Will Rule: Echoes of Apocalypticism and Political Reality in Late Antiquity and Medieval Judaism', in *Endzeiten: Eschatologie in den monotheistischen Weltreligionen*, ed. Wolfram Brandes and Felicitas Schmieder (Berlin: Walter de Gruyter, 2008), 101–18; Bernard Lewis, 'An Apocalyptic Vision of Islamic History', *BSOAS* 13.2 (1950): 308–38; Haggai Ben-Shammai, 'The Attitude of Some Early Karaites Towards Islam', in *Studies in Medieval Jewish History and Literature, Volume II*, ed. Isadore Twersky (Cambridge, MA: Harvard University Press, 1984), 1–40.

41 *Polemical Works of 'Alī al-Ṭabarī*, 420–1.

42 *EI* ^{2}, s.v. 'Nu'aym ibn Ḥammād' (Charles Pellat); van Ess, *Theology and Society*, 2:810–13; David Cook, *'The Book of Tribulations': The Syrian Muslim Apocalyptic Tradition. An Annotated Translation* (Edinburgh: Edinburgh University Press, 2019), xii–xxxiv.

43 Nu'aym b. Ḥammād al-Marwazī, *Kitāb al-Fitan*, ed. Suhayl Zakkār (Beirut: Dār al-Fikr, 2003), 18–19; Cook, *Book of Tribulations*, 7. The *isnād* for this version runs: Muḥammad b. Yazīd al-Kilā'ī (d. *c.* 188/804, Wāsiṭ) > Abū Khalda > Abū al-'Āliya.

invasions and civil wars of the seventh and eighth centuries: apocalyptically-charged times which were frequently characterised in early Islamic literature with the word *fitna* (pl., *fitan*).[44] Other traditions in the *Kitāb al-Fitan* likewise draw upon Daniel's prophetic authority to depict an apocalyptic scenario occurring later than the time of the Islamic conquests, such as a report that 'according to Daniel, the totality of this community – after its prophet Muḥammad up to [the return of] Jesus – will be 274 years'.[45]

Whatever the precise interpretation of Daniel's text, the conquest of the cities of Khūzistān certainly came to be 'described by allusion to apocalyptic ideas' within early Islamic historical traditions.[46] In a report in Muḥammad b. Jarīr al-Ṭabarī's (d. 310/923) *Ta'rīkh al-Rusul wa-l-mulūk* (History of the Prophets and Kings), the conquest of al-Sūs is preceded by the city's Christian monks and priests taunting their Muslim besiegers. These Christians claim that 'our scholars and ancestors have taught us that no one will ever conquer al-Sūs but the Antichrist (al-Dajjāl), or people who have the Antichrist in their midst'.[47] Rather inconveniently, Ṣāfī b. Ṣayyād – a mysterious Antichrist-esque figure who appears in early Islamic traditions about the seventh century – happened to be in the Muslim army besieging al-Sūs.[48] Following the Christians' boasting, Ṣāfī easily kicks the city's gate open, allowing the Muslim army to enter. In this decidedly odd tradition, the successful Muslim conquest fulfils an apocalyptic prophesy that had allegedly circulated among the Christians of al-Sūs.

Daniel's body in Khūzistān perhaps spurred such literary flourishes that connected emergent Islamic history with Jewish and Christian prophecy and

44 David Cook, *Studies in Muslim Apocalyptic* (Princeton: Darwin Press, 2002), 21, 23.

45 Nu'aym b. Ḥammād, *Kitāb al-Fitan*, 420; Cook, *Book of Tribulations*, 426. See also: Nu'aym b. Ḥammād, *Kitāb al-Fitan*, 272, 355; Cook, *Book of Tribulations*, 260, 361.

46 Gerald Hawting, 'Were There Prophets in the Jahiliyya?' in *Islam and Its Past: Jahiliyya, Late Antiquity, and the Qur'an*, ed. Carol Bakhos and Michael Cook (Oxford: Oxford University Press, 2017), 207.

47 al-Ṭabarī, *Ta'rīkh*, 1/5:2,564–5; *The History of al-Ṭabarī. Volume XIII: The Conquest of Iraq, Southwestern Persia, and Egypt*, trans. G. H. A. Juynboll (Albany: State University of New York Press, 1989), 145–6. See discussions in Robinson, 'Conquest of Khūzistān', 29; Sarah Bowen Savant, *The New Muslims of Post-Conquest Iran: Tradition, Memory and Conversion* (New York: Cambridge University Press, 2013), 211; Hawting, 'Were There Prophets', 206–7.

48 Hawting, 'Were There Prophets', 204–7; Cook, *Studies in Muslim Apocalyptic*, 110–17.

apocalypse. The association of this prophet with the conquest of al-Sūs and Tustar enabled a discussion of the Islamic conquests as a manifestation of prophecy and as, in some sense, apocalyptic. Using the occasion of the discovery of an ancient prophet and his book, the feats of the Muslim armies could be placed in terms of prophetic accomplishment and scriptural fulfilment. But the question then became: what should they do with Daniel's body?

Bringing Up the Bodies, Temporarily: Inverted Relic Inventions in Early Islamic Texts

According to the Islamic accounts of the discovery of Daniel in Khūzistān, the Muslim army did not translate the biblical prophet's body to a new place of honour and veneration, but reburied him in anonymity. Notably, Daniel was not the only prophetic corpse that early Muslims treated in this way – uncovering and then re-covering it – as they conquered and consolidated control over much of the Near East. Stories record their coming across the corpses of a variety of prophets, messengers and martyrs at sites sprinkled throughout the Ḥijāz, Yemen, Syria, Egypt and North Africa.

These stories recall a prominent phenomenon, and literary genre, of late antiquity: relic inventions, or *inventiones*.[49] From the fourth century onwards, Christian stories narrate the uncovering of the tombs of biblical prophets and other saints in the Holy Land and elsewhere, long after their ancient resting places had (allegedly) been forgotten to time or had been hidden by disbelievers.[50] Similar themes and topoi are present in these Islamic stories of uncovered holy persons, suggesting an awareness of the late antique genre. Yet, as we will see, important differences appear within the stories, adapted to the early Islamic milieu.

Several topoi of late antique *inventio* narratives appear throughout these Islamic stories of uncovered holy persons. In Christian *inventiones*, an inscription is often found near the body, providing the holy person's name and occasionally the story of his or her martyrdom for their Christian faith.[51] In Islamic texts,

[49] On the genre of *inventio* narrative, see Maraval, *Lieux saints et pèlerinages*, 41–7; Dilley, 'Invention of Christian Tradition', 595–603; Estelle Cronnier, *Les inventions de reliques dans l'Empire romain d'Orient (IVe–VIe s.)* (Turnhout: Brepols, 2015).

[50] Jacobs, *Remains of the Jew*.

[51] Wiśniewski, *Beginnings of the Cult of Relics*, 110; Cronnier, *Les inventions de reliques*, 218–21.

inscriptions likewise identify such individuals; they give the holy person's name, valorise their piety, and describe the rejection by the recalcitrant community that the person had tried to turn towards God. For example, during the caliphate of Muʿāwiya b. Abī Sufyān (r. 41–60/661–80), a corpse was uncovered in Egypt inside a large buried vessel. It carried a Hebrew inscription (given only in Arabic in our texts) near the corpse's head:

> I am Ḥabīb b. Nūbājir – a companion of the messenger of God, Moses b. ʿImrān – who wanted to observe the Great Law [*al-nāmūs al-akbar*, that is, the Torah]. But the Children of Israel opposed this, for they were indifferent to wisdom and acted out of desire. They sold off contentment and abandoned the path that their covenant had imposed upon them.[52]

As discussed above, such saintly bodies are often perfectly preserved, untouched by decay after centuries, with fresh blood still oozing from their ancient wounds. This image appears not only in the case of Daniel at Khūzistān, but also in several other Islamic stories of uncovered corpses. For example, a body was found in the district of Jordan during excavations for stones to be used in the construction of the monumental Umayyad Mosque in Damascus. After the corpse spurted blood where a shovel had struck it – or, alternatively, from the corpse's decapitated head – the body was identified as belonging to Saul, the first king of Israel.[53] Given the strong parallels with Christian relic stories, these Islamic narratives of the discoveries of long-lost prophets and martyrs seem to share in this much wider late antique literary pattern.

[52] Abū Fatḥ Muḥammad b. ʿAlī b. ʿUthmān al-Karājukī, *Kanz al-Fawāʾid*, ed. ʿAbd Allāh Niʿmah, 2 vols (Beirut: Dār al-Aḍwāʾ, 1985), 1:382–3. On this text and author, see Devin J. Stewart, 'An Eleventh-Century Justification of the Authority of Twelver Shiite Jurists', in *Islamic Cultures, Islamic Contexts: Essays in Honor of Professor Patricia Crone*, ed. Behnam Sadeghi, Asad Q. Ahmed, Adam Silverstein and Robert G. Hoyland (Leiden: Brill, 2014), 468–97. On *nāmūs* as a reference to the Torah, see Brannon M. Wheeler, '"This is the Torah that God Sent Down to Moses": Some Early Islamic Views of the Qurʾān and Other Revealed Books', *Graeco-Arabica* 7–8 (1999–2000): 571–604.

[53] Abū Muḥammad al-Ḥasan b. Aḥmad al-Hamdānī, *al-Iklīl: al-juzʾ al-thāmin*, ed. Nabih Amin Faris (Sanaa: Dār al-Kalima, 1940), 172; al-Hamdānī, *The Antiquities of South Arabia*, trans. Nabih Amin Faris (Princeton: Princeton University Press, 1938), 106; al-Karājukī, *Kanz al-Fawāʾid*, 1:383; Ibn ʿAsākir, *Taʾrīkh*, 2:262. Saul's decapitated body recalls the story of his body's desecration by the Philistines at 1 Sam 31:9–13, though seemingly not the body's cremation at Jabesh-Gilead.

However, an important difference from the Christian narrative sequence appears in the Islamic stories. Rather than extracting the ancient relics, ceremoniously transporting them, and installing them in a place of honour – the standard course of events in Christian *inventio* narratives – the Muslim discoverers instead return the corpses to the ground and obscure the graves' locations.[54] As in the story of Daniel in Khūzistān, this instruction to rebury the body sometimes comes from the caliph himself, who stands in for the Christian bishop who often calls for relics to be unearthed in Christian narratives.[55] The narrative of the late antique *inventio* is thus inverted in these stories, with the discovered bodies returned underground and hidden, rather than brought out for display and veneration.

Such stories could rightfully be interpreted as 'informed by iconoclastic concerns', as Chase Robinson has suggested for the stories about Daniel's body. Obscuring Daniel's location appears at the forefront of the Muslims' concerns in several of the narratives about his corpse, such as in Anas b. Mālik's report that 'Umar ordered Daniel to be buried 'in a place that no one knows'. Ibn Jarīr al-Ṭabarī's *Ta'rīkh* similarly relates that 'Umar ordered Abū Mūsā to 'conceal' Daniel's corpse (*tawriyati-hi*).[56] Notably, vocabulary used by Abū al-ʿĀliya in his story of reburying Daniel's body – the 'leveling of graves' (*taswiyat al-qubūr*) – appears within Islamic discussions discouraging the veneration of graves and the dead.[57]

Explicitly 'iconoclastic' comments do not otherwise tend to appear within these stories, but the consistent, almost stereotyped reburial of the bodies is itself noteworthy.[58] The stories' generic quality is noted already in the South

[54] For the Christian narrative patterns of moving and installing the body, see Maraval, *Lieux saints et pèlerinages*, 48–50; Cronnier, *Les inventions de reliques*, 239–66.

[55] Wiśniewski, *Beginnings of the Cult of Relics*, 110; Cronnier, *Les inventions de reliques*, 215–16. A similar point is noted in Khalek, *Damascus after the Muslim Conquest*, 114.

[56] al-Ṭabarī, *Ta'rīkh*, 1/5:2567; *History of al-Ṭabarī*, 13:147.

[57] Halevi, *Muhammad's Grave*, 36, 188; Leisten, 'Between Orthodoxy and Exegesis', 12–18; Beránek and Ťupek, *Temptation of Graves*, 25, 55, 91, 140. For early reports of this discussion, see Ibn Abī Shayba, *Muṣannaf*, 4:560–1 (nos 11,905–11).

[58] The events described in these stories are much less historically well-attested than the discovery of Daniel's body in Khūzistān. They lack outside testimony and many stories appear only in relatively late texts, though cited from earlier authorities.

Arabian historian al-Hamdānī's (d. 334/945) *al-Iklīl* (The Crown), where the author explicitly compares several reports of undecayed saintly bodies.[59] Similarly, the story of the discovery of ʿAbd Allāh b. al-Thāmir's corpse (discussed below) immediately precedes the story of Daniel's within Ibn Bukayr's *sīra* text, suggesting a parallel was seen between these two. So many signifiers recalling late antique *inventiones* appear in these stories – undecayed bodies producing fresh blood, accompanied by inscriptions declaring their faith and/or martyrdom – that their consistent inversion of late antique narrative expectations seems intentional. The avoidance of tomb and relic cult almost certainly lies somewhere within these stories' rhetorical backgrounds, as Robinson notes.

I would suggest, however, that these narratives perform more complex work than simply reporting early Muslims' avoidance of tomb or relic veneration. Using the pervasive late antique symbols of holy relics and relic invention, Muslim storytellers adapted these topoi for their own purposes by fitting them into distinctly Islamic contexts and discussing themes important to early Islamic religious claims. We have seen this already in the utilisation of the prophet Daniel as an apocalyptic predictor of the Islamic conquests, who longed to be buried by Muslims rather than Jews or Christians. In other places, stories of uncovered bodies provide further material evidence – in narrative form – for pre-Islamic sacred history, and for Muslims' inheritance of the Jewish, Christian and Arab monotheistic legacy. While the prophets' and martyrs' bodies themselves may have been reburied underground, the stories of their undecayed corpses bear witness to the monotheistic past that Muslims claimed as their own.

For example, in a report transmitted by the historian Hishām b. Muḥammad al-Kalbī (d. 206/821), the remains of one of the sons of the biblical patriarch and qur'ānic prophet Ishmael are uncovered in Medina. When a well is dug in the territory of the Banū Zurayq tribe, a corpse is found 'sitting as though he were simply talking, and looking nothing like the dead'. The undecayed body evidences the man's piety, illustrated also in the inscription above his body:

> I am Kedar b. Ishmael b. Abraham, the friend of God the Compassionate. I fled in true religion from a community ruled by disbelief. I testify that there is

[59] al-Hamdānī, *Iklīl*, 8:173.

> no god but God, I associate nothing with Him, and I take nothing as a protector apart from Him.[60]

Kedar was a significant figure: Islamic traditions report that 'God spread out the Arabs from Nebaioth b. Ishmael and Kedar b. Ishmael', and that the two men's descendants had settled in the Ḥijāz.[61] Moreover, the Prophet Muḥammad's lineage was traced to Abraham and Ishmael through Kedar (or, alternatively, through Nebaioth),[62] and thus biblical mentions of Kedar were deployed within Islamic apologetics as scriptural predictions of Islam's arrival.[63] Given the importance of Ishmaelite ancestry for formative Arab and Islamic identity in this early period, it was fitting that this ancient progenitor's grave be found in the Prophet's city. Kedar's bodily presence in Medina materially confirmed this connection between the biblical and Arab pasts.

Other stories describe similar discoveries of the corpses of monotheist figures from the pre-Islamic past. The tales demonstrate the expansiveness of that history, as these monotheists had spread throughout the Arabian Peninsula and further into the Near East. The prophets Hūd and Ḥanẓala b. Ṣafwān are both

[60] al-Hamdānī, *al-Iklīl*, 8:173; *Antiquities of South Arabia*, 107; al-Karājukī, *Kanz al-Fawā'id*, 1:382. Ishmael's sons are listed at: Gen 25:13–16; 1 Chron 1:29–31; Ibn Hishām, *Sīra*, 4; Ibn Sa'd, *Ṭabaqāt*, 1:34; al-Azraqī, *Akhbār Makka*, 140–1 (no. 128); al-Ṭabarī, *Ta'rīkh*, 1/1:351–2; *The History of al-Ṭabarī. Volume II: Prophets and Patriarchs*, trans. William M. Brinner (Albany: State University of New York Press, 1987), 132.

[61] al-Azraqī, *Akhbār Makka*, 141 (no. 128); al-Ṭabarī, *Ta'rīkh*, 1/1:352; *History of al-Ṭabarī*, 2:132; Ibn Hishām, *Sīra*, 82.

[62] al-Hamdānī, *Kitāb al-Iklīl min akhbār al-Yaman wa-ansāb Ḥimyar: al-juz' al-awwal*, ed. Muḥammad b. 'Alī b. al-Ḥusayn al-Akwa' (Sanaa: Wizāra al-Thiqāfa wa-l-Siyāḥa, 2004), 135; Ibn Sa'd, *Ṭabaqāt*, 1:38–40; 'Abd Allāh b. Muslim b. Qutayba, *al-Ma'ārif*, ed. Tharwat 'Ukāsha (Cairo: Dār al-Ma'ārif, 1969), 34, 63; Uri Rubin, 'Islamic Retellings of Biblical History', in *Adaptations and Innovations: Studies on the Interaction between Jewish and Islamic Thought and Literature from the Early Middle Ages to the Late Twentieth Century, Dedicated to Professor Joel L. Kraemer*, ed. Y. Tzvi Langermann and Josef Stern (Paris: Peeters, 2007), 305–10.

[63] Ps 120:5; Song 1:5; Isa 21:16–17, 42:11, 60:7; Jer 2:10, 49:28; and Ezek 27:21. These verses are cited and discussed in al-Jāḥiẓ, *Radd 'alā al-Naṣārā*, in *Rasā'il al-Jāḥiẓ*, 3:335; *Polemical Works of 'Alī al-Ṭabarī*, 350–1, 378–81; Nu'aym b. Ḥammād, *Kitāb al-Fitan*, 285, 300; Cook, *Book of Tribulations*, 282, 305; Sabine Schmidtke, 'The Muslim Reception of Biblical

discovered in Yemen,[64] while messengers of the prophet Shuʿayb are uncovered in Midian, Ruṣāfa and North Africa.[65] In the latter case, the story is reported by Ibn al-Kalbī from ʿAbd al-Raḥmān b. Ziyād b. Anʿum al-Ifrīqī (d. 156/772–3 or 161/777–8), a *ḥadīth* scholar and judge who was remembered as 'the first person born into Islam in Africa'.[66] ʿAbd al-Raḥmān reports that, while digging, he and his uncle came upon a man stretched out in an underground chamber. Beside the man's head, an inscription read: 'I am Ḥassān b. Nīsān [alternatively, Sinān] al-Awzāʿī. The messenger of God Shuʿayb sent me to this country in order to call its people to belief. But they called me a liar and killed me.' With this story, North Africa is drawn into the sacred history of places visited by ancient prophets and messengers spreading Islam. In fact, versions of this story appear in some of the earliest Islamic historical/biographical collections on Ifrīqiyya as evidence of the region's monotheistic history.[67]

In some cases, these stories explain points of Islamic history by identifying the uncovered individuals as the prophets or messengers who had been dispatched to peoples and places mentioned in the Qurʾān. Next to the body of Ḥanẓala b. Ṣafwān, a piece of writing declares: 'God sent me to Ḥimyar and the

Materials: Ibn Qutayba and his *Aʿlām al-Nubuwwa*', *Islam and Christian-Muslim Relations* 22.3 (2011): 257; Uri Rubin, *Between Bible and Qurʾān: The Children of Israel and the Islamic Self-Image* (Princeton: Darwin Press, 1999), 16, 21; Camilla Adang, *Muslim Writers on Judaism and the Hebrew Bible: From Ibn Rabban to Ibn Hazm* (Leiden: Brill, 1996), 153, 272–6; Hava Lazarus-Yafeh, *Intertwined Worlds: Medieval Islam and Bible Criticism* (Princeton: Princeton University Press, 1992), 83–5.

64 al-Hamdānī, *al-Iklīl*, 8:131–3, 138–9; *Antiquities of South Arabia*, 78–80, 83–4; al-Karājukī, *Kanz al-Fawāʾid*, 1:380–2.

65 al-Hamdānī, *al-Iklīl*, 8:134, 136; *Antiquities of South Arabia*, 80, 81–2; al-Hamdānī, *al-Juzʿ al-sādis min al-Iklīl*, ed. Muqbil al-Tām ʿĀmir al-Aḥmadī (Sanaa: Arabia Felix Academy, 2020), 37; al-Karājukī, *Kanz al-Fawāʾid*, 1:382–4; Ibn Bābawayh al-Qummī, *Kitāb al-Nubuwwa* (Tehran: Wizārat al-Thaqāfa wa-l-Irshād al-Islāmī, 2002), 139–40.

66 al-Khaṭīb al-Baghdādī, *Taʾrīkh*, 11:475–6 (no. 5,307); al-Dhahabī, *Siyar*, 6:411–12.

67 Abū al-ʿArab Muḥammad b. Aḥmad b. Tamīm, *Ṭabaqāt ʿulamāʾ Ifrīqiyya*, ed. Mohammed Ben Cheneb (Beirut: Dār al-Kitāb al-Lubnānī, n.d.), 7; Abū Bakr ʿAbd Allāh b. Muḥammad al-Mālikī, *Kitāb Riyāḍ al-nufūs fī ṭabaqāt ʿulamāʾ al-Qayrawān wa-Ifrīqiyya wa-zuhhādihim wa-nussākihim wa-siyar min akhbārihim wa-faḍāʾilihim wa-awṣāfihim*, ed. Bashīr al-Bakkūsh and Muḥammad al-ʿArūsī al-Maṭwī, 2 vols (Beirut: Dār al-Gharb al-Islāmī, 1994), 1:9.

Arabs of the people of Yemen, but they denied me and killed me.' The narrator concludes by noting that 'Ḥanẓala b. Ṣafwān was the companion of al-Rass' (*ṣāḥib al-rass*), thus associating him (as well as Ḥimyar and Yemen) with the enigmatic 'people of al-Rass' (*aṣḥāb al-rass*) mentioned at Q 23:38 and 50:12.[68] Similarly, an inscription identifies al-Ḥārith b. ʿAmr (alternatively, al-Ḥārith b. Shuʿayb al-Ghassānī) as 'the messenger of the messenger of God Shuʿayb to the people of Midian' (*rasūl rasūl Allāh Shuʿayb ilā ahl Midyan*).[69] Placed near Wādī al-Qurā in the Ḥijāz, al-Ḥārith's burial spot locates the qurʾānic Midian within Arabian space.

These different threads – the Islamic inheritance of the Jewish and Christian past, the inheritance of pre-Islamic Arab monotheism, and qurʾānic exegesis – are woven together in the story of ʿAbd Allāh b. al-Thāmir's body. Early texts credit ʿAbd Allāh with introducing the Christian faith to the people of Najran in Yemen, and with leading the believers who were killed there. These Yemeni Christians were the sixth-century martyrs often identified with the 'People of the Trench' (*aṣḥāb al-ukhdūd*) mentioned at Q 85:4.[70] In a story set during the caliphate of ʿUmar, diggers in either Najran or Sanaa (in variant versions) uncover ʿAbd Allāh's martyred body, found in a seated position with his hand resting upon his head. When this hand (which bore a ring inscribed with the words *rabbī Allāh*, 'My Lord is God') is moved away from his head, ʿAbd Allāh's

[68] *EI* [3], s.v. 'Ḥanẓala b. Ṣafwān' (Ella Landau-Tasseron); *EQ*, s.v. 'Rass' (Roberto Tottoli); Hawting, 'Were There Prophets', 200–1. The inscription at Ḥanẓala's tomb (but not his corpse) and his identity as 'the prophet of al-Rass' appear in al-Hamdānī, *al-Iklīl*, 1:139–42.

[69] This may be intended to help to resolve Shuʿayb's qurʾānic identification as the prophetic messenger both to Midian (Q. 7:85) and to the 'people of the thicket' (*aṣḥāb al-ayka*) (Q. 26:176–7). While these groups could be exegetically equated, they were also sometimes understood as separate entities: *EQ*, s.v. 'People of the Thicket' (John Nawas); Moshe Gil, 'The Origin of the Jews of Yathrib', *JSAI* 4 (1984): 216–17.

[70] David Cook, 'The *Aṣḥāb al-Ukhdūd*: History and *Ḥadīth* in a Martyrological Sequence', *JSAI* 34 (2008): 125–48; Thomas Sizgorich, '"Become Infidels or We Will Throw You into the Fire": The Martyrs of Najrān in Early Muslim Historiography, Hagiography, and Qurʾānic Exegesis', in Papaconstantinou, Debié and Kennedy, *Writing 'True Stories'*, 125–47; Adam Silverstein, 'Who Are the *Aṣḥāb al-Ukhdūd*? Q 85:4–10 in Near Eastern Context', *Der Islam* 96.2 (2019): 281–323.

head spurts blood from a still-fresh wound there.[71] Similar to the story of Daniel's reburied body, when word is sent to ʿUmar about this discovery, the caliph orders that ʿAbd Allāh's corpse be returned to its grave and covered over.

The version of this story transmitted in Ibn Isḥāq's *sīra* identifies the uncovered corpse as belonging to ʿAbd Allāh b. al-Thāmir, but without explaining how this identification occurred.[72] Another version appears in al-Hamdānī's *al-Iklīl*, in which the ring on the corpse's hand is said to be inscribed: 'I am ʿAbd Allāh b. al-Thāmir.' Unfamiliar with this name, ʿUmar b. al-Khaṭṭāb asks Kaʿb al-Aḥbār about him. Steeped in scriptural wisdom, Kaʿb sagely replies:

> O Commander of the Believers! This is a man of that group who believed in the disciples that followed the religion of Jesus. He had companions whom the king of Yemen burned with fire in a trench: that which God mentions in his book when He says, 'The companions of the trench were killed, the fire well-stoked', et cetera. ʿAbd Allāh b. al-Thāmir was also killed, and he was buried in this state.[73]

[71] Ibn Hishām, *Sīra*, 25; Ibn Isḥāq, *Kitāb al-Siyar*, 66; al-Hamdānī, *al-Iklīl*, 6:36; al-Ṭabarī, *Ta'rīkh*, 1/2:926; *History of al-Ṭabarī*, 5:206. According to the *isnāds*, this story was transmitted to Ibn Isḥāq by ʿAbd Allāh b. Abī Bakr b. Muḥammad b. ʿAmr b. Ḥazm (d. 130/747 or 135/752), a Medinan scholar whose father had served as a governor of Najran. See Horovitz, *Earliest Biographies of the Prophet*, 40–7.

[72] A clearly related story, in which a martyr of the People of the Trench is discovered with a hand resting on his head wound, but without naming him as ʿAbd Allāh b. al-Thāmir, appears in ʿAbd al-Razzāq, *Muṣannaf*, 5:423 (no. 9,751); *Tafsīr ʿAbd al-Razzāq*, ed. Maḥmūd Muḥammad ʿAbduh, 3 vols (Beirut: Dār al-Kutub al-ʿIlmiyya, 1999), 3:414–15; al-Tirmidhī, *al-Jāmiʿ*, 5:362–5 (no. 3,340). A variant of this latter version, telling the martyr's story but without the subsequent discovery of his body, appears in Abū Bakr ʿAbd Allāh b. Muḥammad b. Abī Shayba, *Musnad Ibn Abī Shayba*, ed. ʿĀdil b. Yūsuf al-ʿAzzāzī and Aḥmad Farīd al-Muzaydī, 2 vols (Riyadh: Dār al-Waṭan, 1997), 1:323–6 (no. 482); Muslim, *Ṣaḥīḥ*, 4:2,299–301 (no. 3,005); Ibn Jarīr al-Ṭabarī, *Tafsīr*, 24:273–6. The initial section of the *isnād* for this unnamed martyr version reads: Thābit b. Aslam al-Bunānī (d. 123/740–1 or 127/744–5, Baṣra) > ʿAbd al-Raḥmān b. Abī Laylā (d. 83/702, Kūfa) > Ṣuhayb b. Sinān (d. 38/659). Some of the details present in this version seem to underlie the story of ʿAbd Allāh b. al-Thāmir's unearthed corpse: it is said that this unnamed boy 'placed his hand on his temple and then died' during his martyrdom, thus explaining the placement of ʿAbd Allāh b. al-Thāmir's hand on his own head. See the discussion of the interconnected nature of these different versions in Cook, '*Aṣḥāb al-Ukhdūd*', 130–7.

[73] al-Hamdānī, *al-Iklīl*, 8:134–5; *Antiquities of South Arabia*, 80–1.

After hearing Kaʿb's explanation, ʿUmar commands that the body should be returned to the place where it was, with its location hidden 'so that the grave would not be unearthed'.

This tradition well illustrates the ways that early Islamic texts adapted the topoi of relic inventions for Islamic purposes. In his exegetical role, Kaʿb echoes the Jewish characters in Christian *inventiones*, who frequently reveal the locations and identifications of relics of the biblical past. As those characters had guided their Christian colonisers through the Jewish past, Kaʿb similarly acts as an informant on the relics of the Christian past that preceded the Islamic present. In doing so, Kaʿb not only identifies ʿAbd Allāh b. al-Thāmir's body, but appropriates him for a distinctly Islamic sacred history. ʿAbd Allāh and the Najrānī martyrs are placed within the Qurʾān, and they are no longer simply Christians: instead, they are said to be followers of the true Islamic 'religion of Jesus' (*dīn ʿĪsā*), rather than the deformed version of Jesus' message found in Christianity.[74] Much as Kaʿb had explained Daniel's uncovered book by relating it to the apocalyptic history of early Islam, he here places ʿAbd Allāh b. al-Thāmir within a specifically Islamic understanding of the history of Najran, and of Christianity more generally.

With his story told, ʿAbd Allāh b. al-Thāmir's body is re-deposited underground and covered over so as not to be found again. In this and other Islamic narratives about saintly corpses, the existence of sacred relics throughout the early Islamic world is acknowledged and, in a sense, celebrated. At the same time, these stories 'disembody' the holy person's relics as material objects, turning them into literary devices for the narration of Islamic sacred history.[75]

[74] Sean W. Anthony, 'The Composition of Sayf b. ʿUmar's Account of King Paul and His Corruption of Ancient Christianity', *Der Islam* 85 (2010): 164–202.

[75] We might compare the narration of these stories to the later 'affinities between the circulation of ḥadīth and the circulation of Prophetic relics', and the extent to which 'ḥadīth when recited possessed, like relics, the power to bring individuals into a closer relationship with the sacred power of the Prophet'. Dickinson, 'Ibn al-Ṣalāḥ', 503; Wheeler, *Mecca and Eden*, 75–8; Jean-Jacques Thibon, 'Transmission du hadith et modèle prophétique chez les premiers soufis', *Archives de sciences sociales des religions* 178 (2017): 71–87. Perhaps some similar evocation of prophetic and/or saintly presence might be accomplished through these stories as well.

Akhbār historians and *ḥadīth* scholars seemingly related these stories in order to record and eulogise ancient Islamic and Arab history. Yet there is little indication that many of these figures' tombs were visited and venerated: indeed, the stories suggest such practices would have been nearly impossible. While the bodies are hidden, their stories remained above ground, testifying to the history of Islamic prophets, messengers and martyrs.

Do Not Disturb: Sacred Spaces and Hidden Holy Bodies in the Early Islamic Near East

In the stories studied in the previous section, the norms of the standard late antique *inventio* are inverted, with holy bodies reburied and hidden away, never to be found again. Rather than translated to a new place for veneration – or kept at the same spot, with a shrine built upon them – the bodies are re-deposited underground, with their locations obscured. Instead of providing licence for the veneration of a sacred body in a particular location, the place of burial is purposefully obfuscated, with a story pointing only vaguely towards the holy person's location. The stories of these holy bodies were useful to illustrate regions' ancient histories of receiving monotheistic messengers: but they could not easily be used to commemorate or enforce any cult or sense of sacrality predicated on the precise location of a holy person's remains.

Within some early Islamic narratives, however, the discovery of a holy body was indeed part of a place's commemoration as a significant space. As within Christian *inventiones*, stories of such discoveries utilise the holy person's relics in demarcating and illustrating the sacredness and significance of a particular location. And like Christian *inventiones*, competition and rivalry between different parties were often at work behind these claims to certain spaces' holiness, with relics used to bolster partisan arguments.[76] This included not only intra-Muslim disputes, but also disputes between Muslims and other religious communities.

An example of this phenomenon appears at the most sacred of Islamic spaces, the Kaʿba. In early traditions, a number of prophets are said to be buried around the Kaʿba. The scholar Sālim b. ʿAjlān al-Afṭas (d. 132/750) reports

[76] Wiśniewski, *Beginnings of the Cult of Relics*, 106–14.

that he heard that 'around the Kaʿba are the graves of 300 prophets' who had all fled from disbelieving communities to worship at God's House.[77] In a similar vein, ʿAbd al-Raḥmān b. ʿAbd Allāh b. Sābiṭ (d. 118/736–7) reports that, as he was circumambulating the Kaʿba alongside the Kūfan ascetic ʿAbd Allāh b. Ḍamra al-Salūlī, the latter said to him: 'Under our feet, between the Rukn [that is, the Kaʿba's corner that holds the Black Stone], the Maqām, and Zamzam are the graves of 99 prophets.'[78] Thus, around the Kaʿba – more specifically, around its north-eastern face, near the sacred sites of the Black Stone, the Maqām Ibrāhīm and the well of Zamzam – are said to lie a great number of buried prophets. While these hidden figures are mostly left unidentified, some traditions specify a few of the most famous of the buried prophets, naming the biblical and qur'ānic figures Noah, Hūd, Ṣāliḥ and Shuʿayb as among those buried near the Kaʿba.[79]

The tomb of another important figure also appears in these traditions: the prophet and Arab progenitor Ishmael. In some cases, Ishmael is said to be buried near the other prophets.[80] A tradition attributed to Kaʿb al-Aḥbār, for example, says that 'Ishmael is buried between Zamzam, the Rukn, and the Maqām'.[81] However, this location is disputed in reports that place Ishmael's grave – and its discovery – on the north-western side of the building, in the

[77] Muḥammad b. al-Ḥasan al-Shaybānī, *Kitāb al-Āthār*, ed. Khālid al-ʿAwwād, 2 vols (Kuwait: Dār al-Nawādir, 2008), 1:271 (no. 263); Abū Yūsuf Yaʿqūb b. Ibrāhīm, *Kitāb al-Āthār*, ed. Abū al-Wafā' al-Afghānī (Beirut: Dār al-Kutub al-ʿIlmiyya, 1978), 117 (no. 545); Travis Zadeh, 'The Early Hajj: Seventh–Eighth Centuries CE', in *The Hajj: Pilgrimage in Islam*, ed. Eric Tagliacozzo and Shawkat M. Toorawa (New York: Cambridge University Press, 2016), 53–4. On Sālim b. ʿAjlān al-Afṭas, see van Ess, *Theology and Society*, 2:518–19.

[78] al-Fākihī, *Akhbār Makka*, 2:34 (1,090). Variant versions appear in ʿAbd al-Razzāq, *Muṣannaf*, 5:120 (no. 9,129); al-Azraqī, *Akhbār Makka*, 120–1 (no. 82), 692 (no. 792). See Rubin, *Between Bible and Qur'ān*, 41.

[79] al-Azraqī, *Akhbār Makka*, 121 (no. 83), 691–2 (no. 791); al-Shaybānī, *Kitāb al-Āthār*, 1:272 (no. 264); al-Fākihī, *Akhbār Makka*, 2:291 (no. 1,545); Ibn al-Faqīh, *Kitāb al-Buldān*, 74.

[80] al-Azraqī, *Akhbār Makka*, 129 (no. 102).

[81] ʿAbd al-Razzāq, *Muṣannaf*, 5:119–20 (no. 9,128); al-Fākihī, *Akhbār Makka*, 2:34 (no. 1,090); Abū Nuʿaym al-Iṣbahānī, *Ḥilyat al-awliya' wa ṭabaqāt al-aṣfiyā'*, 10 vols (Cairo: Maṭbaʿat al-Saʿāda, 1974), 6:13; Uri Rubin, 'The Kaʿba: Aspects of Its Ritual Functions and Position in Pre-Islamic and Early Islamic Times', *JSAI* 8 (1986): 109–10.

partially-enclosed area called the Ḥijr.[82] These traditions suggest that Ishmael's grave was part of the Kaʿba's very structure in the Ḥijr, and a constituent component of the Kaʿba's sacred architecture.

According to these traditions, the discovery of Ishmael's grave in the Ḥijr occurred during the 'counter-caliphate' of ʿAbd Allāh b. al-Zubayr (r. 60–73/680–92), in the midst of Ibn al-Zubayr's reconstruction of the Kaʿba, following its damage from Umayyad attacks in 64/683–4.[83] A key component of Ibn al-Zubayr's project was the incorporation of the Ḥijr into the Kaʿba's architectural structure. This was predicated on the notion (discussed below) that the Ḥijr was part of the original Abrahamic Kaʿba, prior to its remodelling by the Quraysh. In a report attributed to Yazīd b. Rūmān (d. 130/747–8), a *mawlā* of the family of Ibn al-Zubayr, we are told:

> I witnessed when Ibn al-Zubayr dug in the Ḥijr. He came upon the House's foundations: they were stones, one closely following another. When the Ḥijr was disturbed, the House [that is, the Kaʿba] itself would quiver. He came upon [the foundations] in the Ḥijr extending from the House six cubits and a measure. There, he also came upon the location of a grave. Ibn al-Zubayr said, 'This is the grave of Ishmael.' He gathered the Quraysh and said to them, 'Bear witness!' Then he began to build.[84]

[82] On the Ḥijr and its association with the Kaʿba, see Hawting, 'Origins of the Muslim Sanctuary', 33–6, 39–44; Gerald Hawting, '"A Plaything for Kings": ʿĀʾisha's *Ḥadīth*, Ibn al-Zubayr, and the Rebuilding of the Kaʿba', in *Islamic Studies Today: Essays in Honor of Andrew Rippin*, ed. Majid Daneshgar and Walid A. Saleh (Leiden: Brill, 2016), 3–21; Rubin, 'The Kaʿba', 100–13. For visual reconstructions of different phases of the Kaʿba's structure, see Simon O'Meara, *The Kaʿba Orientations: Readings in Islam's Ancient House* (Edinburgh: Edinburgh University Press, 2020), 9.

[83] Gerald R. Hawting, 'The Umayyads and the Ḥijāz', *Proceedings of the Seminar for Arabian Studies* 2 (1972): 39–46.

[84] al-Azraqī, *Akhbār Makka*, 310–11 (no. 234). The *isnād* runs: Abū al-Walīd al-Azraqī > Mahdī b. Abī Mahdī (d. unknown, Mecca) > ʿĪsā b. Yūnus [b. Abī Isḥāq] (d. *c.* 191/806–7, Kūfa) > ʿAbd Allāh b. Muslim b. Hurmuz (d. unknown, Mecca) > Yazīd. A shortened version of this report with the same *isnād* (from ʿĪsā b. Yūnus to Yazīd) appears in *Kitāb al-Manāsik*, 492–3. On Yazīd b. Rūmān, see Ibn Khayyāṭ, *Ṭabaqāt*, 260; *The History of al-Ṭabarī. Volume XXXIX: Biographies of the Prophet's Companions and Their Successors*, trans. Ella Landau-Tasseron (Albany: State University of New York Press, 1998), 241. On ʿAbd Allāh b. Muslim b. Hurmuz, see Ibn Khayyāṭ, *Ṭabaqāt*, 283; al-Bukhārī, *Taʾrīkh*, 3/1:190.

This report indicates that the Kaʿba's foundation stones (*asās*) extended in an unbroken line into the Ḥijr area. The Ḥijr's physical connection to the Kaʿba is dramatically illustrated by the fact that the House itself shakes when the Ḥijr is disturbed. In another version of this story, the foundations are compared to 'intertwined fingers or the necks of camels, one joined to another', and it is said that 'disturbing the Ḥijr at the foundations disturbed all the cornerstones' of the Kaʿba.[85] These traditions clearly intend to convey that the Ḥijr was a constituent part of the Kaʿba itself.

The discovery of Ishmael's tomb appears as part of this architectural-cum-archaeological effort to re-build the (allegedly) more original Kaʿba. Embedded in the Ḥijr, discovered alongside its very foundations, is Ishmael's tomb. The tomb further evidences the Ḥijr's ancient origins, intertwined as it is with the very roots of the Kaʿba itself. This theme reappears in another report about the tomb's discovery during Ibn al-Zubayr's rebuilding work, this time narrated by Ṣafwān b. ʿAbd Allāh b. Ṣafwān al-Jumaḥī (d. *c.* 81–90/700–9), a Meccan *ḥadīth* transmitter:

> Ibn al-Zubayr excavated the Ḥijr and found in it a casket made of green stones. He asked the Quraysh who were with him, but found that none of them had any knowledge of it. He then sent to ʿAbd Allāh b. Ṣafwān and asked him. ʿAbd Allāh said, 'This is the grave of Ishmael, so do not disturb it.' Thus, he left it.[86]

In this obscure story, Ishmael's casket is said to be made of green stones, something that only ʿAbd Allāh b. Ṣafwān (d. 73/692–3) – a Meccan Qurashī and a loyal follower of Ibn al-Zubayr – is able to identify.[87] Though it is not

[85] al-Azraqī, *Akhbār Makka*, 301 (no. 227); O'Meara, *Kaʿba Orientations*, 70.

[86] al-Azraqī, *Akhbār Makka*, 431 (no. 389). The *isnād* is: Abū al-Walīd al-Azraqī > Aḥmad b. Muḥammad b. al-Walīd b. ʿUqba b. al-Azraq (d. 222/837) > Khālid b. ʿAbd al-Raḥmān al-Makhzūmī (d. 212/827–8, Mecca) > al-Ḥārith b. Abī Bakr al-Zuhrī (d. unknown, Medina) > Ṣafwān b. ʿAbd Allāh. On Khālid b. ʿAbd al-Raḥmān, see Jamāl al-Dīn Yūsuf al-Mizzī, *Tahdhīb al-kamāl fī asmāʾ al-rijāl*, ed. Bashshār ʿAwwād Maʿrūf, 35 vols (Beirut: Muʾassasat al-Risāla, 1985), 8:124–5. On al-Ḥārith b. Abī Bakr, see Ibn Saʿd, *Ṭabaqāt*, 7:449.

[87] On ʿAbd Allāh b. Ṣafwān and his son Ṣafwān b. ʿAbd Allāh: Ibn Saʿd, *Ṭabaqāt*, 8:26, 35; al-Zubayr b. Bakkār, *Jamharat nasab Quraysh wa-akhbāruhā*, ed. ʿAbbās Hānī al-Jarrāḥ, 2 vols (Beirut: Dār al-Kutub al-ʿIlmiyya, 2010), 2:73–7; al-Mizzī, *Tahdhīb al-kamāl*, 13:197–200, 15:125–7; Rana Mikati, 'On the Identity of the Syrian *abdāl*', *BSOAS* 80 (2017): 29; Mehdy Shaddel, "Abd Allāh ibn al-Zubayr and the Mahdī: Between Propaganda and Historical Memory in the Second Civil War', *BSOAS* 80 (2017): 10–11.

specified here, this story recalls the Quraysh's earlier reconstruction of the Kaʿba, during the Prophet Muḥammad's youth in Mecca. In the account of that event recorded in Ibn Isḥāq's *sīra*, the Kaʿba's uncovered foundations are described as 'green stones, like camel humps [alternatively, teeth] interlocked with one another'.[88] In the description of Ishmael's grave in the Ḥijr, the prophet's casket is seemingly composed of the same, or quite similar, green stones used to construct the Kaʿba's foundations.[89]

Ishmael's tomb is situated in these reports as a constituent element of the Kaʿba's very structure. ʿAbd Allāh b. Ṣafwān's warning not to 'disturb' the tomb points in this direction: as the foundations in the Ḥijr should not be 'disturbed' – or else the whole Kaʿba might shake and fall – Ishmael's tomb should similarly be left in its place. Such a perspective perhaps underlies another report on the tomb's discovery, attributed to a Meccan named Saʿīd b. Ḥarb:

> I witnessed ʿAbd Allāh b. al-Zubayr uprooting the foundations that Abraham laid when he built the House. They came upon some yellow soil near the Ḥaṭīm. Ibn al-Zubayr said, 'This is the grave of Ishmael.' Then he covered it.[90]

As Ibn al-Zubayr digs near the Ḥaṭīm – commonly understood as the semicircular wall enclosing the Ḥijr – some distinct yellow soil alerts him to the presence of Ishmael's grave.[91] The report's tone here is rather restrained, but a variant version finds Ibn al-Zubayr more dramatically crying, 'Bury it, bury

[88] Ibn Hishām, *Sīra*, 124; Ibn Isḥāq, *Kitāb al-Siyar*, 105; al-Ṭabarī, *Taʾrīkh*, 1/3:1137; *The History of al-Ṭabarī. Volume VI: Muḥammad at Mecca*, trans. W. Montgomery Watt and M. V. McDonald (Albany: State University of New York Press, 1988), 58. Ibn Hishām's version compares the stones to 'camel humps' (*asnima*), but Ibn Bukayr's and al-Ṭabarī's have the slight variant 'teeth' (*asinna*).

[89] Modern scholars have noted numerous echoes in the literary accounts of the Qurashī and Zubayrid reconstructions of the Kaʿba: Hawting, 'Origins of the Muslim Sanctuary', 39, 44; O'Meara, *Kaʿba Orientations*, 69–71. I have not found this particular connection noted, however.

[90] Ibn Isḥāq, *Kitāb al-Siyar*, 106. The *isnād* is: Aḥmad b. ʿAbd al-Jabbār al-ʿUṭāridī > Yūnus b. Bukayr > al-Mundhir b. Thaʿlaba (d. unknown, Baṣra) > Saʿīd b. Ḥarb. Another report on Ibn al-Zubayr's rule in Mecca is narrated from Saʿīd b. Ḥarb through his nephew al-Mundhir b. Thaʿlaba in al-Fasawī, *Kitāb al-Maʿrifa*, 3:509.

[91] On the term Ḥaṭīm and its 'conflicting definitions' in early sources, see Hawting, 'Origins of the Muslim Sanctuary', 34–6; Rubin, 'The Kaʿba', 113–18.

it! This is the grave of Ishmael!'[92] While Ibn al-Zubayr's concern may simply lie with the inviolability of the prophet's tomb, the earth-shaking potential of disturbing these foundational structures may also explain his anxious reaction.

The reports about the discovery of Ishmael's tomb in the Ḥijr were pieces of the wider effort waged by Ibn al-Zubayr and his supporters to justify and sacralise his reconstruction of the Kaʿba. As Gerald Hawting has argued, 'there are indications of a dispute about the status of al-Ḥijr', and 'the inclusion of al-Ḥijr inside the bayt is the most striking feature of the sanctuary constructed by Ibn al-Zubayr'.[93] According to reports, Ibn al-Zubayr's changes to the building were controversial, with the majority of Meccans (including prominent Muslim authorities) speaking out against Ibn al-Zubayr's plan. Ibn al-Zubayr's work was predicated, however, on a Prophetic *ḥadīth*, according to which the Prophet had said to his wife 'Āʾisha:

> Your people [the Quraysh] fell short in building the House. Their finances were lacking and they left some cubits of it in the Ḥijr. If it were not that your people were unbelievers until only recently, I would demolish the Kaʿba and restore what they had left out.

According to this *ḥadīth*, 'Ibn al-Zubayr's wish to demolish and rebuild the Kaʿba is explained [. . .] as a consequence of his knowledge that the Prophet himself had expressed a desire to rebuild it'.[94] While the *ḥadīth*'s authenticity was accepted within the corpus of Prophetic traditions, Hawting has drawn attention to the large number of people 'associated with Ibn al-Zubayr and his family' in the *isnād*s transmitting this tradition. Hawting plausibly suggests that 'the 'Āʾisha tradition originated in Zubayrid circles and represents words and ideas attributed to the Prophet rather than originating with him', for the purpose of claiming 'both a Muḥammadan and an Abrahamic sanction for the sanctuary erected by Ibn al-Zubayr'.[95]

[92] *Kitāb al-Manāsik*, 490. The *isnād* is: Faḍl b. Sahl [al-Aʿraj] (d. 255/868–9, Baghdad) > al-Anṣārī [Muḥammad b. 'Abd Allāh b. al-Muthannā] (d. *c.* 214–15/829–31, Baṣra) > al-Mundhir b. Thaʿlaba > Saʿīd b. Ḥarb.

[93] Hawting, 'Origins of the Muslim Sanctuary', 34.

[94] Hawting, 'Plaything for Kings', 4.

[95] Hawting, 'Plaything for Kings', 20–1.

Much like other late antique *inventiones*, the discovery of an ancient holy person's relics here contributes directly to a space's sacredness. While 'Ā'isha's *ḥadīth* about the Ka'ba clearly played a significant role in justifying Ibn al-Zubayr's actions, it is noteworthy that the discovery of Ishmael's body was also evoked in this process. The fact that his discovery occurred in the context of a controversial claim to the Ḥijr's significance and authority highlights the power that a holy person's relics could wield in an early Islamic environment.

Claims about Ishmael's presence in the Ḥijr appear to have been formative for the space's continued veneration. Even after Ibn al-Zubayr's ouster and execution by the Umayyads – and their reconstruction of the Ka'ba, pointedly excluding the Ḥijr from the Ka'ba's architectural structure – traditions continued to circulate about Ishmael's grave in the Ḥijr.[96] By the twelfth century (if not earlier), both Ishmael and Hagar's gravesites were marked with green marble slabs, where 'the people seek blessings by praying at these two spots in the Ḥijr'.[97] Though it was not enshrined, Ishmael's grave was not forgotten, even as the ground around it changed.

Ishmael's *inventio* in the Ḥijr was a component of Ibn al-Zubayr's reformulation of the spatial parameters of the Ka'ba, offering justification for his actions in an intra-Muslim dispute over sacred space. Another *inventio*, occurring a few years later, assisted Umayyad claims to power and authority over what had previously been a Christian space. In the early eighth century, the Umayyad caliph al-Walīd b. 'Abd al-Malik pursued a massive building programme throughout Syria and the Ḥijāz. In addition to the expansion of the Prophet's Mosque in Medina and the continued patronage of the Dome of the Rock and the al-Aqṣā Mosque in Jerusalem, al-Walīd ordered the construction of a large congregational mosque within his capital city, Damascus.[98] Likely as 'a representation of Muslim religious hegemony', the site chosen for this mosque was that of 'the most prominent building in Damascus', the Church

[96] Ibn Hishām, *Sīra*, 5; Ibn Sa'd, *Ṭabaqāt*, 1:35; al-Azraqī, *Akhbār Makka*, 141 (no. 128), 147 (no. 129), 432 (no. 393); Ibn Qutayba, *al-Ma'ārif*, 34.

[97] Ibn Jubayr, *Riḥla*, 88. Earlier reports mention the installation of marble panels in the Ḥijr in 161/777–8, 241/855–6 and 283/896–7, but do not associate these panels with the burial spots of Ishmael and Hagar: al-Azraqī, *Akhbār Makka*, 433, 437–8.

[98] Guidetti, *In the Shadow of the Church*, 19, 41.

of St John the Baptist.[99] In 706 CE, the church building was torn down and construction began on the grand Umayyad Mosque of Damascus, directly on top of the former Christian sacred space.

Stories circulated in the eighth century about an ancient prophetic relic that was uncovered during al-Walīd's construction of the Damascus Mosque. According to a report transmitted from the Damascene scholar Zayd b. Wāqid al-Qurashī (d. 138/755–6), the mosque builders discovered a cave under the old church's floor.[100] When the caliph was informed of this, he himself descended into the cave, where he found 'a delightful little church' with a box inside of it. Opening this box, the caliph discovered a basket containing the decapitated head of John the Baptist (known as Yaḥyā b. Zakariyyā in Islamic tradition), and inscribed with the message, 'This is the head of Yaḥyā b. Zakariyyā'. In another report, Zayd b. Wāqid states that he 'saw the head of Yaḥyā b. Zakariyyā when they were planning the construction of the Damascus Mosque. It was brought out from underneath one of the columns of the [church] dome, and the flesh and hair upon his head had not changed.'[101]

We find here clear parallels to features of other Islamic *inventiones*, such as a prophet's undecayed body and an inscription identifying it. What happens next likewise parallels those *inventio* plots we have encountered so far, though with a distinct twist. After the discovery of John's head, al-Walīd 'ordered that [the head] be restored to its place'. Much as in other cases of uncovered prophetic corpses, the caliph returns John's relic to its previous resting place, without a translation to a new place of honour and worship. However, al-Walīd then

[99] Khalek, *Damascus after the Muslim Conquest*, 112.

[100] 'Alī b. Muḥammad al-Raba'ī, *Faḍā'il al-Shām wa-Dimashq*, ed. Ṣalāḥ al-Dīn al-Munajjid (Damascus: Maṭba'at al-Tarraqī, 1950), 33 (no. 61); Ibn 'Asākir, *Ta'rīkh*, 2:240–1. The passage is translated in Khalek, *Damascus after the Muslim Conquest*, 113–14. On Zayd b. Wāqid, see Ibn 'Asākir, *Ta'rīkh*, 19:524–9; al-Dhahabī, *Siyar*, 6:296–7; van Ess, *Theology and Society*, 1:114–15. This narrative is related through the well-connected Damascene family of Hishām b. Yaḥyā al-Ghassānī. See Khalek, *Damascus after the Muslim Conquest*, 45–52.

[101] al-Raba'ī, *Faḍā'il al-Shām*, 32–3 (no. 60); Ibn 'Asākir, *Ta'rīkh*, 2:241. The *isnād* is: Abū al-Qāsim 'Abd al-Raḥmān b. 'Umar b. Naṣr (d. 415/1024–5, Damascus) > al-Ḥasan b. Ḥabīb al-Ḥaṣā'irī (d. 338/950, Damascus) > Abū 'Abd al-Malik al-Basarī (d. 289/901–2, Damascus) > Mahdī b. Ja'far (d. 230/844–5, Ramla) > al-Walīd b. Muslim (d. 195/810–11, Damascus) > Zayd b. Wāqid.

veers from the standard script: he commands the builders to 'make the column above the cave distinct from the other columns'. Following the caliph's orders, the workmen constructed the column above the cave 'with its top shaped like a basket', visually mimicking the basket that contained John's head. Thus, rather than a totally anonymous burial place, John's head was marked with a special architectural feature within the Umayyad Mosque. Its location there appears to have been well-known, as several eighth-century Syrian scholars are cited as saying that John's head is located 'under the basket-shaped column'.[102]

As Nancy Khalek has demonstrated, the stories of John's head and the column marking its burial place are multilayered symbols of the Umayyad inheritance and reformulation of the Christian past in Damascus. Al-Walīd's active role in both the mosque construction and the relic discovery places him 'as a pivotal figure in the history of Islam', showcasing his strength of resolve and 'a particular claim to religious and political authority'.[103] Moreover, 'the presence of [John's] relics added significantly to the preeminence of the building in the Umayyad period', as the Umayyads 'harness[ed] the physical symbols of political and religious power' that had preceded them.[104] Yet the particular form in which John was incorporated into the mosque offered 'an anti-Trinitarian rejoinder to the sensibilities of the pilgrims and worshippers familiar with the site'.[105] Rather than linking John and the column with Jesus and the cross – that is, the theological, iconographic and cult programmes that were common among Syrian Christians in the preceding centuries – John's column in the Umayyad Mosque was 'emphatically crossless' and devoid of any gesture towards Jesus.[106] The Umayyad discovery and installation of John's head thus deployed the powerful themes of this late antique relic cult, but purposefully sapped it of its Christian connotations.

Though it never carried the significance of the Kaʿba or the Umayyad Mosque, Daniel's burial place was also a subject of dispute: in this case, a dispute about local Khūzistānī issues of space and authority. We saw several

[102] al-Rabaʿī, *Faḍāʾil al-Shām*, 31–2 (nos 56–9); Ibn ʿAsākir, *Taʾrīkh*, 2:241–2.

[103] Khalek, *Damascus after the Muslim Conquest*, 113–14.

[104] Ibid., 94, 98.

[105] Ibid., 97.

[106] Ibid., 98–111, 116.

reports about Daniel's discovery in Tustar, where Abū Mūsa placed him in an anonymous grave. However, in other texts, Daniel is not found in Tustar and is not buried underground. Instead, he is discovered in al-Sūs, and is buried underwater. Quite different from those describing the burial of Daniel in Tustar, these texts provide evidence of a variant tradition regarding the discovery and reburial of Daniel's body during the conquest of Khūzistān.

This alternative story about Daniel's corpse appears in several texts collected around the ninth and tenth centuries. For example, in Ibn Aʿtham al-Kūfī's (fl. early tenth century) *Kitāb al-Futūḥ* (Book of Conquests), Abū Mūsā al-Ashʿarī receives word from ʿUmar to bury Daniel ʻin a place where the people of al-Sūs cannot access his grave'. More ambiguous than ʿUmar's order to ʻhide' Daniel's body, the caliph's command here enables Abū Mūsā to pursue a different strategy:

> When he read ʿUmar's letter, Abū Mūsā ordered the people of al-Sūs to divert their river and to wrap Daniel in a new shroud. He and his Muslim companions prayed over Daniel, then he commanded that Daniel be interred. A grave was dug in the middle of the river of al-Sūs, Daniel was buried inside it, and the water was allowed to flow over it. It is said that Daniel is buried in the river of al-Sūs, with the water flowing over him, up to today. God knows best![107]

Similar stories of Abū Mūsā burying Daniel in the river bed at al-Sūs appear in the historian al-Balādhurī's (d. 279/892) *Futūḥ al-Buldān* (Conquest of the Lands) and in the littérateur Ibn Qutayba's (d. 276/889) *Kitāb al-Maʿārif* (Book of Knowledge).[108] The *Tārīkh-i Qumm* (History of Qum) of Ḥasan b. Muḥammad b. Ḥasan al-Qummī (fl. tenth century) also contains a version of this story, cited from the historians Abū ʿUbayda Maʿmar b. Muthannā (d. *c.* 210/825) and Ibn Isḥāq.[109] These texts indicate that stories about

[107] Ibn Aʿtham, *Kitāb al-Futūḥ*, 2:8–9; al-Thaʿlabī, *Kitāb al-Qiṣaṣ al-anbiyāʾ*, 202.

[108] Aḥmad b. Yaḥyā al-Balādhurī, *Futūḥ al-buldān*, ed. ʿAbd Allāh Anīs al-Ṭabbāʿ and ʿUmar Anīs al-Ṭabbāʿ (Beirut: Muʾassasat al-Maʿārif, 1987), 533; Ibn Qutayba, *al-Maʿārif*, 49. Ibn Qutayba attributes the narrative to Wahb b. Munabbih (d. *c.* 110/728). See Gérard Lecomte, ʻLes citations de l'Ancien et du Nouveau Testament dans l'œuvre d'Ibn Qutayba', *Arabica* 5.1 (1958): 34–46.

[109] Ḥasan b. Muḥammad b. Ḥasan Qummī, *Tārīkh-i Qumm*, ed. Jalāl al-Dīn Ṭihrānī (Tehran: Maṭbaʿat-i Majlis, 1934), 297. This history is now extant only in a Persian translation produced in 805–6/1402–3 by Ḥasan b. ʿAlī b. Ḥasan b. ʿAbd al-Malik Qummī. On this

Daniel's entombment under the river of al-Sūs were circulating by the ninth century, and possibly already in the eighth.

One might think that the outcome of burying Daniel either underground or underwater would be essentially the same: both situations deprive people of physical access to the prophet's body, and negate the possibility of venerating his tomb. But in fact, the story of Daniel's river burial was used in commemorating the prophet's association with al-Sūs, and his continued physical presence there. Ibn Aʿtham notes, for example, that Daniel's location in the river is mentioned 'up to today'. Discussing al-Sūs in his geographical atlas, the writer al-Iṣṭakhrī (fl. *c.* 340/951) provides further information about what was said in his day regarding Daniel's burial spot:

> It has reached me (and God knows best) that they have a coffin that was discovered in the days of Abū Mūsā al-Ashʿarī. They say that it contains the bones of the prophet Daniel, and that the People of the Book used to circulate it in their gathering places, seek blessings from it, and ask for rain through it when suffering from drought. Then Abū Mūsā took it and came to the river near the gate of al-Sūs. He split off a canal [in the river] and placed there three graves encased with bricks. He buried that coffin in one of the graves, secured each one firmly, obscured them, and then opened the gate so that the river concealed the graves. The river flows over them up to today. Someone who descends to the bottom of the water will find those graves.[110]

Here, al-Iṣṭakhrī combines features of the different narratives about Daniel's discovery and reburial, merging the digging of multiple graves with the insertion under the river. Like Ibn Aʿtham, al-Iṣṭakhrī suggests that Daniel's body in the river was still remembered by the community in al-Sūs up to his own day, and could even be seen by one diving to find it.

These divergent traditions suggest that there was disagreement over Daniel's body and its location in Khūzistān. Writing around the same time as al-Iṣṭakhrī,

text, see Robinson, 'Conquest of Khūzistān', 21 n.58; Ann K. S. Lambton, 'An Account of the *Tārīkhi Qumm*', *BSOAS* 12 (1947–8): 586–96; Mimi Hanaoka, *Authority and Identity in Medieval Islamic Historiography: Persian Histories from the Peripheries* (Cambridge: Cambridge University Press, 2016), 55–7, 110–18.

110 Abū Isḥāq Ibrāhīm b. Muḥammad al-Iṣṭakhrī, *Kitāb al-Masālik wa-l-mamālik*, ed. M. J. de Goeje (Leiden: Brill, 1870), 92. The same text appears in Abū al-Qāsim b. Hawqal, *Kitāb Ṣūrat al-Arḍ* (Beirut: Dār Maktabat al-Ḥayāt, 1992), 230.

the geographer al-Muqaddasī (d. *c.* 380/990) highlights this conflict in his discussion of al-Sūs:

> There is partisanship between the people of Tustar and al-Sūs on account of the coffin of Daniel. They relate that when the grave of Daniel was uncovered, the remains were placed in a sarcophagus and carried around to places at which people prayed for rain. They [in al-Sūs] say, 'The coffin was removed from us and returned to Tustar, and they kept it. We sent them ten leaders as hostages for the time of their returning it [to us]. But when they had obtained the coffin again, they stopped this river for it [the coffin], built this vault over it, and then allowed the water to flow over it. They also kept the hostages with them. Since that time, this partisanship has been between us, and because of this the prestige of our leaders has diminished, up to today.'[111]

Here, al-Muqaddasī cites the Khūzistānīs using Daniel's remains to bring rain, but he does not relate the prophet's discovery or reburial to the Muslim conquest at all. Instead, factions of the Khūzistānīs are themselves the ones who both discovered and then reburied Daniel's body. The reburial of Daniel in the river – not agreed upon between the different parties – is blamed for the ongoing 'partisanship between the people of Tustar and al-Sūs'.

This conflict between two Khūzistānī cities in the tenth century recalls many late antique and medieval examples of different locales' competing claims regarding the possession of a holy person's relics. Indeed, the different narratives within the *ḥadīth* and *akhbār* corpus of the eighth and ninth centuries suggest that there were disagreements about Daniel's discovery much earlier than al-Muqaddasī's day. These differences perhaps stemmed from Muslims' differing claims regarding the glory – and revenue – due to them from conquering the cities of Khūzistān. As discussed above, the Muslims who had fought in Khūzistān largely settled in Baṣra and Kūfa, where they disputed their respective cities' contributions to the wars of conquest. Particular disagreement centred on the conquest of Tustar, which was claimed by the inhabitants of both Baṣra and Kūfa.[112]

111 al-Muqaddasī, *Aḥsān al-taqāsīm*, 417; *The Best Divisions for Knowledge of the Regions*, trans. Basil Anthony Collins, rev. Muhammad Hamid al-Tai (Reading: Garnet, 1994), 370–1 (adapted here).

112 Robinson, 'Conquest of Khūzistān', 23.

The tomb of Daniel was drawn into these variant histories of the conquests, perhaps because 'as a source of local pride, as well as a draw for pilgrims, sites such as these were obviously of some value'.[113] In this regard, it is noteworthy that the traditions placing Daniel in Tustar are reported almost exclusively by Baṣran *ḥadīth* transmitters, while those placing him in al-Sūs are mostly narrated by *akhbārī* historians with connections to Kūfa and Baghdad. These different traditions seem to reflect the competing claims of these cities' inhabitants over what happened in the conquests, including what happened to an ancient prophet's body.

Conclusion: A Geography of the Unseen Sacred

In an overview of sources highlighting 'ideas on holy places in the first centuries of Islam and their development during the following centuries', M. J. Kister notes:

> The problem of the graves of prophets is noteworthy. The number of graves of prophets and saints in a given city serves as a measure of its status and position on the map of holy places as drawn by the Muslim community.[114]

Kister adds that 'The expansion of Islam and the rise of the Muslim empire encouraged the establishment of local sanctuaries, places of *ziyārāt*, venerated graves and places of ritual practices'.[115] Yet the relationship between these two developments – the emergence of traditions about prophets' graves, and the ritual veneration of particular spaces associated with such graves – is not entirely clear. What was the relationship between the discourse of unseen prophets' tombs and the ritual practices that emerged around similar sacred spaces? When, and why, were holy persons' tombs hidden from view, versus being venerated 'places of *ziyārāt*'?

As Kister says, traditions emerged that celebrated the multitudes of prophets' tombs in different locales around the early Islamic Near East. Traditions about the great number of prophets (ranging from 70, to 99, to 300) buried around the Kaʿba are attested by the early eighth century. Similar traditions emerged

[113] Ibid., 33.

[114] M. J. Kister, 'Sanctity Joint and Divided: On Holy Places in the Islamic Tradition', *JSAI* 20 (1996): 22.

[115] Kister, 'Sanctity Joint and Divided', 42.

about the tens or hundreds of prophets buried in Syria and Palestine,[116] as did Shīʿī traditions about those buried in the city of Kūfa.[117]

The circulation of such traditions (as well as their contestation) is suggested by an anecdote about an Iraqi delegation that visited the Umayyad caliph Muʿāwiya b. Abī Sufyān in Syria. When the delegation arrived, Muʿāwiya greeted them by extolling his country and himself: 'Welcome! You have arrived in the best place. You have arrived before your caliph, your protector, in the land that contains the prophets' graves, the Holy Land, the land of the gathering [on the Day of Judgement]!' In response, a member of the delegation, Ṣaʿṣaʿa b. Ṣūḥān, dressed down Muʿāwiya point by point. Regarding the prophets buried in Syria, Ṣaʿṣaʿa chided: 'As for your saying, "You have arrived in the land that contains the prophets' graves", more pharaohs have died here than prophets!'[118] Ṣaʿṣaʿa was a Shīʿī partisan, and his pious opposition to Umayyad power likely stands at the forefront of his hostile response to Muʿāwiya. Nonetheless, a critique of the Umayyad sanctification of Palestine is apparent here, including the land's celebration for the many prophets buried there.[119]

Yet these multitudes of prophets' graves throughout cities and regions were not – with some important exceptions – identified or venerated at specific sites in the early centuries. Instead, traditions simply refer to these unseen prophetic graves as a component feature of these locations' holiness. Much like the contagious holiness that saints' bodies diffused according to Christian beliefs, these prophets' buried bodies invisibly diffused *baraka*, or blessing, throughout Islamic regions and cities.[120] As Paul Cobb notes, 'In early Islamic Syria, sacred

[116] Paul M. Cobb, 'Virtual Sacrality: Making Muslim Syria Sacred Before the Crusades', *Medieval Encounters* 8.1 (2002): 45; Hasson, 'Muslim View of Jerusalem', 363.

[117] Yaron Friedman, '"Kūfa is Better": The Sanctity of Kūfa in Early Islam and Shīʿism in Particular', *Le Muséon* 126.1–2 (2013): 213.

[118] Ibn Abī al-Dunyā, *Kitāb Ḥilm Muʿāwiya*, ed. Ibrāhīm Ṣāliḥ (Damascus: Dār al-Bashāʾir, 2002), 32–3 (no. 32); Ibn al-Faqīh, *Kitāb al-Buldān*, 164; Ibn ʿAsākir, *Taʾrīkh*, 24:93; Ibn ʿAbd Rabbihi, *al-ʿIqd al-farīd*, 3:318; Aḥmad b. Yaḥyā al-Balādhurī, *Ansāb al-ashrāf*, vol. 4/1, ed. Iḥsān ʿAbbās (Wiesbaden: Franz Steiner, 1979), 32 (no. 114).

[119] Elad, *Medieval Jerusalem*, 152.

[120] Gustave E. von Grunebaum, 'The Sacred Character of Islamic Cities', in *Islam and Medieval Hellenism: Social and Cultural Perspectives* (London: Variorum Reprints, 1976), 26–7; Meri, *Cult of Saints*, 13–18, 35–6; Béatrice Caseau, 'Sacred Landscapes', in *Late Antiquity: A Guide to the Postclassical World*, ed. G. W. Bowersock, Peter Brown and Oleg Grabar (Cambridge, MA: Belknap Press of Harvard University Press, 1999), 43.

ground was literally underfoot'.[121] The stories discussed throughout this chapter – of bodies discovered and then reburied – similarly suggest that corporeal holiness lay underground throughout the early Islamic world. These stories provide brief, illustrative examples of the numerous prophetic bodies that are hidden away in different places. But rather than becoming objects of veneration, the corpses are returned to their underground tombs, to seep *baraka* into the earth around them.

We thus find a tension in the Islamic re-imagining of the 'ritual networks' of saints' shrines that characterised late antique Christian traditions.[122] The power and holiness of saintly bodies is confirmed in these stories, which proudly highlight the existence of prophetic corpses throughout the early Islamic world. Yet rather than these relics being brought out for believers to revere, they are kept out of sight: the *inventio* is not carried through to enshrinement, but is stopped and inverted. While these stories do not call for a destruction of the prophets' graves, neither are the bodies enshrined for worship. We might compare these stories of holy relics to the qur'ānic accusation of *taḥrīf*: the assertion that Jews and Christians altered the divinely revealed scriptures of the Torah and Gospel. These stories indicate that non-Muslim communities had similarly misunderstood and misused prophetic corpses, whose graves are set aright by true Muslim monotheists through their non-worship and (in most cases) disappearance.

This was not quite the case at all Islamic sites, however. As we saw in the column marking the spot of John the Baptist's head in the Umayyad Mosque in Damascus, something like an enshrinement occurred, even as John's head was kept underground. In fact, we might go so far as to ask if this Islamic treatment of John's head was really so different from how Christians in this period installed and venerated relics in their own sacred spaces. The relics of saints were frequently installed in late antique churches and monasteries in ways such that it was impossible for visitors to touch or see them.[123] Instead, inscriptions or mosaics 'communicated information about the relics in a permanent,

[121] Cobb, 'Virtual Sacrality', 53.

[122] Arietta Papaconstantinou, 'The Cult of Saints: A Haven of Continuity in a Changing World?' in *Egypt in the Byzantine World, 300–700*, ed. Roger S. Bagnall (Cambridge: Cambridge University Press, 2007), 355–8.

[123] Wiśniewski, *Beginnings of the Cult of Relics*, 130–58.

place-bound medium', visually highlighting their presence in these spaces even though the relics themselves were neither visible nor tangible.[124] Comparison can be drawn between these Christian methods of marking relics' invisible but strongly-felt presence and the 'basket-shaped' column that marked the location of John's head. Rather than physically engaging with the remains directly, worshippers could interact with them indirectly, assisted by a visual marker of the relic's location.

Indeed, a close parallel to these Christian practices appears in one Islamic tradition about the Umayyad Mosque. The Syrian Muḥammad b. Shuʿayb (d. *c.* 199/814–15) reports that, as he was entering the mosque alongside a man named Shaddād b. ʿUbayd Allāh, the latter asked him: 'Do you see what is written there in Greek?'[125] 'Yes', Muḥammad answered, then performed two *rakʿa*s of prayer. He then said, 'Here is the head of Yaḥyā b. Zakariyyā.' Like Christians whose religious veneration in churches and shrines was often mediated by decorations indicating where relics were buried, here a Muslim is seemingly led by a Greek inscription to perform prayer in the location of John the Baptist's head. Even though John's head remained unseen, its presence spurred the performance of an act of veneration within the mosque.

[124] Ann Marie Yasin, 'Sacred Installations: The Material Conditions of Relic Collections in Late Antique Churches', in Hahn and Klein, *Saints and Sacred Matter*, 143–6; Ann Marie Yasin, 'Sight Lines of Sanctity at Late Antique Martyria', in *Architecture of the Sacred: Space, Ritual, and Experience from Classical Greece to Byzantium*, ed. Bonna D. Wescoat and Robert G. Ousterhout (Cambridge: Cambridge University Press, 2012), 248–80.

[125] Ibn ʿAsākir, *Taʾrīkh*, 2:242. The modern editor suggests that Ibn ʿAsākir's text should be corrected here to read 'Shaddād b. ʿAbd Allāh', the Syrian scholar also called Abū ʿAmmār. But the original text appears to be correct, since Muḥammad b. Shuʿayb is elsewhere listed as a transmitter from Shaddād b. ʿUbayd Allāh. Ibn ʿAsākir, *Taʾrīkh*, 22:426, 53:246; Ibn Abī Ḥātim, *Kitāb al-Jarḥ wa-l-taʿdīl*, ed. ʿAbd al-Raḥmān b. Yaḥyā al-Muʿallimī, 9 vols (Hyderabad: Dāʾirat al-Maʿārif al-ʿUthmāniyya, 1941–53), 2/1:331 (no. 1,450).

4

PARADOXES AND PROBLEMS OF THE PROPHETIC BODY: MUḤAMMAD'S CORPSE AND TOMB

Early Islamic traditions claimed that there were tens, or even hundreds, of prophets buried in the cities and regions spread throughout the Near Eastern world. One of these many prophets buried underground, unknown and uncelebrated, was Khālid b. Sinān: a wonder-worker from the Arab tribe of ʿAbs, who was said to have appeared in the Ḥijāz in the generations immediately preceding the birth of the Prophet Muḥammad.[1] In a story found in early *ḥadīth* and *akhbār* texts, Khālid's daughter (named Muḥayyāt in some versions) visits Muḥammad in Medina. The Prophet welcomes her: 'Greetings, daughter of my brother, daughter of a prophet abandoned by his people!'[2]

[1] *EI*[2], s.v. 'Khālid b. Sinān' (Charles Pellat); Ella Landau-Tasseron, 'Unearthing a Pre-Islamic Arabian Prophet', *JSAI* 21 (1997): 42–61; Hawting, 'Were There Prophets', 201–4; Christian Julien Robin, 'Les signes de la prophétie en Arabie à l'époque de Muḥammad (fin du VIe début du VIIe siècle de l'ère chrétienne)', in *La Raison des signes: Présages, rites, destin dans les sociétés de la Méditerranée ancienne*, ed. Stella Georgoudi, Renée Koch Piettre and Francis Schmidt (Leiden: Brill, 2012), 433–76; Aziz al-Azmeh, *The Emergence of Islam in Late Antiquity: Allāh and His People* (Cambridge: Cambridge University Press, 2017), 253–4.

[2] Abū ʿUthmān ʿAmr b. Baḥr al-Jāḥiẓ, *Kitāb al-Ḥayawān*, ed. ʿAbd al-Salām Muḥammad Hārūn, 8 vols (Cairo: Maktabat Muṣṭafā al-Bābī al-Ḥalabī, 1938–45), 4:477; Ibn Shabba, *Taʾrīkh*, 421, 423, 426, 433; Ibn Qutayba, *al-Maʿārif*, 62; Ibn ʿAbd al-Ḥakam, *Kitāb Futūḥ Miṣr wa-akhbāruhā*, ed. Charles C. Torrey (New Haven: Yale University Press, 1922), 229 fn.; al-Thaʿālibī, *Thimār al-qulūb*, 460 (no. 943); al-Kulaynī, *al-Kāfī*, 8:342–3 (no. 540).

With this mention of 'a prophet abandoned by his people', Muḥammad evokes the story of Khālid b. Sinān's death and burial, and his grave's abandonment by Khālid's community. According to this story, when Khālid neared death, he called his tribesmen and announced:

> When I die, bury me and watch my grave for three days. A herd of wild donkeys will arrive, including a donkey without a tail, who will sniff and walk around my grave. When you see this, disinter me and I will tell you all that will happen until the end of time.[3]

Three days after Khālid's death and burial, the herd arrived and the tail-less donkey acted just as Khālid had predicted. When his people were on the verge of exhuming Khālid as he had commanded, disagreement broke out among them about the acceptability of disinterring the dead. In several versions, Khālid's family dislike the idea, with Khālid's son worrying that he would be derisively known as Ibn al-Manbūsh, 'Son of the Disinterred'. In other versions, members of Khālid's tribe, the 'Abs, are anxious over what their reputation among the Arabs will be for such actions with the dead. As a result of these reservations, they leave Khālid in his grave: abandoned, and apparently never to be uncovered.[4]

Although Khālid's status as a prophet was debated among early Muslims, traditions indicate that many people (including the Prophet Muḥammad) recognised him as such.[5] With this in mind, Khālid's prediction – that he would emerge after three days with knowledge of all that would happen until the end of time – is compelling. In some versions, Khālid specifies that he will be found 'alive' (*ḥayy*) in his grave after three days.[6] The traditions do not spell out how Khālid would achieve this, nor do they make clear whether or not he was

[3] al-Jāḥiẓ, *Kitāb al-Ḥayawān*, 4:477; Ibn Shabba, *Taʾrīkh*, 422, 424, 425, 426, 432; Ibn Qutayba, *al-Maʿārif*, 62; Ibn ʿAbd al-Ḥakam, *Kitāb Futūḥ Miṣr*, 230 fn.; al-Thaʿālibī, *Thimār al-qulūb*, 460 (no. 943); al-Kulaynī, *al-Kāfī*, 8:342–3 (no. 540); Hawting, 'Were There Prophets', 202; Landau-Tasseron, 'Unearthing', 49.

[4] Later traditions did, however, establish multiple burial places for Khālid, located in Algeria, Tunisia and Syria: Landau-Tasseron, 'Unearthing', 43, 52–9.

[5] On debates about Khālid's status as a prophet, see al-Jāḥiẓ, *Kitāb al-Ḥayawān*, 4:478; Hawting, 'Were There Prophets', 202–3; Landau-Tasseron, 'Unearthing', 45–6.

[6] Ibn Shabba, *Taʾrīkh*, 422, 432.

successful. Yet his accurate prediction of the arrival of a herd of wild donkeys, including the tail-less donkey circling the grave, suggests that Khālid might, in fact, have come back to life. Indeed, Khālid's predicted miracle occurs after a previous series of wondrous feats (including extinguishing a miraculous fire that would spontaneously ignite and kill passers-by) fails to convince his tribe of his identity as a prophet.[7] The intended message of Khālid's story seems to be his tribe's failure to believe him, rather than his own failure to fulfil his prophesy. Khālid's status as 'abandoned' is a reflection of the lack of faith of his people, who would have received prophetic knowledge if only they had believed in their prophet. One wonders what the 'Abs tribe might have thought about all the other buried prophets that dotted the early Islamic landscape.

It is intriguing to consider Khālid's story alongside that of another prophet, whose grave was much better remembered among early Muslims: the Prophet Muḥammad. Within historical reports, Muḥammad's death is a highly traumatic event for the early Muslim community, some of whom deny that the Prophet had died at all. Drawing upon the examples of past prophets like Moses and Jesus – each of whom had temporarily left their respective communities to commune directly with God, or otherwise departed from earth in not entirely permanent ways – some Companions predict that the Prophet would likewise return to them, alive, within a few days. These pious Muslims acknowledge the reality of the Prophet's death only when this predicted return fails to materialise and, in some reports, when the physical decay of the Prophet's corpse illustrates the grim reality of his death. Rather than leaving a resurrected prophet trapped in his grave, as Khālid's unbelieving tribe had (seemingly) done, Muḥammad's believing community only buries its prophet once it seems apparent that his return to life would not be forthcoming.

This story of Muḥammad's death – reluctantly but finally acknowledged by his community – is the one narrated in early biographies of the Prophet. However, many texts also include traditions in which Muḥammad's death is not entirely final. Not only does Muḥammad's corpse fail to display any of the expected signs of decay, but the Prophet does, in fact, eventually return to some form of life in his tomb, not unlike what Khālid b. Sinān claimed would happen. In yet other traditions, the Prophet is not located in his tomb

[7] Landau-Tasseron, 'Unearthing', 47–51.

at all, but he is lifted in body and soul to Paradise, where he is eternally 'praying before God'. A rather complex and contradictory image of the Prophet, his body and his tomb thus appears in these variant traditions from the first centuries of Islam.

This chapter examines these different ideas of the Prophet Muḥammad's post-mortem existence, as well as their effects on a central aspect of his significance for early Muslims: as their intercessor before God. I suggest that early Muslims' variant understandings of Muḥammad's body are paralleled by – and can be contextualised within – the similarly complex images of other late antique holy persons' bodies. Christians and Jews also discussed the post-mortem existences of their saints and rabbis, evoking similarly paradoxical images of these holy persons and their relationships to their tombs. Especially among late antique Christians, these debates over saints' bodies implicated their understandings of these figures' post-mortem intercessions with God on behalf of the faithful. In the eighth and ninth centuries, Muslims likewise discussed the Prophet Muḥammad in ways suggesting that they believed that his body and tomb held significance for his own intercessory abilities. And like other late antique communities, early Muslims came to varied conclusions about the Prophet's status after death.

Conflicts over the Prophet's Corpse in Early *Sīra* and *Ḥadīth* Texts

The stories and statements about the Prophet Muḥammad's corpse found in early *ḥadīth* and *akhbār* display conflicting ideas about Muḥammad's mortal and corporeal status at the time of his death. Some traditions present the Prophet as present in his grave, even mouldering there, like a normal human body. Other traditions suggest that he was a miraculous being: undecaying, and perhaps even raised to heaven and totally transcending death. Likely 'reflect[ing] an ideological conflict within the earliest community', the dramatically different ideas about Muḥammad's existence after death flesh out conflicting conceptions of the nature of the Prophet himself.[8]

[8] Shoemaker, *Death of a Prophet*, 184.

On the one hand, several traditions present a hagiographic portrait of the Prophet Muḥammad's corpse, with his body exhibiting characteristics of a blessed, exceptional status, distinctly different from that of the average human being. As we saw in the previous chapter, the spectacular nature of the prophetic corpse is presaged in a *ḥadīth* in which Muḥammad states that 'God has forbidden the earth to consume the bodies of the prophets'.[9] This idea is actualised in history in *sīra* stories about Muḥammad's death and burial. As he is washing the Prophet's corpse in preparation for burial, 'Alī b. Abī Ṭālib exclaims, 'How fragrant you are, both alive and dead!', and it is narrated that 'nothing was observed on the Messenger of God of what is usually observed on the dead'.[10] The Prophet Muḥammad's body lies uncorrupted by death, demonstrating no signs of decay, and instead exuding the same sort of sweet smell that the living Prophet had exhibited.

On the other hand, several reports present Muḥammad's corpse as distinctly human, displaying a variety of details reflective of his body's natural decomposition. The story of the corpse's sweet fragrance is contradicted by narratives in which the Prophet's uncle al-'Abbās b. 'Abd al-Muṭṭalib (d. *c.* 32/653) argues that the Prophet must be buried since he has, in fact, begun to stink, 'decomposing as people do'.[11] In addition to its scent, the appearance of the Prophet's body is said to have changed, with specifications in some traditions that his fingernails had turned 'greenish' and that his stomach had

[9] Compare the fate of normal human beings' bodies: 'Abd al-Razzāq, *Muṣannaf*, 3:591 (no. 6,759). Commenting on another *ḥadīth* about the status of prophets after death, discussed below, Szilágyi notes that this statement is about 'prophets in general' but suggests that it is 'likely that early Muslims created and circulated these *ḥadīth*s out of interest in Muḥammad's, and not an earlier prophet's, postmortem fate'. This seems relevant to this *ḥadīth* as well. Szilágyi, 'Prophet Like Jesus', 141 and n.34.

[10] Ibn Hishām, *Sīra*, 1,018–19. Translation adapted from Szilágyi, 'Prophet Like Jesus', 157. This tradition is also found in Ibn Sa'd, *Ṭabaqāt*, 2:245; Ibn Abī Shayba, *Muṣannaf*, 13:459 (no. 38,030); al-Balādhurī, *Ansāb al-ashrāf*, 1:569, 571; al-Balādhurī, *Ansāb al-ashrāf*, ed. Suhayl Zakkār and Riyāḍ Ziriklī, 13 vols (Beirut: Dār al-Fikr, 1996), 2:245, 247; Abū Dāwūd Sulaymān b. al-Ash'ath al-Sijistānī, *al-Marāsīl*, ed. Shu'ayb al-Arnā'ūṭ (Beirut: Mu'assasat al-Risāla, 1988), 299 (no. 415). These words are also attributed to Abū Bakr in Ibn Sa'd, *Ṭabaqāt*, 2:232.

[11] Ibn Sa'd, *Ṭabaqāt*, 2:233; 'Abd al-Razzāq, *Muṣannaf*, 5:434–5; al-Dārimī, *Sunan*, 1:220–1 (no. 84); Shoemaker, *Death of a Prophet*, 70, 95, 185–6; Szilágyi, 'Prophet Like Jesus', 150–1.

begun to inflate.[12] In sum, according to these stories, 'death was apparent on him' when the Prophet's body was buried.[13] Instead of an inviolable prophetic body, we find here a very human corpse, subject to corruption and decay.

The differences between an exceptional and an unexceptional body are stark in these traditions. But, rather than being simply variant texts, these divergent representations of Muḥammad's corpse are reflective of larger debates about the very nature of the Prophet himself. Within the historiographical traditions about the events surrounding the Prophet's death, the notion that the Prophet would not simply die a natural death is often associated with the Companion and future caliph ʿUmar b. al-Khaṭṭāb. In Ibn Isḥāq's *Sīra*, ʿUmar recalls the scriptural story of Moses' forty-day meeting with God on Mount Sinai, declaring:

> By God, he is not dead! He has gone to his Lord as Moses b. ʿImrān went and was hidden from his people for forty days, returning to them after it was said that he was dead. By God, the Messenger of God will return, just as Moses returned.[14]

In other versions, ʿUmar suggests that Muḥammad has been 'raised in his spirit' (*ʿurija bi-rūḥi-hi*) as Moses was, perhaps specifying his 'spirit' in order to account for the continued terrestrial presence of the Prophet's body.[15] ʿUmar's disbelief in the possibility of the Prophet's death also appears earlier, in a story set while the Prophet was still on his deathbed. Asked to bring a

[12] Ibn Saʿd, *Ṭabaqāt*, 2:236, 239; Tayeb El-Hibri, *Parable and Politics in Early Islamic History: The Rashidun Caliphs* (New York: Columbia University Press, 2010), 27.

[13] Ibn Saʿd, *Ṭabaqāt*, 2:239; Szilágyi, 'Prophet Like Jesus', 148.

[14] Ibn Hishām, *Sīra*, 1012; al-Ṭabarī, *Tāʾrīkh*, 1/4:1,815–16; *The History of al-Ṭabarī. Volume IX: The Last Years of the Prophet*, trans. Ismail K. Poonawala (Albany: State University of New York Press, 1990), 184; al-Balādhurī, *Ansāb al-ashrāf*, 1:565–6 (no. 1,149). In another version, ʿUmar says that 'his Lord summoned the Messenger of God' as He had summoned Moses: Ibn Saʿd, *Ṭabaqāt*, 2:233, 235; ʿAbd al-Razzāq, *Muṣannaf*, 5:433; Ibn Abī Shayba, *Muṣannaf*, 13:459–60 (no. 38,033). See Shoemaker, *Death of a Prophet*, 91, 94, 179; Szilágyi, 'Prophet Like Jesus', 149–50; El-Hibri, *Parable and Politics*, 28, 40. The qurʾānic mentions of Moses on Mount Sinai (Q 2:51 and 7:142) recall Ex. 24:18 and 34:28.

[15] Ibn Saʿd, *Ṭabaqāt*, 2:233; al-Dārimī, *Sunan*, 1:220–1 (no. 84); al-Balādhurī, *Ansāb al-ashrāf*, 1:567 (no. 1,151). Ibn Saʿd's and al-Dārimī's versions also say that 'they said that he has been raised in his spirit as Moses was', without specifying the speakers.

pen and paper so that the Prophet could record his final wishes, ʿUmar refuses and says: 'Whose, then, will be the cities of Rome? The Prophet will not die until we conquer them, and even if he dies, we shall expect him as the children of Israel expected Moses.'[16] In this tradition, ʿUmar treats the Prophet as an apocalyptic figure, whose death would not occur before the 'cities of Rome' had been conquered by the pious Muslim community.

Early sources attribute similar beliefs to other Companions. In a tradition found in the historian al-Balādhurī's biographical collection *Ansāb al-ashrāf* (Genealogies of the Nobles), the Companion and caliph ʿUthmān b. ʿAffān states, 'The Messenger of God has not died, but he has been raised as Jesus b. Mary was raised', echoing the qurʾānic description of Jesus being raised to God (Q 3:55 and 4:158).[17] The historian Muḥammad b. Saʿd's (d. 230/845) biographical compendium *al-Ṭabaqāt al-kubrā* (Great Book of Generations) includes traditions suggesting that such beliefs were widespread, with the Prophet's Companions wondering among themselves if 'perhaps he was taken up', and 'the people' (*al-nās*) suggesting that the Prophet 'did not die but was raised, as Jesus b. Mary was raised'.[18] These traditions reflect not only denials of Muḥammad's death, but also a belief in the exceptional nature of God's prophet.

Within the canonical narratives of the Prophet's life, these ideas about his death are stopped in their tracks by assertions from prominent members of the early Muslim community that Muḥammad had, in fact, died. In a widely-narrated version, the first caliph Abū Bakr al-Ṣiddīq corrects any misconceptions about the Prophet's death by citing Qurʾān 3:144, which intimates Muḥammad's mortality: 'Muḥammad is only a messenger, before whom many

[16] Ibn Saʿd, *Ṭabaqāt*, 2:215; Said Amir Arjomand, 'Islamic Apocalypticism in the Classic Period', in *The Encyclopedia of Apocalypticism. Volume 2: Apocalypticism in Western History and Culture*, ed. Bernard McGinn (New York: Continuum, 1998), 247. A different interpretation of the narrative appears in Gurdofarid Miskinzoda, 'The Story of "Pen and Paper" and its Interpretation in Muslim Literary and Historical Tradition', in *The Study of Shiʿi Islam: History, Theology and Law*, ed. Farhad Daftary and Gurdofarid Miskinzoda (London: I. B. Tauris in association with the Institute for Ismaili Studies, 2014), 240–1.

[17] al-Balādhurī, *Ansāb al-ashrāf*, 1:567; Szilágyi, 'Prophet Like Jesus', 152.

[18] Ibn Saʿd, *Ṭabaqāt*, 2:236–7; Szilágyi, 'Prophet Like Jesus', 151–2; El-Hibri, *Parable and Politics*, 347 n.7.

messengers have been and gone. If he died or was killed, would you revert to your old ways?'[19] Abū Bakr thus appeals to qur'ānic authority to demonstrate the possibility of the Prophet's death, which should ideally change nothing about the Islamic community's adherence to God's message. In another tradition (mentioned above), al-ʿAbbās asserts, 'The Messenger of God has died. He is a mortal, and he decomposes as mortals do. People, bury your master.' Viscerally pointing to the physical reality of the Prophet's death, al-ʿAbbās argues that the corpse's decay demonstrates that death has occurred, and that his mortality must therefore be acknowledged.

In several texts, ʿUmar himself reacts to these events by recanting his previous statements about the Prophet's death. In a story set during Abū Bakr's nomination as the first caliph, ʿUmar states that his denial of the Prophet's death had been based neither in the Qur'ān nor in any testament from the Prophet. Rather, his comments had emerged from his own mistaken belief 'that the Messenger of God would live until we had passed away, meaning he would be the last of us [alive]',[20] or (in a slightly different version) 'that the Messenger of God would manage our affairs until he was the last of us [alive]'.[21] However, in a later story, set during his time as caliph, ʿUmar says that his belief had in fact emerged from the Qur'ān:

> By God, what brought me to that was when I would recite the verse, 'We have made you into a middle community, so that you may bear witness before others and so that the Messenger may bear witness before you' (Q. 2:143). By God, I thought that the Messenger of God would remain in his community such that he would bear witness to the last of [the community's] actions. That was what brought me to say what I said.[22]

According to this tradition, ʿUmar's own exegesis of the Qur'ān had driven him to believe that the Prophet would not die until an apocalyptic moment. ʿUmar thus offers an eschatological reading of both the Prophet's life and the Islamic scripture.

[19] Shoemaker, *Death of a Prophet*, 179–88; El-Hibri, *Parable and Politics*, 40.

[20] ʿAbd al-Razzāq, *Muṣannaf*, 5:437–8; Ibn Saʿd, *Ṭabaqāt*, 2:236.

[21] Ibn Hishām, *Sīra*, 1,017; al-Ṭabarī, *Tāʾrīkh*, 1/4:1828; *History of al-Ṭabarī*, 9:200.

[22] Ibn Hishām, *Sīra*, 1,018; al-Ṭabarī, *Tāʾrīkh*, 1/4:1,829–30; *History of al-Ṭabarī*, 9:201; al-Balādhurī, *Ansāb al-ashrāf*, 1:568 (no. 1,152).

In these traditions, ʿUmar serves 'as a mouthpiece for the primitive community's belief that Muhammad would live until the Hour', who conveniently repudiates his words within days of the Prophet's death thanks to the counsel of other prominent Companions.[23] Whether or not such disagreements actually occurred immediately following the Prophet's death, these traditions demonstrate that stories about the Companions' reluctance to bury Muḥammad, and belief that he might have been raised to heaven, 'circulated in the entire Caliphate from the early eighth century onwards'.[24] As both Shoemaker and Krisztina Szilágyi argue, it is unlikely that such stories were invented at a late date.[25] The placement of such beliefs within the mouths and minds of the earliest Companions may or may not be a pious fiction, but as Shoemaker notes, 'it is unimaginable that the later Islamic tradition would address such beliefs so directly if in fact they were not widespread within the early community'.[26]

In Heaven and On Earth: Locating the Prophet's Body in the Eighth and Ninth Centuries

It seems, though, that these stories reflect the debates of the eighth and ninth centuries just as much as any arguments contemporaneous with Muḥammad's actual death and burial. Variant ideas about the Prophet are set in opposition to one another in traditions about the Companions, but with the victory of a human image in Muḥammad's mortal death. Yet, despite the quick conclusion presented by these narratives, other texts feature seventh-, eighth- and

[23] Shoemaker, *Death of a Prophet*, 186–8.

[24] Szilágyi, 'Prophet Like Jesus', 153. On the basis of *isnād* analysis, Szilágyi argues that these stories were circulating in Iraq 'by the beginning of the eighth century or earlier' and that stories about the Prophet's belated burial 'circulated in Syria already in the first decades of the eighth century or earlier'. Ibid., 147, 149. Shoemaker similarly suggests that 'a tradition indicating the initial denial of Muḥammad's death by at least some within the earliest Islamic community [. . .] can be traced back to [Ibn Shihāb] al-Zuhrī's teaching', and thus at least to the mid-eighth century. Shoemaker, *Death of a Prophet*, 94–5.

[25] Shoemaker dates the reports to no later than the early eighth century, while Szilágyi suggests they may be rooted in the events immediately following Muḥammad's death. Shoemaker, *Death of a Prophet*, 94–5, 184; Szilágyi, 'Prophet Like Jesus', 154–5.

[26] Shoemaker, *Death of a Prophet*, 187.

ninth-century Muslims professing beliefs about Muḥammad very similar to those that had been attributed to the Companions. While the biographical traditions suggest that beliefs about Muḥammad's exceptional post-mortem status were stamped out at the moment of their genesis, it appears that these ideas did not simply disappear. Instead, we see them living on (or resurfacing) in traditions attributed to later figures in both Sunnī and Shīʿī sources. Rather than an obscure mistake, these traditions 'indicate a belief in Muḥammad's ascension to heaven after his death in some circles in pre-classical Islam', alongside competing conceptions of the Prophet's body.[27]

Claims about the Prophet's ascension after death occur in both Sunnī and Shīʿī sources. For example, the Medinan jurist Saʿīd b. al-Musayyab (d. 94/712–13) reportedly declared that 'no prophet remains in the earth for more than forty days'.[28] The wording here suggests that any prophet, including Muḥammad, would be raised to heaven within forty days. This idea is made more explicit in a variant of Saʿīd's statement, 'No prophet remains in his grave for more than forty nights before he is lifted (*yurfiʿa*)'.[29] A Prophetic *ḥadīth* similarly narrates, 'The prophets do not stay in their graves longer than forty nights, but are praying before God until the horn is blown', meaning until the Day of Judgement.[30] Whether it is a prophet's body or soul that is 'lifted' from the grave is not entirely clear, but the mentions of not remaining 'in the earth' or 'in the grave' suggest that the prophet's body is involved.[31]

Indeed, Shīʿī collections explicitly evoke the prophets' corpses in traditions about God lifting prophets after their deaths. In a collection attributed to the Zaydī scholar Aḥmad b. ʿĪsā b. Zayd (d. 247/861–2), Muḥammad b. al-Ḥanafiyya reports that his father ʿAlī b. Abī Ṭālib said that 'God does not leave a prophet's corpse (*juththa*) under the earth for more than forty nights

[27] Szilágyi, 'Prophet Like Jesus', 145.

[28] ʿAbd al-Razzāq, *Muṣannaf*, 3:576–7 (no. 6,725); Szilágyi, 'Prophet Like Jesus', 142. The *isnād* is: ʿAbd al-Razzāq > Sufyān al-Thawrī (d. 161/778, Kūfa) > Abū al-Miqdām [Thābit b. Hurmuz] (d. unknown, Kūfa) > Saʿīd b. al-Musayyab.

[29] al-Bayhaqī, *Ḥayāt al-anbiyāʾ*, 76–7; Szilágyi, 'Prophet Like Jesus', 142 n.39. The *isnād* is: Sufyān al-Thawrī in his *Jāmiʿ* > 'one of our shaykhs' (*shaykh li-nā*) > Saʿīd b. al-Musayyab.

[30] al-Bayhaqī, *Ḥayāt al-anbiyāʾ*, 75. On the *isnād*, see Szilágyi, 'Prophet Like Jesus', 143–4.

[31] al-Bayhaqī, *Ḥayāt al-anbiyāʾ*, 76 comments that 'it is possible that the meaning is that their bodies were lifted with their spirits'.

before He lifts it to Him'.[32] In the same collection, a report from the Prophet's cousin, the revered scholar ʿAbd Allāh b. ʿAbbās (d. *c.* 68/688), says that 'God does not leave a prophet under the earth for more than forty nights before he lifts [the prophet] to Him'.[33] In Imāmī collections, Jaʿfar al-Ṣādiq declares, 'No prophet or legatee (*waṣī*) remains in the earth for more than three days before

[32] Aḥmad b. ʿĪsā b. Zayd, *Kitāb Raʾb al-ṣadʿ: Amālī al-Imām Aḥmad b. ʿĪsā b. Zayd b. ʿAlī b. al-Ḥusayn b. ʿAlī b. Abī Ṭālib*, ed. ʿAlī b. Ismāʿīl b. ʿAbd Allāh al-Muʿayyad al-Ṣanʿānī, 3 vols (Beirut: Dār al-Nafāʾis, 1990), 2:838 (no. 1,367). On this text, see Najam Haider, *The Origins of the Shīʿa: Identity, Ritual, and Sacred Space in Eighth-Century Kūfa* (Cambridge: Cambridge University Press, 2011), 33–4. The *isnād* is: Muḥammad [b. Manṣūr al-Murādī] (d. *c.* 290/903, Kūfa) > Abū Ṭāhir [Aḥmad b. ʿĪsā b. ʿAbd Allāh b. Muḥammad b. ʿUmar b. ʿAlī b. Abī Ṭālib] (Medina) > his father [ʿĪsā b. ʿAbd Allāh] (Medina) > his father [ʿAbd Allāh b. Muḥammad b. ʿUmar] (d. *c.* 158/775, Medina) > [ʿAbd Allāh b. Muḥammad] Ibn ʿAqīl (Medina, d. after 140/757–8) > Muḥammad b. al-Ḥanafiyya (d. 81/700) > his father [ʿAlī b. Abī Ṭālib]. On Muḥammad b. Manṣūr al-Murādī, see Najam Haider, 'A Kūfan Jurist in Yemen: Contextualizing Muḥammad b. Sulaymān al-Kūfī's *Kitāb al-Muntahab*', *Arabica* 59 (2012): 200–17. On Abū Ṭāhir and his father and grandfather, see Amikam Elad, *The Rebellion of Muḥammad al-Nafs al-Zakiyya in 145/762: Ṭālibīs and Early ʿAbbāsīs in Conflict* (Leiden: Brill, 2016), 8, 80, 401, 469; Tilman Nagel, 'Ein früher Bericht über den Aufstand von Muḥammad b. ʿAbdallāh im Jahre 145 h', *Der Islam* 46 (1970): 242; Ibn Ḥazm, *Jamharat ansāb al-ʿarab*, ed. ʿAbd al-Salām Muḥammad Hārūn (Cairo: Dār al-Maʿārif, 1962), 66; Ibn Saʿd, *Ṭabaqāt*, 7:545; al-Dhahabī, *Mīzān*, 1:148 (no. 476); Ibn Abī Ḥātim, *Kitāb al-Jarḥ*, 1/1:65 (no. 111). On Ibn ʿAqīl, see Ibn Saʿd, *Ṭabaqāt*, 7:481–2; al-Dhahabī, *Siyar*, 6:204–5; Ibn Ḥazm, *Jamharat*, 69; Elad, *Rebellion of Muḥammad*, 268.

[33] Aḥmad b. ʿĪsā b. Zayd, *Raʾb al-ṣadʿ*, 2:838–9 (no. 1,368). The *isnād* is: Muḥammad [b. Manṣūr al-Murādī] > Aḥmad b. Abī ʿAbd al-Raḥmān > al-Ḥasan b. Muḥammad [b. Farqad] > al-Ḥakam b. Ẓuhayr (d. *c.* 180/796–7, Kūfa) > al-Suddī [Ismāʿīl b. ʿAbd al-Raḥmān] (d. 127/744–5, Kūfa) > Abū Mālik [Ghazwān al-Ghifārī] (d. before 100/718–19, Kūfa) > Ibn ʿAbbās. On the obscure Aḥmad b. Abī ʿAbd al-Raḥmān and al-Ḥasan b. Muḥammad, see Aḥmad b. ʿĪsā b. Zayd, *Raʾb al-ṣadʿ*, 3:1898. Al-Ḥakam b. Ẓuhayr was a transmitter criticised by *ḥadīth* critics and accused of *rafḍ* (i.e. rejection of the first two caliphs) and of denigrating the Prophet's Companions: Ibn Abī Ḥātim, *Kitāb al-Jarḥ*, 1/2:118–19 (no. 550); al-Bukhārī, *al-Tārīkh al-Kabīr*, 1/ii: 345 (no. 2,694); Abū Jaʿfar Muḥammad b. ʿAmr al-ʿUqaylī, *Kitāb al-Ḍuʿafāʾ al-kabīr*, ed. ʿAbd al-Muʿṭī Amīn Qalʿajī, 4 vols (Beirut: Dār al-Kutub al-ʿIlmiyya, 1984), 1:259 (no. 316); Muḥammad b. Ḥibbān, *Kitāb al-Majrūḥīn min al-muḥaddithīn*, ed. Ḥamdī ʿAbd al-Majīd al-Salafī, 2 vols (Riyadh: Dār al-Ṣumayʿī, 2000), 1:304; Ibn Ḥajar al-ʿAsqalānī, *Taqrīb al-tahdhīb*, ed. Abū al-Ashbāl Ṣaghīr Aḥmad Shāghif al-Bākistānī (Riyadh: Dār al-ʿĀṣima, 1995), 262 (no. 1,454). Ismāʿīl b. ʿAbd al-Raḥmān al-Suddī was a qurʾānic exegete and preacher, who reportedly denigrated Abū Bakr and ʿUmar and was

he is lifted to the sky in his spirit, his bones, and his flesh.'[34] The implications of this bodily movement are laid out in another Imāmī *ḥadīth*, where Jaʿfar al-Ṣādiq is asked, 'If the grave of al-Ḥusayn were disinterred, would they find anything in it?' Jaʿfar responds, 'If he had been disinterred in his own day, he would have been found [in the grave], but today he is alive with his Lord.'[35] As al-Ḥusayn is said to be living in heaven in 'the house (*manzil*) of the Messenger of God', it seems that the Prophet is likely in heaven as well, though his body may too have once been in its grave.

Other traditions, however, imply that Muḥammad is not located in heaven, but instead is corporeally present in his tomb in Medina. 'The prophets are alive praying in their graves' (*al-anbīyā' aḥyā' fī qubūrihim yuṣallūna*) runs one Prophetic *ḥadīth*, suggesting that prophets such as Muḥammad are terrestrially located in their tombs.[36] Similarly, a *ḥadīth* records Muḥammad's

accused of *tashayyuʿ*: Ibn Abī Ḥātim, *Kitāb al-Jarḥ*, 1/1:184 (no. 625); al-ʿUqaylī, *Kitāb al-Ḍuʿafā'*, 1:87–8 (no. 101); Ibn Ḥajar, *Taqrīb al-tahdhīb*, 141 (no. 467); *EI*², s.v. 'al-Suddī' (G. H. A. Juynboll). Abū Mālik was also associated with qur'ānic exegesis: Ibn Saʿd, *Ṭabaqāt*, 8:412; al-Dhahabī, *Ta'rīkh*, 6 [81–100]:450.

[34] al-Kulaynī, *al-Kāfī*, 4:567; al-Ṣaffār, *Baṣā'ir al-darajāt*, 2:349; Ibn Qūlūya, *Kāmil al-ziyārāt*, ed. Jawād al-Qayyūmī (Qum: Mu'assasat Nashr al-Faqāha, 1997), 544 (*bāb* 108, nos 3–4); Ibn Bābawayh al-Qummī, *Kitāb Man lā yaḥḍuru al-faqīh*, ed. Ḥusayn al-Aʿlamī, 2 vols (Beirut: Mu'assasat al-Aʿlamī li-l-Maṭbūʿāt, 1986), 2:360 (no. 3,161); Abū Jaʿfar Muḥammad b. al-Ḥasan al-Ṭūsī, *Tahdhīb al-aḥkām fī sharḥ al-Muqniʿa li-l-shaykh al-Mufīd*, ed. Muḥammad Jaʿfar Shams al-Dīn, 10 vols (Beirut: Dār al-Taʿāruf li-l-Maṭbūʿāt, 1992), 6:84. Szilágyi, 'Prophet Like Jesus', 145 writes that the *isnād*s found in these traditions – all beginning Aḥmad b. Muḥammad b. ʿĪsā > ʿAlī b. al-Ḥakam b. al-Zubayr > Ziyād b. Abī Ḥilāl > Jaʿfar al-Ṣādiq – suggest that this *ḥadīth* circulated in Kūfa in the late eighth and early ninth centuries. See also Crow, 'Death of al-Ḥusayn', 61 n.47. On Ziyād b. Abī Ḥilāl see Aḥmad b. ʿAlī al-Najāshī, *Rijāl al-Najāshī*, ed. Mūsā al-Shubayrī al-Zanjānī (Qom: Mu'assasat al-Nashr al-Islāmī, 1418 AH [1997–8]), 171 (no. 451). On ʿAlī b. al-Ḥakam, see Hossein Modarressi, *Tradition and Survival: A Bibliographical Survey of Early Shīʿite Literature. Volume One* (Oxford: Oneworld, 2003), 243, 360, 371. On Aḥmad b. Muḥammad b. ʿĪsā, see al-Najāshī, *Rijāl*, 81–3 (no. 198). A slightly variant tradition appears in al-Ṭūsī, *Tahdhīb al-aḥkām*, 6:84. On this version and its *isnād*, see Szilágyi, 'Prophet Like Jesus', 145 with n. 53.

[35] Ibn Qūlūya, *Kāmil al-ziyārāt*, 206 (no. 292), 543–4 (no. 830); Crow, 'Death of al-Ḥusayn', 62–3.

[36] Abū Yaʿlā, *Musnad*, 6:147 (no. 3,425); al-Bazzār, *Musnad*, 13:299–300 (no. 6,888); Ibn ʿAdī, *al-Kāmil*, 2:739; Nūr al-Dīn al-Haythamī, *Majmaʿ al-zawā'id wa-manbaʿ al-fawā'id*,

vision, during his Night Journey, of the prophet Moses standing and praying in his grave.[37] This idea is connected to Muḥammad specifically in traditions where Saʿīd b. al-Musayyab hears a voice performing the call to prayer from within Muḥammad's tomb, suggesting his presence there.[38] In a more risqué speculation about the Prophet's post-mortem activities, a Shīʿī tradition relates that Jaʿfar al-Ṣādiq warned individuals not to climb upon the Prophet's tomb while it was being reconstructed, since 'I am not sure whether or not [such a person] would see something that would take away his sight, or see [the Prophet] standing and performing his prayers, or see him together with one of his wives'.[39]

These descriptions of Muḥammad and other prophets as 'alive in their graves' might appear to grant them an exceptional status, unlike that of normal bodies decaying in the ground. While this is true to an extent, it is necessary to read this image within the context of late antique ideas about the fate of the body after death and the 'punishment of the grave' (*ʿadhāb al-qabr*). As Leor Halevi writes, 'Muslims [. . .] believed in a close connection between body and soul even beyond the moment of death'.[40] According to this post-mortem anthropology, the body and soul are united in the tomb in a (semi-)conscious

ed. Ḥusayn Salīm Asad al-Dārānī, 30 vols (Jeddah: Dār al-Minhāj, 2010), 17:51 (no. 13,833); al-Bayhaqī, *Ḥayāt al-anbiyāʾ*, 69–74; Ibn ʿAsākir, *Taʾrīkh*, 13:326; Katz, 'Prophet Muḥammad in Ritual', 148; Knight, *Muhammad's Body*, 142.

37 ʿAbd al-Razzāq, *Muṣannaf*, 3:577 (no. 6,727); Ibn Abī Shayba, *Muṣannaf*, 13:219 (no. 37,572); Muslim, *Ṣaḥīḥ*, 4:1845 (no. 2,375) (*kitāb faḍāʾil*, *bāb* 42); al-Nasāʾī, *Sunan*, 269–70 (nos 1,631–7); Abū Yaʿlā, *Musnad*, 6:71 (no. 3,325); al-Bayhaqī, *Ḥayāt al-anbiyāʾ*, 79–81; al-Bayhaqī, *Dalāʾil al-nubuwwa*, 2:361, 387; Ibn Balbān, *Ṣaḥīḥ Ibn Ḥibbān*, 1:241–7 (nos 49–50); Ibn Ḥibbān, *Kitāb al-Majrūḥīn*, 1:285–6; Ibn ʿAsākir, *Taʾrīkh*, 61:182–5; Abū Nuʿaym, *Ḥilyat al-awliyaʾ*, 8:333; Amikam El'ad, 'Some Aspects of the Islamic Traditions Regarding the Site of the Grave of Moses', *JSAI* 11 (1988): 1–15.

38 Ibn Saʿd, *Ṭabaqāt*, 7:132; al-Dārimī, *Sunan*, 1:227–8 (no. 94); Abū Nuʿaym, *Dalāʾil al-nubuwwa*, 496. Cf. Szilágyi, 'Prophet Like Jesus', 143 and n.41.

39 al-Kulaynī, *al-Kāfī*, 1:452; Fritz Meier, 'A Resurrection of Muḥammad in Suyūṭī', in *Essays on Islamic Piety and Mysticism*, trans. John O'Kane (Leiden: Brill, 1999), 518–19; Mohammad Ali Amir-Moezzi, The *Divine Guide in Early Shiʿism: The Sources of Esotericism in Islam*, trans. David Streight (Albany: State University of New York Press, 1994), 194 n.375.

40 Halevi, *Muhammad's Grave*, 81, 207–13. For a striking image of the dead body appearing 'alive', see ʿAbd al-Razzāq, *Muṣannaf*, 3:589–90 (no. 6,756); Halevi, *Muhammad's Grave*, 211–12.

state until the day of resurrection. The idea of individuals being 'alive' in their graves was widespread in the Near East at least by the early eighth century, and similar ideas appear in Eastern Christian and Jewish sources on the afterlife.[41]

Notably, both good and evil individuals were believed to experience this 'punishment of the grave', though usually with varying degrees of suffering.[42] A tradition attributed to Jaʿfar al-Ṣādiq states that the Shīʿa will receive the Prophet's intercession on the day of the resurrection, but will nonetheless suffer in the grave during the intervening period.[43] There was fear of this experience even for the righteous: the Prophet himself prayed that he be spared 'the punishment of the grave'.[44] In this sense, prophets being 'alive in their graves' is not exceptional, except that their suffering there is relatively minimal, if not entirely absent.[45] Indeed, the prophets' location in their graves displays their status as mortals, subject to the rules of the resurrection like other human beings. Rather than their being granted a special place in heaven before the resurrection, this image of the prophets offers a more terrestrial and mortal depiction of their post-mortem state.

We thus have a contradictory image of the Prophet. According to some reports, he was raised to heaven; according to others, he remains in his grave awaiting the resurrection. The contradiction is strikingly illustrated by the ascription to both Saʿīd b. al-Musayyab and Jaʿfar al-Ṣādiq of these disparate and seemingly irreconcilable understandings of the Prophet's location. Both men are credited with sayings, discussed above, that indicate that the Prophet was raised to heaven, and, alternatively, with sayings indicating that the Prophet was in his grave. Directly conflicting positions regarding the Prophet's status after death are thus attributed to these authoritative Sunnī and Shīʿī figures.

41 Halevi, *Muhammad's Grave*, 218, 223–5. From rabbinic texts, see *b. Ber.* 18a-b and *b. Shab.* 152b. On 'soul sleep' in late antique Christian texts, see Dal Santo, *Debating the Saints' Cult*, 35, 240–54, 286; Nicholas Constas, '"To Sleep, Perchance to Dream": The Middle State of Souls in Patristic and Byzantine Literature', *DOP* 55 (2001): 91–124.

42 Halevi, *Muhammad's Grave*, 208, 213, 219, 221, 328 n.46.

43 al-Kulaynī, *al-Kāfī*, 3:242; Halevi, *Muhammad's Grave*, 216. The Babylonian Talmud states that the bones of the righteous will not rot, though they will nonetheless be located in the grave until the Day of Judgement (*b. Shab.* 152b).

44 ʿAbd al-Razzāq, *Muṣannaf*, 3:585 (no. 6,743), 3:589 (no. 6,755); Ibn Abī Shayba, *Muṣannaf*, 4:611–14 (nos 12,145–57); Halevi, *Muhammad's Grave*, 218, 220.

45 Halevi, *Muhammad's Grave*, 219.

An explanation for these contradictions may appear in the traditions' *isnāds*, which indicate some degree of regional differences in ideas about the Prophet's post-mortem location. The *isnāds* of Saʿīd b. al-Musayyab's and Jaʿfar al-Ṣādiq's comments indicate that their traditions about prophets' ascension circulated in Kūfa in the mid-to-late eighth century.[46] This is also true of the Zaydī tradition attributed to Ibn ʿAbbās. In contrast, the traditions in which Saʿīd b. al-Musayyab hears a voice from inside the Prophet's tomb were transmitted in this same period by Ḥijāzīs and Syrians.[47] Perhaps, then, the idea of Muḥammad's being lifted to heaven was favoured in Iraq, and especially Kūfa, while the presence of the Prophet's body in his grave was favoured further west.

We might further hypothesise that traditions about the Prophet's location within his grave were expressions of regional pride in the Prophet's grave in the city of Medina.[48] The Prophet's bodily presence within his tomb in Medina

[46] Szilágyi, 'Prophet Like Jesus', 143–6. The fact that both proto-Sunnīs and Shīʿīs in the eighth century transmitted such traditions about the Prophet's resurrected body may indicate that this was a fairly widespread or common idea there, since recent research indicates that there were fairly distinct Shīʿī and non-Shīʿī communities in Kūfa by the early eighth century. Haider, *Origins of the Shīʿa*.

[47] Ibn Saʿd, *Ṭabaqāt*, 7:132: al-Walīd b. ʿAṭāʾ (d. unknown, Ḥijāz) > ʿAbd al-Ḥamīd b. Sulaymān (d. unknown, Medina/Baghdad) > Abū Ḥāzim [Salama b. Dīnār] (d. *c.* 135/752, Medina) > Saʿīd b. al-Musayyab. The same first three links are found in Abū Nuʿaym, *Dalāʾil al-nubuwwa*, 496: Muḥammad b. ʿAbd al-ʿAzīz b. Sahl al-Khashab al-Naysābūrī > Ibrāḥīm b. Isḥāq al-Anmāṭī > Muḥammad b. Sulaymān Luwayn (d. *c.* 246/861, Kūfa and al-Maṣṣīṣa) > ʿAbd al-Ḥamīd b. Sulaymān > Abū Ḥāzim > Saʿīd b. al-Musayyab. The common link here, ʿAbd al-Ḥamīd b. Sulaymān, was considered weak (*ḍaʿīf*) by several *ḥadīth* scholars: Ibn Ḥajar al-ʿAsqalānī, *Tahdhīb al-tahdhīb*, ed. Ibrāhīm al-Zaybaq and ʿĀdil Murshid, 4 vols (Beirut: Muʾassasat al-Risāla, 1995), 2:476; al-Khaṭīb al-Baghdādī, *Taʾrīkh*, 12:335–8. On Muḥammad b. Sulaymān Luwayn see Luke Yarbrough, 'Upholding God's Rule: Early Muslim Juristic Opposition to the State Employment of non-Muslims', *ILS* 19 (2012): 27 n.58, 33 n.82; Benjamin Jokisch, *Islamic Imperial Law: Harun-al-Rashid's Codification Project* (Berlin: Walter de Gruyter, 2007), 387 n.459. A completely different Syrian *isnād* appears in al-Dārimī, *Sunan*, 1:227–8 (no. 94): Marwān b. Muḥammad al-Ṭāṭarī (d. 210/825, Damascus) > Saʿīd b. ʿAbd al-ʿAzīz al-Tanūkhī (d. 167/783–4, Damascus) > Saʿīd b. al-Musayyab. On Saʿīd b. ʿAbd al-ʿAzīz al-Tanūkhī, see: Juynboll, *Muslim Tradition*, 45; El'ad, 'Grave of Moses', 11 n.35, 15.

[48] On regional pride as a factor in early Islamic relic cult, see Shoemaker, *Death of a Prophet*, 260.

certainly undergirds some traditions within early texts. One example is a report attributed to Kaʿb al-Aḥbār:

> No dawn arises without 70,000 angels descending, touching the [Prophet's] grave with their wings and surrounding it. They ask forgiveness for him, give him what contents him, and pray for him until the evening. In the evening, they arise and [another] 70,000 angels descend, touching the grave with their wings and surrounding it. They ask forgiveness for him, give what contents him, and pray for him until morning. So it goes until the Hour. On the Day of Judgment, the Prophet will emerge among 70,000 angels.[49]

The Prophet's body is not explicitly said to be inside his grave, but the angels 'give what contents him', suggesting his presence there in some capacity. The angels demonstrate that the grave is a place of special significance: indeed, it is from here that the Prophet will 'emerge' on the Day of Judgement. Transmitted by Egyptians and Ḥijāzīs, the tradition celebrates the Prophet's grave as a holy site, with angelic visitors and eschatological significance.

A further indication of regional variation – again related to tomb veneration – appears in a version of the Prophet Muḥammad's vision of Moses praying in his grave. In this version, the Prophet says: 'I passed by Moses on the night I was taken up, and he was standing and praying between ʿĀliya and ʿUwayliya.'[50] Here,

[49] ʿAbd Allāh b. al-Mubārak, *Kitāb al-Zuhd wa yalīhi Kitāb al-Raqāʾiq*, ed. Ḥabīb al-Raḥmān al-ʿAẓamī (Beirut: Dār al-Kutub al-ʿIlmiyya, n.d.), 558 (no. 1,600): al-Ḥusayn al-Marwazī (d. 246/860–1, Mecca) > Ibn al-Mubārak > ʿAbd Allāh b. Lahīʿa (d. 174/790, Egypt) > Khālid b. Yazīd (d. 139/757, Egypt) > Saʿīd b. Abī Hilāl (d. 135/753 or 149/766, Egypt and Medina) > Nubayh b. Wahb b. ʿUthmān (d. unknown, Ḥijāz) > Kaʿb al-Aḥbār. The same first four links are found in al-Dārimī, *Sunan*, 1:228 (no. 95): ʿAbd Allāh b. Ṣāliḥ (d. 223/838; Egypt) > al-Layth b. Saʿd (d. 175/791, Egypt) > Khālid b. Yazīd, etc. This *isnād* is also found in Abū Nuʿaym, *Ḥilyat al-awliyaʾ*, 5:390: Ibrāhīm b. ʿAbd Allāh b. al-Junayd (d. unknown, Baghdad) > Muḥammad b. al-Ḥusayn al-Burjulānī (d. 238/852, Baghdad) > Qutayba b. Saʿīd b. Jamīl (d. 240/854, Baghdad) > al-Layth, etc. See also Ismāʿīl b. Isḥāq, *Faḍl al-ṣalāt*, 92 (no. 101); Abū Bakr Aḥmad b. al-Ḥusayn al-Bayhaqī, *al-Jāmiʿ li-shuʿab al-īmān*, ed. Mukhtār Aḥmad al-Narwī, 14 vols (Beirut: Maktabat al-Rushd, 2003), 6:55–6 (no. 3,873). On Ibn Lahīʿa and Egyptian *ḥadīth* scholars: Juynboll, *Muslim Tradition*, 43–4, 80ff., 110, 129, 132. On al-Layth b. Saʿd and ʿAbd Allāh b. Ṣāliḥ: Nabia Abbott, *Studies in Arabic Literary Papyri*, 3 vols (Chicago: University of Chicago Press, 1957–72), 2:102.

[50] Ibn ʿAsākir, *Taʾrīkh*, 61:182, 183.

Moses' burial place is located 'between 'Āliya and 'Uwayliya', a site located to the south of Damascus.[51] Transmitted by Damascene scholars in the eighth century, this tradition was likely part of the emergence of *faḍā'il* traditions related to Syria and Palestine, including celebrating the existence of Moses' tomb there.[52]

Even more strikingly, some attestations of this *ḥadīth* preface the description of Moses praying in his tomb with another Prophetic statement: 'No prophet dies and dwells in his grave for more than forty days without his soul returning to him.'[53] Instead of being bodily raised to heaven – as in the traditions that circulated in Kūfa – the prophets here are seemingly present in their tombs in both body and spirit. This tradition suggests that certain ideas about the prophets' post-mortem status circulated in early Islamic Syria that were quite different from the Kūfan traditions about the prophets being lifted to Paradise.

Perhaps, then, the differing traditions about the prophets' bodies – and particularly the Prophet Muḥammad's body – resulted from regional differences. Early Muslim communities in the Ḥijāz, and further west in regions such as Syria and Egypt, seemingly favoured a conception of the Prophet's corporeal presence on earth, in his grave. On the other hand, Iraqi Muslim groups instead emphasised the Prophet's ascension to Paradise. We might further suggest that this regional variation was connected to the local practices of tomb veneration in the Ḥijaz and Syria, though this is admittedly speculative.

Though regional differences may appear attractive as an explanation, such geographic distinctions are not entirely clear-cut. For example, Ja'far al-Ṣādiq's warning not to climb upon the Prophet's tomb – for fear of seeing his bodily

[51] See the information on the location in Ibn 'Asākir, *Ta'rīkh*, 61:182; El'ad, 'Grave of Moses', 12.

[52] The *isnād* for all these versions begins: al-Ḥasan b. Yaḥyā al-Khushanī (d. *c.* 190/806–7; Damacus) > Sa'īd b. 'Abd al-'Azīz al-Tanūkhī (d. 167/783–4; Damascus) > Yazīd b. 'Abd al-Raḥmān b. Abī Mālik (d. 130/748–9; Damascus) > Anas b. Mālik. On these figures and the *isnāds* for this tradition, see El'ad, 'Grave of Moses', 9–14.

[53] Ibn Ḥibbān, *Kitāb al-Majrūḥīn*, 1:285–6; Ibn al-Jawzī, *Kitāb al-Mawḍū'āt*, ed. 'Abd al-Raḥmān Muḥammad 'Uthmān, 3 vols (Medina: al-Maktaba al-Salafiyya, 1966–8), 1:303. Versions without the mention of the soul returning appear in al-Ṭabarānī, *Musnad al-Shāmiyyīn*, 1:196 (no. 341/2), 2:420–1 (no. 1,614); Abū Nu'aym, *Ḥilyat al-awliya'*, 8:333; Ibn 'Asākir, *Ta'rīkh*, 61:183. These versions all have the same *isnād* as in the previous note, transmitted from the aforementioned scholars by the Damascene Hishām b. Khālid al-Azraq (d. 249/863).

activity there – was transmitted by Shīʿī scholars in Iraq.[54] Iraqi Shīʿa also transmitted traditions about the special qualities of the soil collected near the 'head' and 'feet' of al-Ḥusayn in his grave in Karbalāʾ, suggesting the imam's continued bodily presence there.[55] Such traditions indicate that not all Iraqi Shīʿī communities were strictly wedded to the conception of the Prophet (and the imams) being bodily raised to heaven. They circulated traditions about these figures' presence in the grave alongside traditions about their corporeal ascension.

Beside the Shīʿa, proto-Sunnī circles in Iraq also circulated traditions suggesting that the Prophet's body was located inside his tomb. The *ḥadīth* in which prophets are said to be 'alive praying in their graves' was transmitted in Iraq, and it may have originated in Baṣra.[56] Another example appears in the *Sunan* of al-Dārimī (d. *c.* 255/869) in a tradition that ascribes a distinct importance to the Prophet's earthly presence:

> Abū al-Jawzāʾ Aws b. ʿAbd Allāh said, 'The inhabitants of Medina were suffering a great drought. They turned to ʿĀʾisha, who said: "Look to the Prophet's tomb! Place a hole in it, so that there is no roof between him and the sky."' He [Abū al-Jawzāʾ] said, 'They did so, and it began to rain such that the plants blossomed and the camels fattened nearly to bursting. It was called the Year of Plenty.'[57]

[54] al-Kulaynī, *al-Kāfī*, 1:452. The *isnād* is 'many of our companions' > Aḥmad b. Muḥammad al-Barqī (d. 274/888 or 280/894; Qumm) > Jaʿfar b. al-Muthannā al-Khaṭīb (Kūfa) > Ismāʿīl b. ʿAmmār al-Ṣayrafī (Kūfa). On al-Barqī see Andrew J. Newman, *The Formative Period of Twelver Shīʿism: Ḥadīth as Discourse between Qum and Baghdad* (Richmond: Curzon, 2000), 50ff.; Roy Vilozny, 'Pre-Būyid *Ḥadīth* Literature: The Case of al-Barqī from Qumm (d. 274/888 or 280/894) in Twelve Sections', in Daftary and Miskinzoda, *Study of Shiʿi Islam*, 203–30. Jaʿfar b. al-Muthannā al-Khaṭīb is listed as a Companion of imam ʿAlī al-Riḍā (d. 203/818): Muḥammad b. al-Ḥasan al-Ṭūsī, *Rijāl al-Ṭūsī*, ed. Jawād al-Qayyūmī al-Iṣfahānī (Qom: Muʾassasat al-Nashr al-Islāmī, 1430 AH [2008–9]), 353. Ismāʿīl b. ʿAmmār is listed as a Kūfan Companion of Jaʿfar al-Ṣādiq: ibid., 162.

[55] al-Kulaynī, *al-Kāfī*, 4:588; Muḥammad b. al-Ḥasan al-Ṭūsī, *al-Amālī* (Qum: Dār al-Thaqāfa, 1993), 317.

[56] Nearly all versions begin with the *isnād* al-Mustalim b. Saʿīd (d. unknown, Wāsiṭ) > al-Ḥajjāj b. Abī Ziyād (d. unknown, Baṣra) > Thābit b. Aslam al-Bunānī (d. 123/740–1 or 127/744–5, Baṣra) > Anas b. Mālik (d. 93/712, Baṣra). It was transmitted by Iraqis including al-Ḥasan b. Qutayba al-Madāʾinī (d. unknown, Baghdad) and Yaḥyā b. Abī Bukayr (d. after 200/815–16, Kūfa and Baghdad).

[57] al-Dārimī, *Sunan*, 1:227 (no. 93). The *isnād* runs: Abū al-Nuʿmān Muḥammad b. al-Faḍl al-Sadūsī (d. 224/838–9; Baṣra) > Saʿīd b. Zayd b. Dirham (d. 167/783–4; Baṣra) > ʿAmr b. Mālik al-Nakrī (d. 129/746–7; Baṣra) > Abū al-Jawzāʾ Aws b. ʿAbd Allāh.

In this report, the Prophet Muḥammad's tomb plays a direct role in the provision of rain for the people of Medina, seemingly enabled by his body's directly facing the sky. Reported by Abū al-Jawzā' Aws b. ʿAbd Allāh (an ascetic Qur'ān reciter from Baṣra who died in 83/702–3), the solidly Baṣran *isnād* suggests that ideas about the Prophet's continued presence in his grave were to be found among proto-Sunnī circles in Iraq, perhaps especially in Baṣra.[58] Indeed, the *ḥadīth* describing Moses praying in his grave was also transmitted within proto-Sunnī Baṣran circles (though without the specification of Moses' burial place near Damascus, or the statement that prophets' souls return to them in the grave), further indicating that ideas about the prophets' presence within their graves circulated there.[59]

Meanwhile, the seeming Ḥijāzī emphasis on the Prophet's corporeal presence in his grave is also contradicted by other sources, which are not uniform on this point. For example, the Zaydī tradition saying that 'God does not leave a prophet's corpse under the earth' was transmitted among ʿAlids in Medina. The connection between ʿAlid communities in Medina and Kūfa could perhaps account for the presence of this tradition in Medina. Nonetheless, this report suggests that some traditions of the Prophet's ascension did circulate in the Ḥijāz.

Another illustrative example is a story about Dāwūd b. ʿĪsā b. Mūsā b. Muḥammad b. ʿAlī b. ʿAbd Allāh b. ʿAbbās, who held several positions in the ʿAbbāsid government in the Ḥijāz between 193/808–9 and 197/812–13.[60] During Dāwūd's tenure as governor of Mecca and Medina, a war of words emerged between these holy cities over which of the two was superior.[61] A poet

[58] On Abū al-Jawzā', see Christopher Melchert, *Before Sufism: Early Islamic Renunciant Piety* (Berlin: de Gruyter, 2020), 54; van Ess, *Theology and Society*, 2:4.

[59] The common links of this tradition appear to be the Baṣrans Sulaymān b. Ṭarkhān al-Taymī (d. 143/760–1) and Thābit al-Bunānī, as discussed in El'ad, 'Grave of Moses', 3–7. On Sulaymān b. Ṭarkhān, see van Ess, *Theology and Society*, 2:418–21.

[60] On Dāwūd b. ʿĪsā, see Khalīfa b. Khayyāṭ, *Kitāb al-Ṭārīkh*, ed. Akram Ḍiyā' al-ʿUmarī, 2nd ed. (Riyadh: Dār al-Ṭayba, 1985), 465, 466, 471; *The History of al-Ṭabarī. Volume XXXI: The War between Brothers*, trans. Michael Fishbein (Albany: State University of New York Press, 1992), 19, 91, 120, 124–9, 172, 211; *The History of al-Ṭabarī. Volume XXXII: The Reunification of the ʿAbbāsid Caliphate*, trans. C. E. Bosworth (Albany: State University of New York Press, 1987), 19–21, 28; al-Zubayr b. Bakkār, *Jamharat*, 1:185, 206, 2:16; Ibn ʿAsākir, *Ta'rīkh*, 17:171–80.

[61] al-Fākihī, *Akhbār Makka*, 2:293–300; Ibn ʿAsākir, *Ta'rīkh*, 17:175–80.

named ʿĪsā b. ʿAbd al-ʿAzīz al-Saʿlbūsī composed a laudatory poem (*qaṣīda*) in praise of Mecca, which included the following couplet aimed at Medina:

> If not for the visitation of the Prophet's tomb, you would be like everywhere else,
>
> When the Prophet is not dwelling [in the tomb], but in the midst of gardens most high!

In these satirical lines, we see a glimpse not only of Ḥijāzī inter-city competition, but also a hint of the ideas about the Prophet's body circulating there by the early ninth century. According to this Meccan poet, rather than 'dwelling' (*thāwiyan*) within his tomb, the Prophet is resting in the gardens of heaven. Thus, even the Medinan claim-to-fame of hosting the Prophet's tomb and its 'visitation' (*ziyāra*) is not particularly significant: for, in truth, the Prophet is not even there. Though it is unclear if the poet is referring to his material or spiritual absence from the tomb, there is certainly an idea that the Prophet is not simply lying inside his grave.

With these different conceptions of the Prophet expressed in both Iraq and Arabia, it is difficult to maintain that the divergent traditions about the Prophet's post-mortem existence are a product of variant ideas from different regions. Likewise, the evidence of such ideas' circulation from (seemingly) the time of the Prophet's death right through the ninth century makes it difficult to pinpoint a chronological evolution. As we have seen, any difference between proto-Sunnī and early Shīʿī ideas is similarly difficult to identify, given the presence of variant traditions attributed to authorities from both of these communities. Finally, there is little reason to assume that this was a difference between 'popular' and 'orthodox' Islam: all of these ideas were transmitted among the juristic and scholarly classes of Muslims who were defining the bounds of Islamic belief and practice.

A Gateway to Heaven: The Paradox of Sacred Body and Space in Late Antiquity

What accounts, then, for these conflicting images of the Prophet Muḥammad's body and its location after death? While I suggested above that there was a certain degree of regional variation in ideas about the Prophet's post-mortem location, the available data do not present a completely distinct demarcation between the ideas of scholars from the Ḥijāz and Iraq. Similarly, no clear difference appears in the proto-Sunnī and early Shīʿī positions on this issue, as we find contradictory traditions in the texts of both sectarian groups. Finally, it is worth repeating that there is no evidence in the sources of a distinction between 'elite' and 'popular' ideas.

Rather than trying to distinguish neatly between Ḥijāzī and Iraqi, proto-Sunnī and early Shīʿī, or elite and popular ideas, I suggest that we should read these reports as reflective of a set of paradoxical and essentially irreconcilable notions of the Prophet's body and his location after death. In this respect, early Muslims' ideas about their Prophet shared much with other late antique communities' conceptions of holy persons. Precisely the kinds of debated and conflicting ideas about the Prophet's afterlife that appear in early Islamic sources are also found within the realm of late antique cults of saints and other holy persons.

As Nicholas Constas writes of late ancient Christians, 'The nature of the soul, its relation to the body, and its fate after death are subjects that, despite their importance, were never authoritatively defined or systematically organized in the late antique period'.[62] Alan Avery-Peck notes that Jewish sources likewise display 'inconsistency in the Rabbinic approach to the concept of afterlife' and they 'overall do not yield a cogent or systematic picture' of the nature of existence after death.[63] This was true among early Muslims as well: as Leor Halevi notes, 'No one was all that clear about the precise nature of this connection between spirit and corpse in the grave'.[64] In Christian, Jewish and

[62] Constas, 'Apology for the Cult', 269.

[63] Alan J. Avery-Peck, 'Resurrection of the Body in Early Rabbinic Judaism', in *The Human Body in Death and Resurrection*, ed. Tobias Nicklas, Friedrich V. Reiterer and Joseph Verheyden, in collaboration with Heike Braun (Berlin: Walter de Gruyter, 2009), 243–66. Commenting on the Mishnah and Tosefta, Avery-Peck states, 'the extremely limited and unsystematic discussion of these topics means that the exact nature of the resurrection and the character of the world-to-come remain unexplored, as does the character of the individual's existence after death, a topic that never enters the picture'. Avery-Peck, 'Death and Afterlife in the Early Rabbinic Sources: The Mishnah, Tosefta, and Early Midrash Compilations', in *Judaism in Late Antiquity. Part Four: Death, Life-After-Death, Resurrection and the World-to-Come in the Judaisms of Antiquity*, ed. Alan J. Avery-Peck and Jacob Neusner (Leiden: Brill, 2000), 243–66.

[64] Halevi, *Muhammad's Grave*, 211.

Islamic sources from late antiquity, we see that 'this lacuna provided an opportunity for the free play of the imaginative, the visionary, and the superstitious, as a result of which one may find any number of psychologies and eschatologies strewn about somewhat carelessly across the late antique religious landscape'.[65]

This fluidity was especially pronounced within the post-mortem ontologies of holy persons, whose existence after death was often believed to be particularly lively. According to many late antique Christian theologians, 'the *post-mortem* existence of holy souls was qualitatively different from the rest of humanity'.[66] Rather than remaining at rest or suffering a punishment in the grave until the Resurrection, as other humans do, Christian saints and martyrs 'enjoyed the exceptional privilege of proceeding to immediate post-mortem reward', often understood as some form of existence in Paradise.[67] At the same time, holy persons were also capable of returning to earth after their deaths in order to perform miracles and otherwise engage with the world.[68] Thus, within many texts, 'mutually contradictory beliefs co-exist' regarding the state of human beings after death, with holy persons frequently breaking the fundamental norms expected of the dead.[69]

Similar ideas appear in the Qur'ān, which grants a special post-mortem status to one specific group of holy persons: martyrs. In a verse that was highly influential for Islamic understandings of holy persons' condition after death, Qur'ān 3:169 states: 'Do not think that those who were killed in the path of God are dead. They are alive and receive sustenance with their Lord.' Here and in other verses, the Qur'ān announces that the eschatological scenario planned for other believers (and, of course, for disbelievers) does not apply to martyrs.[70] Rather than waiting in their graves for bodily resurrection

[65] Constas, 'Apology for the Cult', 269–70.

[66] Dal Santo, *Debating the Saints' Cult*, 25, 111.

[67] Tommaso Tesei, 'The *barzakh* and the Intermediate State of the Dead in the Quran', in *Locating Hell in Islamic Traditions*, ed. Christian Lange (Leiden: Brill, 2016), 48; Gabriel Said Reynolds, *The Qur'ān and Its Biblical Subtext* (New York: Routledge, 2010), 164–5; Dal Santo, *Debating the Saints' Cult*, 72–3, 107–18, 285–7.

[68] Dal Santo, *Debating the Saints' Cult*, 108, 164, 172.

[69] Tesei, 'The *barzakh* and the Intermediate State', 47; Dal Santo, *Debating the Saints' Cult*, 268.

[70] Reynolds, *Qur'ān and Its Biblical Subtext*, 156–8.

and divine judgement, the martyrs are granted immediate entry to heaven and an audience before God. As noted by Tommaso Tesei, 'the Quran does not attempt to reconcile the belief in the privileged fate of martyrs with the idea of the dead's inactivity that it professes elsewhere'.[71] Instead, much as in late antique Christian texts, the Qur'ān simply asserts the exceptional state of the martyrs, who are 'alive' with God after their holy deaths.

This exceptional status of the holy person's post-mortem body was complicated and frequently debated within late antique communities.[72] Understood to exist beyond the confines of the grave, the holy person nonetheless was often localised at the site(s) of his or her shrine and/or relics, which were '*loci* where Heaven and Earth met [. . .] where the normal laws of the grave were held to be suspended'.[73] Among Christians, the saint was often understood to be fully present simultaneously in the grave and in heaven.[74] As noted by Peter Brown, the inscription on the grave of Saint Martin of Tours illustrates the 'paradox involved in the graves of saints':

> Here lies Martin the bishop, of holy memory, whose soul is in the hand of God; but he is fully here, present and made plain in miracles of every kind.[75]

While Martin's soul (*anima*) is in heaven, he is fully present (*hic totus est Praesens*) in the tomb too, as evidenced by the miracles performed there. As Sabine MacCormack writes, 'inscriptions marking the tombs of martyrs and saints regularly associate these two themes – the body resting in the tomb and the soul reigning with God in the stars – with one and the same person'.[76]

This 'paradox of the linking of Heaven and Earth' is pushed even further by late ancient Christian writers, who portray saints and their relics transcending

[71] Tesei, 'The *barzakh* and the Intermediate State', 49.

[72] Dal Santo, *Debating the Saints' Cult*, 49–50, 108, 127–8; Miller, *Corporeal Imagination*, 104; Constas, 'To Sleep', 122; Reynolds, *Qur'ān and Its Biblical Subtext*, 159–61; Kohlberg, 'Medieval Muslim Views', 281–307.

[73] Brown, *Cult of the Saints*, 10–11. On Christian discussions of the saints' post-mortem connections to their relics: Dal Santo, *Debating the Saints' Cult*, 290–7, 303, 309–14.

[74] For a later Byzantine rejection of this (fully) simultaneous presence, see Constas, 'To Sleep', 115–16.

[75] Brown, *Cult of the Saints*, 3–4.

[76] MacCormack, 'Loca Sancta', 17.

their tombs while residing within them, and even transcending the distinctions between the material and spiritual realms.[77] Proclus, a fifth-century archbishop of Constantinople, writes in a hymn to Mary that 'with each of the saints [. . .] even though their relics are enclosed within tombs, their power under heaven is not restricted'.[78] An early fifth-century Greek homily, pseudonymously ascribed to John Chrysostom, states of the apostle Thomas that 'nothing is able to conceal him, and he is absent from no place [. . .] he was buried in a tomb but rises everywhere like the sun. The relics of this righteous man have conquered the world, and have appeared as more expansive than creation itself.'[79] These writers provide examples of what Peter Brown describes as a tendency in the late ancient cult of saints 'to raise the physical remains of the saints above the normal associations of place and time' and illustrate that 'at [the saints'] graves, the eternity of paradise and the first touch of the resurrection come into the present'.[80]

Like Christian saints' shrines, the tombs of late ancient rabbis also appear as sites of uncanny linkages between heaven and earth. According to a story in the Babylonian Talmud, Rabbi Joshua b. Levi had a conversation at the entrance to Rabbi Shimon b. Yohai's tomb with both Rabbi Shimon and the prophet Elijah, who told Rabbi Joshua how to meet the Messiah.[81] In addition to such eschatological knowledge, Elijah also granted an unnamed rabbi the ability to see the deceased rabbis of the past 'ascending and descending' from their graves up to the Heavenly Academy and back down to their graves.[82] According to Elijah, while nearly all of the rabbis must be accompanied by angels to accomplish such travels, 'the chariot of Rabbi Ḥiyya ascends and descends of his/its

[77] Brown, *Cult of the Saints*, 78.

[78] Proclus, *hom.* 5.1. Greek text and English translation in Nicholas Constas, *Proclus of Constantinople and the Cult of the Virgin in Late Antiquity: Homilies 1–5, Texts and Translations* (Leiden: Brill, 2003), 256–7.

[79] *PG* 59:498. *BHG* 1838 (2, 302). Translated in Constas, 'Apology for the Cult', 271 n.10. On this text's date, see J. A. de Aldama, *Repertorium Pseudochrysostomicum* (Paris: Éditions du Centre national de la recherche scientifique, 1965), 193 (no. 517).

[80] Brown, *Cult of the Saints*, 78.

[81] *b. San.* 98a; Kristen H. Lindbeck, *Elijah and the Rabbis: Story and Theology* (New York: Columbia University Press, 2010), 87, 123, 187–8.

[82] *b. B.M.* 85a. Lindbeck, *Elijah and the Rabbis*, 51, 127, 175.

own accord', suggesting an autonomy of post-mortem movement on Ḥiyya's part. While these passages do not provide evidence of a cult of the rabbis' tombs on the level witnessed for the Christian saints, they indicate that the rabbis' tombs were places where the line between heaven and earth was flexible, with the rabbis themselves able to criss-cross that boundary with angelic help.

This linkage between heaven and earth also features at the gravesites of holy persons in early Islamic texts. We saw above that daily flocks of angels were said to descend upon the Prophet Muḥammad's tomb in Medina, suggesting a heavenly connection to the site. Early traditions sacralise the space beside the Prophet's tomb and call it 'one of the gardens of Paradise'.[83] Shīʿī traditions similarly call the grave of al-Ḥusayn in Karbalāʾ 'one of the gardens of Paradise' and describe angels ascending and descending from it as at the Prophet's tomb.[84] Such a heavenly connection was also present at the grave of Ishmael in Mecca according to a tradition related by the Umayyad governor of the Ḥijāz (and subsequently caliph) ʿUmar b. ʿAbd al-ʿAzīz. According to him, 'Ishmael complained to God of the heat of Mecca. God revealed to him, "I will open a gate of paradise in the Ḥijr. A breeze will blow onto you from it until the Day of Judgment."'[85] A pleasant breeze is thus said to blow directly onto Ishmael's grave in the Ḥijr, allowing a touch of heaven to enter the space of the prophet's burial place in Mecca.

[83] Juynboll, *Encyclopedia*, 313; van Ess, *Theology and Society*, 4:613; Heribert Busse, 'Die Kanzel des Propheten im Paradiesesgarten', *Die Welt des Islams* 28 (1988): 99–111; Ghazi Izzeddin Bisheh, 'The Mosque of the Prophet at Madīnah throughout the First-Century A.H. with Special Emphasis on the Umayyad Mosque' (PhD., University of Michigan, 1979), 275–6; Barbara Finster, 'Die Mosaiken der Umayyadenmoschee von Damaskus', *Kunst des Orients* 7 (1970–1): 135.

[84] al-Kulaynī, *al-Kāfī*, 4:588; Ibn Qūlūya, *Kāmil al-ziyārāt*, 222 (no. 325), 456–8 (nos 691–6). This motif also appears in traditions about the Masjid al-Kūfa, a very early Shīʿī sacred space. Notably, this mosque was said to contain several non-corporeal prophetic relics, including Moses' staff and Solomon's ring. Ibrāhīm b. Muḥammad b. Saʿīd b. Hilāl al-Thaqafī, *al-Ghārāt*, ed. ʿAbd al-Zahrāʾ al-Ḥusaynī al-Khaṭīb (Beirut: Dār al-Aḍwāʾ, 1987), 285–7; Aḥmad b. Muḥammad al-Barqī, *Kitāb al-Maḥāsin*, ed. Sayyid Jalāl al-Dīn al-Ḥusaynī (Qum: Dār al-Kutub al-Islāmiyya, n.d.), 56 (no. 86); al-Kulaynī, *al-Kāfī*, 3:491–4; Haider, *Origins of the Shīʿa*, 239; Friedman, 'Kūfa is Better', 215.

[85] al-Azraqī, *Akhbār Makka*, 430–1 (no. 388); al-Ṭabarī, *Taʾrīkh*, 1:352. See Hawting, 'Origins of the Muslim Sanctuary', 43; Hawting, 'Plaything for Kings', 15; Bursi, 'Scents of Space', 228–9.

In these traditions, the graves of holy persons are the sites of 'go-betweens [. . .] between the otherworld and this world', and places where paradise is 'truly and fully here on earth'.[86] Much like the slippage between these categories at Christian saints' tombs, the graves of Muslim holy persons were sites where the boundary between heaven and earth was not entirely distinct.

Such heavenly phenomena also attended the Prophet Muḥammad's corpse even before his burial. As we have seen, Muḥammad's corpse often displayed a holiness like that of late antique saints. In this same vein, the pleasant smell of the sacred corpse, 'a common motif in Christian saints' *vitae*', appears in the traditions about Muḥammad's corpse.[87] For example, in the Greek biography of Symeon Stylites ascribed to Antonius, when Symeon was prepared for burial, 'Throughout his body and his garments was a scented perfume which, from its sweet smell, made one's heart merry'.[88] Likewise, the Syriac *Life of Symeon* describes the saint exhibiting a pleasant aroma during his life – 'a cool, refreshing, and very fragrant wind blew as though a heavenly dew were falling on the saint and were sending forth a fragrant scent from him such as has not been spoken of in the world' – that his corpse continued to exhibit after death.[89] These stories parallel the narratives about the preparation of the Prophet's corpse for burial, including one in particular: as ʿAlī washed the Prophet's body, 'a fragrant wind blew, the likes of which they

[86] Christian Lange, *Paradise and Hell in Islamic Traditions* (New York: Cambridge University Press, 2016), 7, 245.

[87] Szilágyi, 'Prophet Like Jesus', 157 and n.95; Shoemaker, *Death of a Prophet*, 95 and 304 n.99; Halevi, *Muhammad's Grave*, 43, 47, 80–1, 270 n.16. Szilágyi and Halevi both cite the example of the fragrant corpse of Symeon Stylites. Several other examples of fragrant saintly corpses are cited in Susan Ashbrook Harvey, *Scenting Salvation: Ancient Christianity and the Olfactory Imagination* (Berkeley: University of California Press, 2006), 325 n.27; Maraval, *Lieux saints et pèlerinages*, 189–91.

[88] H. Lietzmann, *Das Leben des heiligen Symeon Stylites* (Leipzig: Hinrichs, 1908), 66; Robert Doran, *The Lives of Simeon Stylites* (Kalamazoo: Cistercian Publications, 1992), 98.

[89] S. E. Assemani, *Acta Sanctorum Martyrum Orientalium et occidentalium*, 2 vols (Rome: Collini, 1748), 2:382, 392; Doran, *Lives of Simeon Stylites*, 185–6, 193. A slightly different version appears in Paul Bedjan (ed.), *Acta Martyrum et Sanctorum*, 7 vols (Paris: Otto Harrassowitz, 1890–7), 4:630, 641.

had never experienced before'.[90] Muḥammad's corpse appears here as a site of heavenly phenomena, 'radiating its resurrected glory' much as Christian saints' relics did.[91]

Late ancient Christian writers often dealt with the liminal status of the saints by affirming their paradoxical status. In their simultaneous existence on earth and in heaven, their location within their relics while also being present everywhere, 'saintly images deny the dualistic position that splits matter from spirit, body from soul, nature from divine'.[92] This kind of paradoxical state was, seemingly, not explicitly affirmed in most early Islamic discussions of the Prophet's body.[93] Instead of acknowledging paradox, the approach found in the extant sources is the simple juxtaposition of images. For example, in the *Muṣannaf* of the earlier *ḥadīth* collector ʿAbd al-Razzāq b. Hammām (d. 211/827), the chapter on 'wishing peace upon the Prophet's grave' addresses the subject of the Prophet's post-mortem status and location.[94] One tradition finds Saʿīd b. al-Musayyab saying that no prophet remains in his grave for more than forty days; however, another *ḥadīth* in this short chapter says that the Prophet Muḥammad saw Moses 'standing praying in his grave'. Are prophets present in their graves or not? The question appears unanswerable from the data in ʿAbd al-Razzāq's chapter, and perhaps is meant to remain unresolved.

Rather than precisely defining the nature of the Prophet's post-mortem existence, early Islamic sources list conflicting traditions about it, without deciding the issue conclusively. Different notions about the nature and location of the Prophet's body appear in these texts, sometimes directly next to one another. Of course, such variant ideas had conflicting ritual and material

[90] Ibn Saʿd, *Ṭabaqāt*, 2:244. In a similar tradition, ʿĀʾisha says that 'when his soul [*nafsu-hu*] left, I never smelled anything sweeter than it', seemingly referencing the scent of the Prophet's soul itself. Ibn Ḥanbal, *Musnad*, 41:391 (no. 24,905); al-Bayhaqī, *Dalāʾil al-nubuwwa*, 7:213; Knight, *Muhammad's Body*, 143.

[91] Harvey, *Scenting Salvation*, 227.

[92] Miller, *Corporeal Imagination*, 114–15.

[93] Although it is tempting to see purposeful contradiction in the ascription to both Saʿīd b. al-Musayyab and Jaʿfar al-Ṣādiq of diametrically opposed views on the Prophet's post-mortem location.

[94] ʿAbd al-Razzāq, *Muṣannaf*, 3:576–80 (nos 6,724–36).

implications, in the form of Muslims' varied attitudes towards the Prophet's tomb. In many cases, these differing positions on veneration of the tomb were not eased by embrace of paradox, but remained ongoing debates among early Muslim communities. However, as we will see, a paradoxical state does appear in early traditions on the Prophet's relationship to his tomb.

'When You Have Decayed?': The Prophet's Body, Tomb and Intercession

One of the key roles of late antique saints – and one directly implicated by questions of their post-mortem existence – was as their communities' intercessors before God.[95] As Matthew Dal Santo writes, 'In many ways, the later sixth- and seventh-century debate on the saints presents the historian with a debate on intercession – whether and how it was possible, under what conditions, and for what purposes'. Intercession appears to have been a similarly central aspect of early Muslim communities' appreciation of the Prophet Muḥammad 'from a remarkably early date'.[96] Indeed, the importance of Muḥammad's intercession became a central tenet of orthodoxy for Muslim groups, and was enshrined in some of the earliest Sunnī and Shīʿī creeds.[97] However, much as with Christian debates over the saints' post-mortem activities, early Muslims wondered how exactly the Prophet Muḥammad would be able to intercede

[95] Dal Santo, *Debating the Saints' Cult*, 22, 108, 176–87, 208–210, 257–8, 325–7. On rabbinic ideas of the patriarchs and matriarchs as Israel's intercessors, see Ephraim E. Urbach, *The Sages: Their Concepts and Beliefs*, trans. Israel Abrahams (Jerusalem: Magnes Press, 1979), 496–511; J. W. Bowker, 'Intercession in the Qur'an and the Jewish Tradition', *Journal of Semitic Studies* 11 (1966): 69–82; Uri Ehrlich, 'The Ancestors' Prayers for the Salvation of Israel in Early Rabbinic Thought', in *Jewish and Christian Liturgy and Worship: New Insights into History and Interaction*, ed. Albert Gerhards and Clemens Leonhard (Leiden: Brill, 2007), 249–56; Sarit Kattan Gribetz, '*Zekhut Imahot*: Mothers, Fathers, and Ancestral Merit in Rabbinic Sources', *JSJ* 49 (2018): 268–96.

[96] Anthony, *Muhammad and the Empires*, 53. On the Prophet's intercession in the early Islamic period, see Feras Hamza, 'To Hell and Back: A Study of the Concepts of Hell and Intercession in Early Islam' (PhD diss., Oxford University, 2002); Feras Hamza, 'Temporary Hellfire Punishment and the Making of Sunni Orthodoxy', in Günther and Lawson, *Roads to Paradise*, 1:371–406; van Ess, *Theology and Society*, 4:605–12.

[97] Lange, *Paradise and Hell*, 178–9; Hamza, 'To Hell and Back', 184–6; Hamza, 'Temporary Hellfire', 371.

for them after his own death, and how they might ensure their receipt of such intercession. As in Christian communities, different answers were provided for these questions, involving discussions of the Prophet's body, his tomb, and how individuals should engage with them.

The Qur'ān provides ambivalent evidence for the possibility of divine intercession. On the one hand, many passages rail against the idea that any human or divine entity is able to intercede before God.[98] On the other hand, early interpreters read certain verses as implying the Prophet's ability to intercede before God on the Day of Judgement, such as the mention at Q 17:79 of his being raised to 'a praiseworthy station' (*maqāman maḥmūdan*).[99] Both Sunnī and Shīʿī poetry and *ḥadīth* literature contain explicit references to the Prophet's intercessory powers.[100] A seemingly quite early example is an invocation attributed to Ibn ʿAbbās, which reads in part, 'O God, accept Muḥammad's great intercession!'[101] In several traditions, the Prophet asserts that he will intercede for his community in the future, as in his statement that 'Every prophet has been granted a supplication (*daʿwa*) to request something. I intend to preserve my supplication as an intercession for my community on the Day of Resurrection.'[102] While this pronouncement suggests that any

[98] Hawting, *Idea of Idolatry*, 51–4; *EQ*, s.v. 'Intercession' (Valerie J. Hoffman).

[99] *EI*[2], s.v. 'Shafāʿa (I)' (A. J. Wensinck – D. Gimaret); Hamza, 'To Hell and Back', 131–7; van Ess, *Theology and Society*, 4:607–8; Bar-Asher, *Scripture and Exegesis*, 180–9. For some of these traditions, see al-Bukhārī, *Ṣaḥīḥ*, 1171 (kitāb al-tafsīr, bāb 11); al-Tirmidhī, *al-Jāmiʿ*, 5:206 (no. 3,137); Ibn Abī Shayba, *Muṣannaf*, 11:41 (nos 32,277–8); al-Ṭayālisī, *Musnad*, 1:306 (no. 389); Aḥmad b. Abī Khaythama Zuhayr b. Ḥarb, *al-Taʾrīkh al-kabīr al-maʿrūf bi-Taʾrīkh Ibn Abī Khaythama*, ed. Ṣalāḥ b. Fatḥī Halal, 4 vols (Cairo: al-Fārūq al-Ḥadītha, 2004), 1:203–5 (nos 540–55); Ibn al-Mubārak, *Zuhd*, 463 (no. 1,312).

[100] For references within early poetry, see Hamza, 'To Hell and Back', 125–31, 137–40. For examples of the difference between qur'ānic and post-qur'ānic ideas of prophetic intercession, see Hamza Mahmood Zafer, 'Transformation in Early Muslim Prophetology: From Typology to Teleology in Narratives of Jonah and the Ninevites', *Journal of Qur'anic Studies* 22.2 (2020): 1–32.

[101] ʿAbd al-Razzāq, *Muṣannaf*, 2:211–12 (no. 3,104); Ismāʿīl b. Isḥāq, *Faḍl al-ṣalāt*, 58–9 (no. 52).

[102] ʿAbd al-Razzāq, *Muṣannaf*, 11:413 (no. 20,864); Ibn Abī Shayba, *Muṣannaf*, 11:40 (no. 32,273); Muslim, *Ṣaḥīḥ*, 1:188–90 (nos 334–45); Ibn Ḥanbal, *Musnad*, 13:482 (no. 8,132); Ibn Khuzayma, *Kitāb al-Tawḥīd*, 622–37; ʿAlī b. al-Jaʿd, *Musnad Ibn al-Jaʿd*, ed. ʿAbd al-Mahdī b. ʿAbd al-Qādir b. ʿAbd al-Hādī (Kuwait: Maktabat al-Falāḥ, 1985), 549 (no. 1,173).

prophet might choose to use his supplication for the purposes of intercession, other traditions indicate that Muḥammad's intercessory role is unique, since God had not given this precious gift to any previous prophet.[103]

In addition to literary evidence, the material record also indicates that early Muslims believed in Muḥammad's intercession. This honour and responsibility of the Prophet, and its importance for the Muslim *umma*, appears in the Dome of the Rock, constructed in 72/691–2. Near the end of the inscription on the outer arcade are the words: 'Muḥammad is the Messenger of God. May God bless him and accept his intercession for his community on the Day of Resurrection.'[104] Similar phrases are found in several early Arabic rock inscriptions from western Arabia. Near the city of Tabūk, a late seventh-century inscription opens with the words: 'O God, bless the *ummī* Prophet and accept his intercession for his community.'[105] Another text, inscribed in Mecca in the late seventh or early eighth century, opens: 'O God, bless the Prophet Muḥammad and accept his intercession for [someone].'[106] These inscriptions in Jerusalem and Arabia provide further corroboration that Muḥammad's intercession was cited by Muslim communities at the turn of the eighth century.[107]

103 Ibn Abī Shayba, *Muṣannaf*, 11:5–29 (nos 32,171–236), 13:22–3 (nos 36,821, 36,856–7, 36,860, 36,870); Bar-Asher, *Scripture and Exegesis*, 180–1.

104 For the Arabic text, see Christel Kessler, ''Abd al-Malik's Inscription in the Dome of the Rock: A Reconsideration', *JRAS* (1970): 9. On the mention of Muḥammad's intercession in the inscription, see Mathieu Tillier, ''Abd al-Malik, Muḥammad et le Jugement dernier: le dôme du Rocher comme expression d'une orthodoxie islamique', in *Les vivants et les morts dans les sociétés médiévales: Actes du XLVIIIe Congrès de la SHMESP (Jérusalem, 2017)* (Paris: Éditions de la Sorbonne, 2018), 341–65; Hamza, 'To Hell and Back', 124–5, 145–9; van Ess, *Theology and Society*, 1:13; Anthony, *Muhammad and the Empires*, 34, 53.

105 Maysā' bint 'Alī Ibrāhīm al-Ghabbān, 'al-Kitābāt al-Islāmiyya al-mubakkira fī haḍbat Ḥismā bi-minṭaqat Tabūk: dirāsa taḥlīliyya āthāriyya wa-lughawiyya' (PhD diss., King Saud University, 2016–17), 160 (no. 84), 847.

106 Sa'd 'Abd al-'Azīz al-Rāshid, *Kitābāt Islāmiyya min Makka al-Mukarrama: Dirāsa wa-taḥqīq* (Riyadh: Maktabat al-Malik Fahd al-Waṭaniyya, 1995), 149–50 (no. 58).

107 See also the inscriptions in which petitioners ask to be led to the eschatological 'Basin of Muḥammad' (*ḥawḍ Muḥammad*): Anthony, *Muhammad and the Empires*, 53–4. Examples from later centuries are collected in Werner Diem, *The Living and the Dead in Islam: Studies in Arabic Epitaphs. I: Epitaphs as Texts* (Wiesbaden: Harrassowitz, 2004), 162–3, 168–70.

Much of this evidence points to the Prophet's intercessory role for the *umma* on the eschatological Day of Judgement. Yet the Prophet's intercession was not always restricted to the future End Time, but was sometimes represented as an ongoing occurrence throughout the earthly lifetime of the Muslim community. Several traditions connect the Prophet's death with his immediate intercessory activities in the afterlife. For example, in a *mursal ḥadīth* reported by the Baṣran *qāṣṣ* Bakr b. ʿAbd Allāh al-Muzanī (d. 106/724–5 or 108/726–7), the Prophet says:

> My life is a benefit to you, as you can speak [to me] and I can speak to you. But when I die, my death will also be a benefit to you, as your actions will be shown to me. When I see a righteous deed, I will praise God; when I see an evil deed, I will ask God's forgiveness for you.[108]

This *ḥadīth* appears nearly verbatim in an early Shīʿī collection of al-Ṣaffār al-Qummī (d. 290/902–3), where the Prophet's words are reported from imam Muḥammad al-Bāqir (d. 114/732 or 117/735).[109] Another transmission from al-Bāqir is cited in several Shīʿī collections, where the Prophet explains, 'My separation from you will be a benefit to you, for your actions will be shown to me every Monday and Thursday. I will praise God for the good deeds, and I will ask God's forgiveness for the evil ones.'[110] According to these traditions,

[108] Ibn Saʿd, *Ṭabaqāt*, 2:174; Ismāʿīl b. Isḥāq, *Faḍl al-ṣalāt*, 40–2 (nos 25–6); al-Bazzār, *Musnad*, 5:308–9 (no. 1,925); Nūr al-Dīn al-Haythamī, *Bughyat al-bāḥith ʿan zawāʾid musnad al-Ḥārith*, ed. Ḥusayn Aḥmad Ṣāliḥ al-Bākrī (Medina: al-Jāmiʿa al-Islāmiyya bi-Madīna al-Munawwara, 1992), 884 (no. 953). On Bakr b. ʿAbd Allāh al-Muzanī, see Armstrong, *The* Quṣṣāṣ *of Early Islam*, 121, 131, 263, 300. A similar tradition that does not explicitly mention the Prophet's death is in ʿAbd al-Razzāq, *Muṣannaf*, 2:214 (no. 3,111).

[109] al-Ṣaffār, *Baṣāʾir al-darajāt*, 2:347–8. The *isnād* is: Abān b. Muḥammad al-Sindī al-Bazzāz (d. *c.* 250–60/864–73, Kūfa) > ʿĀṣim b. Ḥumayd al-Ḥannāṭ (d. late second/eighth century, Kūfa) > Abū Baṣīr Yaḥyā b. Abī al-Qāsim al-Asadī (d. 149–50/7667, Kūfa) > al-Bāqir. Another version is reported with the *isnād*: Aḥmad b. Muḥammad b. ʿĪsā (third/ninth century, Qum) > ʿAbd al-Raḥmān b. Abī Najrān (active early third/ninth century, Kūfa) > ʿĀṣim b. Ḥumayd > Abū Baṣīr> al-Bāqir. On these figures, see Modarressi, *Tradition and Survival*, 210–11, 215, 230, 390; Derryl N. Maclean, *Religion and Society in Arab Sind* (Leiden: Brill, 1989), 160; Etan Kohlberg, *A Medieval Muslim Scholar at Work: Ibn Ṭāwūs and His Library* (Leiden: Brill, 1992), 121–2.

[110] al-Ṣaffār, *Baṣāʾir al-darajāt*, 2:347–8; ʿAlī b. Ibrāhīm al-Qummī, *Tafsīr*, 1:395–6; al-ʿAyyāshī, *Tafsīr*, 2:192; al-Ṭūsī, *al-Amālī*, 408–9. The transmissions centre on Ḥanān b.

the Prophet continues to benefit believers after his death, much as (if not even more so than) he had done in life. For each evil deed committed by a community member, the Prophet will ask God's forgiveness, seemingly wiping their individual slates clean of sins.[111]

Notably, within both early Sunnī and Shīʿī texts, the Prophet's mortality is evoked as a potential impediment to his performance of such intercessional activities. In several traditions in which Muḥammad encourages his believers to offer prayers for him, and/or assures them of his continuing benefit to them after he has died, his followers ask: how will you accomplish such activities after death? They directly ask the Prophet how he will be able to do these things 'when you have been eradicated', or (as the *ḥadīth* narrator alternatively phrases it) 'when you have decayed'.[112] The Prophet assuages this anxiety by assuring his listeners that 'God has forbidden the earth to consume the bodies of the prophets'. In a version in the Sunnī collector Ibn Mājah's (d. 273/887) *Sunan*, the Prophet Muḥammad adds, 'The prophet of God is alive and receives sustenance', echoing the qurʾānic description of martyrs' post-mortem state.[113]

In these traditions, the question of how the Prophet would be able to receive Muslims' prayers and blessings, and then intercede for them, is directly connected to his corporeal existence. The role of the Prophet's body in the intercessional process is not spelled out, but some believers seem to have understood his bodily integrity as crucial in some respect. Indeed, the Prophet himself reassures his Companions by declaring that his body would never cease to exist. His answer – and the relatively wide circulation of these traditions – suggests that questions about the Prophet's bodily continuity were considered

Sadīr al-Ṣayrafī, a Kūfan active in the late second/eighth century. On him, see Modarressi, *Tradition and Survival*, 240–2. Similar traditions appear in Sunnī collections, but they do not credit the Prophet with asking God's forgiveness: Mālik, *Muwaṭṭa'* [recension of Yaḥyā al-Laythī], 2:495–6 (nos 2,642–3); Muslim, *Ṣaḥīḥ*, 4:1,987 (no. 2,565); and elsewhere.

[111] On the association between the Prophet's 'asking forgiveness' (*istighfār*) and his intercession: Hamza, 'To Hell and Back', 131–7. Note also that early sources indicate that alms (*zakāt*) were 'paid to the Prophet by sinners in return for his prayer and supplication so that they might be purified'. Suliman Bashear, 'On the Origins and Development of the Meaning of *Zakāt* in Early Islam', *Arabica* 40.1 (1993): 84–113.

[112] See the traditions cited in Chapter 3, nn. 17–19.

[113] Ibn Mājah, *Sunan*, 1:524 (no. 1,637); al-Samhūdī, *Wafāʾ al-wafā*, 5:38.

quite reasonable concerns by early Muslims. As Michael Muhammad Knight writes, the Muslim community's 'soteriological welfare' was connected to 'the preservation of Muhammad's post-mortem remains'.[114]

A flurry of traditions emerged over the eighth and ninth centuries related to these questions of the Prophet's post-mortem intercessional activities, and the proper ways of ensuring the individual's receipt of them. These concerns often appear within the context of debates about visiting the Prophet's tomb in Medina. Parallel with other late antique communities in respect of their holy persons' burial places, many Muslims appear to have believed that proximity to the Prophet Muḥammad's grave (and, thus, to his body) was beneficial for their words reaching him. While several reports offer evidence of the prevalence of these ideas among some early Muslims, other reports called these intercessional ideas into question using a variety of techniques.

This debate is directly evoked in a tradition about the Medinan jurist Saʿīd b. al-Musayyab, discussed above. When Ibn al-Musayyab saw a group gathered by the Prophet's tomb to wish him blessings, he declared, 'No prophet remains in the earth for more than forty days.'[115] Here, the Prophet's absent body is offered as a reason not to come to the Prophet's tomb: his corpse is not there, so why visit his tomb?[116] Saʿīd b. al-Musayyab thus discourages pilgrimage to the Prophet's grave explicitly because his body is in heaven, not in his tomb.

Yet even if the Prophet was in Paradise, this did not necessarily mean that Muslims were unable to communicate with him. In a version of Saʿīd b. al-Musayyab's report recorded by the Medinan historian al-Samhūdī (d. 911/1506), Ibn al-Musayyab goes on to offer a message about how the *umma*'s actions are known to the Prophet, even in death. After noting that the Prophet's body is not located in his grave, Ibn al-Musayyab adds: 'No day passes without his *umma* being presented to him in the morning and evening, so that he knows them by their names and their *nisba*s. Through

[114] Knight, *Muhammad's Body*, 140–1.

[115] 'Abd al-Razzāq, *Muṣannaf*, 3:576–7 (no. 6,725).

[116] Although the ascription of these words to Saʿīd is (as Szilágyi notes) 'dubious', the report fits the tenor of other instances in which Ibn al-Musayyab discourages pilgrimage to, and venerational practices at, the Prophet's Mosque. See, for example: 'Abd al-Razzāq, *Muṣannaf*, 8:455 (no. 15,889); Ibn Abī Shayba, *Muṣannaf*, 5:685 (no. 16,114).

this, he testifies for them.'[117] Thus, the Prophet intimately knows his *umma*, even after his heavenly ascension. The Prophet provides testimony before God on behalf of individual members of his community – by their first and last names, as it were – on the basis of their actions, wherever they may have been performed. Visitation of the Prophet's grave is not necessary, as he is 'presented' with information about his community continuously.

We have seen similar ideas in other traditions about the Muslim *umma*'s actions being 'shown' to the Prophet after death. How he receives this information is often left unclear. However, some traditions specify that angels carry the community's prayers to the Prophet. For example, a report from the Baṣran *qāṣṣ* Yazīd b. Abān al-Raqāshī (d. *c.* 110–20/728–37) states: 'Whoever prays for the Prophet, an angel is appointed to report to the Prophet, "So-and-so from your *umma* has prayed for you".'[118] In a rarely-attested report, the Companion Ibn ʿAbbās states: 'None from Muḥammad's *umma* prays for him without it reaching him, through an angel that says to him "So-and-so has prayed for you".'[119] In a more widely-attested *ḥadīth*, the Prophet says, 'God has angels that travel the earth and convey the greetings of my community to me.'[120]

[117] ʿAlī b. ʿAbd Allāh al-Samhūdī, *Khulāṣat al-wafā bi-akhbār Dār al-Muṣṭafā* (Medina: al-Maktaba al-ʿIlmiyya, 1972), 97. This statement is attributed to Saʿīd b. al-Musayyab without narrative context in Ibn al-Mubārak, *Zuhd*, 42 (no. 166) [recension of Nuʿaym b. Ḥammād]. In both cases, the only source named is al-Minhāl b. ʿAmr (d. *c.* 110/728–9, Kūfa).

[118] Ibn Abī Shayba, *Muṣannaf*, 3:602 (no. 8,783); Ismāʿīl b. Isḥāq, *Faḍl al-ṣalāt*, 42 (no. 27). On Yazīd b. Abān al-Raqāshī, see Armstrong, *The* Quṣṣāṣ *of Early Islam*, 300.

[119] al-Bayhaqī, *Shuʿab al-īmān*, 3:141 (no. 1,482); al-Bayhaqī, *Ḥayāt al-anbiyāʾ*, 102–3 (no. 17). A similar *ḥadīth* (extended from Ibn ʿAbbās back to the Prophet) is recorded in Ibn ʿAdī, *al-Kāmil*, 3:1092. In both cases, the *isnād* includes the following figures: Isrāʾīl b. Yūnus b. Abī Isḥāq (d. *c.* 160/776–7, Kūfa) > Abū Yaḥyā al-Qitāt (d. unknown, Kūfa) > Mujāhid b. Jabr > Ibn ʿAbbās.

[120] ʿAbd al-Razzāq, *Muṣannaf*, 2:215 (no. 3,116); Ibn Abī Shayba, *Muṣannaf*, 3:603 (no. 8,789), 11:34 (no. 32,254); Ismāʿīl b. Isḥāq, *Faḍl al-ṣalāt*, 37–8 (no. 21); Ibn Ḥanbal, *Musnad*, 6:183 (no. 3,666), 7:260, 343 (nos 4,210, 4,320); Ibn al-Mubārak, *Zuhd*, 364 (no. 1,028); Abū Yaʿlā, *Musnad*, 9:137 (no. 5,213); al-Bazzār, *Musnad*, 5:307–9 (nos 1,923–5); al-Dārimī, *Sunan*, 3:1826 (no. 2,816); al-Nasāʾī, *Sunan*, 208 (no. 1,282); al-Ṭabarānī, *al-Muʿjam al-kabīr*, 10:270–1 (nos 10,528–31); Ibn Balbān, *Ṣaḥīḥ Ibn Ḥibbān*, 3:195 (no. 914); al-Bayhaqī, *Shuʿab al-īmān*, 3:140 (no. 1,480); Ibn Abī ʿĀṣim, *Kitāb al-Ṣalāt*, 29–30 (no. 28); Ibn ʿAsākir, *Taʾrīkh*, 7:120; al-Khaṭīb al-Baghdādī, *Taʾrīkh*, 10:149–50; Munt, *Holy City of Medina*, 130. The *isnād*s almost all spread out from Sufyān al-Thawrī, who reportedly received it via ʿAbd Allāh b al-Sāʾib al-Kindī (d. unknown, Kūfa) > Zādhān (d. 82/701–2, Kūfa) > Ibn Masʿūd > Prophet.

Notably, these traditions do not actually specify the Prophet's location, and can be read as suggesting his presence in the grave and/or in heaven. Some traditions, however, do provide suggestive hints that the Prophet is present in his grave, or at least that his grave offers an avenue for communication with him. In a *ḥadīth* that circulated in Iraq, the Prophet says:

> God has stationed an angel in my tomb with the ability to hear the creatures of the world. No one shall pray for me up to the Day of Judgment without [that angel] reporting to me his name and his father's name, that 'So-and-so ibn so-and-so has prayed for you.'[121]

Here, an angel in the Prophet's tomb hears the pious activities of the world's living creatures and conveys this information to the Prophet. On the one hand, the tradition might mean that the angel hears the prayers from all over the world (as in the *ḥadīth* above) and conveys them to the Prophet. If so, it would be unnecessary to visit the tomb, as one's prayers would be heard from anywhere in the world. Alternatively, the angel's location *within the Prophet's tomb* might indicate that the angel hears the prayers of those *who come to visit the tomb*, and conveys that information to the Prophet, whether he himself is in the tomb or not. In either case, the angel's location marks the Prophet's tomb as a sacred space, even if the Prophet's location is ambiguous.

In general, however, the message that prayers can reach the Prophet from anywhere in the world seems to have been used to disincentivise pilgrimage to his tomb.[122] This is made clear in a narration attributed to al-Ḥasan b. al-Ḥasan b. ʿAlī (d. *c.* 97/715–16), a grandson of the caliph (and Shīʿī imam) ʿAlī b. Abī Ṭālib, who lived in Medina.[123] When al-Ḥasan saw a group of people clustered

[121] al-Bazzār, *Musnad*, 4:254–5 (nos 1,425–6); Ibn Abī ʿĀṣim, *Kitāb al-Ṣalāt*, 42 (no. 51); al-Bukhārī, *Taʾrīkh*, 3/2:416 (no. 2,831); Ibn Abī Ḥātim, *Kitāb al-Jarḥ*, 3/1:296 (no. 1,644); al-ʿUqaylī, *Kitāb al-Ḍuʿafāʾ*, 3:248–9 (no. 1,246); al-Samhūdī, *Khulāṣat*, 96; Abū al-Shaykh al-Aṣbahānī, *Kitāb al-ʿAẓama*, ed. Riḍāʾ Allāh b. Muḥammad Idrīs al-Mubārakfūrī (Riyadh: Dār al-ʿĀṣima, 1408 AH [1987–8]), 762–3 (no. 339). The *isnāds* spread out from the obscure figure Nuʿaym b. Ḍamḍam, who reports from the equally obscure ʿImrān b. Ḥumayrī, from the Companion ʿAmmār b. Yāsir (d. 37/657), who had settled in Kūfa. According to the *isnāds*, Nuʿaym b. Ḍamḍam transmitted the report to Sufyān b. ʿUyayna, Qabīṣa b. ʿUqba (d. 215/830, Kūfa), ʿAlī b. al-Qāsim al-Kindī (d. unknown, Kūfa) and Abū Aḥmad al-Zubayrī (d. 203/818–19, Kūfa).

[122] Munt, *Holy City of Medina*, 131.

[123] He was also called al-Ḥasan al-Muthannā. On him, see Ahmed, *Religious Elite*, 151ff.

around the Prophet's tomb – in a variant version, it is a single man standing, making invocations and praying there – he upbraided them, saying: 'The Prophet said, "Do not use my grave as a place of celebration, and do not use your own houses as graves! Pray for me wherever you are and your prayers will reach me."'[124] A similar story is told of another grandson of 'Alī's: the fourth Twelver Shīʿī imam, 'Alī b. al-Ḥusayn (d. 95/713–14), called Zayn al-ʿĀbidīn, who also lived in Medina. Seeing a man enter a space by the tomb and make invocations there, 'Alī b. al-Ḥusayn approached him and asked, 'Shall I tell you a *ḥadīth* that I heard from my father, who heard it from my grandfather, who heard it from the Prophet?' He then narrated the same Prophetic statement that al-Ḥasan b. al-Ḥasan cited, ending with the assurance that 'Your prayer will reach me, wherever you are'.[125] These traditions affirm that individual Muslims' own locations are of no consequence for their prayers reaching the Prophet: their words will reach Muḥammad, wherever they are recited.

[124] 'Abd al-Razzāq, *Muṣannaf*, 3:577 (no. 6,726); Ibn Abī Shayba, *Muṣannaf*, 3:366 (no. 7,617), 4:566 (no. 11,929); al-Dhahabī, *Siyar*, 4:483–4; Ibn 'Asākir, *Ta'rīkh*, 13:61–2; al-Samhūdī, *Wafā' al-wafā*, 5:59. The *isnād* is: Muḥammad b. 'Ajlān (d. 148/765, Medina) > Suhayl b. Abī Ṣāliḥ (d. 138/755, Medina) > al-Ḥasan b. al-Ḥasan b. 'Alī. On Muḥammad b. 'Ajlān, see van Ess, *Theology and Society*, 2:761–3. On Suhayl b. Abī Ṣāliḥ, see Eva Collet, 'Dābiq et la frontière du Dār al-Islām: Histoire et représentations (Ier–Ve siècles H./VIIe–XIe siècles)', *RMMM* 144 (2018): 237–68; Juynboll, *Encyclopedia*, 348, 400, 621. From Ibn 'Ajlān, this tradition was transmitted by Sufyān al-Thawrī, Abū Khālid al-Aḥmar [Sulaymān b. Ḥayyān al-Azdī] (d. 189/805, Kūfa) and al-Layth b. Sa'd. A different version appears in Ismāʿīl b. Isḥāq, *Faḍl al-ṣalāt*, 44–5 (no. 30), with the *isnād*: Ibrāhīm b. Ḥamza (d. 230/845, Medina) > 'Abd al-'Azīz b. Muḥammad al-Darāwardī (d. 186/802, Medina) > Suhayl b. Abī Ṣāliḥ. A version without the narrative context appears in Ibn Abī 'Āṣim, *Kitāb al-Ṣalāt*, 29 (no. 27).

[125] Ibn Abī Shayba, *Muṣannaf*, 3:365–6 (no. 7,616); Abū Ya'lā, *Musnad*, 1:361–2 (no. 469); al-Bukhārī, *Ta'rīkh*, 1/2:186 (no. 2,140), 3/2:289 (no. 2,431); Ismāʿīl b. Isḥāq, *Faḍl al-ṣalāt*, 34–5 (no. 20); al-Samhūdī, *Wafā' al-wafā*, 5:59; Ibn Abī 'Āṣim, *Kitāb al-Ṣalāt*, 28–9 (no. 26). The *isnād* is: Ja'far b. Ibrāhīm b. Muḥammad b. 'Alī b. 'Abd Allāh b. Ja'far b. Abī Ṭālib (Medina) > 'Alī b. 'Umar [b. 'Alī b. al-Ḥusayn] (Medina) > his father ['Umar b. 'Alī b. al-Ḥusayn b. 'Alī b. Abī Ṭālib] (d. after 160/776–7, Medina) > 'Alī b. al-Ḥusayn [Zayn al-'Ābidīn]. On Ja'far b. Ibrāhīm, see Ibn Abī Ḥātim, *Kitāb al-Jarḥ*, 1/1:474 (no. 1,928); al-Zubayr b. Bakkār, *Jamharat*, 1:183. On 'Umar b. 'Alī, see Ahmed, *Religious Elite*, 174–6. From Ja'far b. Ibrāhīm, the tradition was transmitted by Zayd b. al-Ḥubāb (d. 203/818–19, Kūfa) and Ismāʿīl b. Abī Uways (d. 226/841, Medina).

On the other hand, several traditions explicitly encourage pilgrimage to the Prophet's tomb, and often directly connect this act with access to the Prophet's intercession. In a report transmitted (and perhaps created) by the Kūfan *mufassir* Muḥammad b. Marwān al-Suddī (d. 186/802), the Prophet says:

> Whoever prays for me at my tomb, I hear him. And whoever prays for me with intention, an angel is appointed to report this to me. He is protected in this world and the hereafter, and I will be a witness and an intercessor for him on the Day of Judgment.[126]

Here, an angel is again appointed to convey information about those who pray for the Prophet, as is found in other traditions. Additionally, though, the Prophet himself hears those who perform the prayer 'at my tomb' (*ʿinda qabrī*), suggesting that prayer there may be considered especially efficacious. But the Prophet will be a 'a witness and an intercessor' for whoever prays for him, explicitly laying out the eschatological benefits of such devotional activity.

In al-Suddī's tradition, the Prophet will intercede for whoever prays for him, whether the prayer is performed at his tomb or elsewhere. Other traditions directly couple the Prophet's intercession with visitation of his tomb. One such report appears in the *Musnad* of the Baṣran scholar Abū Dāwūd al-Ṭayālisī (d. 204/819–20):

> Whoever visits my grave (or whoever visits me), I will be an intercessor (or a witness) for him. And whoever dies in one of the two *ḥarams* [i.e. Mecca or Medina], God will place him among the secure on the Day of Resurrection.[127]

In a variant, the Prophet says that 'Whoever visits me purposefully (*mutaʿammidan*) will be under the protection of God [alternatively, 'my

[126] al-Khaṭīb al-Baghdādī, *Ta'rīkh*, 4:468–9; al-ʿUqaylī, *Kitāb al-Ḍuʿafā'*, 4:136–7 (no. 1,696); al-Bayhaqī, *Shuʿab al-īmān*, 3:140–1 (no. 1,481), 6:50 (no. 3,859); Ibn ʿAsākir, *Ta'rīkh*, 56:301–2; Ibn al-Jawzī, *Kitāb al-Mawḍūʿāt*, 1:303. On Muḥammad b. Marwān al-Suddī, see van Ess, *Theology and Society*, 1:348–50.

[127] al-Ṭayālisī, *Musnad*, 1:66 (no. 65); al-Bayhaqī, *Sunan*, 5:403 (no. 10,273); al-Samhūdī, *Wafā' al-wafā*, 5:19. On al-Ṭayālisī and his *Musnad*, see *EI*^{2}, s.v. 'al-Ṭayālisī' (G. H. A. Juynboll); Munt, *Holy City of Medina*, 133.

protection'] on the Day of Resurrection'.[128] The transmission of this *ḥadīth* centres on an obscure figure identified as Abū al-Jarrāḥ Sawwār b. Maymūn al-ʿAbdī, who reportedly transmitted the *ḥadīth* to the Baṣran proto-Sunnī scholars al-Ṭayālisī, Shuʿba b. al-Ḥajjāj (d. 160/776) and ʿAbd Allāh b. ʿAwn (d. 151/768).[129] In another *ḥadīth*, the Prophet says: 'Whoever visits my grave, my intercession is bound for him' (*wajabat li-hu shafāʿatī*).[130] This *ḥadīth* was transmitted by Mūsā b. Hilāl al-ʿAbdī, a Baṣran active in the late eighth and early ninth centuries.[131]

Throughout the first Islamic centuries, a debate was waged – in part through competing *ḥadīth* statements – regarding prayer for the Prophet, visitation of his grave, and the relationship of these devotional acts to the Prophet's intercession. On the basis of their *isnād*s, it appears that reports linking visitation of the Prophet's tomb with the Prophet's intercession were circulating 'by the early third/ninth century at the latest', and likely decades earlier.[132] Further

[128] al-ʿUqaylī, *Kitāb al-Ḍuʿafāʾ*, 4:361–2 (no. 1,973); al-Dhahabī, *Mīzān*, 5:45; al-Samhūdī, *Wafāʾ al-wafā*, 5:20. Another variant appears in ʿAlī b. ʿUmar al-Dāraquṭnī, *Sunan al-Dāraquṭnī*, ed. Shuʿayb al-Arnaʾūṭ et al., 6 vols (Beirut: Muʾassasat al-Risāla, 2004), 3:333–4 (no. 2,694); Abū Bakr Aḥmad b. Marwān al-Dīnawarī, *al-Mujālasa wa-jawāhir al-ʿilm*, ed. Abū ʿUbayda Mashhūr b. Ḥasan Āl Salmān, 10 vols (Beirut: Dār Ibn Ḥazm, 2002), 1:441–4 (no. 130); al-Dhahabī, *Mīzān*, 5:46; al-Samhūdī, *Wafāʾ al-wafā*, 5:21.

[129] Elsewhere, this transmitter's given name and his father's name are provided in the reverse order, i.e. he is called Maymūn b. Sawwār: Muḥammad b. Ḥibbān al-Bustī, *Kitāb al-Thiqāt*, 9 vols (Hyderabad: Dāʾirat al-Maʿārif al-ʿUthmāniyya, 1973–83), 9:173; Ibn ʿAdī, *al-Kāmil*, 7:2,588.

[130] al-Dāraquṭnī, *Sunan*, 3:334 (no. 2,695); al-ʿUqaylī, *Kitāb al-Ḍuʿafāʾ*, 4:170 (no. 1,744); Ibn ʿAdī, *al-Kāmil*, 6:2,350; al-Dīnawarī, *al-Mujālasa wa-jawāhir*, 1:431–40 (no. 129); Muḥammad b. Aḥmad b. Ḥammād al-Dūlābī, *al-Kunā wa-l-asmāʾ*, ed. Naẓr Muḥammad al-Fāryābī (Beirut: Dār Ibn Ḥazm, 2000), 846; Abū Bakr al-Khaṭīb al-Baghdādī, *Talkhīṣ al-mutashābih fī-l-rasm wa-ḥimāyat mā ashkala minhu ʿan bawādir al-taṣḥīf wa-al-wahm*, ed. Sukayna al-Shihābī (Damascus: Dār Ṭalās, 1980), 581; al-Dhahabī, *Taʾrīkh*, 11 [171–80 AH]:212–13; al-Bayhaqī, *Shuʿab al-īmān*, 6:51–2 (nos 3,862–3); al-Samhūdī, *Wafāʾ al-wafā*, 5:7–12.

[131] Munt, *Holy City of Medina*, 134. Mūsā b. Hilāl is said to have transmitted the tradition to ʿUbayd b. Muḥammad b. al-Qāsim al-Warrāq (d. 255/868–9, Baghdad), Muḥammad b. Ismāʿīl b. Samura (d. 260/873–4, Kūfa), ʿAlī b. Maʿbad b. Nūḥ (d. 259/872–3, Baghdad) and al-Faḍl b. Sahl (d. 255/868–9, Baghdad), among others. On these transmitters, see al-Khaṭīb al-Baghdādī, *Taʾrīkh*, 12:389; Ibn Ḥibbān, *Kitāb al-Thiqāt*, 9:118; Ibn Abī Ḥātim, *Kitāb al-Jarḥ*, 3/2:190 (no. 1,080), 4/1:166 (no. 734).

[132] Munt, *Holy City of Medina*, 135.

upsetting any suggestion of clear 'home town pride' for the Prophet's tomb, Ḥijāzī embrace of pilgrimage to the tomb is mostly absent from these sources. Instead, the most explicit statements of support for pilgrimage to the Prophet's tomb appear in *ḥadīth* that circulated in the cities of Iraq. At the same time, distinctly anti-pilgrimage traditions also circulated in Iraq, such as the *ḥadīth* about angels travelling the earth to collect the *umma*'s prayers. It appears that Iraq was the epicentre of discussion of these ritual and theological issues, with strong statements put forward on each side.

While proto-Sunnī opinions in Iraq were divided, a clear embrace of pilgrimage to the Prophet's tomb appears in Imāmī Shīʿī traditions from Iraq.[133] The *Kitāb* of Muḥammad b. al-Muthannā al-Ḥadramī (a Kūfan Shīʿī active in the early ninth century) includes a tradition in which Jaʿfar al-Ṣādiq commands: 'Pray beside [or 'towards' (*ilā jānib*)] the Messenger of God's tomb, even though a believer's prayer reaches [the Prophet] wherever he is.'[134] Reversing the conclusion found in other reports, Jaʿfar here affirms that the Prophet's tomb should be visited (or at least prayed towards) even though prayers can reach him from elsewhere. This message reappears in another tradition from Jaʿfar al-Ṣādiq directly encouraging pilgrimage to the Prophet's tomb: 'Pass through Medina and greet the Messenger of God from nearby, even though prayer reaches him from afar.'[135] Several Shīʿī traditions associate visitation

[133] George Warner, 'One Thousand *Ḥijaj*: Ritualization and the Margins of the Law in Early Twelver Shiʿi *Ziyāra* Literature', *JAOS* 142.2 (2022): 415–34.

[134] *al-Uṣūl al-sitta ʿashar min al-uṣūl al-awwaliyya: Majmūʿat min kutub al-riwāya al-awwaliyya*, ed. Ḍiyāʾ al-Dīn al-Maḥmūdī (Qom: Dār al-Ḥadīth, 2002), 253 (no. 328). The *isnād* is: Muḥammad b. al-Muthannā al-Ḥadramī > Jaʿfar b. Muḥammad b. Shurayḥ al-Ḥadramī (late second/eighth century, Kūfa) > Dharīḥ al-Muḥāribī (active mid-second/eighth century, Kūfa) > Jaʿfar. On these transmitters, see Modarressi, *Tradition and Survival*, 217–18, 274, 306. On this text and its genre, see Etan Kohlberg, 'Al-Uṣūl Al-Arbaʿumiʾa', *JSAI* 10 (1987): 128–66, esp. 154–5; Hassan Ansari, *L'imamat et l'Occultation selon l'imamisme: Étude bibliographique et histoire de textes* (Leiden: Brill, 2017), 120–2. This tradition also appears, in slightly different form and with a different *isnād*, in al-Kulaynī, *al-Kāfī*, 4:553; al-Ṭūsī, *Tahdhīb al-aḥkām*, 6:8–9.

[135] al-Kulaynī, *al-Kāfī*, 4:552; Munt, *Holy City of Medina*, 131. The *isnād* is: many companions > Sahl b. Ziyād (active 255/869, Rayy) > Aḥmad b. Muḥammad [b. ʿĪsā?] > Ḥammād b. ʿUthmān (d. 190/805–6, Kūfa) > Isḥāq b. ʿAmmār [al-Ṣayrafī] (d. *c.* 181/797–8, Kūfa) > Jaʿfar. On these transmitters, see Modarressi, *Tradition and Survival*, 239, 299; al-Najāshī, *Rijāl*, 185 (no. 490).

of the Prophet's tomb with his intercession, often with language paralleling Sunnī-transmitted traditions discussed above, such as that 'Whoever visits me, my intercession is bound for him'.[136]

These traditions might appear to affirm the Prophet's bodily presence within his grave, as they celebrate visitation of his tomb in Medina and indicate that its visitors are 'nearby' to him. However, other Shīʿī traditions significantly complicate the Prophet's location. Above, we saw the report in which Jaʿfar al-Ṣādiq states: 'No prophet or legatee remains in the earth for more than three days before he is lifted to the sky in his spirit, his bones, and his flesh.' Immediately following these words, Jaʿfar continues:

> But the sites of their traces (*mawāḍiʿu āthārihim*) are arrived at [by visitors], and greetings reach them from afar. They hear [the greetings] at the sites of their traces [as if] from nearby.[137]

In this tradition, the bifurcated location of the prophets and of their legatees – seemingly present both in their graves and in heaven – is addressed directly, though tersely. While their spirits, bones and flesh are raised to heaven, the sites of the prophets' and legatees' traces (*āthār*) nonetheless remain on earth. The sites of these *āthār* offer a communicative portal to the prophets and legatees, who hear the greetings performed at these sites 'from nearby', even though they are far away in the heavens.[138]

As discussed in previous chapters, *āthār* often means 'relics', 'remains' or 'traces'. What the word means in this Shīʿī report is unclear: seemingly the bodies of the prophets and legatees are lifted to heaven, yet some trace of them

[136] al-Kulaynī, *al-Kāfī*, 4:548; al-Ṭūsī, *Tahdhīb al-aḥkām*, 6:6; Ibn Bābawayh, *Kitāb Man lā yaḥḍuru al-faqīh*, 2:353 (no. 3,157). The *isnād* is: 'Alī b. Muḥammad b. Bindār > Ibrāhīm b. Isḥāq (active 269/882–3) > Muḥammad b. Sulaymān al-Daylamī (Baṣra) > Ibrāhīm b. Abī Ḥajar al-Aslamī > Jaʿfar. On these transmitters, see Modarressi, *Tradition and Survival*, 374; al-Najāshī, *Rijāl*, 19 (no. 21), 365 (no. 987).

[137] Translation adapted from Crow, 'Death of al-Ḥusayn', 61.

[138] The Twelver Shīʿī scholar al-Karājukī (d. 449/1057) states that 'our visitation of their shrines is not because [the prophets and imams] are within them, but in order to honor the places'. Within the course of his discussion, al-Karājukī cites a *ḥadīth* about the Prophet's corpse not remaining within the earth for more than three days. See al-Karājukī, *Kanz al-Fawāʾid*, 2:140; Szilágyi, 'Prophet Like Jesus', 140.

is left behind in their graves. At the locations of their traces, they hear visitors' greetings 'from nearby': the traces and/or spaces thus serve as avenues for communicating with the prophets and legatees in heaven. Similar ideas appear in traditions about pilgrimage to al-Ḥusayn's grave in Karbalā'. For example, Ja'far al-Ṣādiq states that 'the actions of his visitors ascend to the sky from [the grave]'.[139] Elsewhere, Ja'far reports that al-Ḥusayn, suspended from God's throne in heaven, 'looks at his visitors [at his grave] and knows them by their names and their fathers' names [. . .] and he asks forgiveness for [such a visitor] and asks his father ['Alī b. Abī Ṭālib] to seek forgiveness for [that visitor]'.[140]

These Shīʿī reports surely reflect the importance of pilgrimage to the imams' tombs for the emergence of Shīʿī communities in the eighth century, as recent scholars have noted.[141] Yet many of these Shīʿī reports present images of the Prophet's grave that are similar to those also found in proto-Sunnī traditions. We might suggest, for example, that al-Suddī's *ḥadīth* ('Whoever prays for me at my grave, I hear him') is not far removed from the idea that the prophets and legatees 'hear at the sites of their traces [as if] from nearby'. Indeed, direct parallels between the Shīʿī and proto-Sunnī sources appear in several of the traditions about the Prophet's intercessory activities after his death, including the benefits gained by those who visit his grave in Medina. There were clearly overlaps and discussions between these Muslim communities, including the significance that some members of these communities placed on visiting the Prophet's tomb in Medina.

These differing traditions suggest that visitation of the Prophet Muḥammad at his tomb – and the role of this practice in acquiring the Prophet's intercession – was the subject of significant dispute among Muslims in the eighth and ninth centuries, especially in Iraq.[142] While some traditions encourage pilgrimage

[139] al-Kulaynī, *al-Kāfī*, 4:588; Ibn Qūlūya, *Kāmil al-ziyārāt*, 457 (no. 694); al-Ṭūsī, *Tahdhīb al-aḥkām*, 6:58–9.

[140] Ibn Qūlūya, *Kāmil al-ziyārāt*, 206 (no. 292), 543–4 (no. 836); Crow, 'Death of al-Ḥusayn', 62–3.

[141] Haider, *Origins of the Shīʿa*, 243–7; Munt, *Holy City of Medina*, 136–7; Warner, 'One Thousand *Ḥijaj*', 422–4.

[142] Versions of several of these reports also circulated in the Ḥijāz, but these seem to focus on the religious merit of making the Hijra to Medina rather than on any benefits accrued from visiting the Prophet's tomb. See 'Abd al-Razzāq, *Muṣannaf*, 9:266–7 (nos 17,161–6); al-Samhūdī, *Wafā' al-wafā*, 5:23–4, 29; Munt, *Holy City of Medina*, 133.

to the tomb and directly tie it to the Prophet's intercession, others indicate that such travel is unnecessary, as the Prophet is able to hear believers' prayers and see their actions wherever they are performed. The Prophet's location is often left unclear in these traditions, with his terrestrial or heavenly existence both possible. Yet his bodily location was not without consequence for these ritual practices, with prominent voices citing his presence or absence there as a reason to visit – or not – the Prophet's grave. The Prophet's body continued to be a site of discussion, whether it was there or not.

Conclusion: A Footnote on the Prophet's Tomb

Among the historical reports about the renovation of the Prophet's Mosque in Medina during the caliphate of al-Walīd b. ʿAbd al-Malik, a 'strange story' appears.[143] During the building project, the chamber that contained the graves of the Prophet Muḥammad and the first two caliphs, Abū Bakr and ʿUmar, either collapsed or was purposefully torn down. As the space was being cleared and rebuilt, a foot appeared among the rubble,[144] or (in another version) a foot with a thigh and knee.[145] The details of the reports differ, but the general tenor of the reactions is conveyed by the version recorded in al-Bukhārī's *Ṣaḥīḥ*: when the builders saw the foot, 'they were frightened, thinking it was the Prophet's foot'.

Scholars have read this story as part of the commentary that emerged around the controversial Umayyad building project at the Prophet's Mosque.[146] Other texts note Medinans' protests at the partial destruction of the Prophet's home that accompanied the incorporation of his burial place into the Mosque. The perceived sacrilege of disturbing the Prophet's resting place conceivably explains the response displayed by ʿUmar b. ʿAbd al-ʿAzīz, the Umayyad governor of the

[143] Halevi, *Muhammad's Grave*, 192.

[144] Ibn Saʿd, *Ṭabaqāt*, 3:342; al-Balādhurī, *Ansāb al-ashrāf*, 10:442–3; al-Bukhārī, *Ṣaḥīḥ*, 336 (kitāb al-janāʾiz, bāb 96); al-Samhūdī, *Wafāʾ al-wafā*, 2:304–5. The *isnād* is: Suwayd b. Saʿīd al-Anbārī (d. 240/855, Iraq) and Farwa b. Abī al-Mughrāʾ (d. 225/839–40, Kūfa) > ʿAlī b. Mushir (d. 189/804–5, Kūfa) > Hishām b. ʿUrwa. The common link here is ʿAlī b. Mushir, on whom see Bursi, 'Holy Heretical Body', 163–5.

[145] al-Ājurrī, *Kitāb al-Sharīʿa*, 5:2,389–90 (no. 1,871); al-Samhūdī, *Wafāʾ al-wafā*, 2:305; Ibn Ḥajar, *Fatḥ al-bārī*, 4:195. On the transmitters of this report, see Chapter 1, note 61.

[146] Halevi, *Muhammad's Grave*, 193; Munt, *Holy City of Medina*, 108.

Ḥijāz and the overseer of the mosque renovation. Informed of the (in this version) two feet discovered in the burial chamber, ʿUmar cries ʿWe belong to God and to Him we shall return!' and strikes his face in agony.[147]

However, the assumption that the builders' reactions emerged from their abject horror at grave desecration is confounded by the story's resolution. Their anxiety was immediately relieved when the scholar ʿUrwa b. al-Zubayr assured them, 'No, by God, this is not the Prophet's foot! It is only ʿUmar's foot!' To many people, the words 'Do not fear! These are the feet of your ancestor, ʿUmar b. al-Khaṭṭāb' would surely not be very reassuring.[148] Yet 'anxiety left ʿUmar b. ʿAbd al-ʿAzīz' at the realisation that the partially uncovered body belonged to his great-grandfather, not to the Prophet.[149]

Why would seeing the Prophet's feet have been considered so much more upsetting than seeing the second caliph's feet? Krisztina Szilágyi provides a plausible explanation, asking: 'why would ʿUmar [b. ʿAbd al-ʿAzīz] be awed to see Muḥammad's foot, but calm down when told it is ʿUmar [b. al-Khaṭṭāb]'s, unless the former was not supposed to be in the grave at all?'[150] In other words, perhaps the builders' fear emerged from their belief that the Prophet's body (including his feet) should not have been found in his grave, since he was 'supposed' to have been lifted to heaven. Were the builders' ideas about the

[147] *Kitāb al-Manāsik*, 375. This version is narrated from Ṣāliḥ b. Muḥammad > Sulaymān b. ʿAbd al-ʿAzīz al-Zuhrī > his father [ʿAbd al-ʿAzīz b. ʿImrān b. ʿAbd al-ʿAzīz] > Jaʿfar b. Wardān al-Bannāʾ > his father [Wardān al-Bannāʾ]. On the transmitters in this *isnād*, see Chapter 1, note 58. For reports from Wardān al-Bannāʾ ('the builder') and his son Jaʿfar, see *Kitāb al-Manāsik*, 365, 367; al-Ṭabarī, *Taʾrīkh*, 2/2:1,192; al-Samhūdī, *Wafāʾ al-wafā*, 2:265, 274, 304.

[148] *Kitāb al-Manāsik*, 369; al-Samhūdī, *Wafāʾ al-wafā*, 2:303; al-Marāghī, *Taḥqīq al-nuṣra*, 82; Munt, *Holy City of Medina*, 108. This version is narrated from Ibn Zabāla > Ibrāhīm b. Muḥammad b. ʿAbd al-ʿAzīz > his father [Muḥammad b. ʿAbd al-ʿAzīz b. ʿUmar al-Zuhrī]. Muḥammad b. ʿAbd al-ʿAzīz was a judge and treasurer in Medina under the ʿAbbāsid caliph al-Manṣūr and 'a useful local ally for the ʿAbbāsids'. His son Ibrāhīm was also a Medinan elite and a *ḥadīth* transmitter with a weak reputation. They are descendants of the Companion ʿAbd al-Raḥmān b. ʿAwf. On these figures, see Ahmed, *Religious Elite*, 57–9; al-Khaṭīb al-Baghdādī, *Taʾrīkh*, 3:605–8 (no. 1,117); Ibn ʿAdī, *al-Kāmil*, 1:250; al-ʿUqaylī, *Kitāb al-Ḍuʿafāʾ*, 1:61 (no. 58).

[149] al-Ājurrī, *Kitāb al-Sharīʿa*, 5:2390 (no. 1,871); al-Samhūdī, *Wafāʾ al-wafā*, 2:305; Ibn Ḥajar, *Fatḥ al-bārī*, 4:195.

[150] Szilágyi, 'Prophet Like Jesus', 146 n.55.

Prophet suddenly thrown into horrible doubt by the sight of this foot? Did the prophecy of the Prophet's empty tomb suddenly appear wrong?

Notably, the Prophet's bodily ascension is directly connected with this story of 'Umar's foot in at least one, significantly later, text. In his *ḥadīth* commentary *al-Badr al-Munīr*, the Shāfiʿī jurist Ibn al-Mulaqqin (d. 804/1401) relates that when the excavators came upon the foot, they 'thought it was the Messenger of God's foot [. . .] and they were panicked, until Saʿīd b. al-Musayyab related to them: "The prophets' corpses do not remain in the earth longer than forty days, then they are raised."'[151] Here, Saʿīd b. al-Musayyab confirms that the foot could not possibly belong to the Prophet, as his body had been raised to Paradise.

Belief in the Prophet's bodily resurrection offers an interesting explanation for these odd stories of horror – followed by relief – caused by the foot in the tomb. However, stories from later in 'Umar b. 'Abd al-ʿAzīz's life complicate things again. In a story transmitted by the Medinan scholar Muḥammad b. Ismāʿīl b. Abī Fudayk (d. *c.* 199–200/814–16), a man named Yazīd b. Abī Saʿīd al-Mihrī reports:

> I met 'Umar b. 'Abd al-ʿAzīz in Syria while he was caliph. When I bade him farewell, he said, 'I need you to do something. When you go to Medina, you will see the Prophet's tomb. Greet him for me.'[152]

Here, 'Umar instructs Yazīd to transmit his greeting to the Prophet at his grave in Medina. Such behaviour is also reported by the Baṣran scholar Ḥātim b. Wardān (d. 184/800), who says that "Umar b. 'Abd al-ʿAzīz would dispatch a messenger to Medina to greet the Prophet for him'.[153] 'Abd Allāh b. Jaʿfar, a

[151] Ibn al-Mulaqqin, *al-Badr al-munīr fī takhrīj al-aḥādīth wa-l-āthār al-wāqiʿa fī al-Sharḥ al-kabīr*, ed. Muṣṭafā Abū al-Ghayṭ et al., 10 vols (Riyadh: Dār al-Hijra, 2004), 5:285; Szilágyi, 'Prophet Like Jesus', 141–2. On this author, see *EI*[3], s.v. 'Ibn al-Mulaqqin' (Nathan Hofer).

[152] al-Bayhaqī, *Shuʿab al-īmān*, 6:54 (no. 3,870); Ibn 'Asākir, *Ta'rīkh*, 65:203–5. The *isnād* runs (in part): Ibn Abī al-Dunyā > Isḥāq b. Ḥātim al-Madāʾinī (d. 252/866–7, Iraq) > Ibn Abī Fudayk > Ribāḥ b. Bashīr > Yazīd b. Abī Saʿīd al-Mihrī. Shortened versions of this narrative appear in the biographies of Yazīd b. Abī Saʿīd in al-Bukhārī, *Ta'rīkh*, 4/2:339 (no. 3,237); Ibn Abī Ḥātim, *Kitāb al-Jarḥ*, 4/2:270 (no. 1,132).

[153] al-Bayhaqī, *Shuʿab al-īmān*, 6:54 (no. 3,869). The *isnād* is: 'Abd Allāh b. Yūsuf al-Iṣfahānī (d. 409/1019, Nishapur) > Ibrāhīm b. Firās (unknown) > Muḥammad b. Ṣāliḥ al-Rāzī (unknown) > Ziyād b. Yaḥyā (d. 254/867–8, Baṣra) > Ḥātim b. Wardān (d. 184/800, Baṣra).

mawlā of the Umayyads, likewise reports that "'Umar would send a messenger to him [the Prophet] from Syria'.[154] If 'Umar b. 'Abd al-'Azīz believed the Prophet had been raised to heaven, he considered it nonetheless worthwhile to greet him at his tomb.

These different traditions may simply reflect different Muslims' variant deployments of the famously pious caliph 'Umar b. 'Abd al-'Azīz for the purposes of justifying particular attitudes towards, and rituals at, the Prophet's grave. Alternatively, perhaps the caliph thought it paradoxically possible that prophets like Muḥammad 'hear at the sites of their traces [as if] from nearby', even when they are in heaven. In either case, the Prophet's tomb was the site of both ritual and debate. As we will see in the next chapter, other locations and objects – or *āthār* – associated with the Prophet's life were likewise discussed and used as places of special significance. And, again like the Prophet's tomb, defining exactly how they should be used was a contentious issue among early Muslim communities.

154 al-Bayhaqī, *Shu'ab al-īmān*, 6:54 (no. 3,870); Ibn 'Asākir, *Ta'rīkh*, 65:204. On 'Abd Allāh b. Ja'far, see al-Bukhārī, *Ta'rīkh*, 3/1:62 (no. 149).

5

PLACES WHERE THE PROPHET PRAYED: RITUALISING THE PROPHET'S TRACES

One day in the late seventh century, the governor of Medina, Marwān b. al-Ḥakam, came to the Prophet's Mosque and found a man pressing his body against the wall of the Prophet's tomb. Indignant at this sight, Marwān grabbed the man by the neck and demanded, 'Do you know what you are doing?' 'Yes', the man replied, looking up, 'I have come to the Messenger of God, not to the stone or the curtain.' The man was Abū Ayyūb al-Anṣārī, a Companion of the Prophet, who had fought bravely in many of the Muslim community's early battles.[1] Eyeing Marwān, Abū Ayyūb said, 'I heard the Messenger of God say, "Do not mourn for the religion (*al-dīn*) when its people govern, but rather mourn for it when other people do."'[2]

[1] On Abū Ayyūb al-Anṣārī, see *EI*[3], s.v. 'Abū Ayyūb al-Anṣārī' (Michael Lecker); Nancy Khalek, 'Dreams of Hagia Sophia: The Muslim Siege of Constantinople in 674 CE, Abū Ayyūb al-Anṣārī, and the Medieval Islamic Imagination', in *The Islamic Scholarly Tradition: Studies in History, Law, and Thought in Honor of Professor Michael Allan Cook*, ed. Asad Q. Ahmed, Behnam Sadeghi and Michael Bonner (Leiden: Brill, 2011), 131–46.

[2] Ibn Ḥanbal, *Musnad*, 38:558 (no. 23,585); Ibn Abī Khaythama, *Ta'rīkh*, 2:76–7 (no. 1,801); al-Ḥākim al-Nisābūrī, *al-Mustadrak 'alā al-Ṣaḥīḥayn*, ed. Yūsuf 'Abd al-Raḥmān al-Mar'ashlī, 5 vols (Beirut: Dār al-Ma'rifa, n.d.), 4:515; Ibn 'Asākir, *Ta'rīkh*, 57:249–50; al-Samhūdī, *Wafā' al-wafā*, 5:107–8.

A similar story is told of a meeting at the Prophet's tomb between Marwān and another Companion: Usāma b. Zayd, the son of the Prophet Muḥammad's adopted son Zayd b. Ḥāritha.[3] When Marwān saw Usāma praying beside the tomb, he yelled, 'You are praying at the Messenger of God's tomb?' Usāma responded 'I love him', prompting Marwān to swear at him with 'vile words' (*qawlan qabīḥan*). With his back turned, Usāma then said, 'O Marwān, I heard the Messenger of God say, "God hates both the obscene and the foul", and you are the obscenest of the foul.'[4]

In these two stories, prominent Muslims face off at the Prophet's tomb, with several themes on display in their narrativised encounters. One key theme is the piety of political rulers. After his tenure as the governor of Medina, Marwān b. al-Ḥakam was a short-reigned caliph (r. 64–5/684–5), whose rule initiated the Marwānid Umayyad dynasty that dominated much of the Islamic world until the 'Abbāsid revolution.[5] In a not-so-subtle critique of the Marwānids and their infamous impieties, Abū Ayyūb cites a Prophetic warning about the rule of people 'other than' the righteous followers of Islam: implicitly, that is, Marwān and his reprobate successors. Indeed, Usāma b. Zayd explicitly connects the Prophet's censorious words to Marwān, and places him in the category of those 'hated' by God. Circulated by proto-Sunnī and Shīʿī transmitters in the eighth to ninth centuries, these reports take part in the wider vilification of Umayyad rule (and of Marwān more specifically) that appears in many sources from this period.[6]

[3] On Usāma b. Zayd, see *EI*², s.v. 'Usāma b. Zayd' (V. Vacca); David S. Powers, *Zayd* (Philadelphia: University of Pennsylvania Press, 2014), 69–94.

[4] Ibn Abī Khaythama, *Ta'rīkh*, 2:75 (no. 1,796); Ibn Balbān, *Ṣaḥīḥ Ibn Ḥibbān*, 12:506–7 (no. 5,694); Ibn 'Asākir, *Ta'rīkh*, 57:248–9; al-Ṭabarānī, *al-Muʿjam al-kabīr*, 1:166 (no. 405); Abū 'Umar Yūsuf b. 'Abd Allāh b. Muḥammad b. 'Abd al-Barr, *al-Istīʿab fī maʿrifat al-aṣḥāb*, ed. 'Alī Muḥammad al-Bajjāwī, 4 vols (Beirut: Dār al-Jīl, 1992), 1:76–7.

[5] On Marwān b. al-Ḥakam, see *EI*², s.v. 'Marwān I b. al-Ḥākam' [*sic*] (C. E. Bosworth); Hawting, *First Dynasty of Islam*, 46–8, 58–9; Henri Lammens, 'L'avènement des Marwānides et le califat de Marwān Ier', *Mélanges de l'Université Saint-Joseph* 12 (1927): 43–147.

[6] The Abū Ayyūb report's common link appears to be Kathīr b. Zayd al-Aslamī (d. 158/774–5, Medina), who transmitted it to Abū 'Āmir al-ʿAqadī 'Abd al-Malik b. 'Umar (d. 205/820–1, Baṣra); Abū Nubāta Yūnus b. Yaḥyā b. Nubāta (d. 207/822–3, Medina); and Sufyān b. Ḥamza al-Aslamī (active late 2nd/8th cent., Medina). Al-Samhūdī reports this tradition from the *Akhbār al-Madīna* of the 'Alid historian Abū al-Ḥusayn Yaḥyā b. al-Ḥasan al-ʿAqīqī (d. 277/890). On

Another theme in these stories is the vexing issue of visiting the Prophet's grave, and what one should (and should not) do there. Marwān appears in these narratives as something of an iconoclast, disparaging men for touching and praying near the Prophet's burial place. As we saw in the discussion of the Maqām Ibrāhīm in Chapter 2, this question of how to engage physically with material remains of the prophetic past was a contested issue among early Muslims. Marwān's angrily yanking Abū Ayyūb away from touching his face to the tomb is quite similar to Ibn al-Zubayr's protest at those whom he sees touching the Maqām: 'You were not commanded to stroke it, but only to pray nearby it!' But in his rebuke of Usāma b. Zayd, Marwān suggests the inappropriateness not only of touching the Prophet's tomb, but even of praying beside it. In Marwān, we see one type of response to the problem of sacred spaces, which exercised many Muslim thinkers from early in Islamic history.

Yet the lines of ritual propriety are thrown somewhat awry in these stories by the identities and reputations of the men involved. The man touching his forehead to the tomb is the devout Companion Abū Ayyūb al-Anṣārī: a paradigm of Islamic virtue, who notes that he has come to visit the Prophet, not to venerate the stones or curtains at his tomb.[7] The one found praying near the tomb is Usāma b. Zayd, often called the 'Beloved of the Messenger of God' (*ḥibb Rasūl Allāh*), who says that his actions at the tomb stem from his own deep love for the Prophet.[8] Could such men be acting ritually improperly? The question of who is, in fact, the pious one in these exchanges is further emphasised by the critique of Marwān and the Umayyads in the Prophetic words that Abū Ayyūb and Usāma each cite. Is Marwān b. al-Ḥakam – a former enemy of the Prophet and the founder of an impious regime – one to say whether a Companion's actions at the Prophet's tomb are incorrect?

the latter, see Munt, *Holy City of Medina*, 11–13, 99–100, 132–3. The Usāma b. Zayd report's common link is Wahb b. Jarīr (d. 206/822, Baṣra), who transmits it from his father Jarīr b. Ḥāzim (d. 175/791, Baṣra), who in turn transmits it from the famous historian Muḥammad b. Isḥāq (d. 150/767). Wahb b. Jarīr and his father appear as transmitters of Ibn Isḥāq traditions elsewhere too: Andersson, *Early Sunnī Historiography*, 111–12, 125, 127.

[7] This is, of course, an argument quite similar to the ones Christians made in defence of their own veneration of relics and icons.

[8] Powers, *Zayd*, 69–70.

This chapter explores these conflicting perspectives about how to engage with the Prophet's relics, or *āthār*, among Muslims of the first centuries of Islam. In the previous chapter, we saw some of this discussion about visiting the Prophet's tomb. Yet the tomb was just one of the many spots in the Ḥijāz that became cherished for their associations with the Prophet. On the basis of reports found in historical and legal texts, it appears that 'the consecration of places connected with the life of the Prophet' was taking place by the early eighth century.[9] Various texts feature lists of 'places where the Prophet prayed', mentions of visitation to these locations by different Muslim groups and individuals, and descriptions of monuments constructed at several sites associated with the Prophet's life. This evidence suggests that an effort was made to promote, and perhaps to control, the veneration of the Prophet in the hallowed landscape of the Ḥijāz throughout the late seventh, eighth and ninth centuries.

In no small part, these efforts at memorialising the Prophetic landscape drew upon the testimony and examples of the Companions.[10] As we see in the reports of Abū Ayyūb and Usāma b. Zayd, such figures could be utilised to authorise places and rituals as authentic, acceptable and even commendable expressions of Islamic piety. Their memories of the Prophet were collected by early historians and used in sacralising locations throughout the geography of the Prophet's life and actions. At the same time, however, Marwān b. al-Ḥakam was not the only early figure found disparaging the visitation and ritualisation of the Prophet's *āthār*. Other prominent Companions and Successors are cited as opponents of such practices, suggesting disagreements among the early generations of Muslims about how exactly to incorporate the places of the Prophet's life into Muslim practice. Desires to commemorate the Prophet's history in the landscape of the Ḥijāz ideologically jostled alongside discomfort with these various venerational activities.

This chapter serves as a final examination of the struggles over relic practices that appeared among early Muslims. Much like the wider late antique contestations over material embodiments of the sacred and pious travel thereto, early Muslims displayed many of the same sorts of debates as occurred among

[9] Miklos Muranyi, 'The Emergence of Holy Places in Early Islam: On the Prophet's Track', *JSAI* 39 (2012): 165–71.

[10] A similar point appears in Khalek, 'Medieval Muslim Martyrs', 92.

contemporaneous Jewish and Christian communities.[11] As within these other religious traditions, trends appeared among early Muslims that encouraged the commemoration of places and objects associated with early Islamic communal history (and especially the life of the Prophet Muḥammad) and treated these as sanctified locations. Simultaneously, other Muslim voices questioned the permissibility of this multiplication of sacred spaces and their visitation. Yet rather than a contest between 'popular practice' and 'orthodox Islam', this was a dialogue between elite voices, with contending perspectives on what Islamic practice could and could not contain.

Following the Prophet's Tracks: Re-tracing the Prophet's Life in the Ḥijāz

Abū Ayyūb al-Anṣārī and Usāma b. Zayd were not the only figures whom we find coming to visit the Prophet's tomb in the seventh century. Probably the tomb's most prolific early visitor was 'Abd Allāh b. 'Umar b. al-Khaṭṭāb (d. 73/692–3), the prominent son of the second caliph. On the basis of many reports, 'Abd Allāh b. 'Umar greatly esteemed the tomb complex in the Medina Mosque, which contained not only the Prophet, but also the first two caliphs Abū Bakr and ('Abd Allāh's father) 'Umar. When he overheard someone asking where 'the ascetics (*zāhidūn*) in this world, who yearn for the afterlife' were, Ibn 'Umar reportedly gestured towards the tomb of the Prophet, Abū Bakr and 'Umar and said, 'You are asking about these men?'[12] Whenever he journeyed away from his home town of Medina, Ibn 'Umar would first pray in the mosque, then come to the tomb and say: 'Peace be upon you, Messenger of God! Peace be upon you, Abū Bakr! Peace be upon you, father!'[13] He did the same when he returned to Medina, coming to greet the three men in the tomb even before setting foot in his own home.[14] In one version of this report,

[11] Brouria Bitton-Ashkelony, *Encountering the Sacred: The Debate on Christian Pilgrimage in Late Antiquity* (Berkeley: University of California Press, 2005); Eyal Ben Eliyahu, 'The Rabbinic Polemic against Sanctification of Sites', *JSJ* 40 (2009): 260–80.

[12] Hannād b. al-Sarī al-Kūfī, *Kitāb al-Zuhd*, ed. 'Abd al-Raḥmān b. 'Abd al-Jabbār al-Farīwā'ī (Kuwait: Dār al-Khulafā' li-l-Kitāb al-Islāmī, 1985), 314–15 (no. 563); Melchert, *Before Sufism*, 11.

[13] Ibn Abī Shayba, *Muṣannaf*, 4:559–60 (no. 11,904); al-Shaybānī, *Muwaṭṭa'*, 306 (no. 948).

[14] Ibn Abī Shayba, *Muṣannaf*, 4:559–60 (no. 11,904); 'Abd al-Razzāq, *Muṣannaf*, 3:576 (no. 6,724); Ibn Sa'd, *Ṭabaqāt*, 4:146; Ismā'īl b. Isḥāq, *Faḍl al-ṣalāt*, 91 (nos 98–9); al-Bayhaqī, *al-Sunan al-kubrā*, 5:402 (no. 10,271).

Ibn ʿUmar is said to move his head with each individual greeting so that he directly faced the Prophet, Abū Bakr and ʿUmar as he spoke to each in turn.[15]

Early sources leave an ambiguous picture regarding whether or not Ibn ʿUmar's frequent visitation of the Prophet's tomb was (or should be) considered a model for other Muslims.[16] Discussing Ibn ʿUmar's habit of visiting the Prophet's tomb whenever he arrived in Medina, the Medinan scholar ʿUbayd Allāh b. ʿUmar b. Ḥafṣ (d. *c.* 140/757–8) notes: 'We know of none of the Prophet's Companions who did that except for Ibn ʿUmar.'[17] Asked if his father, the famous scholar ʿUrwa b. al-Zubayr, would come to the Prophet's grave to wish blessings upon him, the Medinan historian Hishām b. ʿUrwa (d. 146/763–4) simply responded, 'No.'[18]

However, despite the reported rarity of this ritual among the Companions (and perhaps the Successors too), the famed Medinan jurist Mālik b. Anas (d. 179/795) included a report describing Ibn ʿUmar standing beside the tomb and praying for the Prophet, Abū Bakr and ʿUmar in his early legal handbook, the *Muwaṭṭaʾ*, in the chapter 'On prayer for the Prophet'.[19] After recording the tradition in his own recension of the *Muwaṭṭaʾ*, the Iraqi jurist Muḥammad b. al-Ḥasan al-Shaybānī (d. 189/805) comments, 'This is appropriate (*yanbaghī*) to do when arriving in Medina, to go to the Prophet's tomb.'[20] It appears that Ibn ʿUmar's visiting the Prophet's tomb was considered a commendable activity among some proto-Sunnī Muslims by at least the late eighth century.

15 Abū Nuʿaym, *Ḥilyat al-awliyaʾ*, 1:308–9.

16 Munt, *Holy City of Medina*, 130.

17 ʿAbd al-Razzāq, *Muṣannaf*, 3:576 (no. 6,724). ʿUbayd Allāh b. ʿUmar's comment is provoked by a question from Maʿmar b. Rāshid.

18 Ibn Abī Shayba, *Muṣannaf*, 4:559 (no. 11,903).

19 Mālik b. Anas, *al-Muwaṭṭaʾ* [recension of Yaḥyā al-Laythī], 1:235 (no. 458); idem, *al-Muwaṭṭaʾ* [recension of Suwayd], 145 (no. 163); idem, *al-Muwaṭṭaʾ* [recension of Abū Muṣʿab], 1:196 (no. 506); id., *al-Muwaṭṭaʾ* [recension of al-Qaʿnabī], 233 (no. 283); Ismāʿīl b. Isḥāq, *Faḍl al-ṣalāt*, 90 (no. 97); al-Bayhaqī, *al-Sunan al-kubrā*, 5:403 (no. 10272); al-Bayhaqī, *Shuʿab al-īmān*, 6:52 (no. 3,864).

20 al-Shaybānī, *Muwaṭṭaʾ*, 306 (no. 948); Christopher Melchert, 'Al-Shaybānī and Contemporary Renunciant Piety', *Journal of Abbasid Studies* 6 (2019): 75–6. See also Ibn Abī Zayd al-Qayrawānī, *Kitāb al-Jāmiʿ*, 142; idem, *al-Nawādir wa-l-ziyādāt ʿalā mā fī al-Mudawwana min ghayr-hā min al-ummahāt*, ed. ʿAbd al-Fattāḥ Muḥammad al-Ḥulw et al., 15 vols (Beirut: Dār al-Gharb al-Islāmī, 1999), 2:336–7.

In fact, the comment that 'none of the Prophet's Companions' came to the Prophet's grave with Ibn 'Umar's frequency is perhaps meant as a reflection of his great piety, as a sign that Ibn 'Umar venerated the Prophet to a degree that exceeded even that of the other Companions.[21] This fits the extremely devout image found in many biographical reports about Ibn 'Umar, to whom early *ḥadīth* collections devote whole chapters describing his merits (*faḍā'il*) and his asceticism (*zuhd*).[22] The jurist Ṭāwūs b. Kaysān (d. 106/724), for example, reports: 'I have never seen a man more scrupulous (*awra'*) than Ibn 'Umar.'[23] Texts emphasise Ibn 'Umar's ascetic actions: for example, he is said to have bought and freed a thousand slaves, and performed the ḥajj on fifty different occasions.[24] His devoutness extended into profound devotion to the Prophet Muḥammad. Ibn 'Umar was never able to mention the Prophet without tears forming in his eyes, and would only discuss *ḥadīth* when sitting up, in order to give the topic its proper respect.[25] He based his actions closely on the Prophet's precedent and was ravenous for information about him. He 'was mindful of what he had heard from the Messenger of God and, any time that he was absent [from Muḥammad], he asked someone who had been there what the Messenger of God had said and done'.[26]

In several reports, Ibn 'Umar's consummate piety is characterised as his 'following the Prophet's *āthār*' (*ittibā' āthār al-nabī*). The Baṣran judge 'Āṣim b. Sulaymān al-Aḥwal (d. *c.* 141/758–9) reports, 'If you saw Ibn 'Umar, you would think something within him was following the Prophet's *āthār*.'[27] The

[21] Muranyi, 'Emergence of Holy Places', 168 makes a similar point about a report of Ibn 'Umar visiting a different site.

[22] Ibn Abī Shayba, *Muṣannaf*, 11:198, 12:231–6; al-Bukhārī, *Ṣaḥīḥ*, 919 (kitāb faḍā'il aṣḥāb al-nabī, bāb 19); Aḥmad b. Ḥanbal, *Kitāb Faḍā'il al-ṣaḥāba*, ed. Waṣī Allāh b. Muḥammad 'Abbās (Riyadh: Dār Ibn al-Jawzī, 1999), 1,130–3; Lucas, *Constructive Critics*, 19 n.70, 255–6.

[23] al-Fasawī, *Kitāb al-Ma'rifa*, 1:491. The version in Ibn Abī Shayba, *Muṣannaf*, 12:231 (no. 35,633) has *anqā* ('purer') rather than *awra'*.

[24] 'Abd al-Malik b. Ḥabīb, *Kitāb al-Ta'rīj (La Historia)*, ed. Jorge Aguadé (Madrid: Consejo Superior de Investigaciones Científicas, 1991), 160 (no. 487). For reports of his asceticism, see Melchert, *Before Sufism*, 8, 25, 42, 54, 55, 66, 70, 75, 77, 83, 85, 88, 94.

[25] Ibn Ḥabīb, *Kitāb al-Ta'rīj*, 159 (no. 482); al-Dhahabī, *Siyar*, 3:214.

[26] al-Zubayr b. Bakkār, *Jamharat*, 1:558; al-Muṣ'ab b. 'Abd Allāh al-Zubayrī, *Kitāb Nasab al-Quraysh*, ed. E. Lévi-Provençal (Cairo: Dār al-Ma'ārif, 1953), 350.

[27] Ibn Abī Shayba, *Muṣannaf*, 12:232 (no. 35,639); Ibn Sa'd, *Ṭabaqāt*, 4:134; Aḥmad b. Ḥanbal, *al-Zuhd* (Beirut: Dār al-Kutub al-'Ilmiyya, 1983), 239; al-Dhahabī, *Siyar*, 3:237;

Egyptian jurist ʿAbd Allāh b. Wahb (d. 197/813) transmits a report from Mālik b. Anas about Ibn ʿUmar's fastidious piety: "ʿAbd Allāh b. ʿUmar followed the Messenger of God's command (*amr*), his *āthār*, and his manner of being (*ḥāl*). He was so concerned about doing so that it pained his mental state.'[28] Similarly, Ibn ʿUmar's *mawlā*, Nāfiʿ, reports that 'If you watched Ibn ʿUmar when he was following an *athar* of the Prophet, you would say, "This man is possessed (*majnūn*)!"'[29] Ibn ʿUmar's deep reverence for the Prophet appeared, it would seem, rather extreme even to some Muslim traditionists.

The precise meaning of 'following the Prophet's *āthār*' is ambiguous in these reports, as we have often encountered when dealing with the term *āthār*.[30] Ibn ʿUmar is said to have paid close attention to reports – that is, *ḥadīth* or *āthār* – about the Prophet's actions, and he is often presented within Sunnī sources as a prolific and reliable transmitter of such material.[31] But far more than just emulating the Prophet's *sunna* through oral reports, Ibn ʿUmar is said to have literally and physically 'followed the Prophet's tracks' in and around Mecca and Medina.[32] A report from the historian Muṣʿab b. ʿAbd Allāh al-Zubayrī (d. 236/851) lays this out explicitly:

> He followed the Messenger of God's tracks (*āthār*) to every place where the Prophet prayed, and he rode in every road that the Messenger of God had passed through. About this, he said, 'I try to place my camel's feet upon the [same]

Abū Nuʿaym, *Ḥilyat al-awliyaʾ*, 1:310. The tradition's *isnād* is: ʿAbd Allāh b. Numayr (d. 199/815, Kūfa) > ʿĀṣim al-Aḥwal > unnamed narrator. On ʿAbd Allāh b. Numayr and ʿĀṣim al-Aḥwal, see Juynboll, *Encyclopedia*, 9–10 and 134ff.

28 al-Fasawī, *Kitāb al-Maʿrifa*, 1:491; al-Dhahabī, *Siyar*, 3:213. The *isnād* is: Muḥammad b. Abī Zukayr (d. 232/847, Egypt) > ʿAbd Allāh b. Wahb > Mālik b. Anas > unnamed narrator. On Muḥammad b. Abī Zukayr, see al-Dhahabī, *Taʾrīkh al-Islām*, 17 [231–40 AH]:321, 352.

29 Abū Nuʿaym, *Ḥilyat al-awliyaʾ*, 1:310; al-Dhahabī, *Siyar*, 3:213.

30 Juynboll, *Encyclopedia*, 10 notes that Ibn ʿUmar is 'described as having assiduously searched for traces (*āthār*) of the Prophet, however that may be interpreted'.

31 For discussion of his place in the *ḥadīth* canon, see *EI*³, s.v. "Abdallāh b. ʿUmar b. al-Khaṭṭāb' (Andreas Görke); Juynboll, *Muslim Tradition*, 29, 63–4, 143; Joseph Schacht, *The Origins of Muhammadan Jurisprudence* (Oxford: Clarendon Press, 1950), 25, 176–9; Lucas, *Constructive Critics*, 19, 277, 330–1, 333–4.

32 Maribel Fierro glosses the phrase *ittibāʿ āthār al-nabī* as 'the tendency of going to pray in places visited by the Prophet or places that had a special significance during his life, thus transforming them into sanctuaries'. Maribel Fierro, 'The Treatises against Innovations (*kutub al-bidaʿ*)', *Der Islam* 69 (1992): 217.

> places as the Messenger of God's camel.' He had witnessed the Messenger of God's Farewell Pilgrimage and stood with him at ʿArafat. He stood on that same spot during every ḥajj – and he went on many ḥajjs.[33]

Ibn ʿUmar thus closely emulated the Prophet's actions throughout the spaces of his life, such as by standing in the precise spot where the Prophet had performed the ritual of *wuqūf* on ʿArafat during the ḥajj. Ibn ʿUmar's fidelity to the Prophet's model even led to his death in one account: his unwillingness to move from the place of *wuqūf* during a ḥajj annoyed al-Ḥajjāj b. Yūsuf, spurring the infamous Umayyad governor to have him stabbed in the foot with a poisoned spear.

Beyond closely following the Prophet's ḥajj rites, Ibn ʿUmar's emulation reportedly extended into the seemingly more mundane acts and places associated with the Prophet's life. According to Muṣʿab al-Zubayrī's report, Ibn ʿUmar even attempted to make his camel's hooves strike the very spots on the road where the Prophet's camel had trod.[34] In another report, while on a journey, Ibn ʿUmar was found driving his camel around in a circle at a particular spot on the ground. When a man who 'did not know Ibn ʿUmar's merit (*faḍl*)' saw this, he said, 'This old man has lost his way.' Hearing this, Ibn ʿUmar responded, 'Oh, sir! I saw the Messenger of God's camel walk in a circle at this spot in this way, so I wanted my camel to walk in a circle where the Messenger of God's camel did so.'[35] Conversely, while on a journey with Ibn ʿUmar, the Meccan scholar Mujāhid b. Jabr saw him avoid a particular spot as they were passing by it. Asked about this, Ibn ʿUmar replied, 'I saw the Messenger of God do this, so I do it.'[36]

Muṣʿab al-Zubayrī's report specifically connects Ibn ʿUmar's 'following the Prophet's tracks' with his effort to visit 'every place where the Prophet

[33] Muṣʿab al-Zubayrī, *Kitāb Nasab al-Quraysh*, 350–1; al-Zubayr b. Bakkār, *Jamharat*, 1:558; Ibn Ḥajar al-ʿAsqalānī, *al-Iṣāba fī tamyīz al-ṣaḥāba*, ed. ʿAbd Allāh b. ʿAbd al-Muḥsin al-Turkī, 16 vols (Cairo: Markaz Hujr li-l-Buḥūth al-ʿArabiyya wa-al-Islāmiyya, 2008), 6:299.

[34] Similar reports appear in Ibn Abī Shayba, *Muṣannaf*, 12:235 (no. 35,654); al-Bayhaqī, *al-Sunan al-kubrā*, 5:409 (no. 10,301); Abū Nuʿaym, *Ḥilyat al-awliyaʾ*, 1:310.

[35] ʿAbd al-Malik b. Ḥabīb al-Andalusī, *al-Wāḍiḥa: kutub al-ṣalāt wa-kutub al-ḥajj*, ed. Miklos Muranyi (Beirut: Dār al-Bashāʾir al-Islāmiyya, 2010), 103 (no. 196); Muranyi, 'Emergence of Holy Places', 168.

[36] Ibn Ḥanbal, *Musnad*, 8:474–5 (no. 4,870).

prayed'. Ibn 'Umar's son, 'Ubayd Allāh, similarly reports that his father 'followed the Messenger of God's traces to every spot where he prayed, such that – if the Prophet stopped under a tree – Ibn 'Umar would seek it out and water it, so that it would not dry up'.[37] The Medinan historian Mūsā b. 'Uqba (d. 141/758) recalls Ibn 'Umar and the latter's other son, Sālim, visiting several such sites on the way between Mecca and Medina:

> I saw Sālim b. 'Abd Allāh seeking places along the road and praying at them. He reported that his father ['Abd Allāh b. 'Umar] used to pray at them, and that he had seen the Prophet pray at these places. Nāfiʿ also reported to me that Ibn 'Umar would pray at these places.[38]

Ibn 'Umar thus prayed at a series of spots that he associated with the Prophet Muḥammad's actions on the way between the two holy cities. Indeed, the Prophet's wife 'Ā'isha said that 'there was no one who followed the Prophet's tracks to his stopping places (*manāzil*) like Ibn 'Umar followed them'.[39]

According to the medieval historian al-Samhūdī, Ibn 'Umar appears in these reports as a 'symbol' (*sīmā*) for the 'early generations' concern for following the Prophet's *āthār*'.[40] Notably, the Prophet's other Companions are also described following the Prophet's *āthār* in at least one tradition. When the Prophet sends 'Uthmān b. 'Affān to Mecca on a diplomatic mission, 'Uthmān demurs from participating in the local pagan customs, saying, 'We do not do anything until our master [i.e. the Prophet] does, and we follow his track (*athar*).'[41] Here, seemingly the entire Muslim community is characterised as piously following the Prophet's example, using the vocabulary of 'following his *athar*'.

[37] al-Bayhaqī, *al-Sunan al-kubrā*, 5:402 (no. 10,269); al-Dhahabī, *Siyar*, 3:213; Ibn al-Athīr, *Usd al-ghābah fī maʿrifat al-ṣaḥābah* (Beirut: Dār Ibn Ḥazm, 2012), 716. Similar reports appear in Muḥammad b. 'Umar al-Wāqidī, *Kitāb al-Maghāzī*, ed. Marsden Jones, 3 vols (London, Oxford University Press, 1966), 3:1,096.

[38] al-Bukhārī, *Ṣaḥīḥ*, 128–9 (kitāb al-ṣalāt, bāb 89); al-Ṭurṭūshī, *Kitāb al-Ḥawādith*, 310–11 (no. 282).

[39] Ibn Saʿd, *Ṭabaqāt*, 4:135.

[40] al-Samhūdī, *Wafāʾ al-wafā*, 3:167.

[41] Ibn Saʿd, *Ṭabaqāt*, 1:396. Perhaps similarly, the Muslim army 'followed in 'Alī's track [*athar*]' during the conquest of Khaybar: Ibn Hishām, *Sīra*, 762; Ibn 'Asākir, *Taʾrīkh*, 42:89–90.

But even more so than his contemporaries, it is ʿAbd Allāh b. ʿUmar who most often appears as an assiduous follower of the Prophet's *āthār*, sometimes even appearing '*majnūn*' in this regard. Given Ibn ʿUmar's reputation as one who 'followed the precepts of Islam with such scrupulous obedience that he became a pattern for future generations', it seems that his attention to *āthār* was understood by early Muslims as an authentic and commendable mode of revering and commemorating the Prophet.[42] Indeed, traditionists cite these actions as evidence of Ibn ʿUmar's great piety. At the same time, we will see later in this chapter that such behaviour was contested and critiqued by none other than Ibn ʿUmar's father: the caliph ʿUmar b. al-Khaṭṭāb.

'This Shall Not Be Neglected': Commemorating Prophetic Places in Story and Stone

While these reports burnish Ibn ʿUmar's reputation as a devoted follower of the Prophet, this was not the full extent of their usefulness to early Muslims. Narratives about closely following the Prophet's *āthār* served not only as illustrations of Ibn ʿUmar's (and other Companions') great piety in closely emulating the Prophet's actions. These texts were also deployed to authenticate certain spaces' associations with the Prophet Muḥammad, and thus to authorise these places' ritual visitation. The testimony of Companions like Ibn ʿUmar and other authorities provided sanction for these places' commemoration as sites of Prophetic history. But the development of these 'sites of memory' emerged not only from and through ritual and text: these sites were also literally set in stone by power brokers over the course of the seventh and eighth centuries. As we will see, the textual and the built environment operated as interrelated modes of commemorating the places associated with the Prophet.

In several cases, Ibn ʿUmar endeavoured to pray not only in the same buildings or general areas as the Prophet had, but actually to pray at the exact spots where the Prophet had done so. For example, Ibn ʿUmar prayed towards the 'perfumed column' (*al-usṭawāna al-mukhallaqa*) whenever he entered the Qubāʾ mosque in Medina, as 'that had been the prayer spot (*muṣallā*) of the

42 *EI*², s.v. "ʿAbd Allāh b. ʿUmar b. al-Khaṭṭāb' (Laura Veccia Vaglieri). Further on Ibn ʿUmar's reputation in early sources, see Lucas, *Constructive Critics*, 231, 273–4.

Messenger of God'.[43] When he came to the Mosque of the Banū Muʿāwiya (also known as al-Ijāba Mosque) in Medina, Ibn ʿUmar asked, 'Do you know where the Messenger of God prayed in this mosque of yours?' and was shown where the Prophet had done so.[44] In some cases, these locations were directly relevant to discussions of the ḥajj, as the Prophet's actions were models for the performance of the pilgrimage.[45] We saw above, for example, that Ibn ʿUmar stood at the precise spot of the Prophet's *wuqūf* on ʿArafat. In a similar tradition, Ibn ʿUmar's *mawlā* Nāfiʿ reports, 'I saw Ibn ʿUmar standing upon al-Ṣafā at a place that (I think, by God!) he saw the Messenger of God stand.'[46]

Among these locations, the Kaʿba offered a place where Ibn ʿUmar's knowledge of 'where the Prophet prayed' importantly overlapped with the ritual practices of the ḥajj. According to *ḥadīth* reports, on the day of the conquest of Mecca in the year 8/630 (when Ibn ʿUmar was still quite young), he missed the chance to witness what the Prophet had done when he entered the newly liberated Kaʿba. So, Ibn ʿUmar asked an eyewitness, the Companion Bilāl, 'What did the Messenger of God do [in the Kaʿba]?' or (in other versions), 'Where did the Messenger of God pray?'[47] In one case, Ibn ʿUmar characterises his question to Bilāl as his being 'the first of the people to come upon [the

[43] al-Balādhurī, *Futūḥ al-buldān*, 11–12; Ibn Shabba, *Taʾrīkh*, 51, 56; *Kitāb al-Manāsik*, 398; al-Samhūdī, *Wafāʾ al-wafā*, 3:150–8. On the 'perfumed column', see William Popper, *The Cairo Nilometer: Studies in Ibn Taghrî Birdî's Chronicles of Egypt: I* (Berkeley: University of California Press, 1951), 72; Bursi, 'Scents of Space', 212.

[44] Mālik b. Anas, *al-Muwaṭṭaʾ* [recension of Yaḥyā al-Laythī], 1:296 (no. 575); Ibn Shabba, *Taʾrīkh*, 67; al-Samhūdī, *Wafāʾ al-wafā*, 3:180; al-Ṭurṭūshī, *Kitāb al-Ḥawādith*, 310 (no. 282); *Kitāb al-Manāsik*, 402.

[45] The relationship is reflected in Ibn ʿUmar's reputation as an expert in the ḥajj rites (or *manāsik*). For this knowledge, the caliph ʿAbd al-Malik b. Marwān personally recommended Ibn ʿUmar as the person to follow in order to perform the ḥajj most correctly. Mālik b. Anas, *al-Muwaṭṭaʾ* [recension of Yaḥyā al-Laythī], 1:534 (no. 1187); Muṣʿab al-Zubayrī, *Kitāb Nasab al-Quraysh*, 351; al-Zubayr b. Bakkār, *Jamharat*, 1:558; Ibn Ḥajar, *Tahdhīb al-tahdhīb*, 3:699; Ibn ʿAbd al-Barr, *al-Tamhīd li-mā fī-l-Muwaṭṭaʾ min al-maʿānī wa-l-asānīd*, ed. Saʿīd Aḥmad Aʿrāb, 26 vols (Ribat: Wizārat al-Awqāf wa-l-Shuʾūn al-Islāmiyya, 1967–92), 10:8–9; al-Dhahabī, *Siyar*, 5:327.

[46] al-Ḥumaydī, *Musnad*, 1:541 (no. 682).

[47] Gerald R. Hawting, '"We Were Not Ordered with Entering It but Only with Circumambulating It." *Ḥadīth* and *Fiqh* on Entering the Kaʿba', *BSOAS* 47 (1984): 230–1.

Prophet's] *athar*'.[48] In response to Ibn 'Umar's question, Bilāl describes the location in the Ka'ba where the Prophet had prayed. The wording differs in various versions, but reference is usually made to the Prophet standing among the building's columns. Subsequently, Ibn 'Umar would be found praying at this spot inside the Ka'ba, 'aiming for the place where Bilāl reported that the Prophet had prayed'.[49]

Early jurists debated the necessity/acceptability of entering the Ka'ba during pilgrimage, and Ibn 'Umar's reports about the Prophet offered useful fodder within these discussions.[50] Ibn 'Umar's own behaviour was also cited in this context. According to one report, whenever he arrived in Mecca on ḥajj or *'umra* (a non-ḥajj pilgrimage to Mecca), Ibn 'Umar would begin his pilgrimage by entering the Ka'ba to pray there, if he found the building's door open.[51] Conversely, al-Bukhārī provides an *isnād*-less assertion, seemingly in order to refute the practice of entering the Ka'ba: 'Ibn 'Umar went on ḥajj many times and did not enter [the Ka'ba].'[52] However, the Meccan scholar 'Aṭā' b. Abī Rabāḥ told his student Ibn Jurayj (d. 150/767–8) that he saw Ibn 'Umar pray in the Ka'ba, before adding, 'And I also pray in it.'[53]

An important additional detail then appears in 'Aṭā''s report. When Ibn Jurayj asks where exactly in the Ka'ba the Prophet had prayed, 'Aṭā' 'sketched it out for me as he remembered', in terms that echo Bilāl's report about the Prophet praying between the Ka'ba's columns. 'Aṭā' then says: 'It has reached me that he prayed between the two columns, where the disc is placed.' 'Aṭā' thus references a 'disc' (*ḥalqa*) that, he suggests, was located at or near the spot where the Prophet had prayed.

While 'Aṭā' provides no more information about this disc, a similar object marking the Prophet's place of prayer appears in texts that describe the Ka'ba's

[48] al-Bukhārī, *Ṣaḥīḥ*, 132 (kitāb al-ṣalāt, bāb 96); Ibn Abī Shayba, *Muṣannaf*, 5:543 (no. 15,233).

[49] 'Abd al-Razzāq, *Muṣannaf*, 5:81 (no. 9,065); Ibn Hishām, *Sīra*, 822; al-Azraqī, *Akhbār Makka*, 375–6 (no. 321); al-Bukhārī, *Ṣaḥīḥ*, 132 (kitāb al-ṣalāt, bāb 97), 388 (kitāb al-ḥajj, bāb 52).

[50] Hawting, 'We Were Not Ordered'.

[51] al-Azraqī, *Akhbār Makka*, 381–2 (no. 331).

[52] al-Bukhārī, *Ṣaḥīḥ*, 389 (kitāb al-ḥajj, bāb 53).

[53] 'Abd al-Razzāq, *Muṣannaf*, 5:79 (no. 9,062). Notably, 'Abd al-Razzāq comments at the end of the report that he himself also prays in the Ka'ba.

decorative evolution.[54] Ibn Jurayj narrates a report about such an object in an account of the Kaʿba's updating under the caliph al-Walīd b. ʿAbd al-Malik, recorded in the historian al-Azraqī's (d. *c.* 251/865) *Akhbār Makka*:

> Al-Walīd b. ʿAbd al-Malik installed the red, green, and white marble panels that are in [the Kaʿba's] interior [. . .] and he placed the onyx which one encounters when entering the Kaʿba, in front of where one stands when aiming for the place of the Messenger of God's prayer spot (*muṣallā*). He placed a golden hoop (*tawq*) on the onyx.[55]

This onyx stone (*al-jazaʿa*) is described elsewhere as a 'black onyx streaked with white', installed in the wall that one faces when entering via the Kaʿba's doorway.[56] Al-Azraqī reiterates that 'al-Walīd b. ʿAbd al-Malik sent this onyx [to the Kaʿba] and it was placed there'.[57]

Several traditions mention such an onyx as a marker for emulating the Prophet's prayer inside the Kaʿba. Al-Azraqī's *Akhbār Makka* and other historical texts say that the Prophet would face this stone when praying in the Kaʿba, with his right eyebrow directly in front of the onyx stone.[58] Though they do not mention any connection to the caliph al-Walīd, some *ḥadīth*s also seem to reference this onyx. In a version of the report where Ibn ʿUmar asks Bilāl if the Prophet had prayed in the Kaʿba, Bilāl responds: 'Yes, he prayed two *rakaʿ*s facing the onyx stone (*al-jazaʿa*), with the second column on his right.'[59] In another report, Ibn ʿUmar says that the place where the Prophet prayed was 'by the middle column, under the onyx'.[60]

[54] Finbarr Barry Flood, 'Light in Stone: The Commemoration of the Prophet in Umayyad Architecture', in Johns, *Bayt al-Maqdis*, 316–17.

[55] al-Azraqī, *Akhbār Makka*, 308 (no. 228). This account is paralleled in Ibn Rusta, *Kitāb al-Aʿlāk al-nafīsa*, 36, but without mention of the onyx stone marking the Prophet's *muṣallā*.

[56] al-Azraqī, *Akhbār Makka*, 409; Ibn Rusta, *Kitāb al-Aʿlāk al-nafīsa*, 32; Ibn ʿAbd Rabbihi, *al-ʿIqd al-farīd*, 7:284.

[57] al-Azraqī, *Akhbār Makka*, 409.

[58] al-Azraqī, *Akhbār Makka*, 409; Ibn Rusta, *Kitāb al-Aʿlāk al-nafīsa*, 32; Ibn ʿAbd Rabbihi, *al-ʿIqd al-farīd*, 7:284.

[59] al-Dāraquṭnī, *Sunan*, 2:393 (no. 1,747); al-Bayhaqī, *al-Sunan al-kubrā*, 2:465 (no. 3,791).

[60] Abū Yūsuf, *Kitāb al-Āthār*, 117 (no. 546); ʿAbd Allāh b. Muḥammad b. Yaʿqūb b. al-Ḥārith al-Ḥārithī, *Musnad Abī Ḥanīfa*, ed. Abū Muḥammad al-Asyūṭī (Beirut: Dār al-Kutub al-ʿIlmiyya, 2008), 168 (nos 475–6).

Several *ḥadīths* mention a different physical marker of the Prophet's prayer place inside the Kaʿba: a marble slab. We have seen that the caliph al-Walīd b. ʿAbd al-Malik was said to have fitted the interior of the Kaʿba with coloured marbles. Notably, several texts mention a marble panel on the Kaʿba floor being used to mark the Prophet's *muṣallā*. Al-Azraqī, for example, cites a slab of 'white marble' (*rukhāma bayḍāʾ*) on the Kaʿba's floor being 'mentioned as the place where the Prophet prayed'.[61] In a report in al-Bukhārī's *Ṣaḥīḥ*, Bilāl describes the Prophet's praying between the Kaʿba's columns while facing the building's back wall. An unnamed narrator then adds, 'At the place where he prayed, there is a [panel of] red marble' (*marmara ḥamrāʾ*).[62] No further information appears here, but similar descriptions are found in other texts.[63] In Shīʿī *ḥadīths* about entering the Kaʿba, Jaʿfar al-Ṣādiq prescribes praying 'between the two columns, upon the red marble' (*ʿalā al-rukhāma al-ḥamrāʾ*), and imam Mūsā al-Kāẓim (d. 183/799) is described praying at this same location.[64] In one case, Jaʿfar al-Ṣādiq explicitly says that prayer should be performed while standing between the two columns and 'upon the red slab' (*ʿalā al-balāṭa al-ḥamrāʾ*) because 'the Messenger of God prayed upon it'.[65]

In these traditions, early authorities' knowledge and examples are deployed not only to authorise ritual prayer within the Kaʿba, but to promote the performance of the ritual at a particular location associated with the Prophet. Even more strikingly, these traditions indicate that the site of the Prophet's prayer

[61] al-Azraqī, *Akhbār Makka*, 414. Later texts mention a red marble slab: Flood, 'Light in Stone', 318 n.37.

[62] al-Bukhārī, *Ṣaḥīḥ*, 1,077 (kitāb al-maghāzī, bāb 77); al-Bayhaqī, *al-Sunan al-kubrā*, 2:463 (no. 3,783). The *isnād* is Muḥammad [b. Rāfiʿ (d. 245/859–60, Nishapur)?] > Surayj b. al-Nuʿmān (d. 217/832, Baghdad) > Fulayḥ b. Sulaymān (d. 168/782–3, Medina) > Nāfiʿ. On Fulayḥ b. Sulaymān, see Elad, *Rebellion of Muḥammad*, 283–4.

[63] Flood, 'Light in Stone', 317–18.

[64] al-Kulaynī, *al-Kāfī*, 4:529–30; al-Ṭūsī, *Tahdhīb al-aḥkām*, 5:251–3. On Shīʿī discussions about entering the Kaʿba, see Hawting, 'We Were Not Ordered', 237–8.

[65] al-Kulaynī, *al-Kāfī*, 4:528–9. The *isnād* is: Muḥammad b. Yaḥyā > Aḥmad b. Muḥammad > ʿAlī b. al-Ḥakam > al-Ḥusayn b. Abī al-ʿAlāʾ. On the possible identities for Muḥammad b. Yaḥyā, Aḥmad b. Muḥammad and ʿAlī b. al-Ḥakam, see Seyfeddin Kara, *In Search of ʿAlī Ibn Abī Ṭālib's Codex: History and Traditions on the Earliest Copy of the Qurʾān* (Berlin: Gerlach, 2018), 105–8, 118–20, 155–6. On al-Ḥusayn b. Abī al-ʿAlāʾ, a Kūfan transmitter from Jaʿfar al-Ṣādiq, see Modarressi, *Tradition and Survival*, 274–5.

was commemorated by early Muslims not only through transmitted traditions, but through physical demarcations or decorations. Both the onyx stone set in the wall and the marble slab on the floor are associated with prominent figures, thereby lending significant authority to these visual signs of the Prophet's *muṣallā*. It is impossible to prove definitively which came first – the oral traditions about, or the physical sign(s) commemorating, the Prophet's *muṣallā* – but here the textual and ornamental fields are closely intertwined. The *ḥadīth*s point towards the visual object(s) as marking an authentic location where the Prophet prayed, and we can see that these visual markers were sometimes noted by the scholars who narrated *ḥadīth*s. Likewise, the reports from Ibn 'Umar and others were almost certainly cited by those who were themselves 'aiming for the place of the Messenger of God's prayer spot' and believed that the onyx and/or marble offered faithful memories of that location.

Ibn 'Umar's knowledge of the Prophet's *āthār* was also drawn upon in celebrating many other 'places where the Prophet prayed'. We have noted that Ibn 'Umar prayed within the Qubā' mosque to the 'perfumed column', as it was purportedly the Prophet's *muṣallā* there.[66] A more obscure spot was one located six miles outside Medina, called the Plain (al-Baṭḥā') or the Plain of Ibn Azhar.[67] According to *sīra-maghāzī* traditions, while on a military expedition, the Prophet stopped at this plain, prayed under a tree there, and ate a meal cooked in a pot. In one report, Ibn 'Umar himself prays at al-Baṭḥā', looks at the 'trace (*athar*) of the cooking pot, marvels at [this spot], and says, "If God wills, this shall not be neglected!"'[68] Texts report that a mosque was built in the Plain of Ibn Azhar and, according to Ibn Isḥāq's *sīra*, 'the place of the stones of the cooking pot is well-known'.[69] As Miklos Muranyi argues, these traditions

[66] Ibn 'Umar is reported to have gone to pray in Qubā' every week, just as the Prophet had done: Ibn Sa'd, *Ṭabaqāt*, 1:211; Muslim, *Ṣaḥīḥ*, 2:1017 (kitāb al-ḥajj, bāb 97); al-Bayhaqī, *al-Sunan al-kubrā*, 5:408 (no. 10,294); al-Ḥumaydī, *Musnad*, 1:535 (no. 673); al-Samhūdī, *Wafā' al-wafā*, 3:146.

[67] Goldziher, *Muslim Studies*, 2:280. For a collection of sources on this spot: Elad, *Rebellion of Muḥammad*, 201 n.163.

[68] 'Abd Allāh b. Wahb, *al-Ǧāmi': Die Koranwissenschaften*, ed. Miklos Muranyi (Wiesbaden: Otto Harrassowitz, 1992), 233; Muranyi, 'Emergence of Holy Places', 166–7.

[69] Ibn Hishām, *Sīra*, 421; al-Ṭabarī, *Ta'rīkh*, 1/iii:1268 (citing Ibn Isḥāq); Yāqūt al-Ḥamawī, *Mu'jam al-buldān*, 1:446 (also citing Ibn Isḥāq).

about al-Baṭḥā' witness the evolving 'consecration' of this location as 'a celebrated place' associated with the memory of the Prophet.[70] The report of Ibn 'Umar's audible wish that al-Baṭḥā' 'shall not be neglected' was surely intended as an encouragement of the place's commemoration as a site of special significance. Ibn 'Umar is seemingly deployed here as a literary device for 'exhort[ing] later Muslims to visit the site'.[71]

While we do not know when the mosque at al-Baṭḥā' was constructed, the site's physical memorialisation (and perhaps the emergence of a report about Ibn 'Umar visiting it) may have occurred in the context of the caliph al-Walīd's programme of 'commemoration of the Prophet in Muslim religious architecture'.[72] As discussed in previous chapters, al-Walīd and his governor 'Umar b. 'Abd al-'Azīz carried out a major reconstruction of the Prophet's Mosque in Medina, 'turning it into a shrine to the Prophet'.[73] Alongside this substantial undertaking, al-Walīd also installed special stones at locations inside the Medina Mosque and other locations. These stones were, Barry Flood argues, 'intended to commemorate the presence and, more particularly, the *ṣalāt*, of the Prophet'.[74] The onyx stone in the Ka'ba offers one example of the installation of such objects in buildings in Mecca, Medina and Jerusalem: a project that may have been 'motivated, at least in part, by a desire to formalise, if not to regularise, the cultic activity centered on [the Prophet's] person'.[75]

If historical reports are to be believed, al-Walīd's monumentalising of the Prophet's places of prayer extended beyond these grand mosques into several other locations as well. Harry Munt has recently highlighted texts that describe al-Walīd and 'Umar b. 'Abd al-'Azīz 'multiplying the number of sites in Medina connected with the memory of the Prophet through the erection of monuments other than the Prophet's Mosque', and especially 'many mosques said to commemorate where the Prophet had prayed'.[76] The Medinan historian

[70] Muranyi, 'Emergence of Holy Places', 167.

[71] Munt, *Holy City of Medina*, 125.

[72] Flood, 'Light in Stone', 313.

[73] Munt, *Holy City of Medina*, 106.

[74] Flood, 'Light in Stone', 323.

[75] Ibid., 356.

[76] Munt, *Holy City of Medina*, 111.

Abū Ghassān Muḥammad b. Yaḥyā al-Kinānī (d. *c.* 210/825–6) offers perhaps the earliest extant testimony to a local memory of this building project:

> Many of the people of knowledge from the region [of Medina] told me that the mosques of Medina and its environs that are constructed of ornamented, fitted stones were all places where the Prophet had prayed. That was due to ʿUmar b. ʿAbd al-ʿAzīz. When he built the Mosque of the Messenger of God [the Prophet's Mosque], he asked – and the people in those days were numerous – about the mosques in which the Messenger of God had prayed. He then built them with the ornamented, fitted stones.[77]

Abū Ghassān here connects the architectural style of these mosques with that used for the Marwānid reconstruction of the Prophet's Mosque: the latter is also said to have been built with 'ornamented, fitted stones' (*ḥijāra manqūsha muṭābaqa*) in early reports.[78] Later texts ascribe this building programme to al-Walīd's orders, as in a report which says that the caliph wrote to ʿUmar b. ʿAbd al-ʿAzīz: 'Wherever is confirmed among you as being one of the places where the Prophet prayed, build upon it a mosque.'[79] While we cannot verify the historical veracity of these texts, they offer plausible evidence that the Marwānids were interested in commemorating several locations associated with the Prophet's prayer.[80]

The Marwānids' interest in these locations is further suggested by mentions of their visiting several such sites in Medina. For example, when he led the ḥajj in the year 91/710, al-Walīd reportedly visited Medina, where he brought incense and a censer for the Prophet's Mosque, and stood at the Prophet's

[77] Ibn Shabba, *Taʾrīkh*, 74; Ibn Ḥajar, *Fatḥ al-bārī*, 2:234; Munt, *Holy City of Medina*, 113; Miklos Muranyi, 'Visited Places on the Prophet's Track in Mecca and Medina', *JSAI* 49 (2020): 224. On Abū Ghassān, see Munt, *Holy City of Medina*, 98–101; Elad, *Rebellion of Muḥammad*, 415–17.

[78] *Kitāb al-Manāsik*, 364–5; Ibn Rusta, *Kitāb al-Aʿlāk al-nafīsa*, 69; al-Samhūdī, *Wafāʾ al-wafā*, 2:269; Munt, *Holy City of Medina*, 106–7.

[79] Ibn al-Najjār, *al-Durra al-Thamīna*, 191. The text then reads: 'All these *āthār* are *āthār* of the construction of ʿUmar b. ʿAbd al-ʿAzīz.' See also al-Marāghī, *Taḥqīq al-nuṣra*, 138; Munt, *Holy City of Medina*, 113.

[80] Munt, *Holy City of Medina*, 113–14, 138.

tomb.[81] A glimpse of al-Walīd's further activities is attached to a *ḥadīth* describing the route through Medina taken by the Prophet Muḥammad when he visited and returned from the Qubā' mosque. After describing the route, the historian Abū Ghassān adds that his source for this *ḥadīth* says that 'he saw al-Walīd b. 'Abd al-Malik travel this same path when heading to and returning from Qubā''.[82] Retracing the Prophet's steps suggests that al-Walīd was participating in a ritual visitation of the Qubā' mosque, with the route functioning as part of the ritual itself. The caliph here 'follows the Prophet's footsteps' in a manner reminiscent of what we have seen Ibn 'Umar doing.

More evidence of the Marwānids' interest in sites of Prophetic history appears in a report about Sulaymān b. 'Abd al-Malik's visit to Medina during the ḥajj of 82/701. Found in the historian al-Zubayr b. Bakkār's (d. 256/870) *Akhbār al-Muwaffaqiyyāt*, this report is transmitted by the historian al-Wāqidī (d. 207/823), from the Medinan scholar Abū Bakr b. 'Abd Allāh b. Muḥammad b. Abī Sabra (d. 162/778), from someone called 'Abd al-Raḥmān b. Yazīd:[83]

> Sulaymān b. 'Abd al-Malik came to us during the ḥajj of the year 82 when he was the heir apparent [to the caliphate]. He arrived in Medina, and people came and greeted him. He visited the Prophet's sites (*mashāhid*) that he prayed within, as well as where his Companions were attacked at Uḥud. With [Sulaymān] were Abān b. 'Uthmān, 'Amr b. 'Uthmān, and Abū Bakr b. 'Abd Allāh b. Abī Aḥmad. They took him to Qubā', Masjid al-Faḍīkh, Mashrabat

[81] al-Ṭabarī, *Ta'rīkh*, 2/ii:1,233–4; *The History of al-Ṭabarī. Volume XXIII: The Zenith of the Marwānid House*, trans. Martin Hinds (Albany: State University of New York Press, 1990), 180–1.

[82] Ibn Shabba, *Ta'rīkh*, 56–7; al-Samhūdī, *Wafā' al-wafā*, 3:159; Munt, *Holy City of Medina*, 125. The transmitter Isḥāq b. Abī Bakr b. Abī Isḥāq seems to be otherwise unknown. Notably, Qubā' was one of the mosque sites that al-Walīd and 'Umar were said to have (re)built. Munt, *Holy City of Medina*, 113.

[83] On this report, see Maher Jarrar, *Die Prophetenbiographie im islamischen Spanien: Ein Beitrag zur Überlieferungs- und Redaktionsgeschichte* (Frankfurt: Peter Lang, 1989), 15–20, where Jarrar argues that there is little reason to doubt the report's authenticity. At ibid., 49 n.81, Jarrar notes that he was unable to identify this 'Abd al-Raḥmān b. Yazīd. I have not been able to do so with certainty either, but it seems likely to be 'Abd al-Raḥmān b. Yazīd b. Jāriyya (d. 93/711–12), a Medinan noble with an interest in *ḥadīth* who was appointed as judge of the city under 'Umar b. 'Abd al-'Azīz. Cf. Ibn Sa'd, *Ṭabaqāt*, 7:86.

Umm Ibrāhīm, and Uḥud. The whole time he asked them questions, and they reported to him on what was there.[84]

According to this report, the caliphal heir apparent (*walī ʿahd*) visited several 'sites' (*mashāhid*, sing. *mashhad*) in Medina associated with the Prophet and the early Muslim community. Notably, these sites are described as places 'that he [the Prophet] prayed within'. Among these were the Qubāʾ mosque, as well as several other locations: Masjid al-Faḍīkh, where the qurʾānic verses forbidding alcohol were said (by some) to have been revealed to the Prophet;[85] Mashrabat Umm Ibrāhīm, the home of the Prophet's wife Māriyya al-Qibṭiyya where she gave birth to the Prophet's short-lived son Ibrāhīm;[86] and Uḥud, the location of the famed battle in 3/625 between the Muslims of Medina and the pagan Quraysh of Mecca, where many Muslim martyrs were buried. These sites were spread throughout the north and south of Medina and its environs, such that Sulaymān's visitation would have involved a lengthy trek.

Sulaymān was guided around the sites in Medina by local dignitaries. While Ibn ʿUmar was not among them, other Companions' descendants were there, including Abū Bakr b. ʿAbd Allāh b. Abī Aḥmad, the grandson of the early Companion Abū Aḥmad b. Jaḥsh; and Abān b. ʿUthmān and ʿAmr b. ʿUthmān, two sons of the caliph ʿUthmān b. ʿAffān.[87] Among these, Abān b. ʿUthmān (d. *c.* 100/718–19) was a particularly important figure. Not only was he the governor of Medina and the leader of the ḥajj in the year that

[84] al-Zubayr b. Bakkār, *Akhbār al-Muwaffaqiyyāt*, 275.

[85] Ibn Shabba, *Taʾrīkh*, 69; al-Samhūdī, *Wafāʾ al-wafā*, 3:169–72; Munt, *Holy City of Medina*, 112.

[86] Ibn Shabba, *Taʾrīkh*, 69, 173–4; al-Samhūdī, *Wafāʾ al-wafā*, 3:175–7; Ibn Saʿd, *Ṭabaqāt*, 10:201–3; al-Wāqidī, *Kitāb al-Maghāzī*, 378; al-Zubayr b. Bakkār, *Jamharat*, 2:215; Munt, *Holy City of Medina*, 112. On Māriyya al-Qibṭiyya, including discussion of the Mashrabat Umm Ibrāhīm, see Aysha Hidayatullah, 'Māriyya the Copt: Gender, Sex and Heritage in the Legacy of Muhammad's *Umm Walad*', *Islam and Christian–Muslim Relations* 21.3 (2010): 221–43; Maribel Fierro, 'Plants, Mary the Copt, Abraham, Donkeys and Knowledge: Again on Bāṭinism During the Umayyad Caliphate in al-Andalus', in *Difference and Dynamism in Islam. Festschrift for Heinz Halm on his 70th Birthday*, ed. Hinrich Biesterfeldt and Verena Klemm (Würzberg: Ergon, 2012), 133–5; Maribel Fierro, 'Holy Places in Umayyad al-Andalus', *BSOAS* 78 (2015): 129–30.

[87] Muṣʿab al-Zubayrī, *Kitāb Nasab al-Quraysh*, 110; Ibn Saʿd, *Ṭabaqāt*, 7:149–51.

Sulaymān visited, but he was also a *ḥadīth* scholar, and reputedly an expert in the Prophet's biography.[88] It was surely for this latter reason that, after his visit to several sites of the Prophet's life, Sulaymān 'ordered Abān b. 'Uthmān to write down for him the Prophet's *siyar* and his *maghāzī*'.[89] Abān agreed: however, the results proved dissatisfying to Sulaymān and his caliphal father – as Abān's history did not paint their Umayyad ancestors in a sufficiently flattering light – and the pages were burned.

Despite this destructive ending to Abān's story, we see in this narrative that the locations and stories of Prophetic sites were remembered and transmitted by local scholars, and the locations were apparently visited by the ruling authorities.[90] In many cases, traditions about these locations are traced back to quite early authorities: Ibn 'Umar, for example, explains the origin of the name 'Masjid al-Faḍīkh' with an anecdote about how the Prophet was there given *faḍīkh* (a drink made from fermented dates) to drink.[91] Such traditions were collected by at least the eighth century, as suggested not only by Abān's activity, but also by the work of Medinan historians such as Ibrāhīm b. Muḥammad b. Abī Yaḥyā (d. 184/800), Abū Ghassān and Muḥammad b. al-Ḥasan b. Zabāla (d. after 199/814–15).[92] All of these men compiled traditions within their texts about 'places where the Prophet prayed' and other sanctified sites in the Ḥijāz.

[88] M. E. McMillan, *Meaning of Mecca: The Politics of Pilgrimage in Early Islam* (London: Saqi, 2011), 79, 90; Horovitz, *Earliest Biographies of the Prophet*, 6–10; A. A. Duri, *The Rise of Historical Writing Among the Arabs*, trans. and ed. Lawrence I. Conrad (Princeton: Princeton University Press, 1983), 24–5, 96; *EI*[3], s.v. 'Abān b. 'Uthmān b. 'Affān' (Khalil Athamina).

[89] On this aspect of the report, see Jarrar, *Prophetenbiographie*, 15–20; Gregor Schoeler, *The Oral and the Written in Early Islam*, trans. Uwe Vagelpohl (New York: Routledge, 2006), 81, 199 n.504; Schoeler, *Biography of Muḥammad*, 31; Horovitz, *Earliest Biographies of the Prophet*, 10 n.30; Duri, *Rise of Historical Writing*, 24 n.19; Anthony, *Muhammad and the Empires*, 86–8.

[90] Muranyi has drawn attention to the interest of 'local scholars in the early eighth century' with 'the veneration of places where the Prophet has been acting'. Muranyi, 'Visited Places', 227.

[91] Ibn Ḥanbal, *Musnad*, 10:94 (no. 5,844); Abū Ya'lā, *Musnad*, 10:101 (no. 5,733).

[92] On these scholars and their interests in local Medina history, see Maher Jarrar, 'Ibn Abī Yaḥyā: A Controversial Medinan *Akhbārī* of the 2nd/8th Century', in *The Transmission and Dynamics of the Textual Sources of Islam: Essays in Honour of Harald Motzki*, ed. Nicolet Boekhoff-van der Voort, Kees Versteegh and Joas Wagemakers (Leiden: Brill, 2011), 215–18; Harry Munt, 'Writing the History of an Arabian Holy City: Ibn Zabāla and the First Local History of Medina', *Arabica* 59 (2012): 19–20; Munt, *Holy City of Medina*, 97–101; Elad, *Rebellion of Muḥammad*, 411–13, 415–17.

Text and space thus directly overlapped in memorialising the sites of Prophetic activity. Barry Flood notes of the *ḥadīths* about the Prophet's prayer inside the Kaʿba that 'these traditions may well have influenced the manner in which [the Prophet's] praying place was commemorated during the reign of al-Walīd'.[93] If the story of Sulaymān b. ʿAbd al-Malik visiting Medina is any indication, oral/textual traditions likely also influenced how other such Prophetic sites were commemorated in this period too. In this story, visiting the Prophet's *mashāhid* is directly associated (narratively, at least) with the textualisation of Prophetic history. It is easy to imagine how activities at these sites – and the stories told about them – might have also led to their concrete monumentalisations, which al-Walīd and ʿUmar b. ʿAbd al-ʿAzīz reportedly accomplished in the years following Sulaymān's visit. In fact, if the historian Abū Ghassān is believed, the Medinan 'people of knowledge' were directly involved in these places' monumentalisation under the Umayyads.

Such activities were not restricted to the Umayyads, but also occurred in the eighth and ninth centuries under the ʿAbbāsids. Caliphs, governors and other officials constructed and visited monuments at different locations of Prophetic history in the Ḥijāz. This included maintaining and elaborating the Prophet's Mosque (including the tomb structure therein),[94] and the caliph al-Mutawakkil's (r. 232–47/847–61) provision of a new frame for the onyx stone that marked the Prophet's place of prayer inside the Kaʿba.[95]

Beyond these two central shrines, the ʿAbbāsids patronised several other locations as well. ʿAbd al-Ṣamad b. ʿAlī (d. 185/801–2) – a governor of the cities of the Ḥijāz under the caliph al-Manṣūr (r. 136–58/754–75) – reportedly (re)built Masjid ʿĀtika, where the Prophet had performed the first Friday prayer in Medina,[96] and also built a mosque at al-Surar, a spot near Minā that had been praised by the Prophet.[97] ʿĪsā b. Mūsā (d. 167/783–4) – a nephew of the first ʿAbbāsid caliphs and a governor of Kūfa – spent considerable money on the construction of al-Masjid al-Manzila, at the site where the Prophet had

93 Flood, 'Light in Stone', 318.

94 Munt, *Holy City of Medina*, 115–19.

95 Ibn Rusta, *Kitāb al-Aʿlāk al-nafīsa*, 32–3.

96 al-Samhūdī, *Wafāʾ al-wafā*, 3:168; Munt, *Holy City of Medina*, 112, 114, 118. On ʿAbd al-Ṣamad b. ʿAlī, see al-Dhahabī, *Siyar*, 9:129–31.

97 al-Azraqī, *Akhbār Makka*, 815; al-Fākihī, *Akhbār Makka*, 4:30.

prayed during the siege of Khaybar.[98] ʿAbd Allāh b. ʿUbayd Allāh b. al-ʿAbbās b. Muḥammad – a prince of the ʿAbbāsid house – is similarly credited with building a mosque at a location where the Prophet was said to have prayed, near the well of Jubayr b Muṭʿim in Mecca.[99] Perhaps most interestingly of all, al-Khayzurān (d. 173/789) – the wife of the caliph al-Mahdī (r. 158–69/775–85), and mother of the caliphs Mūsā al-Hādī (r. 169–70/785–6) and Hārūn al-Rashīd (r. 170–93/786–809) – made a mosque out of the house in Mecca where the Prophet was born.[100]

In addition to these texts, material evidence directly attests to ʿAbbāsid patronage of one such site from the Prophet's life in Mecca. A pair of inscriptions, still displayed onsite today, commemorate the caliph al-Manṣūr's construction of the 'Mosque of Allegiance' (*masjid al-bayʿa*) at the site where the Prophet and his uncle al-ʿAbbās b. ʿAbd al-Muṭṭalib 'sealed the pact with the Helpers'.[101] One of the inscriptions notes that the caliph ordered the Ḥijāzī governor al-Sārī b. ʿAbd Allāh to construct this building in the year 144 AH (i.e. between 761 and 762 CE) 'for the pilgrim to the House of God and for the traveler'. Though this location was not a required stop on the ḥajj route, it appears that it was considered worth memorialising for pilgrims and other travellers in Mecca.

As with the prayer spaces that had been monumentalised by the Umayyads, oral and textual traditions evidenced these locations' associations with the Prophet, and thereby authorised their commemoration and visitation. Medinan scholars like Abān b. ʿUthmān, Abū Ghassān, Ibn Zabāla and Muḥammad b. Ismāʿīl b. Abī Fudayk all transmitted traditions about Masjid

[98] *Kitāb al-Manāsik*, 540; al-Samhūdī, *Wafāʾ al-wafā*, 3:461.

[99] al-Azraqī, *Akhbār Makka*, 814, 838; al-Fākihī, *Akhbār Makka*, 4:19, 98. The spot is also called al-Biʾr al-ʿUlyā, as appears in a *ḥadīth* mentioning the Prophet's prayer there: Ibn Saʿd, *Ṭabaqāt*, 8:23; Ibn Mājah, *Sunan*, 1:333 (no. 1,050); al-Bukhārī, *Kitāb al-Taʾrīkh al-kabīr*, 4/1:232 (no. 1,000); Ibn ʿAsākir, *Taʾrīkh*, 50:277–8.

[100] al-Azraqī, *Akhbār Makka*, 811–12; al-Fākihī, *Akhbār Makka*, 4:5; Munt, *Holy City of Medina*, 169.

[101] Muḥammad Fahd ʿAbd Allāh al-Faʿr, *Taṭawwur al-kitābāt wa-l-nuqūsh fī-l-Ḥijāz mundhu fajr al-Islām ḥattā muntaṣaf al-qarn al-sābiʿ al-Hijrī* (Jedda: King Faisal Center for Research and Islamic Studies, 1405/1984), 189–95, 384–5; Nāṣr ibn ʿAlī al-Ḥārithī, *al-Āthār al-Islāmiyya fī Makka al-mukarrama* (Riyadh: Dār al-Hilāl, 1430/2009), 216–18. I am very grateful to Mehdy Shaddel for drawing these inscriptions to my attention.

ʿĀtika (also called al-Masjid al-Jumʿa) as the location of the Prophet's first Friday prayer in Medina.[102] In a *ḥadīth* transmitted by Mālik b. Anas, Ibn ʿUmar reports that the Prophet had described al-Surar as having been visited by seventy prophets.[103] Discussing the site of the Prophet's birthplace, the historian al-Fākihī notes that it is 'one of the most sound *āthār* among the Meccans, whose shaykhs have affirmed it to be true'.[104] Meccan and Medinan scholars were thus closely involved in collecting and transmitting knowledge about these locations in the Ḥijāzī cities that were associated with the Prophet's life. Rather than being associated with 'popular' practice, these locations were being collected and remembered by Muslim elites as authentic sites of Islamic history.

Local scholars' knowledge of these locations – as well as ʿAbbāsid interest in them – is well illustrated by an anecdote narrated from the life of the famous historian Muḥammad b. ʿUmar al-Wāqidī (d. 207/823). According to al-Wāqidī's first-person account, the caliph Hārūn al-Rashīd arrived in Medina while on ḥajj and asked the city's inhabitants for someone 'who knew all about Medina and its sites (*mashāhid*); how Gabriel came down to the Prophet, and from which direction he came to him; and the tombs of the martyrs'.[105] Due to his scholarly reputation, al-Wāqidī was nominated for this task, and he guided the caliph and his retinue around Medina such that 'there was not a single place or site that I did not take them to'. At each of these locations, the caliph and his entourage 'prayed and exerted considerable effort in supplication'. Out of gratitude for al-Wāqidī's guiding this pious tour, the caliph rewarded him

[102] Ibn Shabba, *Taʾrīkh*, 68; al-Samhūdī, *Wafāʾ al-wafā*, 3:167–8; *Kitāb al-Manāsik*, 402.

[103] al-Fākihī, *Akhbār Makka*, 4:30–2; Mālik b. Anas, *al-Muwaṭṭaʾ* [recension of Yaḥyā al-Laythī], 1:566–7 (no. 1,274); idem, *al-Muwaṭṭaʾ* [recension of Abū Muṣʿab], 1:558–9 (no. 1,451); idem, *al-Muwaṭṭaʾ* [recension of Suwayd b. Saʿīd], 459–60 (no. 627); Ibn Ḥanbal, *Musnad*, 10:355 (no. 6,233); al-Nasāʾī, *Sunan*, 463 (no. 2,995); Ibn Balbān, *Ṣaḥīḥ Ibn Ḥibbān*, 14:137 (no. 6,244); Abū Nuʿaym, *Ḥilyat al-awliyaʾ*, 6:336. A very different report about al-Surar is in ʿAbd al-Razzāq, *Muṣannaf*, 11:450–1 (no. 20,975). See Goldziher, *Muslim Studies*, 2:318 n.1.

[104] al-Fākihī, *Akhbār Makka*, 4:5.

[105] Ibn Saʿd, *Ṭabaqāt*, 7:604. My translation is slightly adapted from that found in Munt, *Holy City of Medina*, 169. Another translation of this passage appears in Horovitz, *Earliest Biographies of the Prophet*, 96–7.

with 10,000 dirhams, as well as the promise to welcome al-Wāqidī into the caliphal court whenever he desired. This latter gift would prove especially valuable: al-Wāqidī subsequently moved to Baghdad and enjoyed direct ʿAbbāsid patronage throughout his career.[106]

Thus, roughly a century after Abān b. ʿUthmān and the Umayyad caliph-in-waiting Sulaymān b. al-Walīd, another Medinan scholar guided an ʿAbbāsid caliph around the Prophetic sites of Medina. Like Abān's ability to guide Sulaymān, al-Wāqidī's capacity to show these locations to Hārūn al-Rashīd was enabled by his expertise in the history of the Prophet's life. We see this interest in Prophetic geography incorporated into al-Wāqidī's *Kitāb al-Maghāzī*, which includes several traditions about various places where the Prophet had prayed in and around Medina, such as the Plain of Ibn Azhar, discussed above.[107] Several of these traditions are transmitted from ʿAbd Allāh b. ʿUmar, and al-Wāqidī comments that Ibn ʿUmar's tradition about the Masjid al-Fatḥ is 'the most reliable of the reports' (*athbat al-aḥādīth*) on the subject.

Texts such as al-Wāqidī's demonstrate that the traditions transmitted from figures like Ibn ʿUmar were utilised in the early centuries in the process of memorialising places associated with the Prophet's life. These traditions were collected by Muslim scholars and historians and were used to attest to specific locations' significances as sites of Prophetic history. Moreover, in several cases such traditions were cited in order to authorise these sites' visitation and the construction of commemorative architecture there. Much like 'the Christian construction of holy places through narrative, ritual, and cultic buildings' throughout the late antique Near East, these elements similarly formed an interrelated 'package of institutions' that enabled the Prophet's *āthār* to become established as remembered and hallowed spaces.[108] Memories

[106] Horovitz, *Earliest Biographies of the Prophet*, 97–108.

[107] al-Wāqidī, *Kitāb al-Maghāzī*, 1:26. Other traditions in his book describe the Masjid al-Fatḥ on Mount Salʿ, said to be the location where the Prophet prayed during the Battle of the Trench in 5/627; the mosque at al-Manzila where the Prophet had prayed in Khaybar; a mosque constructed at the 'place of the Prophet's prayer' (*muṣallā al-nabī*) in al-Ṭāʾif; and the places where the Prophet prayed on the outskirts of Mecca as he made his way there to perform the Farewell Pilgrimage. al-Wāqidī, *Kitāb al-Maghāzī*, 2:488, 643, 3:927, 1,096–7; Munt, *Holy City of Medina*, 112.

[108] Richard E. Payne, *A State of Mixture: Christians, Zoroastrians, and Iranian Political Culture in Late Antiquity* (Oakland: University of California Press, 2015), 61, 131.

of the events of the Prophet's life, transmitted from the Companions, were concretised in space both by physical buildings and by the rituals performed there by pious visitors.

Tempering Touch: (Mis)remembrance and Regulation of the Prophet's Traces

At the same time as authorities were increasingly patronising the Prophet's *āthār* in Mecca and Medina, jurists were posing questions about how exactly Muslims should engage with these locations. In the previous chapter (and the beginning of this one), we saw some of the debate in the eighth and ninth centuries regarding the appropriateness of visiting and venerating Muḥammad's tomb. Similar issues were raised about the ritualisation of other Prophetic *āthār* in Mecca and Medina. As we saw with Marwān b. al-Ḥakam's altercations with Abū Ayyūb and Usāma b. Zayd, some of this debate took the form of the varying models of Companions and other early figures.[109] In particular, the visitation of Prophetic *āthār* often (but not always) divides our sources between the alleged opinions and actions of ʿAbd Allāh b. ʿUmar, and of his father, the caliph ʿUmar b. al-Khaṭṭab. While the son is often a pious visitant to these locations, the father appears as a critic of their continued remembrance.

The reports about one location of early Islamic history are illustrative of the disputes that surrounded such spaces. According to a report transmitted by the Baṣran proto-Sunnī scholar ʿAbd Allāh b. ʿAwn (d. 151/768) from Ibn ʿUmar's *mawlā* Nāfiʿ, the caliph ʿUmar b. al-Khaṭṭāb heard that people were visiting and praying beneath a tree identified as the location where the Prophet had concluded the Treaty of al-Ḥudaybiyya in the year 6/628.[110] This tree represented a foundational moment: many early believers tied the origins

[109] Khalek, 'Medieval Muslim Martyrs', 92.

[110] Ibn Saʿd, *Ṭabaqāt*, 2:96; Ibn Abī Shayba, *Muṣannaf*, 3:366 (no. 7,619); al-Fākihī, *Akhbār Makka*, 5:78 (no. 2,876); Muḥammad b. Waḍḍāḥ al-Qurṭubī, *Kitāb al-Bidaʿ (Tratado contra las innovaciones)*, ed. and trans. María Isabel Fierro (Madrid: Consejo Superior de Investigaciones Científicas, 1988), 186; al-Ṭurṭūshī, *Kitāb al-Ḥawādith*, 294–5 (no. 265), 308–9 (no. 281). On Ibn ʿAwn, see *EI*[3], s.v. "Abd Allāh b. ʿAwn' (Suleiman A. Mourad); Steven C. Judd, *Religious Scholars and the Umayyads: Piety-Minded Supporters of the Marwānid Caliphate* (New York: Routledge, 2014), 62–70. Ibn ʿAwn transmitted the report to ʿAbd al-Wahhāb b. ʿAṭāʾ (204/819–20 or 206/821–2, Baṣra), Muʿādh b. Muʿādh (d. 196/812, Baṣra), Ibn ʿUlayya (d. 193/809, Baṣra) and ʿĪsā b. Yūnus. On the latter, see the following notes.

of the Muslim community to the oath of allegiance (*bay'a*) that the Prophet Muḥammad's followers had given to him 'under the tree'.[111] Exegetes connected this history with the assertion at Q 48:18 that 'God was pleased with the believers when they swore allegiance to you [Prophet] under the tree'.[112] The event therefore became known as both 'the pledge of [God's] good pleasure' (*bay'at al-riḍwān*) and 'the pledge of the tree' (*bay'at al-shajara*).

Rather than celebrating this location, however, 'Umar reportedly ordered that the tree be cut down. The reason for 'Umar's command does not appear in 'Abd Allāh b. 'Awn's account, but later authorities provided interpretive glosses for the caliph's actions. The Andalusian Mālikī scholar Muḥammad b. Waḍḍāḥ al-Qurṭubī (d. 287/900) quotes a mufti from Tarsus named 'Īsā b. Yūnus (active in the late eighth century) as saying that 'Umar did this 'because the people would come and pray under the tree, and he feared for them that there be *fitna*'.[113] In al-Fākihī's *Akhbār Makka*, a comment appears that, when 'Umar heard that people were praying near and 'glorifying' the tree, the caliph considered this an act of 'innovation' (*ḥadath*).[114] Writing several centuries later, the geographer Yāqūt al-Ḥamawī (d. 626/1229) says that 'Umar learned that 'the people increasingly went to the tree, visited it, and took blessings from it. He feared that [the tree] would be worshipped as [the pre-Islamic goddesses] Allāt and al-'Uzza were.'[115] 'Umar therefore ordered that the tree be cut down and destroyed, such that the 'the people did not see any trace (*athar*) of it'. According to these reports, then, the tree of al-Ḥudaybiyya was destroyed by the second caliph specifically to forestall its visitation and veneration.[116]

111 Mathieu Tillier and Naïm Vanthieghem, 'Recording Debts in Sufyānid Fusṭāṭ: A Reexamination of the Procedures and Calendar in Use in the First/Seventh Century', in *Geneses: A Comparative Study of the Historiographies of the Rise of Christianity, Rabbinic Judaism, and Islam*, ed. John Tolan (London: Routledge, 2019), 148–88.

112 Muqātil, *Tafsīr*, 4:73; Ibn Hishām, *Sīra*, 746, 750; al-Wāqidī, *Kitāb al-Maghāzī*, 618–20.

113 Ibn Waḍḍāḥ, *Kitāb al-Bida'*, 186. On 'Īsā b. Yūnus al-Ṭarasūsī, see al-Mizzī, *Tahdhīb al-kamāl*, 23:76. This is seemingly not the same person as 'Īsā b. Yūnus b. Abī Isḥāq (d. 191/806), regarding whom see Ibn Sa'd, *Ṭabaqāt*, 9:494; Ibn Khayyāṭ, *Ṭabaqāt*, 317–18.

114 al-Fākihī, *Akhbār Makka*, 5:77 (no. 2,875). It is unclear from the text if this comment is part of the *ḥadīth* attributed to Ibn Jurayj, or instead a comment from al-Fākihī himself (or a later compiler or scribe).

115 Yāqūt al-Ḥamawī, *Mu'jam al-buldān*, 3:325.

116 Fierro, 'Treatises against Innovations', 217–18; Fierro, 'Holy Places', 128.

Other texts offer a different, more complicated history of the Ḥudaybiyya tree. The Kūfan Successor Ṭāriq b. ʿAbd al-Raḥmān (active in the late seventh century) reports that, as he travelled through the Ḥijāz on ḥajj, he passed by a group of people praying. When he asked these people what this prayer space (*masjid*) was, they responded, 'This is the tree where the Messenger of God accepted the *bayʿat al-riḍwān*!'[117] However, when Ṭāriq later described this encounter to the famed Medinan jurist Saʿīd b. al-Musayyab, Ibn al-Musayyab responded that his father had been among those who had participated in the *bayʿat al-riḍwān*, and that the participants themselves had forgotten the location of the tree within a year afterwards. Laughing, Saʿīd commented sarcastically: 'Muḥammad's Companions did not know where it was, but you do? You're quite knowledgeable!'

These reports offer conflicting images of the status of the tree of al-Ḥudaybiyya in the seventh century. Contrary to its reported destruction under ʿUmar, Ṭāriq b. ʿAbd al-Raḥmān's account indicates that some people were venerating a tree as the location of the events of al-Ḥudaybiyya still in the late seventh century. However, Saʿīd b. al-Musayyab bedevils things by asserting that the Companions themselves had already lost track of the tree's location not long after the *bayʿat al-riḍwān* itself. A similar tradition is transmitted by the Baṣran Juwayriyya b. Asmāʾ (d. 173/789–90) from Nāfiʿ: when several of the Prophet's Companions went out some years after the events at al-Ḥudaybiyya, 'none of them recognized the tree, and they disagreed among themselves about it'.[118] According to these reports, the tree had not been destroyed by ʿUmar, but its location had simply been forgotten within the lifetimes of the Companions.

The presence of these varying reports suggests either (a) there was no memory of ʿUmar's having destroyed the tree, and another tree was subsequently identified as the location of this moment of Islamic history, or (b) the reports of ʿUmar's destruction of the tree were a later invention, perhaps intended to

[117] Ibn Saʿd, *Ṭabaqāt*, 2:95; al-Bukhārī, *Ṣaḥīḥ*, 1,024 (kitāb al-maghāzī, bāb 35). In both texts, the *isnād* is: ʿUbayd Allāh b. Mūsā (d. *c.* 213/828–9, Kūfa) > Isrāʾīl b. Yūnus b. Abī Isḥāq (d. *c.* 160/777–8, Kūfa) > Ṭāriq. The story is briefly discussed in Goldziher, *Muslim Studies*, 2:280.

[118] Ibn Saʿd, *Ṭabaqāt*, 2:100; al-Bukhārī, *Ṣaḥīḥ*, 730 (kitāb al-jihād wa-l-siyar, bāb 110).

undermine the tree's continued veneration.[119] Either scenario fits the stern and iconoclastic image of 'Umar, who is presented in early Islamic sources as 'the epitome of the rustic Arab of the desert, as well as the austere caliph'.[120] As Tayeb El-Hibri writes, "Umar was carefully chosen to deliver this rebuke to any who wanted to believe in the mystical powers of objects associated with Muḥammad and his practices'.[121]

Whatever the true history of the tree might have been, these stories clearly disparage those who celebrated the location's holiness, and marginalise such visitation as erroneous. These reports marshal the authority of early Muslim figures to offer reasons why the tree should not (indeed, could not) be visited. Unlike the reports in which Companions attest to the Prophet's association with some particular location, these reports instead find Companions obfuscating the tree's location and delegitimising its visitation. Unlike the learned Meccan and Medinan authorities who transmit reports about the Prophet's actions at specific locations, here scholars such as Ibn al-Musayyab and Ibn 'Awn assert that the tree was either lost or destroyed. Notably, a somewhat tepid rejection of the tree's visitation is attributed even to that most *āthār*-inclined of Companions: 'Abd Allāh b. 'Umar. Regarding the Companions' disagreement about the tree's location, Ibn 'Umar reportedly said, 'It was a mercy from God' (*kānat raḥmatan min Allāh*).[122] With these ambiguous words, Ibn 'Umar appears to suggest that the loss of the tree's location was a divine gift to the Muslim community: assumedly because their visiting the tree would have led to *fitna*, innovation and pagan worship.

These reports about the tree of al-Ḥudaybiyya represent some of the most iconoclastic of early Muslims' varied responses to the places commemorating the Prophet's life. Perhaps the nearest comparison to this rejection of a Prophetic trace appears in the story of the stone in the Banū Ẓafar Mosque. According to historical reports and *ḥadīth*s, a stone within the Banū Ẓafar Mosque in Medina was remembered as the spot where the Prophet had sat when he visited this

119 Two further traditions from Sa'īd b. al-Musayyab's father saying that the Companions forgot the location appear in al-Bukhārī, *Ṣaḥīḥ*, 1,024 (kitāb al-maghāzī, bāb 35). They are transmitted from Ibn al-Musayyab by Qatāda b. Di'āma (d. *c.* 117/735–6, Baṣra) and Abū 'Awāna (d. 176/792, Baṣra).

120 Tayeb El-Hibri, "Umar b. al-Khaṭṭāb and the Abbasids', *JAOS* 136.4 (2016): 763–83.

121 El-Hibri, 'Abbasids and the Relics', 88.

122 Ibn Sa'd, *Ṭabaqāt*, 2:100; al-Bukhārī, *Ṣaḥīḥ*, 730 (kitāb al-jihād wa-l-siyar, bāb 110).

mosque.[123] This association with the Prophet led to the stone's usage as a source of blessing: women having trouble conceiving would come to the mosque and sit on the stone, after which they could successfully become pregnant.[124] At one point, the Ḥijāzī governor Ziyād b. ʿUbayd Allāh al-Ḥārithī (r. 133–41/750–9) allegedly ordered that the stone be removed from the Banū Ẓafar Mosque.[125] The governor's reason is not specified, but we might speculate that his order sprang from discomfort with the stone's ritualisation as a Prophetic site, perhaps spurred by the women's visitation there. Yet there is no direct evidence for this: in fact, reports say that when the shaykhs of the Banū Ẓafar told the governor that the Prophet had sat upon the stone, the governor returned it to the mosque. Rather than an example of iconoclasm, this episode instead seems to represent an example of ʿAbbāsid-era patronage of a Prophetic site in Medina.

Indeed, the Prophet Muḥammad's *āthār* do not appear to have undergone frequent campaigns of destruction or purposeful forgetting in the first Islamic centuries. Rather than calling for the places' physical elimination or claiming that their Prophetic identifications were inauthentic, the critics of *āthār* more often critiqued what visitors physically did at these locations/objects. Early jurists appear to have endeavoured to control visitors' modes of interaction with the *āthār*. Instead of targeting the objects and places themselves, Muslim jurists discussed the ways that visitors might appropriately interact with these sites.[126]

[123] Jamāl al-Dīn Muḥammad b. Aḥmad al-Maṭarī, *al-Taʿrīf bi-mā anasat al-hijra min maʿālim dār al-hijra*, ed. Sulaymān al-Ruḥaylī (Riyadh: Dār al-Mālik ʿAbd al-ʿAzīz, 2005), 138–9; al-Marāghī, *Taḥqīq al-nuṣra*, 139; al-Samhūdī, *Wafāʾ al-wafā*, 3:177–8; al-Ṭabarānī, *al-Muʿjam al-kabīr*, 19:243–4; al-Haythamī, *Majmaʿ al-zawāʾid*, 14:96 (no. 10,972). The historical texts relate this narrative from al-Zubayr b. Bakkār > Ibn Zabāla and Yaḥyā b. al-Ḥasan al-ʿAqīqī > Idrīs b. Muḥammad b. Yūnus al-Ẓafarī (active late second/eighth century, Medina) > his grandfather [Yūnus b. Muḥammad b. Anas al-Ẓafarī] (d. 155/771–2, Medina). Al-Ṭabarānī's *ḥadīth* is related through an *isnād* going back to Yūnus b. Muḥammad al-Ẓafarī > his father, Muḥammad b. Anas b. Faḍāla al-Ẓafarī, a Prophetic Companion. This *ḥadīth* notes that 'the stone is in the mosque of the Banū Ẓafar today'.

[124] al-Maṭarī, *al-Taʿrīf*, 139; al-Marāghī, *Taḥqīq al-nuṣra*, 139; al-Samhūdī, *Wafāʾ al-wafā*, 3:177–8; Munt, *Holy City of Medina*, 112, 126, 146.

[125] On Ziyād b. ʿUbayd Allāh, see Ibn Khayyāṭ, *Kitāb al-Tārīkh*, 412–13, 430–1; Patricia Crone, *Slaves on Horses: The Evolution of the Islamic Polity* (Cambridge: Cambridge University Press, 1980), 149.

[126] This dynamic also appears in later periods: Beránek and Ťupek, *Temptation of Graves*, 27.

We have seen something of this dynamic at another prophet's *āthār* in the Ḥijāz: the footprints of Abraham in the Maqām Ibrāhīm. In Chapter 2, we saw that several Muslim jurists and authorities rejected the performance of various rituals at the Maqām, and that they especially baulked at believers' touching and kissing the stone. In this regard, it is noteworthy that Ibn ʿUmar is reported to have prayed at a space of 'one or two men' away from the Maqām.[127] Ibn ʿUmar's authority was thus drawn upon in illustrating the preferred mode of engagement with this powerful object. More specifically, his model was cited for not touching the Maqām, but instead only praying nearby it. Given the debates about haptic ritual at the Maqām, a strong message might have been conveyed by this report that the ritual expert (and *āthār* aficionado) Ibn ʿUmar himself did not touch the stone.

A further glimpse into the debates about how to interact with *āthār* – and the important role of the Companions as model figures for ritual emulation – appears in the reports about Ibn ʿUmar's actions at the Prophet's tomb. We saw above that Ibn ʿUmar often visited the tomb complex in the Prophet's Mosque. One report specifies that he 'would come to the Prophet and place his right hand upon the Prophet's tomb, with his back towards the *qibla*'.[128] Mentioning his 'right hand upon the Prophet's tomb', the report indicates that Ibn ʿUmar physically engaged with the tomb itself, and even turned his back to the *qibla* as he did so. This report is attributed to the Medinan scholar Isḥāq b. Muḥammad al-Farawī (d. 226/840) from another Medinan, ʿUbayd Allāh b. ʿUmar b. Ḥafṣ (d. *c.* 140/757–8), from Ibn ʿUmar's *mawlā* Nāfiʿ.[129]

However, other versions of this report – all of which are likewise attributed to ʿUbayd Allāh b. ʿUmar b. Ḥafṣ from Nāfiʿ – offer very different images of Ibn ʿUmar's behaviour at the Prophet's tomb. In a version transmitted by the Kūfan Muḥammad b. Bishr al-ʿAbdī (d. 203/818–19), it is instead specified that Ibn ʿUmar 'did not touch the tomb' (*lā yamassu al-qabr*) whenever

[127] ʿAbd al-Razzāq, *Muṣannaf*, 5:49 (no. 8,960). The *isnād* is: ʿAbd al-Razzāq > Ibn al-Taymī [Muʿtamir b. Sulaymān] (d. 187/803, Baṣra) > Sulaymān b. Ṭarkhān al-Taymī (d. 143/760, Baṣra) > Bakr b. ʿAbd Allāh al-Muzanī (d. *c.* 106/724–5, Baṣra).

[128] Ismāʿīl b. Isḥāq, *Faḍl al-ṣalāt*, 91–2 (no. 100).

[129] On al-Farawī, see al-Dhahabī, *Siyar*, 10:649–50; al-ʿUqaylī, *Kitāb al-Ḍuʿafāʾ*, 106.

he visited it after returning from a journey.[130] A version transmitted by the Kūfan *muḥaddith* Abū Usāma Ḥammād b. Usāma (d. 201/816–17) says that Ibn ʿUmar 'disapproved of touching the Prophet's tomb' (*yakruhu massa qabri al-nabī*).[131] In a slightly different (and perhaps purposefully reconciliatory) report, another version attributed to Abū Usāma says that Ibn ʿUmar 'disapproved that touching the Prophet's tomb happen frequently' (*yakruhu an yakthura massu qabri al-nabī*).[132] These accounts thus present divergent images of Ibn ʿUmar's interaction with the Prophet's tomb: he alternatively (a) touched the Prophet's tomb, (b) did not touch it, (c) disapproved of touching it, and (d) disapproved of touching it *too much*.

It is difficult to identify any positivistic truth about Ibn ʿUmar's actions from these texts, or to say which of these variant reports is earlier than the others. However, these reports offer witness to early discussions about the proper modes of behaviour at the Prophet's tomb, and the deployment within those discussions of Companions like Ibn ʿUmar. The different reports of Ibn ʿUmar's actions suggest that touching the tomb was a debated practice, with different positions on the issue attributed to this authoritative figure.[133]

If their *isnād*s are reliable, these variant reports likely emerged in the mid- to late eighth century, in the period of the Successors Isḥāq b. Muḥammad al-Farawī, Muḥammad b. Bishr al-ʿAbdī and Abū Usāma. Notably, the Medinan al-Farawī is credited with the version describing Ibn ʿUmar touching the tomb, while the Kūfans Muḥammad b. Bishr and Abū Usāma trans-

[130] al-Bayhaqī, *Shuʿab al-īmān*, 6:45–6 (no. 3,854). On Muḥammad b. Bishr, see I-Wen Su, 'The Early Shīʿī Traditionists' Perspective on the Rightly Guided Caliphs', *JAOS* 141 (2021): 27–47.

[131] Muḥammad b. ʿĀṣim al-Thaqafī, *Juzʾ Muḥammad b. ʿĀṣim al-Thaqafī al-Iṣbahānī*, ed. Mufīd Khālid ʿĪd (Riyadh: Dār al-ʿĀṣima, 1409 AH [1988–9]), 106 (no. 27); al-Dhahabī, *Siyar*, 12:378; al-Dhahabī, *Muʿjam al-shuyūkh*, ed. Muḥammad Ḥabīb al-Hayla, 2 vols (al-Ṭāʾif: Maktabat al-Ṣiddīq, 1988), 1:73.

[132] al-Samhūdī, *Wafāʾ al-wafā*, 5:106. An editorial note indicates that this reading also appears in one of the manuscripts of Muḥammad b. ʿĀṣim, *Juzʾ*, 106 n.158. Alternatively, another manuscript has the reading '*yakthuru*', i.e. 'Ibn ʿUmar 'frequently touched the Prophet's tomb'!

[133] This issue was ongoing long after this period. For example, touching the Prophet's grave was expressly prohibited by the Andalusian Mālikī Abū Bakr al-Ṭurṭūshī (d. 520/1126): al-Ṭurṭūshī, *Kitāb al-Ḥawādith*, 304 (no. 274); Fierro, 'Treatises against Innovations', 221–2.

mit versions in which Ibn ʿUmar is critical of or reticent about touching it. Perhaps we see here – as in Chapter 4 – a degree of regional variation in practice, with Iraqi voices more critical of rituals of veneration/visitation at the Prophet's tomb than Ḥijāzīs were.

Further evidence for some Ḥijāzīs' acceptance of such haptic rituals appears in narratives about Companions' actions at another important relic in the Medina mosque: the Prophet's *minbar*. The Medinan scholars Ibn Abī Fudayk and Ibn Abī Dhiʾb (d. 159/775–6) transmit a report saying that Ibn ʿUmar 'placed his hand upon the Prophet's seat on the *minbar*, then placed [his hand] upon his face'.[134] According to this report, Ibn ʿUmar touched the Prophet's seat and then his own face, seemingly to convey the object's touch more directly onto himself. The *minbar*'s blessing was thus physically accessed through touch. Medinan authorities also transmit a report in which Ibn ʿUmar and another Companion – Saʿd b. Abī Waqqāṣ (d. 55/675) – both take hold of the *minbar*'s pommel (*rummān al-minbar*) before leaving the mosque.[135] The significance of grasping the pommel is not specified, but a similar ritual is described by the Medinan *faqīh* Yazīd b. ʿAbd Allāh b. Qusayṭ (d. 122/739): 'I saw a group of the Prophet's Companions – when the mosque was empty – come to the *minbar*'s pommel, stroke it, and perform *duʿāʾ*'.[136] Yazīd thus reports that several Companions touched the *minbar* as part of their visitation of this space, and did so in combination with the performance of *duʿāʾ*. It appears that touching the *minbar* was seen as a ritually efficacious act, and a place where prayer might be answered. Not only is Ibn ʿUmar associated with

[134] Ibn Saʿd, *Ṭabaqāt*, 1:218; Ibn Ḥibbān, *Kitāb al-Thiqāt*, 4:9. The *isnād* is: Ibn Abī Fudayk > Ibn Abī Dhiʾb > Ḥamza b. Abī Jaʿfar > Ibrāhīm b. ʿAbd al-Raḥmān b. ʿAbd al-Qārī. On the latter two obscure transmitters, see al-Bukhārī, *Kitāb al-Taʾrīkh al-kabīr*, 1/1:297, 2/1:51.

[135] Ibn Saʿd, *Ṭabaqāt*, 7:401; Ibn ʿAsākir, *Taʾrīkh*, 51:192–3. The *isnād* is: Muḥammad b. ʿUmar [al-Wāqidī] > Mūsā b. Muḥammad b. Ibrāhīm (d. 151/768, Medina) > Muḥammad b. Ibrāhīm b. al-Ḥārith al-Taymī (d. 120/737–8, Medina). On these transmitters, see Ibn Saʿd, *Ṭabaqāt*, 7:401, 550; Horovitz, *Earliest Biographies of the Prophet*, 115 n.112.

[136] Ibn Abī Shayba, *Muṣannaf*, 5:685 (no. 16,113); Ibn Saʿd, *Ṭabaqāt*, 1:218–19; al-Samhūdī, *Wafāʾ al-wafā*, 5:104. The report is transmitted by Abū Mawdūd ʿAbd al-ʿAzīz b. Abī Sulaymān (active second/eighth century, Medina), who transmitted it to Zayd b. al-Ḥubāb (d. 203/818–19, Kūfa), Khālid b. Makhlad al-Bajalī (d. 213/828–9, Kūfa) and ʿAbd Allāh b. Maslama b. Qaʿnab al-Ḥārithī (d. 221/835–6, Medina/Baṣra). On Abū Mawdūd, see van Ess, *Theology and Society*, 2:753–4.

such devotional practice at the *minbar* in these traditions, but so are Saʿd b. Abī Waqqāṣ and several unnamed Companions.

On the basis of the reports they transmitted, these eighth- and ninth-century Medinan scholars appear to have approved of such haptic practices at the Prophet's *minbar*, and they drew upon the Companions as exemplars to justify such conduct. The scholars' approval is further indicated by reports in which they themselves carry out similar practices at the Prophet's *minbar*. Yazīd b. ʿAbd Allāh perhaps cited his report about unnamed Companions stroking the pommel as a model for his own practice, as he is reported to have performed the very same ritual at the *minbar*.[137] Yazīd's contemporary, the esteemed Meccan jurist ʿAṭāʾ b. Abī Rabāḥ (d. 114/732–3), is also said to have touched the *minbar*'s pommel and performed *duʿāʾ* there.[138] Within Shīʿī sources, imam Jaʿfar al-Ṣādiq (himself a resident of Medina) prescribes a similar practice for those visiting the Prophet's Mosque in Medina. Jaʿfar says that pilgrims should approach the *minbar* and stroke it with their hands, grasp the two pommels and then wipe their eyes and face (as this is 'a healing for the eye'), and then stand beside the *minbar* and ask God for whatever they need.[139] These rituals at the Prophet's *minbar* thus may have transcended sectarian boundaries among Medinan authorities in the eighth century.

At the same time, other reports suggest that not all Medinans approved of these practices at the Prophet's *minbar*. The jurist Saʿīd b. al-Musayyab – whom we have previously encountered opposing visitation of both the Prophet's tomb

137 Ibn Abī Shayba, *Muṣannaf*, 5:685 (no. 16,113).

138 al-Dhahabī, *Siyar*, 8:54; al-Dhahabī, *Taʾrīkh al-Islām*, 11 [171–80 AH]:319. The *isnād* is: Muṣʿab al-Zubayrī (d. 236/851) > Ibn Abī al-Zubayr > Mālik b. Anas.

139 al-Kulaynī, *al-Kāfī*, 4:553; al-Ṭūsī, *Tahdhīb al-aḥkām*, 6:8; Ibn Bābawayh, *Kitāb Man lā yaḥḍuru al-faqīh*, 2:354. The *isnād* is: ʿAlī b. Ibrāhīm al-Qummī (d. after 307/919, Qum) > his father [Ibrāhīm b. Hāshim] (Kūfa/Qum) > Muḥammad b. Ismāʿīl b. Bazīʿ > al-Faḍl b. Shādhān (d. 260/873–4, Kūfa) > Muḥammad b. Abī ʿUmayr (d. 217/832, Kūfa) > Ṣafwān b. Yaḥyā al-Bajalī (d. *c.* 210/825, Kūfa) > Muʿāwiya b. ʿAmmār al-Duhnī (d. 175/791, Kūfa). On these figures, see Modarressi, *Tradition and Survival*, 170, 327–32; van Ess, *Theology and Society*, 1:451–3; *EI*[3], s.v. 'al-Faḍl b. Shādhān' (Tamima Bayhom-Daou); *EI*[3], s.v. "Alī b. Ibrāhīm al-Qummī' (Mohammad Ali Amir-Moezzi). Najam Haider finds evidence of overlap between Imāmī Shīʿī and Medinan ritual practice: Haider, 'Geography of the *Isnād*: Possibilities for the Reconstruction of Local Ritual Practice in the 2nd/8th Century', *Der Islam* 90.2 (2013): 310, 312, 328, 336–7.

and the Ḥudaybiyya tree – reportedly 'disapproved of placing one's hand upon the *minbar*'.[140] Criticism of the *minbar*'s visitation also colours a *ḥadīth* that circulated in the eighth-century Ḥijāz. In a variant of the Prophet's wish that his grave not be worshipped, the Prophet cries, 'O God, I seek refuge in you if my grave be taken as an idol, or my *minbar* as a place of celebration (*ʿīd*)!'[141] Transmitted by Ḥijāzī scholars such as Ibn Abī Yaḥyā and Ibn Jurayj, this *ḥadīth* likely reflects an ongoing issue in eighth-century Medina. Thus, as we saw in the case of the Prophet's tomb, regional practice fails to provide a clear-cut answer for who did or did not approve of visiting the Prophet's *minbar*.

Muslim scholars from Iraq were also interested in the proper means of interacting with the Prophet's *āthār*, perhaps just as much as the Ḥijāzīs were. The majority of transmitters of the aforementioned traditions about the rejection of the tree of al-Ḥudaybiyya – as well as several of the traditions about touching the Prophet's *minbar*, including Ibn al-Musayyab's rejection of it – are Baṣran and Kūfan.[142] A tradition from the Baṣran scholar Muḥammad b. Sīrīn (d. 110/728–9) provides a rare comment on the treatment of prophets' *āthār* collectively. According to Ibn Sīrīn, 'They disapproved of altering the prophets' *āthār*.'[143] In this ambiguous report, it is not clear what Ibn Sīrīn means by 'altering', or by *āthār*. The context suggests that he was concerned with how Muslims interacted with prophets' remains, in some form or another.

[140] Ibn Abī Shayba, *Muṣannaf*, 5:685 (no. 16,114). The *isnād* is: Ibn Abī Shayba > al-Faḍl b. Dukayn (d. 219/834, Kūfa) > Sufyān al-Thawrī > ʿAbd Allāh b. Yazīd al-Laythī (unidentified) > Saʿīd b. al-Musayyab.

[141] ʿAbd al-Razzāq, *Muṣannaf*, 8:464 (no. 15,916). The *isnād* is: ʿAbd al-Razzāq > Ibrāhīm b. Abī Yaḥyā (d. 184/800, Medina) and Ibn Jurayj (d. 150/767, Mecca) > Ṣafwān b. Salīm (d. 132/749, Medina) > Saʿīd b. Abī Saʿīd *mawlā* al-Mihrī.

[142] The prominent place of Saʿīd b. al-Musayyab in these traditions is noteworthy, as his authority seems to have been sometimes 'deployed by Iraqi jurists' to locate approval of certain ritual practices among the scholars of the Ḥijāz and thereby provide sanction for them. Travis Zadeh, 'An Ingestible Scripture: Qurʾānic Erasure and the Limits of "Popular" Religion', in *Material Culture and Asian Religions: Text, Image, Object*, ed. Benjamin J. Fleming and Richard D. Mann (New York: Routledge, 2014), 104–5. We could have a similar situation here, with Ibn al-Musayyab's purported dislike of *āthār* practices used to justify Iraqī opposition.

[143] Ibn Abī Shayba, *Muṣannaf*, 3:368 (no. 7,625). The *isnād* is: Muʿādh b. Muʿādh (d. 196/812, Baṣra) > Ibn ʿAwn > Ibn Sīrīn.

Ibn Sīrīn's words here are particularly interesting in light of another Iraqi perspective: an Imāmī Shīʿī *ḥadīth*. In this report, imam Jaʿfar al-Ṣādiq asks his Kūfan disciple Muḥammad b. ʿAlī al-Ḥalabī (d. *c.* 148/765–6) if he had 'gone to Masjid Qubāʾ, Masjid al-Faḍīkh, or Mashrabat Umm Ibrāhīm'. After al-Ḥalabī's confirmation that he had done so, Jaʿfar asserts that 'none of the Messenger of God's *āthār* has remained unaltered except for these'.[144] The meaning of 'altering' the *āthār* is again unclear, but it appears that the imam is not in favour of this happening.

Yet it seems impossible that Jaʿfar meant to discourage visitation of these sites. Several Shīʿī traditions find him encouraging visitation of exactly these locations, as well as other sites in Medina, such as the tombs of the martyrs.[145] As he says in one case, 'Do not skip going to all of the *mashāhid*!' Indeed, Shīʿī visitation of these sites in Medina appears to have been a relatively common (or at least strongly encouraged) practice by at least the tenth century, if not earlier.[146] This is suggested not only by the Imāmī texts that encourage such pilgrimage, but also by the presence of a very similar tradition in the North African Ismāʿīlī author al-Qāḍī al-Nuʿmān's (d. 363/974) *Daʿāʾim al-Islām*, in which Jaʿfar al-Ṣādiq lists off these sites as 'the *mashāhid* in Medina that it is appropriate to come see, pray in, and acquaint oneself with'.[147]

What could Ibn Sīrīn have meant, then, about the disapproval of 'altering the prophets' *āthār*'? While the exact meaning remains unclear, it seems he did not intend that such objects or sites should be destroyed, or even that they should be avoided. Perhaps he, and Jaʿfar al-Ṣādiq too, instead mourned the

[144] al-Kulaynī, *al-Kāfī*, 4:561; Munt, *Holy City of Medina*, 114 n.86. The *isnād* is: Abū ʿAlī al-Ashʿarī [Aḥmad b. Idrīs] (d. 306/918–19, Qum) > Muḥammad b. ʿAbd al-Jabbār [aka Muḥammad b. Abī al-Ṣahbān] (Qum) > Ṣafwān b. Yaḥyā al-Bajalī (d. *c.* 210/825, Kūfa) > ʿAbd Allāh b. Muskān (d. *c.* 183/799–800, Kūfa) > al-Ḥalabī. See Modarressi, *Tradition and Survival*, 150–5, 337–8.

[145] al-Kulaynī, *al-Kāfī*, 4:560–1; al-Ṭūsī, *Tahdhīb al-aḥkām*, 6:17; Ibn Qūlūya, *Kāmil al-ziyārāt*, 63–8; Ibn Bābawayh, *Kitāb Man lā yaḥḍuru al-faqīh*, 1:163, 2:358.

[146] Munt, *Holy City of Medina*, 126, 136; Warner, 'One Thousand *Ḥijaj*', 417, 428.

[147] al-Qāḍī al-Nuʿmān b. Muḥammad, *Daʿāʾim al-Islām*, vol. 1, ed. Āṣaf b. ʿAlī Aṣghar Faiḍī (Cairo: Dār al-Maʿārif, 1951), 296–7. For a comparison of this text with Imāmī texts, see Kumail Rajani, 'Between Qum and Qayrawān: Unearthing Early Shii *ḥadīth* sources', *BSOAS* 84.3 (2021): 419–42.

campaigns of aggrandisement of such locations that were carried out under the Umayyads and ʿAbbāsids, as had similarly happened in response to the changes made to the Prophet's Mosque.[148] Alternatively, perhaps there was concern about visitors' touch altering prophetic *āthār*, as had already happened at the Maqām Ibrāhīm in Mecca. Whatever the case, rather than suffering from campaigns of forgetting or destruction, the Prophet Muḥammad's *āthār* generally appear to have been maintained, with jurists recommending certain regulations be followed regarding how visitors interacted with them.

'Each Person Does What He Wants': Visitation of *Āthār* as Supererogatory Ritual

What, then, did Muslim scholars in the first centuries think of the visitation of Prophetic sites? How important was such visitation? How did these rituals interact with other, related practices, such as ritual prayer (*ṣalāt*) and ḥajj? Different answers were offered by different communities and individuals: the early Shīʿa, in particular, strongly encouraged visitation of such sites as a near equivalent of the ḥajj, if their extant *ḥadīth* are reliable sources.[149] In general, though, there is little indication that Muslim scholars understood such visitation as strictly obligatory for all individual Muslims.[150] Indeed, many seem to have been unsure whether these were commendable acts of piety, or if they should be avoided. An important point for many scholars, it seems, was to distinguish visitation of Prophetic *āthār* from the legally prescribed rituals of *ṣalāt* and ḥajj. While visiting *āthār* may or may not have been a good thing, scholars frequently identified such practice as distinct from the required rituals of Muslim identity.

One particularly relevant tradition again finds the caliph ʿUmar as a critic of *āthār*'s visitation. In this report, a Kūfan named al-Maʿrūr b. Suwayd al-Asadī (d. *c.* 80/699–700) narrates that he was on a journey from Mecca to Medina with the caliph ʿUmar b. al-Khaṭṭāb, with some versions specifying that they were returning from the ḥajj.[151] While they were on their way, the

[148] A focus on architectural change is suggested by Munt, *Holy City of Medina*, 114 n.86.

[149] Warner, 'One Thousand *Ḥijaj*', 424–8.

[150] Munt, *Holy City of Medina*, 142.

[151] For a critical perspective on al-Maʿrūr's historicity, see G. H. A. Juynboll, 'The Role of the *Muʿammarūn* in the Early Development of the *Isnād*', *Wiener Zeitschrift für die Kunde des Morgenlandes* 81 (1991): 164.

time for prayer came: they prayed, and then saw people rushing to a particular mosque (*masjid*). When ʿUmar asked what was going on, he was told: 'That is a mosque that the Messenger of God prayed within.' ʿUmar replied: 'But those who came before you – those who took the *āthār* of their prophets as churches and synagogues – have perished! If you are inside one of these mosques when the time for prayer occurs, then pray there: but if not, then pass it by.'[152]

In this tradition, we again find ʿUmar rejecting the veneration of locations associated with the Prophet, as he had done with the tree of al-Ḥudaybiyya. ʿUmar discourages the efforts to pray at the Prophet's places of prayer, saying that the previous communities who did such things 'have perished'. The caliph here specifically connects such practices with Jews and Christians, mentioning those who took their prophet's *āthār* as 'churches' (*kanāʾis*) and 'synagogues' (*biyaʿ*).[153] In some versions of the report, rather than the vague 'those who came before you', ʿUmar explicitly calls these people 'the People of the Book' (*ahl al-kitāb*).[154] As in other texts, the exact meaning of *āthār* is unclear here. Notably, though, some versions find ʿUmar criticising the Jews and Christians not only for taking their prophets' *āthār* as worship spaces, but also for 'following their prophets' *āthār*'.[155] Thus, he seemingly characterises the veneration of spaces associated with a holy person as 'following' their *āthār*. This is, of course, the exact activity that the caliph's son, ʿAbd Allāh b. ʿUmar, reportedly performed so prolifically.

ʿUmar emphasises that attention should be paid to the times of ritual prayer, rather than to the places where it is performed. If a prayer time were to occur while one was in one of the Prophet's worship spots, then one should pray there: but one should not go out of one's way to pray in such a location specifically. Rather than these locations being sought out for ritual prayer, they should be 'passed by', with no attention paid to their Prophetic significance.

[152] Ibn Waḍḍāḥ, *Kitāb al-Bidaʿ*, 185; Ibn Abī Shayba, *Muṣannaf*, 3: 367–8 (no. 7,624); ʿAbd al-Razzāq, *Muṣannaf*, 2:118–19 (no. 2,734); Ibn Ḥajar, *Fatḥ al-bārī*, 2:231; Ibn Baṭṭāl, *Sharḥ Ṣaḥīḥ al-Bukhārī*, ed. Abū Tamīm Yāsir b. Ibrāhīm, 10 vols (Riyadh: Maktabat al-Rushd, 2000), 2:126. On this tradition, see Munt, *Holy City of Medina*, 128.

[153] On the multiple possible meanings of *biyaʿ*, see Bursi, 'Fluid Boundaries', 480 n.5.

[154] Ibn Abī Shayba, *Muṣannaf*, 3:367–8 (no. 7,624); Ibn Ḥajar, *Fatḥ al-bārī*, 2:231; Ibn Baṭṭāl, *Sharḥ*, 2:126.

[155] Ibn Waḍḍāḥ, *Kitāb al-Bidaʿ*, 185; Ibn Ḥajar, *Fatḥ al-bārī*, 2:231; Ibn Baṭṭāl, *Sharḥ*, 2:126.

The importance is in performing the ritual prayer at the correct times, not in doing so at particular locations. Indeed, in one version, ʿUmar even says, 'If the time for prayer does not occur while you are in [one of these locations], then do not pray.'[156] This might suggest that additional, supererogatory prayer in such locations is discouraged.

This is certainly a different and more disapproving attitude towards worship at the Prophet's places of prayer than the perspective attributed to ʿUmar's son. Importantly, though, the caliph does not call here for these Prophetic places of prayer to be destroyed like the Ḥudaybiyya tree. Instead, these sites of Prophetic activity are simply to be treated as normal places of worship, like any other. These sites should not be specifically sanctified, and to do so would risk repeating the errors of the Jews and Christians. Yet the sites are not themselves represented as inherently dangerous places of blasphemy or idolatrous veneration. Instead, emphasis is placed on controlling the activity that is performed there, and specifically the importance of only worshipping there at the canonical times of prayer. According to this tradition, participation in the sacred time of the *ṣalāt* is far more important than visitation of the purportedly sacred place of the Prophet's *muṣallā*.

This tradition about ʿUmar originally circulated in Iraq, and likely reflects views among some eighth-century proto-Sunnī Iraqis regarding visitation of Prophetic sites.[157] Several reports offer further evidence of Iraqi scholars' rejection of these practices. For example, the Kūfan scholar Sufyān al-Thawrī (d. 161/778) appears to have discouraged pilgrimage to Medina: when someone told him of plans to visit the city, al-Thawrī responded, 'Do not do that!'[158] His

[156] Ibn Abī Shayba, *Muṣannaf*, 3:367–8 (no. 7,624).

[157] In almost every *isnād*, this report is transmitted from its Kūfan narrator al-Maʿrūr to the Kūfan Sulaymān b. Mihrān al-Aʿmash (d. *c.* 148/765–6), from whom it then passed to the Baṣrans Jarīr b. Ḥāzim and Maʿmar b. Rāshid and the Kūfan Abū Muʿāwiya Muḥammad b. Khāzim (d. *c.* 195/810–11). The sole exception to this pattern is Ibn Baṭṭāl's text, where al-Maʿrūr is instead said to have transmitted the report to the Baṣran Sulaymān al-Taymī (d. 143/760–1). Juynboll, *Encyclopedia*, 78 notes that these two Sulaymāns – al-Aʿmash and al-Taymī – were sometimes confused, but it is not clear if that has happened here.

[158] ʿAbd al-Razzāq, *Muṣannaf*, 5:134 (no. 9,169); Munt, *Holy City of Medina*, 128–9; M. J. Kister, 'You Shall Only Set Out for Three Mosques: A Study of an Early Tradition', *Le Muséon* 82 (1969): 188.

aversion to visiting *āthār* specifically is noted in the case of Jerusalem, where al-Thawrī prayed in the city's congregational mosque but 'did not follow the *āthār* and did not pray at them'.[159] His Kūfan colleague Wakīʿ b. al-Jarrāḥ acted in much the same way in Jerusalem: he prayed in the congregational mosque, but did not visit any of the sacred sites there.[160] Similarly, Sufyān b. ʿUyayna transmits a tradition, through a Baṣran *isnād*, in which the caliph ʿUmar (or Ibn ʿUmar, in variant versions) responds to a questioner asking about visiting al-Ṭūr, meaning Mount Sinai: 'Abandon al-Ṭūr and do not go there!'[161] These sources indicate some proto-Sunnī Iraqis' rejection of ritual visitation of such sites, perhaps especially those in Medina and Jerusalem.

Such attitudes were not limited to Iraq, as we find several similar opinions among Ḥijāzīs as well. When Hammām b. Nāfiʿ al-Ḥimyārī told the Meccan scholar al-Muthannā b. al-Ṣabbāḥ (d. 149/766–7) that he planned to travel to Medina, al-Muthannā told him: 'Do not do that! I heard ʿAṭā' [b. Abī Rabāḥ] say to a man, "Seven circumambulations of the House are better than your trip to Medina."'[162] Several reports record ʿAṭā' expressing such sentiments about

[159] Ibn Waḍḍāḥ, *Kitāb al-Bidaʿ*, 186. Notably, however, Sufyān's visitation of sites in Jerusalem seems to have been disputed, with varying accounts of whether he visited the Dome of the Rock. See Shihāb al-Dīn Abū Maḥmūd b. Tamīm al-Maqdisī, *Muthīr al-Gharām ilā Ziyārat al-Quds wa-l-Shām*, ed. Aḥmad al-Khuṭaymī (Beirut, Dār al-Jīl, 1994), 352; Ofer Livne-Kafri, 'The Muslim Traditions "In Praise of Jerusalem" (*Faḍā'il al-Quds*): Diversity and Complexity', *Università degli Studi di Napoli L'Orientale* 58 (1998): 171–3. On the identification of the Jerusalemite holy sites in this period, see Elad, *Medieval Jerusalem*, 67–8.

[160] Ibn Waḍḍāḥ, *Kitāb al-Bidaʿ*, 186; al-Wāsiṭī, *Faḍā'il*, 76 (no. 124); Ibn al-Murajjā, *Faḍā'il*, 243 (no. 363); al-Maqdisī, *Muthīr al-Gharām*, 356–7; Elad, *Medieval Jerusalem*, 67. Both al-Thawrī and Wakīʿ also transmitted traditions, related from earlier Kūfan authorities, that display clear disparagement of the visitation of Jerusalem: ʿAbd al-Razzāq, *Muṣannaf*, 5:134 (nos 9,166–7); Ibn Abī Shayba, *Muṣannaf*, 3:364 (nos 7,607–9); Kister, 'You Shall Only Set Out', 182–3.

[161] Ibn Abī Shayba, *Muṣannaf*, 3:365 (no. 7,613); ʿAbd al-Razzāq, *Muṣannaf*, 5:135 (no. 9,171); Kister, 'You Shall Only Set Out', 177; Kister, 'Sanctity Joint and Divided', 19. The *isnād* in Ibn Abī Shayba is: Ibn ʿUyayna > ʿAmr [b. Dīnār] > Ṭalq [b. Ḥabīb] (Baṣra) > Qazaʿa [b. Yaḥyā, Abū al-Ghādiyya] (Baṣra). In ʿAbd al-Razzāq, it is: Ibn ʿUyayna > ʿAmr b. Dīnār > ʿArfaja [b. ʿAbd Allāh (Kūfa)?].

[162] ʿAbd al-Razzāq, *Muṣannaf*, 5:134 (no. 9,168); Kister, 'You Shall Only Set Out', 187–8; Munt, *Holy City of Medina*, 128.

visiting various sites, such as when he is asked about going to 'the tree' (likely referencing the tree of al-Ḥudaybiyya near Medina) and making an *'umra* from there. To this idea, 'Aṭā' responds, 'No!'[163] Asked about someone who has made a vow to walk from Baṣra to Jerusalem, 'Aṭā' says, 'You were commanded [to come to] this House [i.e. the Ka'ba], so walk to this House.'[164] Similarly, when the Meccan Ṭāwūs b. Kaysān was asked about someone having vowed to walk to or make a 'visit' (*ziyāra*) to Jerusalem, Ṭāwūs responded: 'Mecca is incumbent upon you.'[165]

Negative attitudes towards the visitation of various sites thus appeared among scholars in both Iraq and the Ḥijāz in the eighth century. Explicit rejection occurs in some reports, such as in the command 'Abandon al-Ṭūr and do not go there!'. In other cases, rather than complete rejection, the scholars express their preference for the performance of certain rituals, especially the ḥajj to Mecca, instead of these acts of pious visitation. While the reports do not state early scholars' reasoning regarding the avoidance of practices of ritual visitation to different sites, we can see some themes at play.

One important point is that these reports clearly reflect early controversies about pilgrimage within the emergent Islamic sacred geography. Debates over these issues included the relative status of the shrines in Mecca, Medina and Jerusalem, as well as the permissibility of visiting 'minor sanctuaries', such as Mount Sinai, the Qubā' mosque, and many other such sites.[166] Discussions of these issues often pivoted around a seemingly quite early Prophetic *ḥadīth*, 'Do not set out except for three mosques: al-Masjid al-Ḥarām [in Mecca], Masjid al-Aqṣā [in Jerusalem], and my mosque', that is, the Prophet's Mosque in Medina.[167] Interpreters often understood this *ḥadīth* as prohibiting pious travel to any sites other than these three locations. Yet Jerusalem and Medina's merits as destinations for pilgrimage were also disputed, as we see in several of the traditions above.

[163] 'Abd al-Razzāq, *Muṣannaf*, 5:134–5 (no. 9,170).

[164] Ibid., 8:454 (no. 15,886).

[165] 'Abd al-Razzāq, *Muṣannaf*, 8:456 (no. 15,892).

[166] Kister, 'You Shall Only Set Out', 174–5.

[167] Kister, 'You Shall Only Set Out', 173; Shoemaker, *Death of a Prophet*, 229; Elad, *Medieval Jerusalem*, 147–8, 153–7.

At the same time, total rejection of travel to, and veneration of, different sites is not the only position found in the early reports. A theme in some traditions is the principle of *rukhṣa*: 'concession', that is, modifications to ritual prescriptions 'designed to soften their harshness'.[168] For example, in many traditions, the Prophet Muḥammad and early scholars do not encourage practices of intense self-exertion during pilgrimage, such as walking the whole way to Mecca for the ḥajj, or crawling on the ground during circumambulation of the Kaʿba.[169] Discussing the prohibition of such acts of self-mortification, Ibn Jurayj cites the Prophet's words: 'There is no celibacy nor monasticism in Islam.'[170]

This attitude of 'concession' may explain some of the traditions in which scholars discourage individuals from visiting locations such as the Prophet's Mosque in Medina or the city of Jerusalem. Rather than absolutely condemning those sites, scholars in several cases appear to offer a form of concession by suggesting that worshipping in a nearer site is just as meritorious as doing so at a far-away one. Thus, in one tradition, Saʿīd b al-Musayyab says: 'One who vows to worship in Masjid Īliyāʾ [Jerusalem], let him worship in the Prophet's Mosque in Medina, for it suffices him; and one who vows to worship in the Prophet's Mosque, let him worship in al-Masjid al-Ḥarām, for it suffices him.'[171] Like the caliph ʿUmar's flattening of worship spaces regardless of their Prophetic histories, these traditions appear to equalise sites of pious visitation, regardless of how far individuals must exert themselves to worship at them.[172]

As we see in Ibn al-Musayyab's report, early discussions about the acceptability or necessity of visiting sacred spaces were often framed around questions

[168] Kister, 'On "Concessions" and Conduct', 89.

[169] Kister, 'On "Concessions" and Conduct', 103; Norman Calder, '*Ḥinth*, *Birr*, *Tabarrur*, *Taḥannuth*: An Inquiry into the Arabic Vocabulary of Vows', *BSOAS* 51.2 (1988): 227–8.

[170] ʿAbd al-Razzāq, *Muṣannaf*, 8:448 (no. 15,860). At the same time, there was also an acceptance of some such rigorous practices – especially travelling on ḥajj by foot – as virtuous acts of piety: Kister, 'On "Concessions" and Conduct', 103–4; Melchert, *Before Sufism*, 88–9; Calder, 'Vocabulary of Vows', 226.

[171] ʿAbd al-Razzāq, *Muṣannaf*, 8:455 (no. 15,889); Ibn Baṭṭāl, *Sharḥ*, 3:179.

[172] Melchert, *Before Sufism*, 90 makes a similar point about some early Muslim renunciants' discomfort with the ḥajj because 'it was so tied to a particular time and place, whereas their ascetic outlook tended to insist on the equality of times and places'.

about fulfilling pious vows. Like other late antique religious practitioners, early Muslims made vows to voyage on pilgrimage to sacred sites – often in far-away locations – as embodied acts of gratitude, repentance, and/or supplication to God.[173] In their turn, Muslim jurists debated questions that such vows evoked, such as: how imperative was it to fulfil a vow to worship in some particular location, usually involving long and strenuous travel to get there?[174]

In many cases, early Muslim jurists offered concessions that loosened the difficulties of individuals' self-imposed hardships. When asked about a person who had vowed to walk to Jerusalem, the Syrian jurist al-Awzāʿī (d. 157/774) suggested that the person ride there instead, and then give away that riding animal as charity (*ṣadaqa*).[175] Similarly, when asked about a man who had vowed to walk to the Kaʿba, ʿAlī b. Abī Ṭālib reportedly said: 'Let him walk – but, if it is too difficult, then ride and bring a camel to be sacrificed (*jazūr*).'[176] Likewise, when the Shīʿī imam Muḥammad al-Bāqir is asked about a man who has vowed to walk to the Kaʿba, but is unable to do so, al-Bāqir replies, 'Let him go on ḥajj riding!'[177]

The concessions that scholars offered suggest their views on the relative importance and acceptability of worship at different sites. For example, we saw that Ibn al-Musayyab said that a vow to worship in Jerusalem could be fulfilled by doing so in Medina, and a vow to worship in Medina could be fulfilled in Mecca. This may suggest a certain equivalence between, and acceptance of, worship at these different locations. On the other hand, we saw above that ʿAṭāʾ b. Abī Rabāḥ and Ṭāwūs b. Kaysān both dismissed vows to worship in Jerusalem and commanded individuals to worship in Mecca instead. Their

[173] Maraval, *Lieux saints et pèlerinages*, 150; Bitton-Ashkelony, *Encountering the Sacred*, 96, 151; Jane L. Kanarek, 'Pilgrimage and Piety: Rabbinic Women and Vows of Valuation: Mishnah *ʿArakhin* 5:1, Tosefta *ʿArakhin* 3:1, BT *ʿArakhin* 19a', *Nashim* 28 (2015): 61–74.

[174] Calder, 'Vocabulary of Vows', 226–34.

[175] al-Wāsiṭī, *Faḍāʾil*, 30 (no. 42); Ibn al-Murajjā, *Faḍāʾil*, 167 (no. 229); Calder, 'Vocabulary of Vows', 226–7. On al-Awzāʿī, see Judd, *Awzaʿi*.

[176] ʿAbd al-Razzāq, *Muṣannaf*, 8:450 (no. 15,869); al-Fākihī, *Akhbār Makka*, 1:350 (no. 723). These two slightly different traditions are ascribed to ʿAlī via Ibrāhīm al-Nakhaʿī (d. 96/714), on whom, see Christopher Melchert, 'Ibrāhīm al-Naḫaʿī (Kufan, d. 96/714)', *Arabica* 67 (2020): 60–81.

[177] al-Kulaynī, *al-Kāfī*, 7:458.

reports advocate for the visitation of Mecca rather than Jerusalem, regardless of any vow, and suggest a hostility towards veneration of Jerusalem. This likely reflects the contest between these two cities in the early eighth century.

Another example appears in a *sīra-maghāzī* tradition about the Prophet Muḥammad. After the Muslim army's successful conquest of Mecca in 8/630, a man told the Prophet that he had vowed to go pray in Jerusalem if God would grant victory to the Muslims. With the battle won, the man was now prepared to fulfil this vow. The Prophet told him to 'pray here' in Mecca instead, for such a prayer would be sufficient for his vow, even if he did not travel all the way to Jerusalem.[178] The Prophet's answer can be read in different ways: either as a promotion of Mecca over Jerusalem, or, alternatively, as an assertion of their relative equality, with a concession offered that negates the need for travel. Notably, some (but not all) versions of the report add pro-Meccan comments to the Prophet's words, as when the Prophet says 'Here is better' than Jerusalem, and 'A prayer here is better than a thousand like it in other lands'.[179]

A related factor appears in the juristic distinction between obligatory and supererogatory ritual acts. Within Islamic law, obligatory rituals (*wājib*, pl. *wajā'ib*; or *farḍ*, pl. *farā'iḍ*) are those whose performance is required by God, while supererogatory acts (*nāfila*, pl. *nawāfil*) are non-required, additional pious acts, such as prayers beyond the obligatory five daily performances of *ṣalāt*.[180] Some early jurists categorised pilgrimage to non-Meccan sites as a

[178] 'Abd al-Razzāq, *Muṣannaf*, 5:122 (no. 9,140), 8:455–6 (nos 15,890–1); Ibn Ḥanbal, *Musnad*, 23:185–6 (no. 14,919), 38:234–5 (no. 23,169); al-Bukhārī, *Ta'rīkh*, 3/2:171 (no. 2,066); Abū Dāwūd, *Sunan*, 4:98–9 (nos 3,298–9); al-Dārimī, *Sunan*, 3:1509 (no. 2,384); Abū Ya'lā, *Musnad*, 4:88–9, 158 (nos 2,116, 2,224); Ibn al-Murajjā, *Faḍā'il*, 167 (no. 230). The most widely attested version appears to have originated with 'Aṭā' b. Abī Rabāḥ, and was transmitted from him to many via Ḥammād b. Salama (d. 167/783–4, Baṣra) > Ḥabīb b. Abī Qarība al-Mu'allim (d. 130/747–8, Baṣra). A less common version has the *isnād*: Ibn Jurayj > Yūsuf b. al-Ḥakam b. Abī Sufyān (Ḥijāz) > Ḥafṣ b. 'Umar b. 'Abd al-Raḥmān b. 'Awf (Medina) > 'Umar b. 'Abd al-Raḥmān b. 'Awf (Medina). On the latter two transmitters, see Ahmed, *Religious Elite*, 56, 217–18.

[179] al-Wāqidī, *Kitāb al-Maghāzī*, 2:866.

[180] *EI*², s.v. 'Farḍ' (Theodoor W. Juynboll); Weiss, *Spirit of Islamic Law*, 18–19; Michael Ebstein, 'The Organs of God: *Ḥadīth al-Nawāfil* in Classical Islamic Mysticism', *JAOS* 138.2 (2018): 271–89.

supererogatory ritual: commendable, but not required. In the midst of a discussion of the 'three mosques' *ḥadīth*, al-Shāfiʿī (d. 204/820), a foundational figure of Islamic law, notes that the fulfilment of a vow to go to Mecca is the accomplishment of an obligation (*farḍ*), while the fulfilment of a vow to go to Medina or Jerusalem was merely a supererogatory act (*nāfila*).[181] Neither rejecting the visitation of Medina and Jerusalem nor equating the two cities with Mecca, al-Shāfiʿī places the visitation of these different sites in different categories of necessity.

A similar discussion appears in the Mālikī legal digest *al-Mudawwana al-kubrā* of the Qayrawānī jurist Saḥnūn (d. 240/854). Saḥnūn reports that – in the case of someone who has vowed to walk to the Prophet's Mosque or to the Aqṣā Mosque – Mālik b. Anas ruled that such a person should ride, rather than travel by foot, to those locations.[182] However, this concession was not offered to someone who had vowed to walk to the Kaʿba: such a person must complete their vow and travel by foot. Much as in al-Shāfiʿī's comment on these issues, we see here a hierarchy of sacred spaces, with Mecca at the top. At the same time, the two mosques in Medina and Jerusalem were considered important places of visitation and worship, and travel to them was required if a vow had been made. Indeed, Mālik explicitly states that one who has vowed to pray in one or both of these two mosques is obligated (*wajaba ʿalayhi*) to carry out the vow.

While visitation of Medina and Jerusalem is thus encouraged by Mālik, an effort 'to control and limit the sites of pilgrimage' is likewise apparent in Saḥnūn's discussion of vows.[183] According to Mālik, vows to travel to worship in the three sacred mosques at Mecca, Medina and Jerusalem were fundamentally different from vows to worship in other locations, such as the mosques of Kūfa or Baṣra. In the latter cases, the vow could be fulfilled simply by praying 'in the spot where one is'.[184] This represents a clear priority given to the 'three

[181] Muḥammad b. Idrīs al-Shāfiʿī, *al-Umm*, ed. Rifʿat Fawzī ʿAbd al-Muṭṭalib, 11 vols (Mansoura: Dār al-Wafāʾ, 2001), 3:663; Ibn Baṭṭāl, *Sharḥ*, 3:179; Calder, 'Vocabulary of Vows', 230.

[182] Saḥnūn b. Saʿīd al-Tanūkhī, *al-Mudawwana al-kubrā*, 16 vols (Riyadh: Wizārat al-Shuʾūn al-Islāmiyya wa-l-Awqāf wa-l-Daʿwa wa-l-Irshād, n.d.), 3:86–7; Calder, 'Vocabulary of Vows', 229.

[183] Calder, 'Vocabulary of Vows', 230.

[184] Saḥnūn, *al-Mudawwana*, 3:86.

mosques' over any other destinations of pious travel. Though it is not stated explicitly, we can assume that vows to visit other locations, such as the sites of the Prophet's *āthār*, likewise need not be fulfilled literally.

Just such a discussion appears in the earliest extant commentary on al-Bukhārī's *Ṣaḥīḥ*, composed by the traditionist Ḥamd b. Muḥammad al-Khaṭṭābī (d. *c.* 388/998).[185] Discussing the 'three mosques' *ḥadīth*, al-Khaṭṭābī writes that the Prophet's words pertain to the question of 'the obligation (*al-ījāb*) when a person has vowed to perform prayer in sites where blessing is sought from among the *mashāhid*, the mosques, and the domains of [divine] proximity'.[186] According to al-Khaṭṭābī, fulfilling such a vow is not obligatory (*lā yalzam*) if one must cover a long distance (i.e. 'set out') in order to pray in one of these locations. The individual has the choice either to go and pray at the vowed spot, or instead to pray in a place nearby.

On the other hand, the three mosques mentioned in the Prophet's *ḥadīth* are all places to which travel is encouraged, if not in fact required. According to al-Khaṭṭābī, going to al-Masjid al-Ḥarām is a component of the Islamic obligation (*farḍ*) to perform the ḥajj; visiting the Prophet's Mosque is a 'collective responsibility, according to some of the *'ulama'*; and visiting Jerusalem is 'a virtue and recommended'.[187] Al-Khaṭṭābī thus distinguishes between sacred spaces to which travel is required, and those to which it is not required but encouraged. He posits a scale of necessity in visiting these locations, with the great mosques in Mecca, Medina and Jerusalem in a different, more important category than other sacred spaces. However, he does not regard the Prophet's *ḥadīth* about the three mosques as criticising or forbidding the visitation of 'sites where blessing is sought', such as the various *mashāhid* and mosques.

185 On this text and author, see Vardit Tokatly, 'The *A'lām al-ḥadīth* of al-Khaṭṭābī: A Commentary on al-Bukhārī's *Ṣaḥīḥ* or a Polemical Treatise?', *Studia Islamica* 92 (2001): 53–91.

186 Abū Sulaymān Ḥamd b. Muḥammad al-Khaṭṭābī, *A'lām al-ḥadīth fī sharḥ Ṣaḥīḥ al-Bukhārī*, ed. Muḥammad b. Sa'd b. 'Abd al-Raḥmān Āl Sa'ūd (Mecca: Jāmi'at Umm al-Qurā, 1988), 647. I thank Eyad Abuali, Simon Leese, Ali Altaf Mian and Antonio Musto for help with the phrase *mawāṭin al-qurb/qurab* found here.

187 'Collective responsibility' (here *wājiba 'alā al-kifāya*, more often *farḍ kifāya*) refers to duties that are incumbent upon the community as a whole to perform, but which are not required of all individual Muslims.

Notably, though, al-Khaṭṭābī adds that 'another interpretation' of the 'three mosques' *ḥadīth* also exists.[188] According to this second reading, the Prophet's words indicate that one must 'not set out to perform a pious retreat (*al-iʿtikāf*) except at these three mosques'. Al-Khaṭṭābī reports that 'Some of the forebears (*baʿḍ al-salaf*) held the view that pious retreat was not permissible (*lā yaṣiḥḥu*) except at [the three mosques], but not at other mosques'. Al-Khaṭṭābī spends only a few lines on this interpretation and does not appear to consider it to be as important as the more lenient position. Nonetheless, he posits an argument – ascribed to some Muslim ancestors – that such worship was 'not permissible' other than at the mosques of Mecca, Medina and Jerusalem.

A distinction between obligatory and non-obligatory places of visitation is used more explicitly when discussing visitation of the Prophet's prayer spaces and other *āthār*. In his commentary on al-Bukhārī's *Ṣaḥīḥ*, the Andalusian Mālikī scholar Ibn Baṭṭāl (d. 449/1057) cites the caliph ʿUmar's discouragement of seeking out Prophetic prayer spaces and explains it in this way: 'ʿUmar feared that the people would keep coming to pray in these places and confuse those that came after them, who might think this was obligatory (*wājib*).'[189] Rather than flatly banning the visitation of these locations, ʿUmar's concern was that later generations would confuse such righteous deeds with their being legally necessary, causing themselves undue hardship. In this same vein, the great Shāfiʿī jurist Ibn Ḥajar al-ʿAsqalānī (d. 852/1449) writes in his own commentary on the *Ṣaḥīḥ* that ʿUmar 'feared this would be confusing for one who did not know the truth of the matter and think that [praying in these locations] was obligatory'.[190]

Writing in the tenth, eleventh and fifteenth centuries respectively, al-Khaṭṭābī, Ibn Baṭṭāl and Ibn Ḥajar offer explanations reflecting different time periods and, thus, different engagements with these issues from those of Muslim scholars in the earliest centuries. Nonetheless, the issues that they bring up seem to have characterised Muslim scholars' thoughts on pious visitation in earlier centuries as well, such as distinguishing the ritually necessary from the unnecessary.

188 al-Khaṭṭābī, *Aʿlām al-ḥadīth*, 648.

189 Ibn Baṭṭāl, *Sharḥ*, 2:126.

190 Ibn Ḥajar, *Fatḥ al-bārī*, 2:231.

Indeed, the question of influencing later Muslims, cited by Ibn Baṭṭāl and Ibn Ḥajar, also appears as an explicit concern affecting some early scholars' engagements with Prophetic *āthār*. Writing in the ninth century, Ibn Waḍḍāḥ reports that 'Mālik b. Anas and other *ʿulamāʾ* of Medina disapproved of coming to (*ityān*) these prayer spaces and these *āthār* of the Prophet in Medina, other than Qubāʾ and Uḥud'.[191] Mālik b. Anas's disciple Ashhab b. ʿAbd al-ʿAzīz (d. 204/819–20) similarly reports that 'when Mālik was asked about prayer in the places where the Messenger of God had prayed, [Mālik] said, "That does not please me, except for the mosque of Qubāʾ."'[192] Mālik and other Medinan scholars thus reportedly discouraged visitation of Prophetic sites in Medina, with exceptions such as Qubāʾ and Uḥud.

But even these accepted locations were questioned, due to worries that their visitation might be interpreted as an authoritative precedent, or *sunna*, for people to follow. As Ibn Waḍḍāḥ reports:

> Mālik disapproved of going to Jerusalem, fearing that this be taken as a *sunna*. He also disapproved of going to the graves of the martyrs [in Uḥud] and going to Qubāʾ, fearing the same thing. Traditions had been transmitted from the Prophet that encouraged doing that (*bi-l-raghbati fī dhālika*), but because the *ʿulamāʾ* feared the result of [doing] it, they abandoned them.[193]

Thus, according to Ibn Waḍḍāḥ, even the existence of Prophetic reports that supported visitation of these sites could not forestall anxieties over such practices, and specifically their being seen as a *sunna*. On this subject, Mālik's student Ibn Kināna (d. *c.* 185/801–2) similarly reports regarding the *āthār* in Medina: 'The most reliably attested amongst us is Qubāʾ, but Mālik disapproved of going to it, fearing it be taken as a *sunna*.'[194]

[191] Ibn Waḍḍāḥ, *Kitāb al-Bidaʿ*, 186; al-Ṭurṭūshī, *Kitāb al-Ḥawādith*, 295 (no. 265); Fierro, 'Treatises against Innovations', 218; Fierro, 'Holy Places', 128–9.

[192] Ibn Baṭṭāl, *Sharḥ*, 2:127. On Ashhab, see *EI*[3], s.v. 'Ashhab' (Jonathan Brockopp). A similar report appears in Ibn Abī Zayd al-Qayrawānī, *Kitāb al-Jāmiʿ*, 142.

[193] Ibn Waḍḍāḥ, *Kitāb al-Bidaʿ*, 187.

[194] Ibn Waḍḍāḥ, *Kitāb al-Bidaʿ*, 187. ʿUthmān b. ʿĪsā b. Kināna was considered Mālik's 'successor after his death as the head of the Medinese school'. Umar F. Abd-Allah Wymann-Landgraf, *Mālik and Medina: Islamic Legal Reasoning in the Formative Period* (Leiden: Brill, 2013), 447.

A different attitude appears in a work of the North African Mālikī jurist Ibn Abī Zayd al-Qayrawānī (d. 386/996). In the midst of a discussion of rituals to be performed when visiting the Prophet's grave in Medina, Ibn Abī Zayd quotes the Andalusian scholar and jurist ʿAbd al-Malik b. Ḥabīb (d. 238/852–3): 'Do not skip (*lā tadaʿ*) going to the mosque of Qubāʾ and to the graves of the martyrs [in Uḥud].'[195] A frequently cited source among Mālikī jurists, Ibn Ḥabīb studied with several students of Mālik b. Anas.[196] The locations he mentions (Qubāʾ and the graves of the martyrs) correspond with traditions transmitted elsewhere about Mālik's preferences. Yet Ibn Ḥabīb presents a perspective much more inclined towards visiting these locations than the hesitancy displayed elsewhere by Mālik and his students. Indeed, the command to 'not skip going' echoes the Shīʿī traditions in which imam Jaʿfar al-Ṣādiq similarly commands his followers to visit all the Prophet's sites in Medina.

We see in these reports that Muslim scholars displayed a diversity of opinions regarding visitation of sites associated with the Prophet's life and history, as well as other sites, in the first centuries. A stray comment from the Baṣran scholar Muʾammal b. Ismāʿīl (d. 206/822) about visitation of sites in Jerusalem offers another formulation regarding these issues. In a report transmitted by the Tunisian scholar Jaʿfar b. Musāfir (d. 254/868), Muʾammal visits Jerusalem and is guided around holy sites by locals, much as we saw with the caliphal visitors to Medina. In the midst of this trip, Muʾammal's son points out that Wakīʿ b. al-Jarrāḥ had come to Jerusalem without making this course of the city's holy sites. Muʾammal responds simply: 'Each person does what he wants.'[197] Here, ritual visitation is clearly represented as a positive act, and one that Muʾammal himself participates in. But it is not incumbent on the individual in the same way as rituals such as the ḥajj are: instead, 'each person does what he wants'.

A similar viewpoint on related issues is attributed to the famed jurist Aḥmad b. Ḥanbal (d. 241/855). Ibn Ḥanbal was asked by his son ʿAbd Allāh about someone 'who touches the Prophet's *minbar*, seeking blessing from

[195] Ibn Abī Zayd al-Qayrawānī, *al-Nawādir wa-l-ziyādāt*, 2:337.

[196] *EI*[3], s.v. "Abd al-Malik b. Ḥabīb' (Miklos Muranyi); Wymann-Landgraf, *Mālik and Medina*, 18 n.44, 83.

[197] al-Wāsiṭī, *Faḍāʾil*, 76 (no. 124); Ibn al-Murajjā, *Faḍāʾil*, 243 (no. 363); Elad, *Medieval Jerusalem*, 67.

touching and kissing it, or who does something similar with the [Prophet's] tomb, wanting by that to come near to God'. Ibn Ḥanbal reportedly responded that there was 'Nothing wrong with that' (*lā ba's bi-dhālika*).[198] While not providing a ringing endorsement of touching and kissing the Prophet's tomb and *minbar*, Ibn Ḥanbal suggests there is literally 'no problem' with doing so.

Conclusion

Visiting sites associated with the Prophet Muḥammad was a point of contestation among Muslims in the first centuries. Political authorities' patronage of physical monuments at these locations – and scholars' recording of traditions about them – suggest a level of acceptance, and indeed promotion, of these sites' remembrance. Yet jurists were unsure about the activities at these places, and even suggested their visitation was 'disapproved' in several cases. In a notable tradition, the caliph 'Umar b. al-Khaṭṭāb even compares Muslim efforts to pray in these locations to the erroneous practices of Christians and Jews. Like the Prophet cursing Christians and Jews who took their prophets' burial places as mosques, 'Umar similarly condemns them for taking their prophets' *āthār* as churches and synagogues. Here, again, ideas about Christian and Jewish venerational practices are used to distinguish what Islamic ritual should not be.

At the same time, there was the caliph's son, 'Abd Allāh b. 'Umar, who was well-remembered for his assiduous efforts to 'follow the Prophet's *āthār*'. His intense interest in these matters appears to veer into the obsessive in some reports. But his ritual model was an important one for early Sunnism, and he is often praised for his careful attention to Prophetic precedent. While 'following the Prophet's *āthār*' seems to have become negatively connotated for some thinkers, this was not the case for others. While visiting the Prophet's prayer spaces did not become a required component of Islamic ritual identity, many looked upon such acts as manifestations of piety.

In fact, another prominent authority was also said to have literally followed the Prophet's footsteps, at least in the world of dreams: the *ḥadīth* master

[198] Aḥmad Ibn Ḥanbal, *Kitāb al-'Ilal wa-ma'rifat al-rijāl*, ed. Waṣī Allāh b. Muḥammad 'Abbās, 4 vols (Beirut: al-Maktab al-Islāmī, 1988), 2:492 (no. 3,243); al-Samhūdī, *Wafā' al-wafā*, 5:107; al-Dhahabī, *Mu'jam al-shuyūkh*, 1:73.

Muḥammad b. Ismāʿīl al-Bukhārī. In reports attributed to al-Bukhārī's close student, Muḥammad b. Yūsuf al-Firabrī (d. 320/932), individuals describe seeing the Prophet Muḥammad in a dream, with al-Bukhārī following right behind him.[199] In one case, al-Bukhārī's copyist Muḥammad b. Abī Ḥātim al-Warrāq narrates a dream in which he saw al-Bukhārī 'walking behind the Prophet, and whenever the Prophet lifted his foot, Abū 'Abd Allāh Muḥammad b. Ismāʿīl [al-Bukhārī] would place his foot in that place'.[200] In another version, a man named al-Najm b. al-Fuḍayl says that he 'saw the Prophet in a dream [. . .] and Muḥammad b. Ismāʿīl [al-Bukhārī] was behind him. When the Prophet took a step, Muḥammad would step and place his foot on the footprint of the Prophet and follow his track (*yattabiʿu athara-hu*).'[201]

These dream stories form part of the hagiographical material that quickly emerged around the scholarly figure of al-Bukhārī.[202] That he closely follows the Prophet's footprints may simply imply his close fidelity to the Prophet's righteous model of behaviour. Yet the particular vocabulary of 'following his track' nonetheless evokes the ways that such emulation could involve issues of sacred space, as we have seen in several other traditions. Indeed, al-Bukhārī was at least somewhat sympathetic to these kinds of practices, as he included in his *Ṣaḥīḥ* traditions about Ibn ʿUmar seeking out 'the places where the Prophet prayed', as well as several others about the commemoration of such Prophetic locations.[203] In this respect, it is noteworthy that hagiographic

[199] On al-Firabrī, the primary transmitter of al-Bukhārī's *Ṣaḥīḥ*, see al-Dhahabī, *Siyar*, 15:10–13; Melchert, 'Bukhārī and his *Ṣaḥīḥ*', 429, 445.

[200] al-Khaṭīb al-Baghdādī, *Taʾrīkh*, 2:328; Ibn ʿAsākir, *Taʾrīkh*, 52:77; Ibn Ḥajar, *Hady al-sārī*, 1309. The ascription to Muḥammad b. Abī Ḥātim al-Warrāq is an educated guess on my part, as the narrator is identified in the different texts as: Muḥammad al-Bukhārī, Muḥammad b. al-Bukhārī and Muḥammad b. Ḥātim *warrāq* al-Bukhārī. It is possible that the narrator is meant to be al-Bukhārī himself, speaking in the third person.

[201] Ibn ʿAdī, *al-Kāmil*, 1:140; al-Khaṭīb al-Baghdādī, *Taʾrīkh*, 2:328; Ibn ʿAsākir, *Taʾrīkh*, 52:77–8; al-Dhahabī, *Siyar*, 12:405; Ibn Ḥajar, *Hady al-sārī*, 1309. This al-Najm b. al-Fuḍayl seems to be otherwise unknown, and is identified only as one of the 'people of understanding' (*ahl al-fahm*).

[202] Jonathan Brown, *The Canonization of al-Bukhārī and Muslim: The Formation and Function of the Sunnī Ḥadīth Canon* (Leiden: Brill, 2007), 86.

[203] al-Bukhārī, *Ṣaḥīḥ*, 128–9 (kitāb al-ṣalāt, bāb 89), 132 (kitāb al-ṣalāt, bāb 96–7), 388 (kitāb al-ḥajj, bāb 52), 1,077 (kitāb al-maghāzī, bāb 77).

traditions also say that al-Bukhārī copy-edited his famous *Ṣaḥīḥ* collection inside the Prophet's Mosque in Medina, 'between the tomb of the Prophet and his *minbar*'.[204] Visiting these kinds of sacred spaces was not only for the uneducated masses, but – for many individuals – part of the early Islamic scholarly tradition itself.

[204] al-Khaṭīb al-Baghdādī, *Ta'rīkh*, 2:327; Ibn 'Asākir, *Ta'rīkh*, 52:71; al-Dhahabī, *Siyar*, 12:404; Ibn Ḥajar, *Hady al-sārī*, 1309; Munt, *Holy City of Medina*, 187. The tradition is attributed to Ibn 'Adī (d. 365/975–6), related from the otherwise unknown 'Abd al-Quddūs b. Hammām, but I have not been able to locate it in Ibn 'Adī's text. Al-Bukhārī is also said to have organised his *Tārīkh* beside the Prophet's tomb: al-Khaṭīb al-Baghdādī, *Ta'rīkh*, 2:325; al-Dhahabī, *Siyar*, 12:400.

EPILOGUE

This book has explored the complex significance of relics and tombs within formative Islamic ritual and thought. Rather than rejecting them completely, many Muslims not only venerated material religious objects and spaces, but used them in conceptualising ideas about the Islamic community. These items and locations, and their varied significances, included the footsteps of Abraham in the Maqām Ibrāhīm as a marker of history, prayer and pilgrimage in Mecca; the corpses of unseen prophets sacralising the landscape of the emergent Islamic empire; the Prophet Muḥammad's tomb as a destination for pilgrimage and intercession in Medina; and the places where the Prophet stopped and prayed in the Ḥijāz as sites of communal memory, emulation and visitation. Rather than innovations of later centuries, many rituals and ideas that surrounded these places and objects were practised and discussed by early generations of Muslims, in the seventh, eighth and ninth centuries. The manifold 'traces' of the prophets were memorialised, visited, prayed at and debated by Muslims from very early in Islamic history.

At the same time, the avoidance of tomb and relic cult was undeniably a distinct and prominent theme within early Islamic juristic discussions and historical texts. Many figures criticised their fellow Muslims for touching the Maqām Ibrāhīm, for worshipping at the Prophet Muḥammad's tomb, and for visiting and praying at the Prophet's *āthār*. In no small part, the avoidance of such practices was presented as a rejection of Christian and Jewish tendencies towards the veneration of holy people. Efforts to distinguish Muslims from their near-others cannot totally and comprehensively account for these condemnatory attitudes towards the veneration of tombs and relics. Nonetheless, the enactment of Muslim difference was certainly an important component in the rhetorical framing of Muslim positions on the complex bundle of social, ritual and theological issues provoked by tomb and relic veneration.

Later Muslims would continue to perform rituals with relics and tombs, as well as to contest the validity of such practices. The continuing vitality of this debate is suggested, for example, by contemporary phenomena at the site in Mecca believed to be the place of the Prophet Muḥammad's birth, briefly discussed above.[1] At this location – which was converted into the Makka al-Mukarrama Library in the mid-twentieth century – multilingual signage warns visitors against performing worship practices there, and even against 'visiting this library as an act of worship' at all.[2] It is stated, for example, that 'pursuing blessing through this place, or specifying this place for prayer or supplication, is not permissible'. The reasoning offered for such prohibitions varies on the different signs: one asserts that there is simply no proof that the location was the actual birthplace of the Prophet; another specifies that practices like performing *duʿāʾ* near the library or touching its walls (for blessing, we can assume) are 'innovations and offences' (*min al-bidaʿ wa-l-mukhālafāt*). The question of what to do with and at spaces like this one, hallowed in Muslim memory, has not lost its pertinence.[3]

* * *

[1] On this site in the early twentieth century, see Beránek and Ťupek, *Temptation of Graves*, 113, 125; Saud al-Sarhan, 'The Saudis as Managers of the Hajj', in Tagliacozzo and Toorawa, *Hajj*, 205–6.

[2] Beránek and Ťupek, *Temptation of Graves*, 134. For photos, see Richard Mortel, photographer, 'Admonitions at the site of the birthplace of the Prophet Muhammad, Mecca, Saudi Arabia', 4 December 2020, https://commons.wikimedia.org/wiki/File:Admonitions_at_the_site_of_the_birthplace_of_the_Prophet_Muhammad,_Mecca,_Saudi_Arabia.jpg (last accessed 7 June 2023); Saudi Press Agency, '200,000 Educational Publications for Pilgrims at Guidance Center for the Committee for the Promotion of Virtue' (200 Alf maṭbūʿa tawʿawiyya li-l-ḥujjāj fī-l-markaz al-tawjīhī al-tābiʿ li-hayʾat al-amr bi-l-maʿrūf), 2 November 2011, https://sp.spa.gov.sa/viewfullstory.php?lang=ar&newsid=940284 (last accessed 7 June 2023).

[3] On the continuing contestation over this site, see Rosie Bsheer, *Archive Wars: The Politics of History in Saudi Arabia* (Stanford: Stanford University Press, 2020), 201–4.

While this book has covered many different instances and types of *āthār* – and could discuss many more – one particularly iconic trace has been left unmentioned so far: the Prophet Muḥammad's sandals (sing., *naʿl*; dual, *naʿlayn*). I close this book with a discussion of these items, as an indication of the connection between early Islamic phenomena and the events and habits of later centuries, as well as a sign of where scholarship might proceed in studying issues of material religion in both early and later Islam.

Beginning around the twelfth or thirteenth century, the Prophet's sandals began to receive extensive veneration in different forms, eventually becoming 'among the most popular relics in Islam'.[4] The most well-attested cult around the Prophet's sandals emerged in Damascus, where the Ayyubid emir al-Ashraf Mūsā (r. 626–35/1229–37) installed a sandal of the Prophet at his newly endowed Dār al-Ḥadīth al-Ashrafiyya, a school for instruction in the Prophet's *ḥadīth*.[5] Students and scholars, as well as pilgrims more generally, came to see and even rub and kiss the sandal at its bi-weekly times of public display. The sandal did not always stay in its case, but was occasionally brought out for veneration. In 711/1312, for example, it was carried in a procession of merchants and religious scholars protesting the tax policies of the Mamluk government.

In addition to direct encounters with the Prophet's sandal, an important form of contact relic emerged in these centuries: drawings of the sandal's outline. These tracings were treated as extensions of the sandal, and considered capable of healing illnesses and repelling the evil eye.[6] The images circulated widely throughout the Islamic world, and many authors composed texts in celebration of the Prophet's sandal.[7] The sandal's image was incorporated

[4] Hiba Abid, 'Material Images and Mental *Ziyāra*: Depicting the Prophet's Grave in North African Devotional Books (*Dalāʾil al-Khayrāt*)', *Journal of Material Cultures in the Muslim World* 1 (2020): 344.

[5] Goldziher, *Muslim Studies*, 2:327–8; Meri, *Cult of Saints*, 109–11, 116; Meri, 'Relics of Piety', 107–11; Talmon-Heller, *Islamic Piety*, 203–5; Dickinson, 'Ibn al-Ṣalāḥ', 481–4; McGregor, *Islam and the Devotional Object*, 101, 131–2, 163–4; Wheeler, *Mecca and Eden*, 79–80.

[6] Richard McGregor, 'Repetition and Relics: Tracing the Lives of Muhammad's Sandals', in Bigelow, *Islam Through Objects*, 49–64; Meri, 'Relics of Piety', 108–9; Flood, 'Bodies and Becoming', 470–1.

[7] Meri, 'Relics of Piety', 108; Annemarie Schimmel, *And Muhammad is His Messenger: The Veneration of the Prophet in Islamic Piety* (Chapel Hill: University of North Carolina Press, 1985), 40–2.

into devotional texts, such as the *Dalā'il al-Khayrāt*, a popular compilation of prayers for the Prophet composed by the Moroccan Sufi Muḥammad b. Sulaymān al-Jazūlī (d. 869/1465).[8] In pilgrimage scrolls, the sandal appeared alongside other iconic objects and spaces, such as the Prophet's tomb and *minbar*.[9] In several cases, these sandal images 'show clear signs of wear from kissing or touching', physically illustrating their tactile usage by Muslim worshippers.[10] More durable versions were painted on Ottoman-period tiles, which were frequently installed on the *qibla* wall of mosques.[11] Today, the sandal can be found on a variety of media, ranging from prayer beads and skull caps to key chains, backpacks and gift bags.[12]

These extensive institutional and iconographic developments in devotion shown to the Prophet's sandals are, admittedly, dateable to much later than the period covered in this book. One might argue that devotion to these objects was a novel feature of these subsequent centuries, as is sometimes suggested within discussions of relics in Islam more generally. Indeed, the focus on the Prophet's sandals, and especially images of them, can plausibly be read within the context of 'the intensification of Prophet-centred patterns of piety in different cultural fields since the fourteenth century, which can be observed in virtually all regions of the Muslim world'.[13]

[8] Abid, 'Material Images', 344; Jan Just Witkam, 'Mecca and Medina Revisited: The Manuscripts of the *Dalā'il al-Khayrāt* by al-Ǧazūlī and Their Ornamental Addition', *Journal of Islamic Manuscripts* 12 (2021): 396–432.

[9] Flood, 'Bodies and Becoming', 470–1; Mounia Chekhab-Abudaya, Amélie Couvrat Desvergnes and David J. Roxburgh, 'Sayyid Yusuf's 1433 Pilgrimage Scroll (*Ziyārātnāma*) in the Collection of the Museum of Islamic Art, Doha', *Muqarnas* 33 (2016): 345–407; Rachel Milstein, 'Futuh-i Haramayn: Sixteenth-Century Illustrations of the Hajj Route', in *Mamluks and Ottomans: Studies in Honour of Michael Winter*, ed. David J. Wasserstein and Ami Ayalon (London: Routledge, 2006), 169.

[10] Flood, 'Bodies and Becoming', 471; Meri, 'Relics of Piety', 100 n.52.

[11] Charlotte Maury, 'Depictions of the Haramayn on Ottoman Tiles: Content and Context', in *The Hajj: Collected Essays*, ed. Venetia Porter and Liana Saif (London: British Museum, 2013), 143–59.

[12] See, for example: 'The Blessed Sandals', Nalayn, https://nalayn.com/ (last accessed 7 June 2023).

[13] Rachida Chih, David Jordan and Stefan Reichmuth, 'The Presence of the Prophet: General Introduction', in *The Presence of the Prophet in Early Modern and Contemporary Islam. Volume 1. The Prophet Between Doctrine, Literature and Arts: Historical Legacies and Their Unfolding*, ed. Denis Gril, Stefan Reichmuth and Dilek Sarmis (Leiden: Brill, 2022), 7.

At the same time, however, mentions of the Prophet's sandals thread throughout earlier sources, hinting towards these medieval and modern developments. The sandals were treasured objects, kept by descendants of the Prophet's Companions.[14] In some cases, the sandals seemingly endowed their owners with authority. For example, the Prophet's descendants, the Shīʿī imams Muḥammad al-Bāqir[15] and Jaʿfar al-Ṣādiq,[16] are each said to display a sandal (or two) of the Prophet's for visitors. Imam Jaʿfar's report appears in Twelver Shīʿī literature alongside mentions of the imams' inheritance of several other Prophetic objects, including his swords, the possession of which was used 'as the core argument for the right of this specific Ḥusaynī house to rule'.[17] In Sunnī texts, the Prophet's Companion and servant Anas b. Mālik is described bringing out a pair of sandals to show a visitor, causing the Baṣran scholar Thābit al-Bunānī to remark, 'These are the Prophet's sandals.'[18] Anas is identified as the 'keeper of the Prophet's sandal' (*ṣāḥib naʿl Rasūl Allāh*),

[14] Fāṭima bt. ʿUbayd Allāh, daughter of the Companion ʿUbayd Allāh b. al-ʿAbbās b. ʿAbd al-Muṭṭalib, was said to own one of the Prophet's sandals: Ibn Saʿd, *Ṭabaqāt*, 1:411–12; Abū Dāwūd, *al-Marāsīl*, 313 (no. 442). The family of the Companion Shaddād b. Aws was said to possess a pair of his sandals: al-Dhahabī, *Siyar*, 2:463; Ibn ʿAsākir, *Taʾrīkh*, 22:409–10.

[15] Ibn Saʿd, *Ṭabaqāt*, 1:411. The *isnād* is: ʿUbayd Allāh b. Mūsā (d. *c*. 213/828–9, Kūfa) > Isrāʾīl [b. Yūnus b. Abī Isḥāq] (d. *c*. 160/777–8, Kūfa) > Jābir [b. Yazīd al-Juʿfī] (d. *c*. 127/744–5, Kūfa) > Muḥammad b. ʿAlī [al-Bāqir].

[16] al-Ṣaffār, *Baṣāʾir al-darajāt*, 1:364. The *isnād* is: Aḥmad b. Muḥammad [b. ʿĪsā? (third/ninth century, Qum)] > ʿAlī b. al-Ḥakam [b. al-Zubayr?] > Ismāʿīl b. [Ibrāhīm b.] Burra (Companion of Jaʿfar al-Ṣādiq, Kūfa) > ʿĀmir b. [ʿAbd Allāh b.] Judhāʿa (Companion of Jaʿfar al-Ṣādiq, Kūfa). On Ismāʿīl b. Burra, see al-Najāshī, *Rijāl*, 30 (no. 61); al-Ṭūsī, *Rijāl*, 160 (no. 1,792). On ʿĀmir b. Judhāʿa, see al-Najāshī, *Rijāl*, 293–4 (no. 794); al-Ṭūsī, *Rijāl*, 255 (no. 3,606), 635 (no. 6,227); Muḥammad b. al-Ḥasan al-Ṭūsī, *Ikhtiyār maʿrifat al-rijāl al-maʿrūf bi-Rijāl al-Kashshī*, ed. Jawād al-Qayyūmī al-Iṣfahānī (Qom: Muʾassasat al-Nashr al-Islāmī, 1427 AH [2006–7]), 22 (no. 20).

[17] Elad, *Rebellion of Muḥammad*, 435–40.

[18] al-Bukhārī, *Ṣaḥīḥ*, 766 (kitāb farḍ al-khums, bāb 5), 1479 (kitāb al-libās, bāb 41); Ibn Saʿd, *Ṭabaqāt*, 1:411. The *isnād*s are respectively: (1) ʿAbd Allāh b. Muḥammad [al-Juʿfī al-Musnadī] (d. 229/844, Bukhārā) > Muḥammad b. ʿAbd Allāh [b. al-Zubayr b. Darham] al-Asadī (d. 203/818–19, Kūfa) > ʿĪsā b. Ṭahmān (d. before 160/776–7, Baṣra/Kūfa); (2) Muḥammad [b. Muqātil] (d. 226, Merv/Baghdad) > ʿAbd Allāh [b. al-Mubārak] > ʿĪsā b. Ṭahmān; and (3) al-Faḍl b. Dukayn (d. 219/834, Kūfa) > ʿĪsā b. Ṭahmān.

suggesting that his position was worth noting.[19] Owning the Prophet's sandals thus seems to have been a marker of status in different communities in the early period, as it would be also in later centuries.

Indeed, reports suggest that the sandal's keepers might deploy them as emblems of the Prophet Muḥammad. In reports transmitted by eighth- and ninth-century Muslim scholars, the Prophet's wife ʿĀʾisha brandishes the Prophet's sandal to chastise and shame her political opponents.[20] Lifting the sandal, she yells: 'You have abandoned the *sunna* of the Messenger of God, the owner of this sandal!'[21] In another situation, she brings out several relics and says: 'How quickly you have abandoned the *sunna* of your Prophet, when this hair, shirt, and sandal of his have not yet decayed!'[22] Like the fourteenth-century Damascenes wielding the Prophet's sandal against the Mamluk government, these reports indicate that earlier Muslims might have drawn upon the sandal's talismanic authority to criticise political rulers and advocate for justice.

Another political usage of the Prophet's sandals is recorded in a surprising place: the *Chronicle* of Theophanes the Confessor. In his entry for the year 6246 Annus Mundi (753–4 CE), Theophanes reports how the ʿAbbāsid al-Manṣūr 'achieved the kingship' (i.e. the caliphate), following the death of his brother al-Ṣaffāḥ.[23] As part of his consolidation of power, al-Manṣūr

[19] Ibn Saʿd, *Ṭabaqāt*, 1:414. The *isnād* is: al-Faḍl b. Dukayn (d. 219/834, Kūfa) > Yūnus b. Abī Isḥāq (d. 159/775–6, Kūfa) > al-Minhāl b. ʿAmr (d. *c.* 110/728–9, Kūfa). He was also said to possess the Prophet's waterskin.

[20] On these reports and their background, see Wilferd Madelung, *The Succession to Muhammad: A Study of the Early Caliphate* (New York: Cambridge University Press, 1997), 96–7, 100–1.

[21] Abū al-Faraj ʿAlī b. al-Ḥusayn al-Iṣfahānī, *Kitāb al-Aghānī*, ed. Iḥsān ʿAbbās, Ibrāhīm al-Saʿāfīn and Bakr ʿAbbās, 25 vols (Beirut: Dār al-Ṣādir, 2002), 5:87. The *isnād* is: Aḥmad [b. Yaḥyā al-Balādhurī] > ʿUmar [b. Shabba] (d. *c.* 262/875–6) > al-Madāʾinī (d. *c.* 228/842–3) > al-Waqqāṣī [ʿUthmān b. ʿAbd al-Raḥmān b. ʿUmar] (d. before 193/809) > [Ibn Shihāb] al-Zuhrī.

[22] al-Balādhurī, *Ansāb al-ashrāf*, 6:161–2, 208–9. The *isnād*s are: (1) ʿAbbās b. Hishām b. Muḥammad [al-Kalbī] > Abū Mikhnaf (d. *c.* 157/773–4, Kūfa); and (2) Aḥmad b. Ibrāhīm al-Dawraqī (d. 246/860, Baghdad) > Wahb b. Jarīr (d. 206/822, Baṣra) > Jarīr b. Ḥāzim (d. 175/791, Baṣra) > Yūnus b. Yazīd al-Aylī (d. *c.* 159/775–6) > [Ibn Shihāb] al-Zuhrī.

[23] *Theophanis Chronographia*, 1:428–9; *Chronicle of Theophanes*, 592–3 (adapted here). On the basis of parallels with other Christian historical texts, this section of Theophanes' *Chronicle* is thought to come from the end of the Syriac Common Source, a lost text now commonly

assassinated the Muslim general (and governor of the province of Khurāsān) Abū Muslim.[24] In order to carry out this plot, al-Manṣūr called upon Abū Muslim to visit him, using 'persuasive arguments and supplications, and even the abominable symbols of their kingship – I mean the staff and sandals of the false prophet Mouamed'. According to this text, the Prophet Muḥammad's relics were used as 'symbols of kingship' by Muslim rulers, and were mobilised by al-Manṣūr specifically as icons of persuasive authority. While clearly set within a polemical frame, Theophanes' narrative suggests that the Prophet's sandals, alongside his staff, offered a powerful political representation of the Prophet by perhaps as early as the mid-eighth century.[25]

Beyond these scattered mentions, the social significance of the Prophet's sandals, and what was actually done with them in the first centuries, is unclear. Al-Bukhārī placed the report about Anas b. Mālik displaying the sandals in his *Ṣaḥīḥ*'s section on clothing. Like the strands of the Prophet's dyed hair kept by the Muslim community, his sandals provided physical documentation of the Prophet's *sunna*: in this case, what kind of footwear he used. A focus on ascertaining what style of shoes the Prophet had worn also characterises several of the reports found in the section on the Prophet's sandals in Ibn Saʿd's *Ṭabaqāt*. These texts thus suggest an emphasis on the 'textualisation' of the Prophet's physical remains, with his behavioural model as a key implication of reports about his sandals.

attributed to Theophilus of Edessa, a Christian astrologer at the court of the caliph al-Mahdī. However, Theophanes' version includes additional details (including mention of the Prophet's relics) not recorded elsewhere, suggesting that he here draws upon the Greek continuation of Theophilus' text, thought to be written by a Syrian Christian working in the late eighth century. On the Syriac Common Source and Theophilus of Edessa, see Hoyland, *Seeing Islam*, 400–9; Lawrence I. Conrad, 'The Conquest of Arwād: A Source-Critical Study in the Historiography of the Early Medieval Near East', in Cameron and Conrad, *Byzantine and Early Islamic Near East*, 331–2. On the Greek continuation as a source used by Theophanes, see Hoyland, *Seeing Islam*, 405–6, 431–2; Conrad, 'Conquest of Arwād', 336–8.

[24] *EI*^{2}, s.v. 'Abū Muslim' (S. Moscati).

[25] The Prophet's staff appears as a symbol of caliphal authority already in the Umayyad-era panegyrics of al-Farazdaq (d. *c*. 110/728–9). See Nadia Jamil, 'Caliph and Quṭb: Poetry as a Sources for Interpreting the Transformation of the Byzantine Cross on Steps on Umayyad Coinage', in Johns, *Bayt al-Maqdis*, 11–57.

Notably, however, al-Bukhārī also placed the report about Anas b. Mālik in another part of his text. The heading for this particular chapter reads, in part: 'his hair, his sandal, and his drinking vessels, through which his Companions and others sought blessing (*tabarraka*) after his death'.[26] While the meanings and implications of al-Bukhārī's chapter headings (*tarājim*) have long been disputed, they have frequently been said to offer glimpses of al-Bukhārī's guiding authorial-editorial voice.[27] In this case, the chapter heading suggests that these Prophetic objects were not understood simply as pieces of evidence for reconstructing the Prophet's sartorial choices or drinking habits. Rather, his hair, sandals and other relics were considered to be items that the Companions and others had used to 'seek blessing' after the Prophet's death. In this important *ḥadīth* compilation of the ninth century, we find a sign that veneration of the Prophet's sandal (and other items) was occurring, and was even believed to have been practised by the Prophet's Companions. Rather than just textualised pieces of data, the sandals were also real, material objects that could be used to acquire blessing.

Yet al-Bukhārī's text provides a slight complication to such assertions. The chapter heading stating that the Companions and others 'sought blessings' from the Prophet's relics is found only in certain versions of al-Bukhārī's *Ṣaḥīḥ*. In other transmissions of the book, a variant text appears in the chapter heading, which instead states that the Companions and others 'shared' (*sharika*) the Prophet's hair, sandal and drinking vessels.[28] Only a one-word difference, this slight textual discrepancy perhaps reflects tension among early scholarly circles regarding the Prophet Muḥammad's relics. Saying that the Prophet's

[26] al-Bukhārī, *Ṣaḥīḥ*, 765 (kitāb farḍ al-khums, bāb 5). For commentary on this heading, see Ibn Baṭṭāl, *Sharḥ*, 5:265–6; Ibn Ḥajar, *Fatḥ al-bārī*, 7:369.

[27] On al-Bukhārī's chapter headings, see Goldziher, *Muslim Studies*, 2:216–18; Joel Blecher, *Said the Prophet of God: Hadith Commentary across the Millennium* (Oakland: University of California Press, 2018), 5, 111–15; Brown, *Canonization*, 72–3, 385–6; Stephen R. Burge, 'Reading between the Lines: The Compilation of *Ḥadīṯ* and the Authorial Voice', *Arabica* 58 (2011): 168–97.

[28] al-Bukhārī, *Ṣaḥīḥ al-Imām al-Bukhārī al-musammā bi-l-Jāmiʿ al-musnad al-ṣaḥīḥ al-mukhtaṣar min umūr Rasūl Allāh wa-sunani-hi wa-ayyāmi-hi*, ed. Muḥammad Zuhayr b. Nāṣir al- Nāṣir, 9 vols (Beirut: Dār al-Ṭawq al-Najā, 2001), 4:82 n.8. These differences in the text are discussed in Ibn Ḥajar, *Fatḥ al-bārī*, 7:369.

material traces were merely 'shared' among the members of the Muslim community – rather than used as sources of blessing – arguably diminishes the power and significance of these objects. While neither reading can be proven to be earlier or more original than the other, the existence of the two variants suggests questions over the status of objects like the Prophet's sandals in the ritual lives of Muslims.

Such questions also animate a story about the 'Abbāsid caliph al-Mahdī, whom we earlier encountered drinking water from the Maqām Ibrāhīm. In a report related from al-Mahdī's servant Ḥasan, while the caliph was sitting with a group of people, a man approached him holding a sandal wrapped in a handkerchief. The man said, 'Oh Commander of the Believers, this is the Messenger of God's sandal, which I give to you!' The caliph ordered the man to bring the sandal to him, and al-Mahdī kissed it and pressed it to his eyes. He commanded that the unnamed man be rewarded with 10,000 dirhams, which the man accepted; he then left. Turning to his companions, al-Mahdī said: 'Do you think I don't know that the Messenger of God never looked at this sandal, much less wore it?' The caliph explains that, had he rejected the gift as a fake, the man likely would have said harmful things about him among the caliph's subjects. By taking the sandal, he instead 'bought his tongue, accepted his gift, and trusted his words'.[29]

Commentators have often emphasised al-Mahdī's political skill in this story.[30] The caliph accepts the sandal for the public goodwill it will afford him, despite private reservations about the authenticity of the purported Prophetic relic. We seem to have here an example in miniature of the oft-prevailing

[29] al-Khaṭīb al-Baghdādī, *Ta'rīkh*, 3:386–7. The *isnād* is: Muḥammad b. 'Abd al-Wāḥid b. Muḥammad al-Akbar [Abū al-Faraj al-Dārimī] (d. 448/1057, Baghdad) > Muḥammad b. al-'Abbās [Abū 'Umar Ibn Ḥayyawayh] (d. 382/992, Baghdad) > Muḥammad b. Khalaf b. al-Marzubān (d. 309/921–2, Baghdad) > Muḥammad b. al-Faḍl [Abū Bakr al-Nasā'ī (d. 265/878–9, Baghdad)?] > one of the *ahl al-adab* > Ḥasan al-Waṣīf. On (al-)Ḥasan al-Waṣīf, see *The History of al-Ṭabarī. Volume XXIX: Al-Manṣūr and al-Mahdī*, trans. Hugh Kennedy (Albany: State University of New York Press, 1990), 170, 211–12, 250.

[30] El-Hibri, 'Abbasids and the Relics', 89 n.79; McGregor, 'Repetition and Relics', 53; Dickinson, 'Ibn al-Ṣalāḥ', 482. This is not exclusively a modern interpretation, as Ibn al-Jawzī includes the report in his *Akhbār al-adhkiyā'* (Stories of Cunning People). Ibn al-Jawzī, *Akhbār al-adhkiyā'*, ed. Bassām 'Abd al-Wahhāb al-Jābī (Beirut: Dār Ibn Ḥazm, 2003), 71.

wisdom about relics, both in Islam and in other traditions: that relics were the concern of 'common people', but not of savvier elites, such as scholars and rulers. Yet we should be careful how far we let one story carry such a weighty conclusion. As we saw with his veneration of the Maqām Ibrāhīm, al-Mahdī elsewhere appears quite solicitous of *āthār*; indeed, he is recorded in another story seeking to possess sandals of the Prophet's that had been kept in a Companion's family.[31] Perhaps al-Mahdī was not distrustful of *all* relics per se but, rather, was sceptical of one brought to him by a stranger.

Indeed, whatever al-Mahdī believed about the sandal in his hand, he nonetheless kissed it and rubbed it against his eyes. However sincere the caliph's actions were or were not, this devotional ritual was accessible and legible to al-Mahdī and his audience, as it was one practised by many communities in late antiquity, including Muslims.[32] Rather than the exclusive terrain of Jews and Christians, such actions were meaningful also to Muslim devotees, who kissed and clasped objects like the Prophet Muḥammad's hair, *minbar* and sandals, and the stone containing Abraham's footprints, as well as other sanctified objects and places. As within other religious traditions, such objects, places and practices were the subject of intense debates among Muslims. Yet they would continually influence the material and intellectual lives of Muslims, in a variety of ways, from the beginning of the tradition onwards.

[31] al-Dhahabī, *Siyar*, 2:463; Ibn 'Asākir, *Ta'rīkh*, 22:409–10.

[32] On Christians kissing and touching their eyes to saints' relics, see Roland Betancourt, *Sight, Touch, and Imagination in Byzantium* (Cambridge: Cambridge University Press, 2018), 69–71, 256–63.

BIBLIOGRAPHY

Primary Sources

ʿAbd Allāh b. Aḥmad b. Ḥanbal. *Masāʾil al-Imām Aḥmad ibn Ḥanbāl*. Edited by Zuhayr al-Shāwīsh. Beirut: al-Maktab al-Islāmī, 1981.

ʿAbd al-Malik b. Ḥabīb al-Andalusī. *Kitāb al-Taʾrīj (La Historia)*. Edited by Jorge Aguadé. Madrid: Consejo Superior de Investigaciones Científicas, 1991.

ʿAbd al-Malik b. Ḥabīb al-Andalusī. *al-Wāḍiḥa: kutub al-ṣalāt wa-kutub al-ḥajj*. Edited by Miklos Muranyi. Beirut: Dār al-Bashāʾir al-Islāmiyya, 2010.

ʿAbd al-Razzāq b. Hammām al-Ṣanʿānī. *al-Muṣannaf*. Edited by Ḥabīb al-Raḥmān al-Aʿẓamī. 11 vols. Beirut: al-Maktab al-Islāmī, 1983.

ʿAbd al-Razzāq b. Hammām al-Ṣanʿānī. *Tafsīr ʿAbd al-Razzāq*. Edited by Maḥmūd Muḥammad ʿAbduh. 3 vols. Beirut: Dār al-Kutub al-ʿIlmiyya, 1999.

al-Ābī, Abū Saʿd Manṣūr b. al-Ḥusayn. *Nathr al-durr*. Edited by Khālid ʿAbd al-Ghanī Maḥfūẓ. 7 vols. Beirut: Dār al-Kutub al-ʿIlmiyya, 2004.

Abū al-ʿArab Muḥammad b. Aḥmad b. Tamīm. *Ṭabaqāt ʿulamāʾ Ifrīqiyya*. Edited by Mohammed Ben Cheneb. Beirut: Dār al-Kitāb al-Lubnānī, n.d.

Abū ʿAwāna Yaʿqūb b. Isḥāq. *Musnad Abī ʿAwāna*. Edited by Ayman b. ʿĀrif al-Dimashqī. 5 vols. Beirut: Dār al-Maʿrifa, 1998.

Abū Dāwūd Sulaymān b. al-Ashʿath al-Sijistānī. *al-Marāsīl*. Edited by Shuʿayb al-Arnāʾūṭ. Beirut: Muʾassasat al-Risāla, 1988.

Abū Dāwūd Sulaymān b. al-Ashʿath al-Sijistānī. *Kitāb al-Sunan*. Edited by Muḥammad ʿAwwāma. 5 vols. Jedda: Dār al-Qibla li-l-Thaqāfa al-Islāmiyya, 1998.

Abū al-Faraj al-Iṣfahānī, ʿAlī b. al-Ḥusayn. *Kitāb al-Aghānī*. Edited by Iḥsān ʿAbbās, Ibrāhīm al-Saʿāfīn and Bakr ʿAbbās. 25 vols. Beirut: Dār al-Ṣādir, 2002.

Abū Nuʿaym al-Iṣbahānī. *Ḥilyat al-awliya' wa ṭabaqāt al-aṣfiyā'*. 10 vols. Cairo: Maṭbaʿat al-Saʿāda, 1974.

Abū Nuʿaym al-Iṣbahānī. *Kitāb Dalā'il al-nubuwwa*. Hyderabad: Dā'irat al-Maʿārif al-ʿUthmāniyya, 1977.

Abū al-Shaykh al-Aṣbahānī. *Kitāb al-ʿAẓama*. Edited by Riḍā' Allāh b. Muḥammad Idrīs al-Mubārakfūrī. Riyadh: Dār al-ʿĀṣima, 1408 AH [1987–8].

Abū ʿUbayd al-Qāsim b. Sallām. *Kitāb al-Amwāl*. Edited by Muḥammad ʿImāra. Beirut: Dār al-Shurūq, 1989.

Abū Yaʿlā Aḥmad b. ʿAlī al-Muthannā al-Taymī. *Musnad Abī Yaʿlā al-Mawṣilī*. Edited by Ḥusayn Salīm Asad al-Dārānī. 16 vols. Beirut: Dār al-Ma'mūn li-l-Turāth, 1984–90.

Abū Yūsuf Yaʿqūb b. Ibrāhīm. *Kitāb al-Āthār*. Edited by Abū al-Wafā' al-Afghānī. Beirut: Dār al-Kutub al-ʿIlmiyya, 1978.

Acts of Anastasios the Persian = Flusin, Bernard. *Saint Anastase le Perse et l'histoire de la Palestine au début du VIIe siècle*. 2 vols. Paris: Centre National de la Recherche Scientifique, 1992.

Agapius of Manbij. *Kitāb al-ʿUnwān* [*Agapius Episcopus Mabbugensis Historia universalis*]. Edited by Louis Cheikho. CSCO 65, Scriptores Arabici 5. Beirut: Typographeo Catholico, 1912.

Aḥmad b. ʿĪsa b. Zayd. *Kitāb Ra'b al-ṣadʿ: Amālī al-Imām Aḥmad b. ʿĪsā b. Zayd b. ʿAlī b. al-Ḥusayn b. ʿAlī b. Abī Ṭālib*. Edited by ʿAlī b. Ismāʿīl b. ʿAbd Allāh al-Muʿayyad al-Ṣanʿānī. 3 vols. Beirut: Dār al-Nafā'is, 1990.

al-Ājurrī, Abū Bakr Muḥammad b. al-Ḥasan. *Kitāb al-Sharīʿa*. Edited by ʿAbd Allāh b. ʿUmar b. Sulaymān al-Dumayjī. 6 vols. Riyadh: Dār al-Waṭan, 1997.

ʿAlī b. Ibrāhīm al-Qummī. *Tafsīr al-Qummī*. Edited by Sayyid Muḥammad Bāqir al-Muwaḥḥid al-Abṭaḥī et al. 3 vols. Qum: Mu'assasat al-Imām al-Mahdī, 2014.

Assemani, S. E. *Acta Sanctorum Martyrum Orientalium et occidentalium*. 2 vols. Rome: Collini, 1748.

al-ʿAyyāshī, Abū al-Naṣr Muḥammad b. Masʿūd. *Tafsīr al-ʿAyyāshī*. Edited by Hāshim al-Rasūlī al-Maḥallātī. 2 vols. Beirut: Mu'assasat al-Aʿlamī, 1991.

al-Azraqī, Abū al-Walīd Muḥammad b. ʿAbd Allāh b. Aḥmad. *Akhbār Makka wa-mā jā'fīhā min al-āthār*. Edited by ʿAbd al-Malik b. ʿAbd Allāh b. Duhaysh. Mecca: Maktabat al-Asadī, 2003.

al-Balādhurī, Aḥmad b. Yaḥyā. *Ansāb al-ashrāf*, volume 1. Edited by Muḥammad Ḥamīdullāh. Cairo: Dār al-Maʿārif, 1959.

al-Balādhurī, Aḥmad b. Yaḥyā. *Ansāb al-ashrāf*, volume 4/1. Edited by Iḥsān ʿAbbās. Wiesbaden: Franz Steiner, 1979.

al-Balādhurī, Aḥmad b. Yaḥyā. *Ansāb al-ashrāf*. Edited by Suhayl Zakkār and Riyāḍ Ziriklī. 13 vols. Beirut: Dār al-Fikr, 1996.

al-Balādhurī, Aḥmad b. Yaḥyā. *Futūḥ al-buldān*. Edited by ʿAbd Allāh Anīs al-Ṭabbāʿ and ʿUmar Anīs al-Ṭabbāʿ. Beirut: Muʾassasat al-Maʿārif, 1987.

al-Barqī, Aḥmad b. Muḥammad. *Kitāb al-Maḥāsin*. Edited by Sayyid Jalāl al-Dīn al-Ḥusaynī. Qum: Dār al-Kutub al-Islāmiyya, n.d.

al-Bayhaqī, Abū Bakr Aḥmad b. al-Ḥusayn. *Dalāʾil al-nubuwwa wa-maʿrifat aḥwāl ṣāḥib al-sharīʿa*. Edited by ʿAbd al-Muʿṭī Qalʿajī, 7 vols. Beirut: Dār al-Kutub al-ʿIlmiyya, 1985.

al-Bayhaqī, Abū Bakr Aḥmad b. al-Ḥusayn. *Ḥayāt al-anbiyāʾ baʿda wafāti-him*. Edited by Aḥmad b. ʿAṭiyya al-Ghāʾirī. Medina: Maktabat al-ʿUlūm wa-l-Ḥikm, 1993.

al-Bayhaqī, Abū Bakr Aḥmad b. al-Ḥusayn. *al-Jāmiʿ li-shuʿab al-īmān*. Edited by Mukhtār Aḥmad al-Narwī. 14 vols. Beirut: Maktabat al-Rushd, 2003.

al-Bayhaqī, Abū Bakr Aḥmad b. al-Ḥusayn. *al-Sunan al-kubrā*. Edited by Muḥammad ʿAbd al-Qādir ʿAṭā. 11 vols. Beirut: Dār al-Kutub al-ʿIlmiyya, 2003.

al-Bazzār, Abū Bakr Aḥmad b. ʿAmr b. ʿAbd al-Khāliq al-ʿAtakī. *al-Baḥr al-zakhkhār al-maʿrūf bi-Musnad al-Bazzār*. Edited by Maḥfūẓ al-Raḥmān Zayn Allāh et al. 20 vols. Medina: Maktabat al-ʿUlūm wa-l-Ḥikam, 1988–2009.

Bedjan, Paul (ed.). *Acta Martyrum et Sanctorum*. 7 vols. Paris: Otto Harrassowitz, 1890–7.

al-Bukhārī, Muḥammad b. Ismāʿīl. *Ṣaḥīḥ al-Bukhārī*. Damascus: Dār Ibn Kathīr, 2002.

al-Bukhārī, Muḥammad b. Ismāʿīl. *Ṣaḥīḥ al-Imām al-Bukhārī al-musammā bi-l-Jāmiʿ al-musnad al-ṣaḥīḥ al-mukhtaṣar min umūr Rasūl Allāh wa-sunani-hi wa-ayyāmi-hi*. Edited by Muḥammad Zuhayr b. Nāṣir al- Nāṣir. 9 vols. Beirut: Dār al-Ṭawq al-Najā, 2001.

al-Bukhārī, Muḥammad b. Ismāʿīl. *Kitāb al-Taʾrīkh al-kabīr*. 4 vols. in 8. Hyderabad: Dāʾirat al-Maʿārif al-ʿUthmāniyya, 1941–64.

Cave of Treasures = La Caverne des Trésors: les deux recensions syriaques. Edited by Su-Min Ri. CSCO 486, Scriptores Syri 207. Louvain: Peeters, 1987.

al-Damīrī, Muḥammad b. Mūsā. *Ḥayāt al-ḥayawān al-kubrā*. 2 vols. Cairo: Sharikat Maktabat wa-Maṭbaʿa Muṣṭafā al-Bābī al-Ḥalabī wa-Awlāduhu, 1978.

al-Dāraquṭnī, ʿAlī b. ʿUmar. *al-ʿIlal*. Edited by Muḥammad b. Ṣāliḥ b. Muḥammad al-Dabbāsī, 10 vols. Muʾassasat al-Rayyān, 2011.

al-Dāraquṭnī, ʿAlī b. ʿUmar. *Sunan al-Dāraquṭnī*. Edited by Shuʿayb al-Arnaʾūṭ et al. 6 vols. Beirut: Muʾassasat al-Risāla, 2004.

al-Dārimī, ʿAbd Allāh b. ʿAbd al-Rahṃān. *Musnad al-Dārimī al-maʿrūf bi-Sunan al-Dārimī*. Edited by Ḥusayn Salīm Asad al-Dārānī, 4 vols. (Riyadh: Dār al-Mughnī, 2000.

al-Dhahabī, Shams al-Dīn Muḥammad b. Aḥmad. *Mīzān al-iʿtidāl fī naqd al-rijāl*. Edited by Muḥammad Riḍwān ʿIrqsūsī, 5 vols. Beirut: Dār al-Risāla al-ʿĀlamiyya, 2009.

al-Dhahabī, Shams al-Dīn Muḥammad b. Aḥmad. *Muʿjam al-shuyūkh*. Edited by Muḥammad Ḥabīb al-Hayla. 2 vols. al-Ṭāʾif: Maktabat al-Ṣiddīq, 1988.

al-Dhahabī, Shams al-Dīn Muḥammad b. Aḥmad. *Siyar aʿlām al-nubalāʾ*. Edited by Shuʿayb al-Arnāʾūṭ et al. 25 vols. Beirut: Muʾassasat al-Risāla, 1981–8.

al-Dhahabī, Shams al-Dīn Muḥammad b. Aḥmad. *Taʾrīkh al-Islām wa-wafayāt al-mashāhīr wa-l-aʿlām*. Edited by ʿUmar ʿAbd al-Salām al-Tadmurī. 53 vols. Beirut: Dār al-Kitāb al-ʿArabī, 1987–2000.

al-Dīnawarī, Abū Bakr Aḥmad b. Marwān. *al-Mujālasa wa-jawāhir al-ʿilm*. Edited by Abū ʿUbayda Mashhūr b. Ḥasan Āl Salmān. 10 vols. Beirut: Dār Ibn Ḥazm, 2002.

al-Dīnawarī, Abū Ḥanīfa Aḥmad b. Dāwūd. *Kitāb al-Akhbār al-Ṭiwāl*. Edited by Vladimir Guirgass. Leiden: Brill, 1888.

Disputation between a Muslim and a Monk of Bēt Ḥālē = Taylor, David G. K. 'The Disputation between a Muslim and a Monk of Bēt Ḥālē: Syriac Text and Annotated English Translation'. In *Christsein in der islamischen Welt: Festschrift für Martin Tamcke zum 60. Geburtstag*, edited by Sidney H. Griffith and Sven Grebenstein, 187–242. Wiesbaden: Harrassowitz, 2015.

al-Dūlābī, Muḥammad b. Aḥmad b. Ḥammād. *al-Kunā wa-l-asmāʾ*. Edited by Naẓr Muḥammad al-Fāryābī. Beirut: Dār Ibn Ḥazm, 2000.

Doran, Robert. *The Lives of Simeon Stylites*. Kalamazoo: Cistercian Publications, 1992.

Eutychius of Alexandria. *The Book of the Demonstration (Kitāb al-Burhān)*. Edited by Pierre Cachia. Translated by W. Montgomery Watt. 4 vols. CSCO 192–3 and 209–10. Louvain: Secrétariat du CorpusSCO, 1960–1.

al-Fākihī, Abū ʿAbd Allāh Muḥammad b. Isḥāq b. al-ʿAbbās. *Akhbār Makka fī qadīm al-dahr wa-ḥadīthihi*. Edited by ʿAbd al-Malik b. ʿAbd Allāh b. Duhaysh. 2nd ed. 6 vols. Beirut: Dār Khiḍr, 1994.

al-Fasawī, Yaʿqūb b. Sufyān. *Kitāb al-Maʿrifa wa-l-taʾrīkh*. Edited by Akram Ḍiyāʾ al-ʿUmarī. 4 vols. Medina: Maktabat al-Dār, 1989.

Furāt b. Ibrāhīm b. Furāt al-Kūfī. *Tafsīr Furāt al-Kūfī*. Edited by Muḥammad al-Kāẓim. 2 vols. Beirut: Muʾassasat al-Tārīkh al-ʿArabī, 2011.

al-Ḥākim al-Nisābūrī. *al-Mustadrak ʿalā al-Ṣaḥīḥayn*. Edited by Yūsuf ʿAbd al-Raḥmān al-Marʿashlī. 5 vols. Beirut: Dār al-Maʿrifa, n.d.

al-Hamdānī, Abū Muḥammad al-Ḥasan b. Aḥmad. *The Antiquities of South Arabia*. Translated by Nabih Amin Faris. Princeton: Princeton University Press, 1938.

al-Hamdānī, Abū Muḥammad al-Ḥasan b. Aḥmad. *Kitāb al-Iklīl min akhbār al-Yaman wa-ansāb Ḥimyar: al-juzʾ al-awwal*. Edited by Muḥammad b. ʿAlī b. al-Ḥusayn al-Akwaʿ. Sanaa: Wizāra al-Thiqāfa wa-l-Siyāḥa, 2004.

al-Hamdānī, Abū Muḥammad al-Ḥasan b. Aḥmad. *al-Juzʿ al-sādis min al-Iklīl*. Edited by Muqbil al-Tām ʿĀmir al-Aḥmadī. Sanaa: Arabia Felix Academy, 2020.

al-Hamdānī, Abū Muḥammad al-Ḥasan b. Aḥmad. *al-Iklīl: al-juzʾ al-thāmin*. Edited by Nabih Amin Faris. Sanaa: Dār al-Kalima, 1940.

Hannād b. al-Sarī al-Kūfī. *Kitāb al-Zuhd*. Edited by ʿAbd al-Raḥmān b. ʿAbd al-Jabbār al-Farīwāʾī. Kuwait: Dār al-Khulafāʾ li-l-Kitāb al-Islāmī, 1985.

al-Ḥārithī, ʿAbd Allāh b. Muḥammad b. Yaʿqūb b. al-Ḥārith. *Musnad Abī Ḥanīfa*. Edited by Abū Muḥammad al-Asyūṭī. Beirut: Dār al-Kutub al-ʿIlmiyya, 2008.

al-Ḥasan al-Baṣrī (attrib.). *Faḍāʾil Makka wa-l-sakan fīhā*. Edited by Sāmī Makkī al-ʿĀnī. Kuwait: Maktabat al-Falāḥ, 1980.

Ḥasan b. Muḥammad b. Ḥasan Qummī. *Tārīkh-i Qumm*. Edited by Jalāl al-Dīn Ṭihrānī. Tehran: Maṭbaʿat-i Majlis, 1934.

al-Haythamī, Nūr al-Dīn. *Bughyat al-bāḥith ʿan zawāʾid musnad al-Ḥārith*. Edited by Ḥusayn Aḥmad Ṣāliḥ al-Bākrī. Medina: al-Jāmiʿa al-Islāmiyya bi-Madīna al-Munawwara, 1992.

al-Haythamī, Nūr al-Dīn. *Majmaʿ al-zawāʾid wa-manbaʿ al-fawāʾid*. Edited by Ḥusayn Salīm Asad al-Dārānī. 30 vols. Jeddah: Dār al-Minhāj, 2010.

Hūd b. Muḥakkam al-Hawwārī. *Tafsīr Kitāb Allāh al-ʿazīz*. Edited by Bālḥāj b. Saʿīd al-Sharīfī. 4 vols. Beirut: Dār al-Gharb al-Islāmī, 1990.

al-Ḥumaydī, Abū Bakr ʿAbd Allāh b. al-Zubayr al-Qurashī. *Musnad al-Ḥumaydī*. Edited by Ḥusayn Salīm Asad al-Dārānī. 2 vols. Damascus: Dār al-Saqā, 1996.

Ibn ʿAbd al-Barr, Abū ʿUmar Yūsuf b. ʿAbd Allāh b. Muḥammad. *al-Istīʿab fī maʿrifat al-aṣḥāb*. Edited by ʿAlī Muḥammad al-Bajjāwī. 4 vols. Beirut: Dār al-Jīl, 1992.

Ibn ʿAbd al-Barr, Abū ʿUmar Yūsuf b. ʿAbd Allāh b. Muḥammad. *al-Tamhīd li-mā fī-l-Muwaṭṭaʾ min al-maʿānī wa-l-asānīd*. Edited by Saʿīd Aḥmad Aʿrāb. 26 vols. Ribat: Wizārat al-Awqāf wa-l-Shuʾūn al-Islāmiyya, 1967–92.

Ibn ʿAbd al-Ḥakam. *Kitāb Futūḥ Miṣr wa-akhbāruhā*. Edited by Charles C. Torrey. New Haven: Yale University Press, 1922.

Ibn ʿAbd Rabbihi al-Andalusī. *al-ʿIqd al-farīd*. Edited by Mufīd Muḥammad Qumayḥa et al. 9 vols. Beirut: Dār al-Kutub al-ʿIlmiyyah, 1983.

Ibn Abī ʿArūba, Abū al-Naḍr Saʿīd al-ʿAdawī. *Kitāb al-Manāsik*. Edited by ʿĀmir Ḥasan Ṣabrī. Beirut: Dār al-Bashāʾir al-Islāmiyya, 2000.

Ibn Abī ʿĀṣim, Abū Bakr Aḥmad b. ʿAmr. *al-Āḥād wa-l-mathānī*. Edited by Bāsim Fayṣal Aḥmad al-Jawābira, 6 vols. Riyadh: Dār al-Rāya, 1991.

Ibn Abī ʿĀṣim, Abū Bakr Aḥmad b. ʿAmr. *Kitāb al-Ṣalāt ʿalā al-nabī*. Edited by Ḥamdī ʿAbd al-Majīd al-Salafī. Damascus: Dār al-Maʾmūn li-l-Turāth, 1995.

Ibn Abī al-Dunyā. *Kitāb Ḥilm Muʿāwiya*. Edited by Ibrāhīm Ṣāliḥ. Damascus: Dār al-Bashāʾir, 2002.

Ibn Abī al-Dunyā. *Kitāb al-Mawt wa-Kitāb al-Qubūr*. Edited and reconstructed by Leah Kinberg. Haifa: University of Haifa, 1983.

Ibn Abī al-Dunyā. *Kitāb al-Qubūr*. Edited by Ṭāriq Muḥammad Saklūʿ al-ʿUmūdī. Medina: Maktabat al-Ghurabāʾ al-Athariyya, 2000.

Ibn Abī Ḥātim. *Kitāb al-Jarḥ wa-l-taʿdīl*. Edited by ʿAbd al-Raḥmān b. Yaḥyā al-Muʿallimī. 9 vols. Hyderabad: Dāʾirat al-Maʿārif al-ʿUthmāniyya, 1941–53.

Ibn Abī Khaythama, Aḥmad Zuhayr b. Ḥarb. *al-Taʾrīkh al-kabīr al-maʿrūf bi-Taʾrīkh Ibn Abī Khaythama*. Edited by Ṣalāḥ b. Fatḥī Halal. 4 vols. Cairo: al-Fārūq al-Ḥadītha, 2004.

Ibn Abī Shayba, Abū Bakr ʿAbd Allāh b. Muḥammad. *al-Muṣannaf*. Edited by Ḥamad b. ʿAbd Allāh al-Jumʿa and Muḥammad b. Ibrāhīm al-Luḥaydān. 16 vols. Riyadh: Maktabat al-Rushd, 2004.

Ibn Abī Shayba, Abū Bakr ʿAbd Allāh b. Muḥammad. *Musnad Ibn Abī Shayba*. Edited by ʿĀdil b. Yūsuf al-ʿAzzāzī and Aḥmad Farīd al-Muzaydī. 2 vols. Riyadh: Dār al-Waṭan, 1997.

Ibn Abī Zayd al-Qayrawānī. *Kitāb al-Jāmiʿ fī al-sunan wa-l-ādāb wa-l-māghāzī wa-l-tārīkh*. Edited by Muḥammad Abū al-Ajfān and ʿUthmān Baṭṭīkh. Beirut: Muʾassasat al-Risāla, 1983.

Ibn Abī Zayd al-Qayrawānī. *al-Nawādir wa-l-ziyādāt ʿalā mā fī al-Mudawwana min ghayr-hā min al-ummahāt*. Edited by ʿAbd al-Fattāḥ Muḥammad al-Ḥulw, et al. 15 vols. Beirut: Dār al-Gharb al-Islāmī, 1999.

Ibn ʿAdī, ʿAbd Allāh al-Jurjānī. *al-Kāmil fī ḍuʿafāʾ al-rijāl*. 7 vols. Beirut: Dār al-Fikr, 1984.

Ibn ʿAsākir. *Taʾrīkh Madīnat Dimashq*. Edited by Muḥibb al-Dīn Abū Saʿīd ʿUmar b. Gharāma al-ʿAmrawī. 80 vols. Beirut: Dār al-Fikr: 1995–2001.

Ibn Aʿtham, Aḥmad al-Kūfī. *Kitāb al-Futūḥ*. Edited by Muḥammad ʿAbd al-Muʿīd Khān et al. 8 vols. Hyderabad: Maṭbaʿat Jamʿiyyat Dāʾirat al-Maʿārif al-ʿUthmāniyya, 1968–75.

Ibn al-Athīr. *Usd al-ghābah fī maʿrifat al-ṣaḥābah*. Beirut: Dār Ibn Ḥazm, 2012.

Ibn Bābawayh al-Qummī. *Amālī al-Ṣadūq*. Introduced by Muḥammad Mahdī al-Mūsawī al-Kharsān. Najaf: al-Maṭbaʿa al-Ḥaydariyya, 1970.

Ibn Bābawayh al-Qummī. *Kitāb Man lā yaḥḍuru al-faqīh*. Edited by Ḥusayn al-Aʿlamī. 2 vols. Beirut: Muʾassasat al-Aʿlamī li-l-Maṭbūʿāt, 1986.

Ibn Bābawayh al-Qummī. *Kitāb al-Nubuwwa*. Tehran: Wizārat al-Thaqāfa wa-l-Irshād al-Islāmī, 2002.

Ibn Balbān, ʿAlāʾ al-Dīn ʿAlī al-Fārisī. *al-Iḥsān fī taqrīb Ṣaḥīḥ Ibn Ḥibbān*. Edited by Shuʿayb al-Arnaʾūṭ. 18 vols. Beirut: Muʾassasat al-Risāla, 1988.

Ibn Baṭṭāl, ʿAlī b. Khalf. *Sharḥ Ṣaḥīḥ al-Bukhārī*. Edited by Abū Tamīm Yāsir b. Ibrāhīm. 10 vols. Riyadh: Maktabat al-Rushd, 2000.

Ibn al-Faqīh al-Hamadhānī. *Kitāb al-Buldān*. Edited by Yūsuf al-Hādī. Beirut: ʿĀlam al-Kutub, 1996.

Ibn Ḥajar al-ʿAsqalānī. *Fatḥ al-bārī bi-sharḥ Ṣaḥīḥ al-Bukhārī*. Edited by Abū Qutayba Naẓar Muḥammad al-Fāryābī. 17 vols. Riyadh: Dār al-Ṭayba, 2005.

Ibn Ḥajar al-ʿAsqalānī. *Hady al-sārī muqaddimat Fatḥ al-bārī*. Edited by Abū Qutayba Naẓar Muḥammad al-Fāryābī, 2 vols. Riyadh: Dār al-Ṭayba, 2006.

Ibn Ḥajar al-ʿAsqalānī. *al-Iṣāba fī tamyīz al-ṣaḥāba*. Edited by ʿAbd Allāh b. ʿAbd al-Muḥsin al-Turkī. 16 vols. Cairo: Markaz Hujr li-l-Buḥūth al-ʿArabiyya wa-al-Islāmiyya, 2008.

Ibn Ḥajar al-ʿAsqalānī. *Tahdhīb al-tahdhīb*. Edited by Ibrāhīm al-Zaybaq and ʿĀdil Murshid. 4 vols. Beirut: Muʾassasat al-Risāla, 1995.

Ibn Ḥajar al-ʿAsqalānī. *Taqrīb al-tahdhīb*. Edited by Abū al-Ashbāl Ṣaghīr Aḥmad Shāghif al-Bākistānī. Riyadh: Dār al-ʿĀṣima, 1995.

Ibn Ḥanbal, Aḥmad. *Kitāb Faḍāʾil al-ṣaḥāba*. Edited by Waṣī Allāh b. Muḥammad ʿAbbās. Riyadh: Dār Ibn al-Jawzī, 1999.

Ibn Ḥanbal, Aḥmad. *Kitāb al-ʿIlal wa-maʿrifat al-rijāl*. Edited by Waṣī Allāh b. Muḥammad ʿAbbās. 4 vols. Beirut: al-Maktab al-Islāmī, 1988.

Ibn Ḥanbal, Aḥmad. *Musnad al-Imām Aḥmad ibn Ḥanbal*. Edited by Shuʿayb al-Arnaʾūṭ et al. 50 vols. Beirut: Muʾassasat al-Risālah, 1993–2001.

Ibn Ḥanbal, Aḥmad. *al-Zuhd*. Beirut: Dār al-Kutub al-ʿIlmiyya, 1983.

Ibn Hawqal, Abū al-Qāsim. *Kitāb Ṣūrat al-Arḍ*. Beirut: Dār Maktabat al-Ḥayāt, 1992.

Ibn Ḥazm, ʿAlī b. Aḥmad b. Saʿīd. *Jamharat ansāb al-ʿarab*. Edited by ʿAbd al-Salām Muḥammad Hārūn. Cairo: Dār al-Maʿārif, 1962.

Ibn Ḥibbān, Muḥammad al-Tamīmī al-Bustī. *Kitāb al-Majrūḥīn min al-muḥaddithīn*. Edited by Ḥamdī ʿAbd al-Majīd al-Salafī. 2 vols. Riyadh: Dār al-Ṣumayʿī, 2000.

Ibn Ḥibbān, Muḥammad al-Tamīmī al-Bustī. *Kitāb al-Thiqāt*. 9 vols. Hyderabad: Dāʾirat al-Maʿārif al-ʿUthmāniyya, 1973–83.

Ibn Hishām, ʿAbd al-Malik. *Kitāb Sīrat Rasūl Allāh: Das Leben Muhammed's nach Muhammed Ibn Isḥāk bearbeitet von Abd el-Malik Ibn Hischām*. Edited by Ferdinand Wüstenfeld. 2 vols. Göttingen: Dieterichsche Universitäts-Buchhandlung, 1858–60.

Ibn Isḥāq, Muḥammad. *Kitāb al-Siyar wa-l-maghāzī*. Edited by Suhayl Zakkār. Damascus: Dār al-Fikr, 1978.

Ibn al-Jaʿd, ʿAlī. *Musnad Ibn al-Jaʿd*. Edited by ʿAbd al-Mahdī b. ʿAbd al-Qādir b. ʿAbd al-Hādī. Kuwait: Maktabat al-Falāḥ, 1985.

Ibn al-Jawzī, Abū al-Faraj ʿAbd al-Raḥmān b. ʿAlī. *Akhbār al-adhkiyā'*. Edited by Bassām ʿAbd al-Wahhāb al-Jābī. Beirut: Dār Ibn Ḥazm, 2003.

Ibn al-Jawzī, Abū al-Faraj ʿAbd al-Raḥmān b. ʿAlī. *Kitāb al-Mawḍūʿāt*. Edited by ʿAbd al-Raḥmān Muḥammad ʿUthmān. 3 vols. Medina: al-Maktaba al-Salafiyya, 1966–8.

Ibn al-Jawzī, Abū al-Faraj ʿAbd al-Raḥmān b. ʿAlī. *Virtues of the Imām Aḥmad ibn Ḥanbal*. Edited and translated by Michael Cooperson. 2 vols. New York: New York University Press, 2013–15.

Ibn Jubayr, Abū al-Ḥusayn Muḥammad b. Aḥmad. *Riḥla*. Edited by William Wright. 2nd rev. ed. by M. J. de Goeje. Leiden: Brill, 1907.

Ibn al-Kalbī, Hishām b. Muḥammad. *Nasab Maʿadd wa-l-Yaman al-kabīr*. Edited by Nājī Ḥasan. 2 vols. Beirut: ʿĀlam al-Kutub, 1988.

Ibn Kathīr. *al-Bidāya wa-l-nihāya*. 14 vols. Beirut: Maktabat al-Maʿārif, 1990.

Ibn Khayyāṭ, Khalīfa. *Kitāb al-Ṭabaqāt*. Edited by Akram Ḍiyā' al-ʿUmarī. Baghdad: Maṭbaʿat al-ʿĀnī, 1967.

Ibn Khayyāṭ, Khalīfa. *Kitāb al-Ṭārīkh*. Edited by Akram Ḍiyā' al-ʿUmarī. 2nd ed. Riyadh: Dār al-Ṭayba, 1985.

Ibn Khuzayma, Muḥammad b. Isḥāq. *Ṣaḥīḥ Ibn Khuzayma*. Edited by Muḥammad Muṣṭafa al-Aʿẓamī. Beirut: al-Maktab al-Islāmī, 2003.

Ibn Khuzayma, Muḥammad b. Isḥāq. *Kitāb al-Tawḥīd wa-ithbāt ṣifāt al-rabb ʿazza wa-jalla*. Edited by ʿAbd al-ʿAzīz b. Ibrāhīm al-Shahwān. Riyadh: Dār al-Rushd, 1988.

Ibn Mājah, Abū ʿAbd Allāh Muḥammad b. Yazīd al-Qazwīnī. *Sunan Ibn Mājah*. Edited by Muḥammad Fu'ād ʿAbd al-Bāqī. 2 vols. Cairo: ʿĪsā al-Bābī al-Ḥalabī, 1972.

Ibn al-Mubārak, ʿAbd Allāh. *Kitāb al-Zuhd wa yalīhi Kitāb al-Raqā'iq*. Edited by Ḥabīb al-Raḥmān al-ʿAẓamī. Beirut: Dār al-Kutub al-ʿIlmiyya, n.d.

Ibn al-Murajjā, Abū al-Maʿālī al-Musharraf al-Maqdisī. *Faḍā'il Bayt al-Maqdis wa-l-Khalīl wa-faḍā'il al-Shām*. Edited by Ofer Livne-Kafri. Shafā ʿAmr: Dār al-Mashriq, 1995.

Ibn al-Najjār. *al-Durra al-Thamīna fī ta'rīkh al-Madīna*. Edited by Muḥammad Zaynahum Muḥammad ʿAzab. Cairo: Maktabat al-Thaqāfa al-Dīniyya, 1995.

Ibn Qayyim al-Jawziyya. *Ighāthat al-lahfān fī maṣā'id al-shayṭān*. Edited by Muḥammad ʿUzayr Shams et al. Mecca: Dār ʿĀlam al-Fawā'id, 2010.

Ibn Qūlūya. *Kāmil al-ziyārāt*. Edited by Jawād al-Qayyūmī. Qum: Mu'assasat Nashr al-Faqāha, 1997.

Ibn Qutayba, ʿAbd Allāh b. Muslim. *The Excellence of the Arabs*. Edited by James Montgomery and Peter Webb. Translated by Sarah Bowen Savant and Peter Webb. New York: New York University Press, 2017.

Ibn Qutayba, ʿAbd Allāh b. Muslim. *al-Maʿārif*. Edited by Tharwat ʿUkāsha. Cairo: Dār al-Maʿārif, 1969.

Ibn Rāhwayh, Isḥāq b. Ibrāhīm b. Makhlad al-Ḥanẓalī al-Marwazī. *Musnad Isḥāq ibn Rāhwayh*. Edited by ʿAbd al-Ghafūr ʿAbd al-Ḥaqq Ḥusayn Burr al-Balūshī. 5 vols. Medina: Maktabat Dār al-Īmān: 1991–5.

Ibn Rajab al-Ḥanbalī. *Kitāb Aḥkām al-khawātīm wa-mā yataʿallaq bi-hā*. Edited by Abū al-Fidāʾ ʿAbd Allāh al-Qāḍī. Beirut: Dār al-Kutub al-ʿIlmiyya, 1985.

Ibn Rusta. *Kitāb al-Aʿlāk al-nafīsa*. Edited by M. J. de Goeje. Leiden: Brill, 1892.

Ibn Saʿd, Muḥammad. *Kitāb al-Ṭabaqāt al-kabīr*. Edited by ʿAlī Muḥammad ʿUmar. 11 vols. Cairo: Maktabat al-Khānjī, 2001.

Ibn Shabba, ʿUmar. *Taʾrīkh al-Madīna al-munawwara*. Edited by Fahīm Muḥammad Shaltūt. 4 vols. Beirut: Dār al-Turāth, 1990.

Ibn Shahrāshūb, Muḥammad b. ʿAlī. *Manāqib Āl Abī Ṭālib*. Edited by Muḥammad Kāẓim al-Kutubī. 3 vols. Najaf: al-Maṭbaʿa al-Ḥaydariyya, 1956.

Ibn Taymiyya. *Iqtiḍāʾ al-ṣirāṭ al-mustaqīm li-mukhālafat aṣḥāb al-jaḥīm*. Edited by Nāṣir b. ʿAbd al-Karīm al-ʿAql. 2 vols. Riyadh: Dār Ishbīliyyā, 1998.

Ibn Taymiyya. *Majmūʿ al-fatāwā*. Edited by ʿAbd al-Raḥmān b. Muḥammad b. Qāsim and Muḥammad b. ʿAbd al-Raḥmān b. Muḥammad. 37 vols. Medina: Mujammaʿ al-Malik Fahd li-Ṭibāʿat al-Muṣḥaf al-Sharīf, 2004.

Ibn Waḍḍāḥ, Muḥammad al-Qurṭubī. *Kitāb al-Bidaʿ (Tratado contra las innovaciones)*. Edited and translated by María Isabel Fierro. Madrid: Consejo Superior de Investigaciones Científicas, 1988.

Ibn Wahb, ʿAbd Allāh al-Qurashī. *al-Ǧāmiʿ: Die Koranwissenschaften*. Edited by Miklos Muranyi. Wiesbaden: Otto Harrassowitz, 1992.

Ibn Wahb, ʿAbd Allāh al-Qurashī. *al-Jāmiʿ fī-l-ḥadīth*. Edited by Muṣṭafā Ḥasan Ḥusayn Muḥammad Abū al-Khayr. 2 vols. Riyadh: Dār Ibn al-Jawzī, 1996.

Ibn Wahb, ʿAbd Allāh al-Qurashī. *Kitāb al-Muḥāraba min al-Muwaṭṭaʾ*. Edited by Miklos Muranyi. Beirut: Dār al-Gharb al-Islāmī, 2002.

Ibn Zanjawayh, Ḥumayd. *Kitāb al-Amwāl*. Edited by Shākir Dhīb Fayyāḍ. Riyadh: Markaz al-Malik Fayṣal li-l-Buḥūth wa-l-Dirāsāt al-Islāmiyya, 1986.

Ismāʿīl b. Isḥāq al-Azdī. *Faḍl al-ṣalāt ʿalā al-nabī*. Edited by Ḥusayn Muḥammad ʿAlī Shukrī. Beirut: Dār al-Kutub al-ʿIlmiyya, 2008.

al-Iṣṭakhrī, Abū Isḥāq Ibrāhīm b. Muḥammad. *Kitāb al-Masālik wa-l-mamālik*. Edited by M. J. de Goeje. Leiden: Brill, 1870.

al-Jāḥiẓ, Abū ʿUthmān ʿAmr b. Baḥr. *al-Bayān wa-l-tabyīn*. Edited by ʿAbd al-Salām Muḥammad Hārūn. 4 vols. Cairo: Maktabat al-Khānijī, 1968.

al-Jāḥiẓ, Abū ʿUthmān ʿAmr b. Baḥr. *Kitāb al-Ḥayawān*. Edited by ʿAbd al-Salām Muḥammad Hārūn. 8 vols. Cairo: Maktabat Muṣṭafā al-Bābī al-Ḥalabī, 1938–45.

al-Jāḥiẓ, Abū ʿUthmān ʿAmr b. Baḥr. *Rasāʾil al-Jāḥiẓ*. Edited by ʿAbd al-Salām Muḥammad Hārūn. 4 vols. Cairo: Maktabat al-Khānjī, 1964–79.

al-Jāḥiẓ, Abū ʿUthmān ʿAmr b. Baḥr. *Kitāb al-Tarbīʿ wa-l-tadwīr*. Edited by Charles Pellat. Damascus: Institut Français de Damas, 1955.

John Rufus, *Vita Petri Iberii = The Lives of Peter the Iberian, Theodosius of Jerusalem, and the Monk Romanus*. Edited and translated by Cornelia B. Horn and Robert R. Phenix Jr. Atlanta: Society of Biblical Literature, 2008.

al-Karājukī, Abū Fatḥ Muḥammad b. ʿAlī b. ʿUthmān. *Kanz al-Fawāʾid*. Edited by ʿAbd Allāh Niʿmah. 2 vols. Beirut: Dār al-Aḍwāʾ, 1985.

al-Khallāl, Abū Bakr Aḥmad b. Muḥammad. *Ahl al-milal wa-l-ridda wa-l-zanādiqa wa-tārik al-ṣalāt wa-l-farāʾiḍ min Kitāb al-Jāmiʿ*. Edited by Ibrāhīm b. Ḥamad b. Sulṭān. 2 vols. Riyadh: Maktabat al-Maʿārif, 1996.

al-Khaṭīb al-Baghdādī, Abū Bakr Aḥmad b. ʿAlī. *Talkhīṣ al-mutashābih fī-l-rasm wa-ḥimāyat mā ashkala minhu ʿan bawādir al-taṣḥīf wa-al-wahm*. Edited by Sukayna al-Shihābī. Damascus: Dār Ṭalās, 1980.

al-Khaṭīb al-Baghdādī, Abū Bakr Aḥmad b. ʿAlī. *Taʾrīkh Madīnat al-Salām*. Edited by Bashshār ʿAwwād Maʿrūf. 16 vols. Beirut: Dār al-Gharb al-Islāmī, 2001.

al-Khaṭṭābī, Abū Sulaymān Ḥamd b. Muḥammad. *Aʿlām al-ḥadīth fī sharḥ Ṣaḥīḥ al-Bukhārī*. Edited by Muḥammad b. Saʿd b. ʿAbd al-Raḥmān Āl Saʿūd. Mecca: Jāmiʿat Umm al-Qurā, 1988.

Khūzistān Chronicle = Nasir al-Kaʿbi. *A Short Chronicle on the End of the Sasanian Empire and Early Islam 590–660 A.D.* Piscataway, NJ: Gorgias Press, 2016; *Chronica Minora, pars prior*. Edited by Ignazio Guidi. 2 vols. Paris: Typographeo Reipublicae, 1903.

al-Kindī, Abū ʿUmar Muḥammad b. Yūsuf al-Miṣrī. *Kitāb al-Wulāt wa-kitāb al-quḍāt*. Edited by Rhuvon Guest. Leiden: Brill, 1912.

Kitāb al-Manāsik wa-amākin ṭuruq al-ḥajj wa-maʿālim al-jazīra. Edited by Ḥamad al-Jāsir. Riyadh: Manshūrāt Dār al-Yamāma li-l-Baḥth wa-l-Tarjama wa-l-Nashr, 1969.

Kitāb Sulaym b. Qays al-Hilālī. Edited by Muḥammad Bāqir al-Anṣārī al-Zanjānī. Qom: Nashr al-Hādī, 1420 AH [1999–2000].

al-Kulaynī, Muḥammad b. Yaʿqūb b. Isḥāq al-Rāzī. *al-Kāfī*. Edited by ʿAlī Akbar al-Ghaffārī. 8 vols. Tehran: Dār al-Kutub al-Islāmiyya, 1388–9 AH [1968].

Lietzmann, H. *Das Leben des heiligen Symeon Stylites*. Leipzig: Hinrichs, 1908.

The Life of Timothy of Kākhushtā: Two Arabic Texts. Edited and translated by John C. Lamoreaux and Cyril Cairala. *PO* 48.4. Turnhout: Brepols, 2000.

Mālik b. Anas. *al-Muwaṭṭaʾ*. Recension of ʿAbd Allāh b. Maslama al-Qaʿnabī. Edited by ʿAbd al-Majīd Turkī. Beirut: Dār al-Gharb al-Islāmī, 1999.

Mālik b. Anas. *al-Muwaṭṭaʾ*. Recension of Abū Muṣʿab al-Zuhrī al-Madanī. Edited by Bashshār ʿAwwād Maʿrūf and Maḥmūd Muḥammad Khalīl. 2 vols. Beirut: Muʾassasat al-Risāla, 1998.

Mālik b. Anas. *al-Muwaṭṭaʾ*. Recension of Suwayd b. Saʿīd al-Hadathānī. Edited by ʿAbd al-Majīd Turkī. Beirut: Dār al-Gharb al-Islāmī, 1994.

Mālik b. Anas. *al-Muwaṭṭaʾ*. Recension of Yaḥyā b. Yaḥyā al-Laythī al-Andalusī. Edited by Bashshār ʿAwwād Maʿrūf. 2 vols. Beirut: Dār al-Gharb al-Islāmī, 1997.

al-Mālikī, Abū Bakr ʿAbd Allāh b. Muḥammad. *Kitāb Riyāḍ al-nufūs fī ṭabaqāt ʿulamāʾ al-Qayrawān wa-Ifrīqiyya wa-zuhhādihim wa-nussākihim wa-siyar min akhbārihim wa-faḍāʾilihim wa-awṣāfihim*. Edited by Bashīr al-Bakkūsh and Muḥammad al-ʿArūsī al-Maṭwī. 2 vols. Beirut: Dār al-Gharb al-Islāmī, 1994.

al-Maqdisī, Shihāb al-Dīn Abū Maḥmūd b. Tamīm. *Muthīr al-Gharām ilā Ziyārat al-Quds wa-l-Shām*. Edited by Aḥmad al-Khuṭaymī. Beirut, Dār al-Jīl, 1994.

al-Marāghī, Abū Bakr b. al-Ḥusayn b. ʿUmar. *Taḥqīq al-nuṣra bi-talkhīṣ maʿālim dār al-hijra*. Edited by Muḥammad ʿAbd al-Jawwād al-Aṣmaʿī. Medina: al-Maktaba al-ʿIlmiyya, 1955.

Masāʾil al-imām Aḥmad riwāyat Abī Dāwūd Sulaymān ibn al-Ashʿath al-Sijistānī. Edited by Ṭāriq b. ʿAwaḍ Allāh b. Muḥammad. Cairo: Maktabat Ibn Taymiyya, 1999.

Masāʾil al-imām Aḥmad ibn Ḥanbal wa-Isḥāq ibn Rāhwayh bi-riwāyat Isḥāq ibn Manṣūr al-Marwazī. Edited by Muḥammad b. ʿAbd Allāh al-Zāḥim et al. Medina: al-Jāmiʿa al-Islāmiyya, 2004.

al-Masʿūdī, ʿAlī b. al-Ḥusayn. *Murūj al-dhahab wa-maʿādin al-jawhar*. Edited and translated by C. Barbier de Meynard and J.-B. Pavet de Courteille. 9 vols. Paris: Imprimerie impériale, 1861–77.

al-Maṭarī, Jamāl al-Dīn Muḥammad b. Aḥmad. *al-Taʿrīf bi-mā anasat al-hijra min maʿālim dār al-hijra*. Edited by Sulaymān al-Ruḥaylī. Riyadh: Dār al-Mālik ʿAbd al-ʿAzīz, 2005.

Migne, Jacques-Paul (ed.). *Patrologiae cursus completus. Series graeca*. Paris: Imprimerie Catholique, 1857–66.

al-Mizzī, Jamāl al-Dīn Yūsuf. *Tahdhīb al-kamāl fī asmāʾ al-rijāl*. Edited by Bashshār ʿAwwād Maʿrūf. 35 vols. Beirut: Muʾassasat al-Risāla, 1985.

Muḥammad b. ʿĀṣim al-Thaqafī. *Juzʾ Muḥammad b. ʿĀṣim al-Thaqafī al-Iṣbahānī*. Edited by Mufīd Khālid ʿĪd. Riyadh: Dār al-ʿĀṣima, 1409 AH [1988–9].

Mujāhid b. Jabr (attrib.). *Tafsīr al-imām Mujāhid ibn Jabr*. Edited by Muḥammad ʿAbd al-Salām Abū al-Nīl. Cairo: Dār al-Fikr al-Islāmī al-Ḥadītha, 1989.

al-Muqaddasī, Shams al-Dīn. *Aḥsān al-taqāsīm fī maʿrifat al-aqālīm*. Edited by M. J. de Goeje. 2nd ed. Leiden: Brill, 1906.

al-Muqaddasī, Shams al-Dīn. *The Best Divisions for Knowledge of the Regions*. Translated by Basil Anthony Collins. Revised by Muhammad Hamid al-Tai. Reading: Garnet, 1994.

Muqātil b. Sulaymān (attrib.). *Tafsīr Muqātil b. Sulaymān*. Edited by ʿAbd Allāh Maḥmūd Shiḥāta. 5 vols. Beirut: Muʾassasat al-Tārīkh al-ʿArabī, 2002.

al-Muṣʿab b. ʿAbd Allāh al-Zubayrī. *Kitāb Nasab al-Quraysh*. Edited by E. Lévi-Provençal. Cairo: Dār al-Maʿārif, 1953.

Muslim b. al-Ḥajjāj al-Qushayrī, *Ṣaḥīḥ Muslim*. Edited by Muḥammad Fuʾād ʿAbd al-Bāqī. 5 vols. Cairo: Dār Iḥyāʾ al-Kutub al-ʿArabiyya, 1955.

al-Najāshī, Aḥmad b. ʿAlī. *Rijāl al-Najāshī*. Edited by Mūsā al-Shubayrī al-Zanjānī. Qom: Muʾassasat al-Nashr al-Islāmī, 1418 AH [1997–8].

al-Nasāʾī, Aḥmad b. Shuʿayb. *Kitāb al-Sunan al-Kubrā*. Edited by Ḥasan ʿAbd al-Munʿim Shalbī. 12 vols. Beirut: Muʾassasat al-Risāla, 2001.

al-Nasāʾī, Aḥmad b. Shuʿayb. *Sunan al-Nasāʾī*. Edited by Muḥammad Nāṣir al-Dīn al-Albānī and Abū ʿUbayda Mashhūr b. Ḥasan Āl Salmān. Riyadh: Maktabat al-Maʿārif li-l-Nashr wa-l-Tawzīʿ, 1988.

Nuʿaym b. Ḥammād al-Marwazī. *Kitāb al-Fitan*. Edited by Suhayl Zakkār. Beirut: Dār al-Fikr, 2003.

Pirke de-Rabbi Elieser: Nach der Edition Venedig 1544 unter Berücksichtigung der Edition Warschau 1852. Edited by Dagmer Börner-Klein. Berlin: de Gruyter, 2004.

al-Qāḍī al-Nuʿmān b. Muḥammad. *Daʿāʾim al-Islām*. Volume 1. Edited by Āṣaf b. ʿAlī Aṣghar Faiḍī. Cairo: Dār al-Maʿārif, 1951.

al-Rabaʿī, ʿAlī b. Muḥammad. *Faḍāʾil al-Shām wa-Dimashq*. Edited by Ṣalāḥ al-Dīn al-Munajjid. Damascus: Maṭbaʿat al-Tarraqī, 1950.

Revelatio Sancti Stephani = S. Vanderlinden, '*Revelatio Sancti Stephani* (BHG 7850–6)'. *Revue des études byzantines* 4 (1946): 178–216.

al-Ṣaffār, Abū Jaʿfar Muḥammad b. al-Ḥasan b. Farrūkh. *Baṣāʾir al-Darajāt fī faḍāʾil āl Muḥammad*. Edited by al-Sayyid Muḥammad al-Sayyid al-Ḥasan al-Muʿallim. 2 vols. Qum: Maktabat al-Ḥaydariyya, 2005.

Saḥnūn b. Saʿīd al-Tanūkhī. *al-Mudawwana al-kubrā*. 16 vols. Riyadh: Wizārat al-Shuʾūn al-Islāmiyya wa-l-Awqāf wa-l-Daʿwa wa-l-Irshād, n.d.

al-Samhūdī, ʿAlī b. ʿAbd Allāh. *Khulāṣat al-wafā bi-akhbār Dār al-Muṣṭafā*. Medina: al-Maktaba al-ʿIlmiyya, 1972.

al-Samhūdī, ʿAlī b. ʿAbd Allāh. *Wafāʾ al-wafā bi-akhbār Dār al-Muṣṭafā*. Edited by Qāsim al-Sāmarrāʾī. 5 vols. London: Muʾassasat al-Furqān li-l-Turāth al-Islāmī, 2001.

Sebeos (attrib.). *The Armenian History attributed to Sebeos*. Translated and commentary by R. W. Thomson, James Howard-Johnston and Tim Greenwood. Liverpool: Liverpool University Press, 1999.

al-Shāfiʿī, Muḥammad b. Idrīs. *al-Umm*. Edited by Rifʿat Fawzī ʿAbd al-Muṭṭalib. 11 vols. Mansoura: Dār al-Wafāʾ, 2001.

al-Shaybānī, Muḥammad b. al-Ḥasan. *Kitāb al-Āthār*. Edited by Khālid al-ʿAwwād. 2 vols. Kuwait: Dār al-Nawādir, 2008.

al-Shaybānī, Muḥammad b. al-Ḥasan. *Muwaṭṭaʾ al-imām Mālik*. Edited by ʿAbd al-Wahhāb ʿAbd al-Laṭīf. Cairo: Wizārat al-Awqāf, 1994.

al-Suyūṭī, Jalāl al-Dīn. *al-Khaṣāʾiṣ al-kubrā*. Edited by Muḥammad Khalīl Harrās. 3 vols. Cairo: Dār al-Kutub al-Ḥadītha, 1967.

al-Ṭabarānī, Sulaymān b. Aḥmad. *al-Muʿjam al-kabīr*. Edited by Ḥamdī ʿAbd al-Majīd al-Salafī. 25 vols. Cairo: Maktabat Ibn Taymiyya, 1983.

al-Ṭabarānī, Sulaymān b. Aḥmad. *Musnad al-Shāmiyyīn*. Edited by Ḥamdī ʿAbd al-Majīd al-Salafī, 4 vols. Beirut: Muʾassasat al-Risāla, 1989.

al-Ṭabarī, ʿAlī b. Rabban. *The Polemical Works of ʿAlī al-Ṭabarī*. Edited and translated by Rifaat Ebied and David Thomas. Leiden: Brill, 2016.

al-Ṭabarī, Muḥammad b. Jarīr. *The History of al-Ṭabarī. Volume II: Prophets and Patriarchs*. Translated by William M. Brinner. Albany: State University of New York Press, 1987.

al-Ṭabarī, Muḥammad b. Jarīr. *The History of al-Ṭabarī. Volume V: The Sāsānids, the Byzantines, the Lakmids, and Yemen*. Translated by C. E. Bosworth. Albany: State University of New York Press, 1999.

al-Ṭabarī, Muḥammad b. Jarīr. *The History of al-Ṭabarī. Volume VI: Muḥammad at Mecca*. Translated by W. M. Watt and M. V. McDonald. Albany: State University of New York Press, 1988.

al-Ṭabarī, Muḥammad b. Jarīr. *The History of al-Ṭabarī. Volume IX: The Last Years of the Prophet*. Translated by Ismail K. Poonawala. Albany: State University of New York Press, 1990.

al-Ṭabarī, Muḥammad b. Jarīr. *The History of al-Ṭabarī. Volume XIII: The Conquest of Iraq, Southwestern Persia, and Egypt*. Translated by G. H. A. Juynboll. Albany: State University of New York Press, 1989.

al-Ṭabarī, Muḥammad b. Jarīr. *The History of al-Ṭabarī. Volume XXIII: The Zenith of the Marwānid House*. Translated by Martin Hinds. Albany: State University of New York Press, 1990.

al-Ṭabarī, Muḥammad b. Jarīr. *The History of al-Ṭabarī. Volume XXIX: Al-Manṣūr and al-Mahdī*. Translated by Hugh Kennedy. Albany: State University of New York Press, 1990.

al-Ṭabarī, Muḥammad b. Jarīr. *The History of al-Ṭabarī. Volume XXXI: The War between Brothers*. Translated by Michael Fishbein. Albany: State University of New York Press, 1992.

al-Ṭabarī, Muḥammad b. Jarīr. *The History of al-Ṭabarī. Volume XXXII: The Reunification of the 'Abbāsid Caliphate*. Translated by C. E. Bosworth. Albany: State University of New York Press, 1987.

al-Ṭabarī, Muḥammad b. Jarīr. *The History of al-Ṭabarī. Volume XXXIV: Incipient Decline*. Translated by Joel L. Kraemer. Albany: State University of New York Press, 1989.

al-Ṭabarī, Muḥammad b. Jarīr. *The History of al-Ṭabarī. Volume XXXIX: Biographies of the Prophet's Companions and Their Successors*. Translated by Ella Landau-Tasseron. Albany: State University of New York Press, 1998.

al-Ṭabarī, Muḥammad b. Jarīr. *Ta'rīkh al-rusul wa-l-mulūk* [*Annales quos scripsit Abu Djafar Mohammed ibn Djarir at-Tabari*]. Edited by M. J. de Goeje. 3 series in 15 vols. Leiden: Brill, 1879–1901.

al-Ṭabarī, Muḥammad b. Jarīr. *Tafsīr al-Ṭabarī: Jāmi' al-Bayān 'an ta'wīl āy al-Qur'ān*. 26 vols. Edited 'Abd Allāh b. 'Abd al-Muḥsin al-Turkī et al. Cairo: Dār Hajar, 2001.

al-Ṭayālisī, Abū Dāwūd Sulaymān b. Dāwūd al-Jārūd. *Musnad Abī Dāwūd al-Ṭayālisī*. Edited by Muḥammad b. 'Abd al-Muḥsin al-Turkī. 4 vols. Cairo: Ḥajar, 1999.

al-Tha'ālibī, Abū Manṣūr 'Abd al-Malik b. Muḥammad b. Ismā'īl. *Thimār al-qulūb fī-l-muḍāf wa-l-mansūb*. Edited by Muḥammad Abū al-Faḍl Ibrāhīm. Sidon: al-Maktaba al-'Aṣriyya, 2003.

al-Tha'labī, Aḥmad b. Muḥammad b. Ibrāhīm. *'Arā'is al-Majālis fī Qiṣaṣ al-Anbiyā' or 'Lives of the Prophets'*. Translated by William M. Brinner. Leiden: Brill, 2002.

al-Tha'labī, Aḥmad b. Muḥammad b. Ibrāhīm. *Kitāb al-Qiṣaṣ al-anbiyā' al-musammā bi-l-'Arā'is*. Cairo: al-Maṭba'a al-'Āmira al-Sharafiyya, 1906.

al-Thaqafī, Ibrāhīm b. Muḥammad b. Sa'īd b. Hilāl. *al-Ghārāt*. Edited by 'Abd al-Zahrā' al-Ḥusaynī al-Khaṭīb. Beirut: Dār al-Aḍwā', 1987.

Theophanes the Confessor. *The Chronicle of Theophanes Confessor: Byzantine and Near Eastern History AD 284–813*. Translated by Cyril Mango and Roger Scott with Geoffrey Greatrex. Oxford: Clarendon Press, 1997.

Theophanes the Confessor. *Theophanis Chronographia*. Edited by Carolus de Boor. 2 vols. Leipzig: 1883–5.

al-Tirmidhī, Muḥammad b. 'Īsā. *al-Jāmi' al-kabīr*. Edited by Bashshār 'Awwād Ma'rūf. 6 vols. Beirut: Dār al-Gharb al-Islāmī, 1996.

al-Ṭurṭūshī, Abū Bakr. *Kitāb al-Ḥawādith wa-l-bida'*. Edited by 'Abd al-Majīd Turkī. Beirut: Dār al-Gharb al-Islāmī, 1990.

al-Ṭūsī, Abū Ja'far Muḥammad b. al-Ḥasan. *al-Amālī*. Qum: Dār al-Thaqāfa, 1993.

al-Ṭūsī, Abū Ja'far Muḥammad b. al-Ḥasan. *Ikhtiyār ma'rifat al-rijāl al-ma'rūf bi-Rijāl al-Kashshī*. Edited by Jawād al-Qayyūmī al-Iṣfahānī. Qom: Mu'assasat al-Nashr al-Islāmī, 1427 AH [2006–7].

al-Ṭūsī, Abū Jaʿfar Muḥammad b. al-Ḥasan. *Rijāl al-Ṭūsī*. Edited by Jawād al-Qayyūmī al-Iṣfahānī. Qom: Mu'assasat al-Nashr al-Islāmī, 1430 AH [2008–9].

al-Ṭūsī, Abū Jaʿfar Muḥammad b. al-Ḥasan. *Tahdhīb al-aḥkām fī sharḥ al-Muqniʿa li-l-shaykh al-Mufīd*. Edited by Muḥammad Jaʿfar Shams al-Dīn. 10 vols. Beirut: Dār al-Taʿāruf li-l-Maṭbūʿāt, 1992.

al-ʿUqaylī, Abū Jaʿfar Muḥammad b. ʿAmr. *Kitāb al-Ḍuʿafāʾ al-kabīr*. Edited by ʿAbd al-Muʿṭī Amīn Qalʿajī. 4 vols. Beirut: Dār al-Kutub al-ʿIlmiyya, 1984.

al-Uṣūl al-sitta ʿashar min al-uṣūl al-awwaliyya: Majmūʿat min kutub al-riwāya al-awwaliyya. Edited by Ḍiyāʾ al-Dīn al-Maḥmūdī. Qom: Dār al-Ḥadīth, 2002.

Vööbus, Arthur (ed. and trans.). *The Synodicon in the West Syrian Tradition*. 4 vols. Louvain: Secrétariat du CorpusSCO, 1975–6.

Wahb b. Munabbih (attrib.). *Wahb b. Munabbih. Der Heidelberger Papyrus PSR Heid Arab 23*. Edited by R. G. Khoury. 2 vols. Wiesbaden: Otto Harrassowitz, 1972.

al-Wāqidī, Muḥammad b. ʿUmar. *Kitāb al-Maghāzī*. Edited by Marsden Jones. 3 vols. London: Oxford University Press, 1966.

al-Warjlānī, Abū Yaʿqūb Yūsuf b. Ibrāhīm. *Kitāb al-Tartīb fī-l-ṣaḥīḥ min ḥadīth al-rasūl*. Edited by Nūr al-Dīn ʿAbd Allāh b. Ḥumayd al-Sālimī. Muscat: Maktabat Masqaṭ, 2003.

al-Wāsiṭī, Abū Bakr Muḥammad b. Aḥmad. *Faḍāʾil al-Bayt al-Muqaddas*. Edited by Isaac Hasson. Jerusalem: Magness Press, 1979.

al-Yaʿqūbī, Aḥmad b. Abī Yaʿqūb b. Jaʿfar b. Wahb b. Wāḍiḥ. *Taʾrīkh*. Edited by Martijn T. Houtsma. 2 vols. Leiden: Brill, 1883.

al-Yaʿqūbī, Aḥmad b. Abī Yaʿqūb b. Jaʿfar b. Wahb b. Wāḍiḥ. *The Works of Ibn Wāḍiḥ al-Yaʿqūbī: An English Translation*. Edited by Matthew S. Gordon et al. 3 vols. Leiden: Brill, 2018.

Yāqūt al-Ḥamawī. *Muʿjam al-buldān*. 5 vols. Beirut: Dār Ṣādir, 1977.

al-Zubayr b. Bakkār. *Akhbār al-Muwaffaqiyyāt*. Edited by Sāmī Makkī al-ʿĀnī. 2nd ed. Beirut: ʿĀlam al-Kutub, 1996.

al-Zubayr b. Bakkār. *Jamharat nasab Quraysh wa-akhbāruhā*. Edited by ʿAbbās Hānī al-Jarrāḥ. 2 vols. Beirut: Dār al-Kutub al-ʿIlmiyya, 2010.

Secondary Sources

Abbott, Nabia. *Studies in Arabic Literary Papyri*. 3 vols. Chicago: University of Chicago Press, 1957–72.

Abid, Hiba. 'Material Images and Mental *Ziyāra*: Depicting the Prophet's Grave in North African Devotional Books (*Dalāʾil al-Khayrāt*)'. *Journal of Material Cultures in the Muslim World* 1 (2020): 331–54.

Adang, Camilla. *Muslim Writers on Judaism and the Hebrew Bible: From Ibn Rabban to Ibn Hazm*. Leiden: Brill, 1996.

Adelman, Rachel. 'Midrash, Myth, and Bakhtin's Chronotope: The Itinerant Well and the Foundation Stone in *Pirqe de-Rabbi Eliezer*'. *Journal of Jewish Thought and Philosophy* 17.2 (2009): 143–76.

Ahmed, Asad Q. *The Religious Elite of the Early Islamic Ḥijāz: Five Prosopographical Case Studies*. Oxford: Prosopographica et Genealogica, 2011.

Ahmed, Shahab. *What Is Islam? The Importance of Being Islamic*. Princeton: Princeton University Press, 2016.

Aigrain, René. *L'hagiographie: ses sources, ses méthodes, son histoire*. Paris: Bloud et Gay, 1953.

Alexander, Philip S. 'Jerusalem as the *Omphalos* of the World: On the History of a Geographical Concept'. *Judaism* 46 (1997): 147–58.

Amir-Moezzi, Mohammad Ali. The *Divine Guide in Early Shi'ism: The Sources of Esotericism in Islam*. Translated by David Streight. Albany: State University of New York Press, 1994.

Andersson, Tobias. *Early Sunnī Historiography: A Study of the* Tārīkh *of Khalīfa b. Khayyāṭ*. Leiden: Brill, 2019.

Ansārī, Hassan. *L'imamat et l'Occultation selon l'imamisme: Étude bibliographique et histoire de textes*. Leiden: Brill, 2017.

Anthony, Sean W. 'The Composition of Sayf b. 'Umar's Account of King Paul and His Corruption of Ancient Christianity'. *Der Islam* 85 (2010): 164–202.

Anthony, Sean W. *Crucifixion and Death as Spectacle: Umayyad Crucifixion in its Late Antique Context*. New Haven: American Oriental Society, 2014.

Anthony, Sean W. *Muhammad and the Empires of Faith: The Making of the Prophet of Islam*. Oakland: University of California Press, 2020.

Anthony, Sean W. 'Was Ibn Wāḍiḥ al-Ya'qūbī a Shi'ite Historian? The State of the Question'. *Al-'Uṣūr al-Wusṭā* 24 (2016): 15–41.

Arjomand, Said Amir. 'Islamic Apocalypticism in the Classic Period'. In *The Encyclopedia of Apocalypticism. Volume 2: Apocalypticism in Western History and Culture*, edited by Bernard McGinn, 238–83. New York: Continuum, 1998.

Armstrong, Lyall R. *The* Quṣṣāṣ *of Early Islam*. Leiden: Brill, 2017.

Atkin, Albert. 'Peirce on the Index and Indexical Reference'. *Transactions of the Charles S. Peirce Society* 41 (2005): 161–88.

Avery-Peck, Alan J. 'Death and Afterlife in the Early Rabbinic Sources: The Mishnah, Tosefta, and Early Midrash Compilations'. In *Judaism in Late Antiquity. Part Four: Death, Life-After-Death, Resurrection and the World-to-Come in the Judaisms of Antiquity*, edited by Alan J. Avery-Peck and Jacob Neusner, 243–66. Leiden: Brill, 2000.

Avery-Peck, Alan J. 'Resurrection of the Body in Early Rabbinic Judaism'. In *The Human Body in Death and Resurrection*, edited by Tobias Nicklas, Friedrich V. Reiterer and Joseph Verheyden, in collaboration with Heike Braun, 243–66. Berlin: Walter de Gruyter, 2009.

Avner, Rina. 'The Dome of the Rock in Light of the Development of Concentric Martyria in Jerusalem: Architecture and Architectural Iconography'. *Muqarnas* 27 (2010): 31–49.

Avner, Rina. 'The Kathisma: A Christian and Muslim Pilgrimage Site'. *ARAM* 18–19 (2006–7): 541–57.

Aydın, Hilmi. *The Sacred Trusts: Pavilion of the Sacred Relics, Topkapı Palace Museum, Istanbul*. Somerset, NJ: The Light, 2004.

Ayyad, Essam S. 'An Historiographical Analysis of the Arabic Accounts of Early Mosques: With Special Reference to those at Madina, Baṣra and Kūfa'. *Journal of Islamic Studies* 30.1 (2019): 1–33.

Ayyad, Essam S. *The Making of the Mosque: A Survey of Religious Imperatives*. Piscataway, NJ: Gorgias, 2019.

al-Azmeh, Aziz. *The Emergence of Islam in Late Antiquity: Allāh and His People*. Cambridge: Cambridge University Press, 2017.

Bar-Asher, Meir M. *Scripture and Exegesis in Early Imāmī-Shiism*. Leiden: Brill, 1999.

Bar-Ilan, Meir. 'The Hand of God: A Chapter in Rabbinic Anthropomorphism'. In *Rashi 1040–1990: Hommage à Ephraïm E. Urbach. Congrès européen des études juives*, edited by Gabrielle Sed-Rajna, 321–35. Paris: Éditions du CERF, 1993.

Bashear, Suliman. 'On the Origins and Development of the Meaning of *Zakāt* in Early Islam'. *Arabica* 40.1 (1993): 84–113.

Bashear, Suliman. 'Qibla Musharriqa and Early Muslim Prayer in Churches'. *Muslim World* 81.3–4 (1991): 267–82.

Ben-Eliyahu, Eyal. '"On That Day, His Feet Will Stand on the Mount of Olives": The Mount of Olives and Its Hero between Jews, Christians, and Muslims'. *Jewish History* 30 (2016): 29–42.

Ben-Eliyahu, Eyal. 'The Rabbinic Polemic against Sanctification of Sites'. *JSJ* 40 (2009): 260–80.

Ben-Shammai, Haggai. 'The Attitude of Some Early Karaites Towards Islam'. In *Studies in Medieval Jewish History and Literature, Volume II*, edited by Isadore Twersky, 1–40. Cambridge, MA: Harvard University Press, 1984.

Beránek, Ondřej and Pavel Ťupek. *The Temptation of Graves in Salafi Islam: Iconoclasm, Destruction and Idolatry*. Edinburgh: Edinburgh University Press, 2018.

Berkey, Jonathan P. 'Tradition, Innovation and the Social Construction of Knowledge in the Medieval Islamic Near East'. *Past & Present* 146 (1995): 38–65.

Betancourt, Roland. *Sight, Touch, and Imagination in Byzantium*. Cambridge: Cambridge University Press, 2018.

Bhabha, Homi K. *Location of Culture*. London: Routledge, 1991.

Bigelow, Anna (ed.). *Islam Through Objects*. London: Bloomsbury, 2021.

Bisheh, Ghazi Izzeddin. 'The Mosque of the Prophet at Madīnah throughout the First-Century A.H. with Special Emphasis on the Umayyad Mosque'. PhD., University of Michigan, 1979.

Bitton-Ashkelony, Brouria. *Encountering the Sacred: The Debate on Christian Pilgrimage in Late Antiquity*. Berkeley: University of California Press, 2005.

Blecher, Joel. *Said the Prophet of God: Hadith Commentary across the Millennium*. Oakland: University of California Press, 2018.

Boekhoff-van der Voort, Nicolet. 'Untangling the "Unwritten Documents" of the Prophet Muḥammad. An *Isnād-cum-Matn* Analysis of Interwoven Traditions'. *Religions* 12.8 (2021): https://doi.org/10.3390/rel12080579 (last accessed 7 June 2023).

Boustan, Ra'anan. 'Jewish Veneration of the "Special Dead" in Late Antiquity and Beyond'. In Hahn and Klein, *Saints and Sacred Matter*, 61–81.

Boustan, Ra'anan. 'The Spoils of the Jerusalem Temple at Rome and Constantinople: Jewish Counter-Geography in a Christianizing Empire'. In *Antiquity in Antiquity: Jewish and Christian Pasts in the Greco-Roman World*, edited by Gregg Gardner and Kevin L. Osterloh, 327–72. Tübingen: Mohr Siebeck, 2008.

Bowker, J. W. 'Intercession in the Qur'an and the Jewish Tradition'. *Journal of Semitic Studies* 11 (1966): 69–82.

Bowman, Bradley. 'Refuge in the Bosoms of the Mountains: A Ninth-Century Muslim Appraisal of Monastic Piety'. *Islam and Christian-Muslim Relations* 30.4 (2019): 459–82.

Boyarin, Daniel. *Border Lines: The Partition of Judaeo-Christianity*. Philadelphia: University of Pennsylvania Press, 2004.

Boyarin, Daniel. *Sparks of the Logos: Essays in Rabbinic Hermeneutics*. Leiden: Brill, 2003.

Bräunlein, Peter J. 'Thinking Religion Through Things: Reflections on the Material Turn in the Scientific Study of Religion\s'. *Method and Theory in the Study of Religion* 28 (2016): 365–99.

Brock, Sebastian. 'The *Lives of the Prophets* in Syriac: Some Soundings'. In *Biblical Traditions in Transmission: Essays in Honour Michael A. Knibb*, edited by Charlotte Hempel and Judith M. Lieu, 21–37. Leiden: Brill, 2006.

Brockopp, Jonathan E. (ed.). *The Cambridge Companion to Muḥammad*. New York: Cambridge University Press, 2010.

Brockopp, Jonathan E. *Muhammad's Heirs: The Rise of Muslim Scholarly Communities, 622–950*. Cambridge: Cambridge University Press, 2017.

Brown, Jonathan. *The Canonization of al-Bukhārī and Muslim: The Formation and Function of the Sunnī Ḥadīth Canon*. Leiden: Brill, 2007.

Brown, Peter. *The Cult of the Saints: Its Rise and Function in Latin Christianity*. Chicago: University of Chicago Press, 1981.

Brown, Peter. 'The Rise and Function of the Holy Man in Late Antiquity'. *Journal of Roman Studies* 61 (1971): 80–101.

Bsheer, Rosie. *Archive Wars: The Politics of History in Saudi Arabia*. Stanford: Stanford University Press, 2020.

Burge, Stephen R. 'Reading between the Lines: The Compilation of *Ḥadīṯ* and the Authorial Voice'. *Arabica* 58 (2011): 168–97.

Bursi, Adam. 'Fluid Boundaries: Christian Sacred Space and Islamic Relics in an Early *Ḥadīth*'. *Medieval Encounters* 27.6 (2021): 478–510.

Bursi, Adam. 'A Hair's Breadth: The Prophet Muhammad's Hair as Relic in Early Islamic Texts'. In *Religious Competition in the Greco-Roman World*, edited by Nathaniel P. DesRosiers and Lily C. Vuong, 219–31. Atlanta: SBL Press, 2016.

Bursi, Adam. 'A Holy Heretical Body: Ṭalḥa b. 'Ubayd Allāh's Corpse and Early Islamic Sectarianism'. *Studies in Late Antiquity* 2.2 (2018): 147–79.

Bursi, Adam. 'Scents of Space: Early Islamic Pilgrimage, Perfume, and Paradise'. *Arabica* 67 (2020): 200–34.

Bursi, Adam. '"You Were Not Commanded to Stroke It, But to Pray Nearby It": Debating Touch within Early Islamic Pilgrimage'. *Senses and Society* 17.1 (2022): 8–21.

Busse, Heribert. 'Jerusalem in the Story of Muhammad's Night Journey and Ascension'. *JSAI* 14 (1991): 1–40.

Busse, Heribert. 'Die Kanzel des Propheten im Paradiesesgarten'. *Die Welt des Islams* 28 (1988): 99–111.

Bynum, Caroline Walker. *Christian Materiality: An Essay on Religion in Late Medieval Europe*. New York: Zone Books, 2011.

Bynum, Caroline Walker. 'Footprints: The Xenophilia of a European Medievalist'. *Common Knowledge* 24.2 (2018): 291–311.

Calder, Norman. '*Ḥinth*, *Birr*, *Tabarrur*, *Taḥannuth*: An Inquiry into the Arabic Vocabulary of Vows'. *BSOAS* 51.2 (1988): 214–39.

Cameron, Averil and Lawrence I. Conrad (eds). *The Byzantine and Early Islamic Near East. I. Problems in the Literary Source Material*. Princeton: Darwin Press, 1992.

Caseau, Béatrice. 'Sacred Landscapes'. In *Late Antiquity: A Guide to the Postclassical World*, edited by G. W. Bowersock, Peter Brown and Oleg Grabar, 21–59. Cambridge, MA: Belknap Press of Harvard University Press, 1999.

Charlesworth, James H. (ed.). *The Old Testament Pseudepigrapha*. 2 vols. Garden City, NY: Doubleday, 1983–5.

Chekhab-Abudaya, Mounia, Amélie Couvrat Desvergnes and David J. Roxburgh. 'Sayyid Yusuf's 1433 Pilgrimage Scroll (*Ziyārātnāma*) in the Collection of the Museum of Islamic Art, Doha'. *Muqarnas* 33 (2016): 345–407.

Chrysostomides, Anna. '"There Is No Harm in It": Muslim Participation in Levantine Christian Religious Festivals (750–1000)'. *Al-Masāq* 33.2 (2021): 117–38.

Clark, Elizabeth A. *History, Theory, Text: Historians and the Linguistic Turn*. Cambridge, MA: Harvard University Press, 2004.

Clark, Gillian. 'Victricius of Rouen: Praising the Saints'. *JECS* 7.3 (1999): 365–99.

Cobb, Paul M. 'Virtual Sacrality: Making Muslim Syria Sacred Before the Crusades'. Medieval Encounters 8.1 (2002): 35–55.

Cohen, Mark R. 'What Was the Pact of 'Umar? A Literary-Historical Study'. *JSAI* 23 (1999): 100–57.

Collet, Eva. 'Dābiq et la frontière du Dār al-Islām: Histoire et représentations (Ier–Ve siècles H./VIIe–XIe siècles)'. *RMMM* 144 (2018): 237–68.

Collinet, Annabelle, Sepideh Parsapajouh and Michel Boivin. 'Bodies & Artefacts. Relics and Other Devotional Supports in Shi'a Societies in the Indic and Iranian World: An Introduction'. *Journal of Material Cultures in the Muslim World* 1 (2020): 191–8.

Conrad, Lawrence I. 'The Conquest of Arwād: A Source-Critical Study in the Historiography of the Early Medieval Near East'. In Cameron and Conrad, *Byzantine and Early Islamic Near East*, 317–401.

Constas, Nicholas. 'An Apology for the Cult of the Saints in Late Antiquity: Eustratius Presbyter of Constantinople, *On the State of Souls after Death* (CPG 7522)'. *JECS* 10 (2002): 267–85.

Constas, Nicholas. *Proclus of Constantinople and the Cult of the Virgin in Late Antiquity: Homilies 1–5, Texts and Translations*. Leiden: Brill, 2003.

Constas, Nicholas. '"To Sleep, Perchance to Dream": The Middle State of Souls in Patristic and Byzantine Literature'. *DOP* 55 (2001): 91–124.

Cook, David. 'The *Aṣḥāb al-Ukhdūd*: History and *Ḥadīth* in a Martyrological Narrative'. *JSAI* 34 (2008): 125–48.

Cook, David. *'The Book of Tribulations': The Syrian Muslim Apocalyptic Tradition. An Annotated Translation*. Edinburgh: Edinburgh University Press, 2019.

Cook, David. *Studies in Muslim Apocalyptic*. Princeton: Darwin Press, 2002.

Costa, José. 'The Body of God in Ancient Rabbinic Judaism: Problems of Interpretation'. *Revue de l'histoire des religions* 227.3 (2010): 283–316.

Crone, Patricia. 'The *Book of Watchers* in the Qur'ān'. In *The Qur'ānic Pagans and Related Matters: Collected Studies in Three Volumes*, edited by Hanna Siurua, 1:183–218. 3 vols. Leiden: Brill, 2016.

Crone, Patricia. *God's Rule: Government and Islam*. New York: Columbia University Press, 2004.

Crone, Patricia. *Slaves on Horses: The Evolution of the Islamic Polity*. Cambridge: Cambridge University Press, 1980.

Cronnier, Estelle. *Les inventions de reliques dans l'Empire romain d'Orient (IVe–VIe s.)*. Turnhout: Brepols, 2015.

Crow, Douglas Karim. 'The Death of al-Ḥusayn b. 'Alī and Early Shī'ī Views of the Imamate'. In *Shī'ism: Origins and Early Development*, edited by Etan Kohlberg, 41–86. Aldershot: Ashgate Variorum, 2003.

Daftary, Farhad and Gurdofarid Miskinzoda (eds). *The Study of Shi'i Islam: History, Theology and Law*. London: I. B. Tauris in association with the Institute for Ismaili Studies, 2014.

Dal Santo, Matthew. *Debating the Saints' Cult in the Age of Gregory the Great*. Oxford: Oxford University Press, 2012.

de Aldama, J. A. *Repertorium Pseudochrysostomicum*. Paris: Éditions du Centre national de la recherche scientifique, 1965.

Diamond, Eliezer. 'Lions, Snakes and Asses: Palestinian Jewish Holy Men as Masters of the Animal Kingdom'. In Kalmin and Schwartz, *Jewish Culture and Society under the Christian Roman Empire*, 251–83.

Dickinson, Eerik. 'Ibn al-Ṣalāḥ al-Shahrazūrī and the Isnād'. *JAOS* 122.3 (2002): 481–505.

Diem, Werner. *The Living and the Dead in Islam: Studies in Arabic Epitaphs. I: Epitaphs as Texts*. Wiesbaden: Harrassowitz, 2004.

Dilley, Paul C. 'Christian Icon Practice in Apocryphal Literature: Consecration and the Conversion of Synagogues into Churches'. *Journal of Roman Archaeology* 23 (2010): 285–302.

Dilley, Paul C. 'The Invention of Christian Tradition: "Apocrypha", Imperial Policy, and Anti-Jewish Propaganda'. *Greek, Roman, and Byzantine Studies* 50 (2010): 586–615.

DiTommaso, Lorenzo. *The Book of Daniel and the Apocryphal Daniel Literature*. Brill: Leiden, 2005.

Drijvers, H. J. W. 'The Gospel of the Twelve Apostles: A Syriac Apocalypse from the Early Islamic Period'. In Cameron and Conrad, *Byzantine and Early Islamic Near East*, 189–213.

Duri, A. A. *The Rise of Historical Writing Among the Arabs*. Translated and edited by Lawrence I. Conrad. Princeton: Princeton University Press, 1983.

Ebstein, Michael. 'The Organs of God: *Ḥadīth al-Nawāfil* in Classical Islamic Mysticism'. *JAOS* 138.2 (2018): 271–89.

Ehinger, Jessica Lee. 'Revolutionizing the Status Quo: Appeals to Pre-Islamic Christianity in the Writings of Anastasius of Sinai'. *Studies in Late Antiquity* 3 (2019): 17–35.

Ehrlich, Uri. 'The Ancestors' Prayers for the Salvation of Israel in Early Rabbinic Thought'. In *Jewish and Christian Liturgy and Worship: New Insights into History and Interaction*, edited by Albert Gerhards and Clemens Leonhard, 249–56. Leiden: Brill, 2007.

Eilberg-Schwartz, Howard (ed.). *People of the Body: Jews and Judaism from an Embodied Perspective*. Albany: State University of New York Press, 1992.

Elad, Amikam. *Medieval Jerusalem and Islamic Worship: Holy Places, Ceremonies, Pilgrimage*. Leiden: Brill, 1995.

Elad, Amikam. *The Rebellion of Muḥammad al-Nafs al-Zakiyya in 145/762: Ṭālibīs and Early ʿAbbāsīs in Conflict*. Leiden: Brill, 2016.

Elad, Amikam [as El'ad, Amikam]. 'Some Aspects of the Islamic Traditions Regarding the Site of the Grave of Moses'. *JSAI* 11 (1988): 1–15.

Elad, Amikam. 'Why Did ʿAbd al-Malik Build the Dome of the Rock? A Re-Examination of the Muslim Sources'. In Raby and Johns, *Bayt al-Maqdis*, 33–58.

El Cheikh, Nadia Maria. *Byzantium Viewed by the Arabs*. Cambridge, MA: Harvard University Press, 2004.

El-Hibri, Tayeb. 'The Abbasids and the Relics of the Prophet'. *Journal of Abbasid Studies* 4 (2017): 62–96.

El-Hibri, Tayeb. *Parable and Politics in Early Islamic History: The Rashidun Caliphs*. New York: Columbia University Press, 2010.

El-Hibri, Tayeb. ''Umar b. al-Khaṭṭāb and the Abbasids'. *JAOS* 136.4 (2016): 763–83.

Elliott, Alison Goddard. *Roads to Paradise: Reading the Lives of the Early Saints*. Hanover: University Press of New England, 1987.

El Shamsy, Ahmed. 'The Curious Case of Early Muslim Hair Dyeing'. In *Islam at 250: Studies in Memory of G. H. A. Juynboll*, edited by Petra M. Sijpesteijn and Camilla Adang, 187–206. Leiden: Brill, 2020.

Encyclopaedia of Islam. 2nd ed. Edited by P. J. Bearman, T. Bianquis, C. E. Bosworth, E. van Donzel, W. P. Heinrichs et al. Leiden: Brill, 1954–2009.

Encyclopaedia of Islam. 3nd ed. Edited by Gudrun Krämer, Denis Matringe, John Nawas and Everett Rowson. Leiden: Brill, 2007–.

Encyclopaedia of the Qur'ān. Edited by Jane Dammen McAuliffe. 6 vols. Leiden: Brill, 2001–6.

Fahd, Toufic. *La divination Arabe. Études religieuses, sociologiques et folkloriques sur la milieu natif de l'Islam*. Leiden: Brill, 1966.

al-Faʿr, Muḥammad Fahd ʿAbd Allāh. *Taṭawwur al-kitābāt wa-l-nuqūsh fī-l-Ḥijāz mundhu fajr al-Islām ḥattā muntaṣaf al-qarn al-sābiʿ al-Hijrī*. Jedda: King Faisal Center for Research and Islamic Studies, 1405/1984.

Fierro, Maribel. 'Holy Places in Umayyad al-Andalus'. *BSOAS* 78 (2015): 121–33.

Fierro, Maribel. 'Plants, Mary the Copt, Abraham, Donkeys and Knowledge: Again on Bāṭinism During the Umayyad Caliphate in al-Andalus'. In *Difference and Dynamism in Islam. Festschrift for Heinz Halm on his 70th Birthday*, edited by Hinrich Biesterfeldt and Verena Klemm, 125–44. Würzberg: Ergon, 2012.

Fierro, Maribel. 'The Treatises against Innovations (*kutub al-bidaʿ*)'. *Der Islam* 69 (1992): 204–46.

Finster, Barbara. 'Die Mosaiken der Umayyadenmoschee von Damaskus'. *Kunst des Orients* 7 (1970–1): 83–141.

Firestone, Reuven. 'The Problematic of Prophecy: 2015 IQSA Presidential Address'. *JIQSA* 1 (2016): 11–22.

Flood, Finbarr Barry. 'Bodies and Becoming: Mimesis, Mediation, and the Ingestion of the Sacred in Christianity and Islam'. In *Sensational Religion: Sensory Cultures in Material Practice*, edited by Sally M. Promey, 459–93. New Haven: Yale University Press, 2014.

Flood, Finbarr Barry. 'Light in Stone: The Commemoration of the Prophet in Umayyad Architecture'. In Johns, *Bayt al-Maqdis*, 311–59.

Flood, Finbarr Barry. *Technologies de dévotion dans les arts de l'Islam*. Paris: Hazan, 2019.

Flusin, Bernard. 'Construire une nouvelle Jérusalem: Constantinople et les reliques'. In *L'Orient dans l'histoire religieuse de l'Europe: L'invention des origines*, edited by Mohammad Ali Amir-Moezzi and John Scheid, 51–70. Turnhout: Brepols, 2000.

Flusin, Bernard. 'Démons et Sarrasins: l'auteur et le propos des *Diègèmata stèriktika* d'Anastase le Sinaïte'. *Travaux et Mémoires* 11 (1991): 381–409.

Fowden, Elizabeth Key. *The Barbarian Plain: Saint Sergius between Rome and Iran*. Berkeley: University of California Press, 1999.

Fowden, Elizabeth Key. 'Sharing Holy Places'. *Common Knowledge* 8.1 (2002): 124–46.

Fowden, Elizabeth Key. 'Shrines and Banners: Paleo-Muslims and their Material Inheritance'. In *Encompassing the Sacred in Islamic Art*, edited by Lorenz Korn and Çiğdem İvren, 5–23. Wiesbaden: Reichert Verlag, 2020.

Francesca, Ersilia. 'The Formation and Early Development of the Ibāḍī Madhhab'. *JSAI* 28 (2003): 260–77.

Frank, Georgia. *The Memory of the Eyes: Pilgrims to Living Saints in Christian Late Antiquity*. Berkeley: University of California Press, 2000.

Friedman, Yaron. '"Kūfa is Better": The Sanctity of Kūfa in Early Islam and Shīʿism in Particular'. *Le Muséon* 126.1–2 (2013): 203–37.

Gaiser, Adam. '*Ballaghanā ʿan an-Nabī*: Early Basran and Omani Ibāḍī Understandings of *Sunna* and *Siyar*, *Āthār* and *Nasab*'. *BSOAS* 83.3 (2020): 437–48.

Gaiser, Adam. 'A Narrative Identity Approach to Islamic Sectarianism'. In *Sectarianization: Mapping the New Politics of the Middle East*, edited by Nader Hashemi and Danny Postel, 61–75. New York: Oxford University Press, 2017.

Gaiser, Adam. *Shurāt Legends, Ibāḍī Identities: Martyrdom, Asceticism, and the Making of an Early Islamic Community*. Columbia: University of South Carolina Press, 2016.

Geary, Patrick. *Furta Sacra: Thefts of Relics in the Central Middle Ages*. Revised ed. Princeton: Princeton University Press, 1990.

Geary, Patrick. 'Sacred Commodities: The Circulation of Medieval Relics'. In *The Social Life of Things: Commodities in Cultural Perspective*, edited by Arjan Appadurai, 169–91. Cambridge: Cambridge University Press, 1986.

Gero, Stephen. *Byzantine Iconoclasm during the Reign of Leo III, with Particular Attention to the Oriental Sources*. CSCO 346, Subsidia 41. Louvain: Secrétariat du CorpusSCO, 1973.

al-Ghabbān, Maysāʾ bint ʿAlī Ibrāhīm. 'al-Kitābāt al-Islāmiyya al-mubakkira fī haḍbat Ḥismā bi-minṭaqat Tabūk: dirāsa taḥlīliyya āthāriyya wa-lughawiyya'. PhD diss., King Saud University, 2016–17.

Gil, Moshe. 'The Origin of the Jews of Yathrib', *JSAI* 4 (1984): 203–24.

Ginzberg, Louis. *The Legends of the Jews*. Translated by Henrietta Szold et al. 7 vols. Philadelphia: Jewish Publication Society of America, 1909–38.

Goldziher, Ignaz. *Muslim Studies*. Edited and translated by S. M. Stern and C. R. Barber. 2 vols. London: 1967–71.

Goudarzi, Mohsen. 'The Ascent of Ishmael: Genealogy, Covenant, and Identity in Early Islam'. *Arabica* 66 (2019): 415–84.

Grabar, Oleg. 'The Earliest Islamic Commemorative Structures, Notes and Documents'. *Ars Orientalis* 6 (1966): 7–46.

Grehan, James. *Twilight of the Saints: Everyday Religion in Ottoman Syria and Palestine*. Oxford: Oxford University Press, 2014.

Gribetz, Sarit Kattan. '*Zekhut Imahot*: Mothers, Fathers, and Ancestral Merit in Rabbinic Sources'. *JSJ* 49 (2018): 268–96.

Griffith, Sidney H. 'Crosses, Icons and the Image of Christ in Edessa: The Place of Iconophobia in the Christian-Muslim Controversies of Early Islamic Times'. In *Transformations of Late Antiquity: Essays for Peter Brown*, edited by Philip Rousseau and Manolis Papoutsakis, 63–84. Burlington: Aldershot, 2009.

Gril, Denis. 'Le corps du Prophète'. *RMMM* 113–14 (2006): 37–57.

Gril, Denis, Stefan Reichmuth and Dilek Sarmis (eds). *The Presence of the Prophet in Early Modern and Contemporary Islam. Volume 1. The Prophet Between Doctrine, Literature and Arts: Historical Legacies and Their Unfolding*. Leiden: Brill, 2022

Gruber, Christine. *The Praiseworthy One: The Prophet Muhammad in Islamic Texts and Images*. Bloomington: Indiana University Press, 2019.

Gruendler, Beatrice. *The Rise of the Arabic Book*. Cambridge, MA: Harvard University Press, 2020.

Grypeou, Emmanouela and Helen Spurling. *The Book of Genesis in Late Antiquity: Encounters between Jewish and Christian Exegesis*. Brill: Leiden, 2013.

Guidetti, Mattia. *In the Shadow of the Church: The Building of Mosques in Early Medieval Syria*. Leiden: Brill, 2017.

Günther, Sebastian and Todd Lawson (eds). *Roads to Paradise: Eschatology and Concepts of the Hereafter in Islam*. 2 vols. Leiden: Brill, 2017.

Hahn, Cynthia. *The Reliquary Effect: Enshrining the Sacred Object*. London: Reaktion, 2017.

Hahn, Cynthia and Holger A. Klein (eds). *Saints and Sacred Matter: The Cult of Relics in Byzantium and Beyond*. Washington, DC: Dumbarton Oaks Research Library and Collection, 2015.

Haider, Najam. 'Geography of the *Isnād*: Possibilities for the Reconstruction of Local Ritual Practice in the 2nd/8th Century'. *Der Islam* 90.2 (2013): 306–46.

Haider, Najam. 'A Kūfan Jurist in Yemen: Contextualizing Muḥammad b. Sulaymān al-Kūfī's *Kitāb al-Muntaḥab*'. *Arabica* 59 (2012): 200–17.

Haider, Najam. *The Origins of the Shī'a: Identity, Ritual, and Sacred Space in Eighth-Century Kūfa*. New York: Cambridge University Press, 2011.

Haider, Najam. *The Rebel and the Imām in Early Islam: Explorations in Muslim Historiography*. Cambridge: Cambridge University Press, 2019.

Halevi, Leor. *Muhammad's Grave: Death Rites and the Making of Islamic Society* (New York: Columbia University Press, 2007.

Hall, Isaac H. 'The Lives of the Prophets'. *Journal of the Society of Biblical Literature and Exegesis* 7.1 (1887): 28–40.

Hamza, Feras. 'Temporary Hellfire Punishment and the Making of Sunni Orthodoxy'. In Günther and Lawson, *Roads to Paradise*, 1:371–406.

Hamza, Feras. 'To Hell and Back: A Study of the Concepts of Hell and Intercession in Early Islam'. PhD diss., Oxford University, 2002.

Hanaoka, Mimi. *Authority and Identity in Medieval Islamic Historiography: Persian Histories from the Peripheries*. Cambridge: Cambridge University Press, 2016.

al-Ḥārithī, Nāṣr ibn ʿAlī. *al-Āthār al-Islāmiyya fī Makka al-mukarrama*. Riyadh: Dār al-Hilāl, 1430/2009.

Harvey, Susan Ashbrook. *Scenting Salvation: Ancient Christianity and the Olfactory Imagination*. Berkeley: University of California Press, 2006.

Hasson, Izhak. 'The Muslim View of Jerusalem: The Qur'ān and Ḥadīth'. In *The History of Jerusalem: The Early Muslim Period, 638–1099*, edited by Joshua Prawer and Haggai Ben-Shammai, 349–85. Jerusalem: Yad Izhak Ben-Zvi, 1996.

Hawting, Gerald. 'The Case of Jaʿd b. Dirham and the Punishment of "Heretics" in the Early Caliphate'. In *Public Violence in Islamic Societies: Power, Discipline, and the Construction of the Public Sphere, 7th–19th Centuries* CE, edited by Christian Lange and Maribel Fierro, 27–41. Edinburgh: Edinburgh University Press, 2009.

Hawting, Gerald. *The First Dynasty of Islam: The Umayyad Caliphate* AD *661–750*. 2nd ed. London: Routledge, 2000.

Hawting, Gerald. 'The Ḥajj in the Second Civil War'. In *Golden Roads: Migration, Pilgrimage and Travel in Mediaeval and Modern Islam*, edited by Ian Richard Netton, 31–42. Richmond: Curzon Press, 1993.

Hawting, Gerald. *The Idea of Idolatry and the Emergence of Islam: From Polemic to History*. Cambridge: Cambridge University Press, 1999.

Hawting, Gerald. 'The Origins of the Muslim Sanctuary at Mecca'. In Juynboll, *Studies on the First Century of Islamic Society*, 23–47.

Hawting, Gerald. '"A Plaything for Kings": ʿĀ'isha's *Ḥadīth*, Ibn al-Zubayr, and the Rebuilding of the Kaʿba'. In *Islamic Studies Today: Essays in Honor of Andrew Rippin*, edited by Majid Daneshgar and Walid A. Saleh, 3–21. Leiden: Brill, 2016.

Hawting, Gerald. 'The Umayyads and the Ḥijāz'. *Proceedings of the Seminar for Arabian Studies* 2 (1972): 39–46.

Hawting, Gerald. '"We Were Not Ordered with Entering It but Only with Circumambulating It." *Ḥadīth* and *Fiqh* on Entering the Kaʿba'. *BSOAS* 47 (1984): 228–42.

Hawting, Gerald. 'Were There Prophets in the Jahiliyya?' In *Islam and Its Past: Jahiliyya, Late Antiquity, and the Qur'an*, edited by Carol Bakhos and Michael Cook, 186–212. Oxford: Oxford University Press, 2017.

Hayes, Edmund. 'The Institutions of the Shīʿī Imāmate: Towards a Social History of Early Imāmī Shiʿism'. *Al-Masāq* 33.2 (2021): 188–204.

Hazard, Sonia. 'The Material Turn in the Study of Religion'. *Religion and Society: Advances in Research* 4 (2013): 58–78.

Hazard, Sonia. 'Thing'. *Early American Studies* 16.4 (2018): 792–800.

Heinzelmann, Martin. *Translationsberichte und andere Quellen des Reliquienkultes*. Turnhout: Brepols, 1979.

Hidayatullah, Aysha. 'Māriyya the Copt: Gender, Sex and Heritage in the Legacy of Muhammad's *Umm Walad*'. *Islam and Christian-Muslim Relations* 21.3 (2010): 221–43.

Hillenbrand, Robert. *Islamic Architecture: Form, Function and Meaning*. New York: Columbia University Press, 1994.

Holtzman, Livnat. *Anthropomorphism in Islam: The Challenge of Traditionalism (700–1350)*. Edinburgh: Edinburgh University Press, 2018.

Horovitz, Josef. *The Earliest Biographies of the Prophet and their Authors*. Edited by Lawrence I. Conrad. Princeton: Darwin Press, 2002.

Hoyland, Robert. 'Early Islam as a Late Antique Religion'. In Johnson, *Oxford Handbook of Late Antiquity*, 1,053–77.

Hoyland, Robert. 'Physiognomy in Islam'. *JSAI* 30 (2005): 361–402.

Hoyland, Robert. *Seeing Islam as Others Saw It: A Survey and Evaluation of Christian, Jewish, and Zoroastrian Writings on Early Islam*. Princeton: Darwin Press, 1997.

Hughes, Aaron W. *An Anxious Inheritance: Religious Others and the Shaping of Sunnī Orthodoxy*. New York: Oxford University Press, 2022.

Hunter, David G. 'Vigilantius of Calagurris and Victricius of Rouen: Ascetics, Relics, and Clerics in Late Roman Gaul'. *JECS* 7.3 (1999) 401–30.

Inglis, Erik. 'Inventing Apostolic Impression Relics in Medieval Rome'. *Speculum* 96 (2021): 309–66.

Jacobs, Andrew S. 'The Remains of the Jew: Imperial Christian Identity in the Late Ancient Holy Land'. *Journal of Medieval and Early Modern Studies* 33.1 (2003): 23–45.

Jacobs, Andrew S. *Remains of the Jews: The Holy Land and Christian Empire in Late Antiquity*. Stanford: Stanford University Press, 2004.

James, Liz. 'Bearing Gifts from the East: Imperial Relic Hunters Abroad'. In *Eastern Approaches to Byzantium*, ed. Antony Eastmond, 119–31. London: Routledge, 2001.

Jamil, Nadia. 'Caliph and Quṭb: Poetry as a Sources for Interpreting the Transformation of the Byzantine Cross on Steps on Umayyad Coinage'. In Johns, *Bayt al-Maqdis*, 11–57.

Jarrar, Maher. 'Ibn Abī Yaḥyā: A Controversial Medinan *Akhbārī* of the 2nd/8th Century'. In *The Transmission and Dynamics of the Textual Sources of Islam: Essays in Honour of Harald Motzki*, edited by Nicolet Boekhoff-van der Voort, Kees Versteegh and Joas Wagemakers, 197–227. Leiden: Brill, 2011.

Jarrar, Maher. *Die Prophetenbiographie im islamischen Spanien: Ein Beitrag zur Überlieferungs- und Redaktionsgeschichte*. Frankfurt: Peter Lang, 1989.

Johns, Jeremy (ed.). *Bayt al-Maqdis: Jerusalem and Early Islam*. Oxford: Oxford University Press, 1999.

Johnson, Scott Fitzgerald (ed.). *The Oxford Handbook of Late Antiquity*. Oxford: Oxford University Press, 2012.

Jokisch, Benjamin. *Islamic Imperial Law: Harun-al-Rashid's Codification Project*. Berlin: Walter de Gruyter, 2007.

Judd, Steven. *ʿAbd al-Rahman b. ʿAmr al-Awzaʿi*. London: Oneworld, 2019.

Judd, Steven. 'Muslim Persecution of Heretics during the Marwānid Period (64–132/684–750)'. *Al-Masāq* 23 (2011): 1–14.

Judd, Steven. *Religious Scholars and the Umayyads: Piety-Minded Supporters of the Marwānid Caliphate*. New York: Routledge, 2014.

Jullien, Christelle and Florence Jullien. 'Du *ḥnana* ou la bénédiction contestée'. In *Sur les pas des Araméens chrétiens: Mélanges offerts à Alain Desreumaux*, edited by Françoise Briquel Chatonnet and Muriel Debié, 333–49. Paris: Geuthner, 2010.

Juynboll, G. H. A. 'Dyeing the Hair and Beard in Early Islam: A Ḥadīth-Analytical Study'. *Arabica* 33.1 (1986): 49–75.

Juynboll, G. H. A. *Encyclopedia of Canonical Ḥadīth*. Leiden: Brill, 2007.

Juynboll, G. H. A. *Muslim Tradition: Studies in Chronology, Provenance and Authorship of Early* Ḥadīth. Cambridge: Cambridge University Press, 1983.

Juynboll, G. H. A. 'The Role of the *Muʿammarūn* in the Early Development of the *Isnād*'. *Wiener Zeitschrift für die Kunde des Morgenlandes* 81 (1991): 155–75.

Juynboll, G. H. A. (ed.). *Studies on the First Century of Islamic Society*. Carbondale and Edwardsville: Southern Illinois University Press, 1982.

Kaegi, Walter Emil Jr. 'Initial Byzantine Reactions to the Arab Conquest'. *Church History* 38.2 (1969): 139–49.

Kalmin, Richard. 'Holy Men, Rabbis, and Demonic Sages in Late Antiquity'. In Kalmin and Schwartz, *Jewish Culture and Society under the Christian Roman Empire*, 213–49.

Kalmin, Richard and Seth Schwartz (eds). *Jewish Culture and Society under the Christian Roman Empire*. Leuven: Peeters, 2003.

Kanarek, Jane L. 'Pilgrimage and Piety: Rabbinic Women and Vows of Valuation: Mishnah *ʿArakhin* 5:1, Tosefta *ʿArakhin* 3:1, BT *ʿArakhin* 19a'. *Nashim* 28 (2015): 61–74.

Kara, Seyfeddin. *In Search of ʿAlī Ibn Abī Ṭālib's Codex: History and Traditions on the Earliest Copy of the Qurʾān*. Berlin: Gerlach, 2018.

Karamustafa, Ahmet T. 'Shiʾis, Sufis, and Popular Saints'. In *The Wiley Blackwell History of Islam*, edited by Armando Salvatore et al., 159–75. Oxford: Wiley Blackwell, 2018.

Katz, Marion Holmes. *Body of Text: The Emergence of the Sunnī Law of Ritual Purity*. Albany: State University of New York Press, 2002.

Katz, Marion Holmes. 'The Prophet Muḥammad in Ritual'. In Brockopp, *Cambridge Companion to Muḥammad*, 139–57.

Keim, Katharina E. *Pirqei deRabbi Eliezer: Structure, Coherence, Intertextuality*. Leiden: Brill, 2017.

Kessler, Christel. '"Abd al-Malik's Inscription in the Dome of the Rock: A Reconsideration'. *JRAS* (1970): 2–14.

Khalek, Nancy. *Damascus after the Muslim Conquest: Text and Image in Early Islam*. New York: Oxford University Press, 2011.

Khalek, Nancy. 'Dreams of Hagia Sophia: The Muslim Siege of Constantinople in 674 CE, Abū Ayyūb al-Anṣārī, and the Medieval Islamic Imagination'. In *The Islamic Scholarly Tradition: Studies in History, Law, and Thought in Honor of Professor Michael Allan Cook*, edited by Asad Q. Ahmed, Behnam Sadeghi and Michael Bonner, 131–46. Leiden: Brill, 2011.

Khalek, Nancy. '"He Was Tall and Slender, and His Virtues Were Numerous": Byzantine Hagiographical Topoi and the Companions of Muḥammad in al-Azdī's *Futūḥ al-Shām*'. In Papaconstantinou, *Writing 'True Stories': Historians and Hagiographers in the Late Antique and Medieval Near East*, 105–23.

Khalek, Nancy. 'Medieval Muslim Martyrs to the Plague: Venerating the Companions of Muhammad in the Jordan Valley'. In Hahn and Klein, *Saints and Sacred Matter*, 83–97.

Khoury, R. G. 'Quelques remarques suppleméntaires concernant la papyrus de Wahb b. Munabbih'. *BSOAS* 40.1 (1977): 15–24.

Kister, M. J. '"Do Not Assimilate Yourselves . . ." *Lā tashabbuhū . . .*' *JSAI* 12 (1989): 321–71.

Kister, M. J. 'Maqām Ibrāhīm: A Stone with an Inscription'. *Le Muséon* 84 (1971): 477–91.

Kister, M. J. 'On "Concessions" and Conduct: A Study in Early *Ḥadīth*'. In Juynboll, *Studies on the First Century of Islamic Society*, 89–107.

Kister, M. J. 'On the Papyrus of Wahb b. Munabbih'. *BSOAS* 37.3 (1974): 545–71.

Kister, M. J. 'On the Papyrus of Wahb b. Munabbih: An Addendum'. *BSOAS* 40.1 (1977): 125–7.

Kister, M. J. 'Sanctity Joint and Divided: On Holy Places in the Islamic Tradition'. *JSAI* 20 (1996): 18–65.

Kister, M. J. 'You Shall Only Set Out for Three Mosques: A Study of an Early Tradition'. *Le Muséon* 82 (1969): 173–96.

King, Anya H. *Scent from the Garden: Musk and the Medieval Islamic World*. Leiden: Brill, 2017.

Kinnard, Jacob N. *Places in Motion: The Fluid Identities of Temples, Images, and Pilgrims*. Oxford: Oxford University Press, 2014.

Klasova, Pamela. 'Ḥadīth as Common Discourse: Reflections on the Intersectarian Dissemination of the Creation of the Intellect Tradition'. *Al-ʿUṣūr al-Wusṭā* 28 (2020): 297–345.

Klein, Holger A. 'Sacred Relics and Imperial Ceremonies at the Great Palace of Constantinople'. In *Visualisierungen von Herrschaft: Frühmittelalterliche Residenzen – Gestalt und Zeremoniell*, edited by Franz Alto Bauer, 79–99. Istanbul: Ege Yayınları, 2006.

Knight, Michael Muhammad. *Muhammad's Body: Baraka Networks and the Prophetic Assemblage*. Chapel Hill: University of North Carolina Press, 2020.

Kohlberg, Etan. 'Al-Uṣūl Al-Arbaʿumiʾa'. *JSAI* 10 (1987): 128–66.

Kohlberg, Etan. *A Medieval Muslim Scholar at Work: Ibn Ṭāwūs and His Library*. Leiden: Brill, 1992.

Kohlberg, Etan. 'Medieval Muslim Views on Martyrdom'. *Mededelingen van de Afdeling Letterkunde* 60 (1997): 281–307.

Koltun-Fromm, Naomi. 'Jerusalem Sacred Stones from Creation to Eschaton'. *Journal of Late Antiquity* 10.2 (2018): 405–31.

Korom, Frank J. 'The Presence of Absence: Using Stuff in a South Asian Sufi Movement'. *AAS Working Papers in Anthropology* 23 (2012): 1–19.

Krauss, Samuel. 'Jewish Giants in the Gentile Folklore'. *Jewish Quarterly Review* 38.2 (1947): 135–49.

Krueger, Derek. 'The Religion of Relics in Late Antiquity and Byzantium'. In *Treasures of Heaven: Saints, Relics, and Devotion in Medieval Europe*, edited by Martina Bagnoli, Holger A. Klein, C. Griffith Mann and James Robinson, 5–17. Baltimore: Walters Art Museum, 2010.

Lambton, Ann K. S. 'An Account of the *Tārīkhi Qumm*'. *BSOAS* 12 (1947–8): 586–96.

Lammens, Henri. 'L'avènement des Marwānides et le califat de Marwān Ier'. *Mélanges de l'Université Saint-Joseph* 12 (1927): 43–147.

Landau-Tasseron, Ella. 'Unearthing a Pre-Islamic Arabian Prophet'. *JSAI* 21 (1997): 42–61.

Lange, Christian. *Paradise and Hell in Islamic Traditions*. New York: Cambridge University Press, 2016.

Lapin, Hayim. 'Rabbis and Public Prayers for Rain in Later Roman Palestine'. In *Religion and Politics in the Ancient Near East*, edited by Adele Berlin, 105–29. Bethesda: University Press of Maryland, 1996.

Lazarus-Yafeh, Hava. *Intertwined Worlds: Medieval Islam and Bible Criticism*. Princeton: Princeton University Press, 1992.

Lecomte, Gérard. 'Les citations de l'Ancien et du Nouveau Testament dans l'œuvre d'Ibn Qutayba'. *Arabica* 5.1 (1958): 34–46.

Leisten, Thomas. 'Between Orthodoxy and Exegesis: Some Aspects of Attitudes in the Shari'a toward Funerary Architecture'. *Muqarnas* 7 (1990): 12–22.

Levinson, Joshua. 'There Is No Place Like Home: Rabbinic Responses to the Christianization of Palestine'. In *Jews, Christians, and the Roman Empire: The Poetics of Power in Late Antiquity*, edited by N. Dohrmann and Annette Yoshiko Reed, 99–120. Philadelphia: University of Pennsylvania Press, 2013.

Levy-Rubin, Milka. *Non-Muslims in the Early Islamic Empire: From Surrender to Coexistence*. Cambridge: Cambridge University Press, 2011.

Levy-Rubin, Milka. 'Why Was the Dome of the Rock Built? A New Perspective on a Long-Discussed Question'. *BSOAS* 80.3 (2017): 441–64.

Lewis, Agnes Smith. *Catalogue of the Syriac Manuscripts in the Convent of S. Catharine on Mount Sinai*. London: C. J. Clay & Sons, 1894.

Lewis, Bernard. 'An Apocalyptic Vision of Islamic History', *BSOAS* 13.2 (1950): 308–38.

Lindbeck, Kristen H. *Elijah and the Rabbis: Story and Theology*. New York: Columbia University Press, 2010.

Livne-Kafri, Ofer. 'Jerusalem in Early Islam: The Eschatological Aspect'. *Arabica* 53.3 (2006): 382–403.

Livne-Kafri, Ofer. 'The Muslim Traditions "In Praise of Jerusalem" (*Faḍāʾil al-Quds*): Diversity and Complexity'. *Università degli Studi di Napoli L'Orientale* 58 (1998): 165–92.

Lowry, Joseph E. 'The Prophet as Lawgiver and Legal Authority'. In Brockopp, *Cambridge Companion to Muḥammad*, 83–102.

Lucas, Scott C. *Constructive Critics,* Ḥadīth *Literature, and the Articulation of Sunnī Islam: The Legacy of the Generation of Ibn Saʿd, Ibn Maʿīn, and Ibn Ḥanbal*. Leiden: Brill, 2004.

McGregor, Richard J. A. *Islam and the Devotional Object: Seeing Religion in Egypt and Syria*. Cambridge: Cambridge University Press, 2020.

McGregor, Richard J. 'Repetition and Relics: Tracing the Lives of Muhammad's Sandals'. In Bigelow, *Islam Through Objects*, 49–64.

Maclean, Derryl N. *Religion and Society in Arab Sind*. Leiden: Brill, 1989.

McMillan, M. E. *The Meaning of Mecca: The Politics of Piety in Early Islam*. London: Saqi, 2011.

Madelung, Wilferd. *The Succession to Muhammad: A Study of the Early Caliphate*. New York: Cambridge University Press, 1997.

Maraval, Pierre. *Lieux saints et pèlerinages d'Orient: histoire et géographie des origines à la conquête arabe*. Paris: Cerf, 1985.

Margoliouth, David S. 'The Relics of the Prophet Mohammed'. *The Moslem World* 27 (1937): 20–7.

Markus, Robert A. 'How on Earth Could Places Become Holy?' *JECS* 2.3 (1994): 257–71.

Marsham, Andrew. 'Public Execution in the Umayyad Period: Early Islamic Punitive Practice and Its Late Antique Contexts'. *JAIS* 11 (2011): 101–36.

Martin, Dale B. and Patricia Cox Miller (eds). *The Cultural Turn in Late Antique Studies: Gender, Asceticism, and Historiography*. Durham, NC: Duke University Press, 2005.

Maury, Charlotte. 'Depictions of the Haramayn on Ottoman Tiles: Content and Context'. In *The Hajj: Collected Essays*, edited by Venetia Porter and Liana Saif, 143–59. London: British Museum, 2013.

Meier, Fritz. 'A Resurrection of Muḥammad in Suyūṭī'. In *Essays on Islamic Piety and Mysticism*, 505–47. Translated by John O'Kane with the editorial assistance of Bernd Radtke. Leiden: Brill, 1999.

Melchert, Christopher. 'Al-Shaybānī and Contemporary Renunciant Piety'. *Journal of Abbasid Studies* 6 (2019): 52–85.

Melchert, Christopher. *Before Sufism: Early Islamic Renunciant Piety*. Berlin: de Gruyter, 2020.

Melchert, Christopher. 'Bukhārī and his *Ṣaḥīḥ*'. *Le Muséon* 123.3–4 (2010): 425–54.

Melchert, Christopher. 'Ibrāhīm al-Nakhaʿī (Kufan, d. 96/714)'. *Arabica* 67 (2020): 60–81.

Melchert, Christopher. 'Whether to Keep Unbelievers Out of Sacred Zones: A Survey of Medieval Islamic Law'. *JSAI* 40 (2013): 177–94.

Mellon Saint-Laurent, Jeanne-Nicole. 'Bones in Bags: Relics in Syriac Hagiography'. In *Syriac Encounters*, edited by Maria Doerfler, Emanuel Fiano and Kyle Smith, 439–54. Leuven: Peeters, 2015.

Memon, Muhammad Umar. *Ibn Taimīya's Struggle Against Popular Religion: With an Annotated Translation of his Kitāb al-Iqtiḍā' aṣ-ṣirāt al-mustaqīm mukhālafat aṣḥāb al-jaḥīm*. The Hague: Mouton, 1976.

Meri, Josef W. *The Cult of Saints among Muslims and Jews in Medieval Syria*. Oxford: Oxford University Press, 2002.

Meri, Josef W. 'Relics of Piety and Power in Islam'. In *Relics and Remains*, edited by Alexandra Walsham, 97–120. *Past & Present* Supplement 5. Oxford: Oxford University Press, 2010.

Mikati, Rana. 'On the Identity of the Syrian *abdāl*'. *BSOAS* 80 (2017): 21–43.
Miller, Patricia Cox. *The Corporeal Imagination: Signifying the Holy in Late Ancient Christianity*. Philadelphia: University of Pennsylvania Press, 2009.
Miller, Patricia Cox. *In the Eye of the Animal: Zoological Imagination in Ancient Christianity*. Philadelphia: University of Pennsylvania Press, 2018.
Milstein, Rachel. 'Futuh-i Haramayn: Sixteenth-Century Illustrations of the Hajj Route'. In *Mamluks and Ottomans: Studies in Honour of Michael Winter*, ed. David J. Wasserstein and Ami Ayalon, 166–94. London: Routledge, 2006.
Mirza, Sarah Z. 'The Peoples' Hadith: Evidence for Popular Tradition on Hadith as Physical Object in the First Centuries of Islam'. *Arabica* 63 (2016): 30–63.
Miskinzoda, Gurdofarid. 'The Story of "Pen and Paper" and its Interpretation in Muslim Literary and Historical Tradition'. In Daftary and Miskinzoda, *Study of Shi'i Islam*, 231–49.
Modarressi, Hossein. *Tradition and Survival: A Bibliographical Survey of Early Shī'ite Literature. Volume One*. Oxford: Oneworld, 2003.
Motzki, Harald. 'Abraham, Hagar and Ishmael at Mecca: A Contribution to the Problem of Dating Muslim Traditions'. In *Books and Written Culture of the Islamic World: Studies Presented to Claude Gilliot on the Occasion of His 75th Birthday*, edited by Andrew Rippin and Roberto Tottoli, 361–84. Leiden: Brill, 2015.
Motzki, Harald. *The Origins of Islamic Jurisprudence: Meccan Fiqh before the Classical Schools*. Translated by Marion H. Katz. Leiden: Brill, 2002.
Motzki, Harald, Nicolet Boekhoff-van der Voort and Sean W. Anthony. *Analysing Muslim Traditions: Studies in Legal, Exegetical and Maghāzī Ḥadīth*. Leiden: Brill, 2010.
Munt, Harry. *The Holy City of Medina: Sacred Space in Early Islamic Arabia*. Cambridge: Cambridge University Press, 2014.
Munt, Harry. '"No Two Religions": Non-Muslims in the Early Islamic Ḥijāz'. *BSOAS* 78 (2015): 249–69.
Munt, Harry. 'What Did Conversion to Islam Mean in Seventh-Century Arabia?' In *Islamisation: Comparative Perspectives from History*, edited by A. C. S. Peacock, 83–101. Edinburgh: Edinburgh University Press, 2017.
Munt, Harry. 'Writing the History of an Arabian Holy City: Ibn Zabāla and the First Local History of Medina'. *Arabica* 59 (2012): 1–34.
Muranyi, Miklos. 'The Emergence of Holy Places in Early Islam: On the Prophet's Track'. *JSAI* 39 (2012): 165–71.
Muranyi, Miklos. 'Ibn Isḥāq's *Kitāb al-Maġāzī* in der *riwāya* von Yūnus b. Bukair. Bemerkungen zur frühen Überlieferungsgeschichte'. *JSAI* 14 (1991): 214–75.

Muranyi, Miklos. 'Visited Places on the Prophet's Track in Mecca and Medina'. *JSAI* 49 (2020): 217–30.

Neis, Rafael Rachel. 'Religious Lives of Image-Things, *Avodah Zarah*, and Rabbis in Late Antique Palestine'. *Archiv für Religionsgeschichte* 17 (2016): 91–121.

Neis, Rafael Rachel. *The Sense of Sight in Rabbinic Culture: Jewish Ways of Seeing in Late Antiquity*. Cambridge: Cambridge University Press, 2013.

Newby, Gordon D. 'Imitating Muhammad in Two Genres: Mimesis and Problems of Genre in Sîrah and Sunnah'. *Medieval Encounters* 3.3 (1997): 266–83.

Newman, Andrew J. *The Formative Period of Twelver Shīʿism: Ḥadīth as Discourse between Qum and Baghdad*. Richmond: Curzon, 2000.

Noth, Albrecht. 'Problems of Differentiation between Muslims and Non-Muslims: Re-Reading the "Ordinances of ʿUmar" (*al-Shurūṭ al-ʿUmariyya*)'. Translated by Mark Muelhaeusler. In *Muslims and Others in Early Islamic Society*, edited by Robert Hoyland, 103–24. Aldershot: Ashgate, 2004.

O'Meara, Simon. *The Kaʿba Orientations: Readings in Islam's Ancient House*. Edinburgh: Edinburgh University Press, 2020.

Papaconstantinou, Arietta. 'The Cult of Saints: A Haven of Continuity in a Changing World?' In *Egypt in the Byzantine World, 300–700*, edited by Roger S. Bagnall, 350–67. Cambridge: Cambridge University Press, 2007.

Papaconstantinou, Arietta (ed.), in collaboration with Muriel Debié and Hugh Kennedy. *Writing 'True Stories': Historians and Hagiographers in the Late Antique and Medieval Near East*. Turnhout, Belgium: Brepols, 2010.

Patel, Youshaa. *The Muslim Difference: Defining the Line between Believers and Unbelievers from Early Islam to the Present*. New Haven: Yale University Press, 2022.

Patrizi, Luca. 'Impronte, ritratti e reliquie di profeti nell'Islam'. In *Sacre impronte e oggetti «non fatti da mano d'uomo» nelle religioni*, edited by Adele Monaci Castagno, 81–94. Alessandria: Edizioni dell'Orso, 2011.

Payne, Richard E. *A State of Mixture: Christians, Zoroastrians, and Iranian Political Culture in Late Antiquity*. Oakland: University of California Press, 2015.

Peers, Glenn. 'Object Relations: Theorizing the Late Antique Viewer'. In Johnson, *Oxford Handbook of Late Antiquity*, 970–93.

Penn, Michael Philip. 'Demons Gone Wild: An Introduction and Translation of the Syriac *Qenneshre Fragment*'. *Orientalia Christiana Periodica* 27 (2013): 367–99.

Penn, Michael Philip. *Envisioning Islam: Syriac Christians and the Early Muslim World*. Philadelphia: University of Pennsylvania Press, 2015.

Penn, Michael Philip. *When Christians First Met Muslims: A Sourcebook of the Earliest Syriac Writings on Islam*. Oakland: University of California Press, 2015.

Pierce, Matthew. *Twelve Infallible Men: The Imams and the Making of Shīʿism*. Cambridge, MA: Harvard University Press, 2016.

Plate, S. Brent. *A History of Religion in 5½ Objects: Bringing the Spiritual to Its Senses*. Boston: Beacon Press, 2014.

Popper, William. *The Cairo Nilometer: Studies in Ibn Taghrî Birdî's Chronicles of Egypt: I*. Berkeley: University of California Press, 1951.

Powers, David S. *Law, Society, and Culture in the Maghrib, 1300–1500*. Cambridge: Cambridge University Press, 2002.

Powers, David S. *Zayd*. Philadelphia: University of Pennsylvania Press, 2014.

Qian, Ailin. 'Delights in Paradise: A Comparative Survey of Heavenly Food and Drink in the Quran'. In Günther and Lawson, *Roads to Paradise*, 1:251–70.

Raby, Julian. 'In Vitro Veritas: Glass Pilgrim Vessels from 7th-Century Jerusalem'. In Johns, *Bayt al-Maqdis*, 113–90.

Raby, Julian and Jeremy Johns (eds). *Bayt al-Maqdis: ʿAbd al-Malik's Jerusalem*. Oxford: Oxford University Press, 1992.

Rāġib, Yūsuf. 'Les premiers monuments funéraires de l'Islam'. *Annales Islamologiques* 9 (1970): 21–36.

Rajani, Kumail. 'Between Qum and Qayrawān: Unearthing Early Shii *ḥadīth* Sources'. *BSOAS* 84.3 (2021): 419–42.

al-Rāshid, Saʿd ʿAbd al-ʿAzīz. *Kitābāt Islāmiyya min Makka al-Mukarrama: Dirāsa wa-taḥqīq*. Riyadh: Maktabat al-Malik Fahd al-Waṭaniyya, 1995.

Reynolds, Gabriel Said. *The Qur'ān and Its Biblical Subtext*. New York: Routledge, 2010.

Robin, Christian Julien. 'Les signes de la prophétie en Arabie à l'époque de Muḥammad (fin du VIe début du VIIe siècle de l'ère chrétienne)'. In *La Raison des signes: Présages, rites, destin dans les sociétés de la Méditerranée ancienne*, edited by Stella Georgoudi, Renée Koch Piettre and Francis Schmidt, 433–76. Leiden: Brill, 2012.

Robinson, Chase. *ʿAbd al-Malik*. Oxford: OneWorld, 2005.

Robinson, Chase. 'The Conquest of Khūzistān: A Historiographical Reassessment'. *BSOAS* 67.1 (2004): 14–39.

Robinson, Chase. *Islamic Historiography*. Cambridge: Cambridge University Press, 2003.

Roggema, Barbara. 'Muslims as Crypto-Idolaters – A Theme in the Christian Portrayal of Islam in the Near East'. In *Christians at the Heart of Islamic Rule: Church Life and Scholarship in ʿAbbasid Iraq*, edited by David Thomas, 3–11. Leiden: Brill, 2003.

Rubenstein, Jeffrey L. 'From Mythic Motifs to Sustained Myth: The Revision of Rabbinic Traditions in Medieval Midrashim'. *HTR* 89.2 (1996): 131–59.

Rubenstein, Jeffrey L. 'Hero, Saint, and Sage: The Life of R. Elazar b. R. Shimon in Pesiqta de Rab Kahana 11'. In *The Faces of Torah: Studies in the Texts and Contexts of Ancient Judaism in Honor of Steven Fraade*, edited by Michal Bar-Asher Siegal, Tzvi Novick and Christine Hayes, 509–28. Göttingen: Vandenhoeck & Ruprecht, 2017.

Rubenstein, Jeffrey L. 'A Rabbinic Translation of Relics'. In *Crossing Boundaries in Early Judaism and Christianity. Ambiguities, Complexities, and Half-Forgotten Adversaries: Essays in Honor of Alan F. Segal*, edited by Kimberly B. Stratton and Andrea Lieber, 314–32. Leiden: Brill, 2016.

Rubin, Uri. 'Between Arabia and the Holy Land: A Mecca–Jerusalem Axis of Sanctity'. *JSAI* 34 (2008): 345–62.

Rubin, Uri. *Between Bible and Qur'ān: The Children of Israel and the Islamic Self Image*. Princeton: Darwin Press, 1999.

Rubin, Uri. *The Eye of the Beholder: The Life of Muḥammad as Viewed by the Early Muslims. A Textual Analysis*. Princeton: Darwin Press, 1995.

Rubin, Uri. 'Islamic Retellings of Biblical History'. In *Adaptations and Innovations: Studies on the Interaction between Jewish and Islamic Thought and Literature from the Early Middle Ages to the Late Twentieth Century, Dedicated to Professor Joel L. Kraemer*, edited by Y. Tzvi Langermann and Josef Stern, 299–313. Paris: Peeters, 2007.

Rubin, Uri. 'The Kaʿba: Aspects of Its Ritual Functions and Position in Pre-Islamic and Early Islamic Times'. *JSAI* 8 (1986): 97–131.

Rubin, Uri. 'The Life of Muḥammad and the Qur'ān: The Case of Muḥammad's Hijra'. *JSAI* 28 (2003): 40–64.

Ruffle, Karen G. 'Presence in Absence: The Formation of Reliquary Shiʿism in Qutb Shahi Hyderabad'. *Material Religion* 13.3 (2017): 329–53.

Rytter, Mikkel. 'The Hair of the Prophet: Relics and Affective Presence of the Absent Beloved among Sufis in Denmark'. *Contemporary Islam* 13 (2019): 49–65.

Sahner, Christian C. 'The First Iconoclasm in Islam: A New History of the Edict of Yazīd II (AH 104/AD 723)'. *Der Islam* 94.1 (2017): 5–56.

al-Salimi, Abdulrahman. *Early Islamic Law in Basra in the 2nd/8th Century:* Aqwāl Qatāda b. Diʿāma as-Sadūsī. Leiden: Brill, 2018.

al-Sarhan, Saud. 'The Saudis as Managers of the Hajj'. In Tagliacozzo and Toorawa, *Hajj*, 196–212.

Satran, David. *Biblical Prophets in Byzantine Palestine: Reassessing the* Lives of the Prophets. Leiden: Brill, 1995.

Savant, Sarah Bowen. *The New Muslims of Post-Conquest Iran: Tradition, Memory and Conversion*. New York: Cambridge University Press, 2013.

Schacht, Joseph. *The Origins of Muhammadan Jurisprudence*. Oxford: Clarendon Press, 1950.

Schadler, Peter. *John of Damascus and Islam: Christian Heresiology and the Intellectual Background to Earliest Christian–Muslim Relations*. Leiden: Brill, 2018.

Schimmel, Annemarie. *And Muhammad is His Messenger: The Veneration of the Prophet in Islamic Piety*. Chapel Hill: University of North Carolina Press, 1985.

Schmidtke, Sabine. 'The Muslim Reception of Biblical Materials: Ibn Qutayba and his *Aʿlām al-Nubuwwa*'. *Islam and Christian–Muslim Relations* 22.3 (2011): 249–74.

Schoeler, Gregor. *The Biography of Muḥammad: Nature and Authenticity*. Translated by Uwe Vagelpohl. Edited by James E. Montgomery. New York: Routledge, 2011.

Schoeler, Gregor. *The Oral and the Written in Early Islam*. Translated by Uwe Vagelpohl. Edited by James E. Montgomery. New York: Routledge, 2006.

Schopen, Gregory. 'Burial "Ad Sanctos" and the Physical Presence of the Buddha in Early Indian Buddhism: A Study in the Archeology of Religions'. *Religion* 17 (1987): 193–225.

Schopen, Gregory. 'Relic'. In *Critical Terms for Religious Studies*, edited by Mark C. Taylor, 256–68. Chicago: University of Chicago Press, 1998.

Schwartz, Seth. *Imperialism and Jewish Society from 200 B.C.E. to 650 C.E.* Princeton: Princeton University Press, 2001.

Shaddel, Mehdy. ''Abd Allāh ibn al-Zubayr and the Mahdī: Between Propaganda and Historical Memory in the Second Civil War'. *BSOAS* 80 (2017): 1–19.

Sharf, Robert H. 'On the Allure of Buddhist Relics'. *Representations* 66 (1999): 75–99.

Sharon, Moshe. 'The "Praises of Jerusalem" as a Source for the Early History of Jerusalem'. *Bibliotheca Orientalis* 49 (1992): 56–67.

Shaw, Wendy M. K. 'Between the Secular and the Sacred: A New Face for the Department of the Holy Relics at the Topkapı Palace Museum'. *Material Religion* 6.1 (2010): 129–31.

Shoemaker, Stephen J. 'Christmas in the Qur'ān: The Qur'ānic Account of Jesus' Nativity and Palestinian Local Tradition'. *JSAI* 28 (2003): 11–39.

Shoemaker, Stephen J. *The Death of a Prophet: The End of Muhammad's Life and the Beginnings of Islam* (Philadelphia: University of Pennsylvania Press, 2012.

Shoshan, Boaz. 'High Culture and Popular Culture in Medieval Islam'. *Studia Islamica* 73 (1991): 67–107.

Siegal, Michal Bar-Asher. *Early Christian Monastic Literature and the Babylonian Talmud*. New York: Cambridge University Press, 2013.

Silverstein, Adam. 'Who are the *Aṣḥāb al-Ukhdūd*? Q 85:4–10 in Near Eastern Context'. *Der Islam* 96.2 (2019): 281–323.

Sizgorich, Thomas. '"Become Infidels or We Will Throw You Into the Fire": The Martyrs of Najran in Early Muslim Historiography, Hagiography and Qur'anic Exegesis'. In Papaconstantinou, *Writing 'True Stories': Historians and Hagiographers in the Late Antique and Medieval Near East*, 125–47.

Sizgorich, Thomas. *Violence and Belief in Late Antiquity: Militant Devotion in Christianity and Islam*. Philadelphia: University of Pennsylvania Press, 2009.

Sourdel, Dominique. 'Un pamphlet musulman anonyme d'époque 'Abbāside contre les Chrétiens'. *Revue des études islamiques* 34 (1966): 1–33.

Stafford, Samuel A. 'Constructing Muḥammad's Legitimacy: Arabic Literary Biography and the Jewish Pedigree of the Companion 'Abd Allāh b. Salām (d. 43/633)'. *JSAI* 47 (2019): 133–86.

Stafford, Samuel A. 'The Conversions of 'Abdallāh ibn Salām (d. 43/633): A Legendary Moment in the Biography of Muḥammad's Jewish Companion'. *BSOAS* 84.2 (2021): 237–61.

Stewart, Devin J. 'An Eleventh-Century Justification of the Authority of Twelver Shiite Jurists'. In *Islamic Cultures, Islamic Contexts: Essays in Honor of Professor Patricia Crone*, edited by Behnam Sadeghi, Asad Q. Ahmed, Adam Silverstein and Robert G. Hoyland, 468–97. Leiden: Brill, 2014.

Strack, H. L. and Günter Stemberger. *Introduction to the Talmud and Midrash*. Edited and translated by Markus Bockmuehl. 2nd ed. Minneapolis: Fortress Press, 1996.

Su, I-Wen. 'The Early Shīʿī Traditionists' Perspective on the Rightly Guided Caliphs'. *JAOS* 141 (2021): 27–47.

Szilágyi, Krisztina. 'After the Prophet's Death: Christian-Muslim Polemic and the Literary Images of Muhammad'. PhD diss., Princeton University, 2014.

Szilágyi, Krisztina. 'A Prophet Like Jesus? Christians and Muslims Debating Muḥammad's Death'. *JSAI* 36 (2009): 131–71.

Tagliacozzo, Eric and Shawkat M. Toorawa (eds). *The Hajj: Pilgrimage in Islam*. New York: Cambridge University Press, 2016.

Talmon-Heller, Daniella. 'Historiography in the Service of the *Muftī*: Ibn Taymiyya on the Origins and Fallacies of *Ziyāra*'. *ILS* 26 (2019): 227–51.

Talmon-Heller, Daniella. *Islamic Piety in Medieval Syria: Mosques, Cemeteries and Sermons under the Zangids and Ayyūbids (1146–1260)*. Leiden: Brill, 2007.

Talmon-Heller, Daniella. *Sacred Place and Sacred Time in the Medieval Islamic Middle East: A Historical Perspective*. Edinburgh: Edinburgh University Press, 2020.

Tannous, Jack. *The Making of the Medieval Middle East: Religion, Society, and Simple Believers*. Princeton: Princeton University Press, 2018.

Taylor, Christopher S. *In the Vicinity of the Righteous: Ziyāra and the Veneration of Muslim Saints in Late Medieval Egypt*. Leiden: Brill, 1999.

Taylor, Christopher S. 'Reevaluating the Shi'i Role in the Development of Monumental Islamic Funerary Architecture: The Case of Egypt'. *Muqarnas* 9 (1992): 1–10.

Taylor, David G. K. 'The Syriac Baptism of St John: A Christian Ritual of Protection for Muslim Children'. In *The Late Antique World of Early Islam: Muslims among Christians and Jews in the East Mediterranean*, edited by Robert G. Hoyland, 437–59. Princeton: Darwin Press, 2015.

Tesei, Tommaso. 'The *barzakh* and the Intermediate State of the Dead in the Quran'. In *Locating Hell in Islamic Traditions*, edited by Christian Lange, 31–55. Leiden: Brill, 2016.

Thibon, Jean-Jacques. 'Transmission du hadith et modèle prophétique chez les premiers soufis'. *Archives de sciences sociales des religions* 178 (2017): 71–87.

Thomas, David and Barbara Roggema (eds). *Christian–Muslim Relations: A Bibliographic History. Volume 1 (600–900)*. Leiden: Brill, 2009.

Tillier, Matthew. "Abd al-Malik, Muḥammad et le Jugement dernier: le dôme du Rocher comme expression d'une orthodoxie islamique'. In *Les vivants et les morts dans les sociétés médiévales: Actes du XLVIIIe Congrès de la SHMESP (Jérusalem, 2017)*, 341–65. Paris: Éditions de la Sorbonne, 2018.

Tillier, Matthew. 'Deux papyrus judiciaires de Fusṭāṭ (IIe/VIIIe siècle)'. *Chronique d'Égypte* 89, fasc. 178 (2014): 412–45.

Tillier, Mathieu and Naïm Vanthieghem, 'Recording Debts in Sufyānid Fusṭāṭ: A Reexamination of the Procedures and Calendar in Use in the First/Seventh Century'. In *Geneses: A Comparative Study of the Historiographies of the Rise of Christianity, Rabbinic Judaism, and Islam*, ed. John Tolan, 148–88. London: Routledge, 2019.

Tokatly, Vardit. 'The *A'lām al-ḥadīth* of al-Khaṭṭābī: A Commentary on al-Bukhārī's *Ṣaḥīḥ* or a Polemical Treatise?' *Studia Islamica* 92 (2001): 53–91.

Urbach, Ephraim E. *The Sages: Their Concepts and Beliefs*. Translated by Israel Abrahams. Jerusalem: Magnes Press, 1979.

van Bekkum, Wout Jacques. 'Four Kingdoms Will Rule: Echoes of Apocalypticism and Political Reality in Late Antiquity and Medieval Judaism'. In *Endzeiten: Eschatologie in den monotheistischen Weltreligionen*, edited by Wolfram Brandes and Felicitas Schmieder, 101–18. Berlin: Walter de Gruyter, 2008.

van Ess, Josef. "Abd al-Malik and the Dome of the Rock: An Analysis of Some Texts'. In Raby and Johns, *Bayt al-Maqdis*, 89–103.

van Ess, Josef. *Kleine Schriften*. Edited by Hinrich Biesterfeldt. 3 vols. Leiden: Brill, 2018.

van Ess, Josef. *Theology and Society in the Second and Third Centuries of the Hijra: A History of Religious Thought in Early Islam*. Translated by John O'Kane and Gwendolin Goldbloom. 4 vols. Leiden: Brill, 2017–19.

van Reenen, Daan. 'The *Bilderverbot*, a new survey'. *Der Islam* 67.1 (1990): 27–77.

von Grunebaum, Gustave E. *Islam and Medieval Hellenism: Social and Cultural Perspectives*. London: Variorum Reprints, 1976.

Vilozny, Roy. 'Pre-Būyid *Ḥadīth* Literature: The Case of al-Barqī from Qumm (d. 274/888 or 280/894) in Twelve Sections'. In Daftary and Miskinzoda, *Study of Shiʿi Islam*, 203–30.

Waardenburg, Jacques. 'Official and Popular Religion in Islam'. *Social Compass* 25 (1978): 315–41.

Waldman, Marilyn. *Prophecy and Power: Muhammad and the Qur'an in the Light of Comparison*. Sheffield: Equinox, 2012.

Warner, George. 'One Thousand *Ḥijaj*: Ritualization and the Margins of the Law in Early Twelver Shiʿi *Ziyāra* Literature'. *JAOS* 142.2 (2022): 415–34.

Webb, Peter. *Imagining the Arabs: Arab Identity and the Rise of Islam*. Edinburgh: Edinburgh University Press, 2016.

Weiss, Bernard. *The Spirit of Islamic Law*. Athens: University of Georgia Press, 1998.

Weltecke, Dorothea. 'Multireligiöse Loca Sancta und die mächtigen Heiligen der Christen'. *Der Islam* 88.1 (2012): 73–95.

Wheeler, Brannon M. *Mecca and Eden: Ritual, Relics, and Territory in Islam*. Chicago: University of Chicago Press, 2006.

Wheeler, Brannon M. *Prophets in the Quran: An Introduction to the Quran and Muslim Exegesis*. London: Continuum, 2002.

Wheeler, Brannon M. '"This is the Torah that God Sent Down to Moses": Some Early Islamic Views of the Qurʾān and Other Revealed Books'. *Graeco-Arabica* 7–8 (1999–2000): 571–604.

Wilkinson, John. *Jerusalem Pilgrims before the Crusades*. Jerusalem: Ariel, 1977.

Wilkinson, John C. 'Ibāḍī Ḥadīth: An Essay on Normalization'. *Der Islam* 62.2 (1985): 231–59.

Williams, Wesley. 'A Body Unlike Bodies: Transcendent Anthropomorphism in Ancient Semitic Tradition and Early Islam'. *JAOS* 129 (2009): 19–44.

Wills, Lawrence M. *Not God's People: Insiders and Outsiders in the Biblical World*. Lanham: Rowman & Littlefield, 2008.

Wiśniewski, Robert. *The Beginnings of the Cult of Relics*. Oxford: Oxford University Press, 2019.

Witkam, Jan Just. 'Mecca and Medina Revisited: The Manuscripts of the *Dalāʾil al-Khayrāt* by al-Ǧazūlī and Their Ornamental Addition'. *Journal of Islamic Manuscripts* 12 (2021): 396–432.

Wortley, John. 'Iconoclasm and Leipsanoclasm: Leo III, Constantine V and the Relics'. *Byzantinische Forschungen* 8 (1982): 253–79.

Wymann-Landgraf, Umar F. Abd-Allah. *Mālik and Medina: Islamic Legal Reasoning in the Formative Period*. Leiden: Brill, 2013.

Yarbrough, Luke. 'Origins of the *Ghiyār*'. *JAOS* 134.1 (2014): 113–21.

Yarbrough, Luke. 'Upholding God's Rule: Early Muslim Juristic Opposition to the State Employment of Non-Muslims'. *ILS* 19 (2012): 11–85.

Yasin, Ann Marie. 'Sacred Installations: The Material Conditions of Relic Collections in Late Antique Churches'. In Hahn and Klein, *Saints and Sacred Matter*, 133–51.

Yasin, Ann Marie. *Saints and Church Spaces in the Late Antique Mediterranean: Architecture, Cult, and Community*. Cambridge: Cambridge University Press, 2009.

Yasin, Ann Marie. 'Sight Lines of Sanctity at Late Antique Martyria'. In *Architecture of the Sacred: Space, Ritual, and Experience from Classical Greece to Byzantium*, edited by Bonna D. Wescoat and Robert G. Ousterhout, 248–80. Cambridge: Cambridge University Press, 2012.

Zadeh, Travis. 'The Early Hajj: Seventh–Eighth Centuries CE'. In Tagliacozzo and Toorawa, *Hajj*, 42–64.

Zadeh, Travis. 'An Ingestible Scripture: Qur'ānic Erasure and the Limits of "Popular" Religion'. In *Material Culture and Asian Religions: Text, Image, Object*, edited by Benjamin J. Fleming and Richard D. Mann, 97–119. New York and London: Routledge, 2014.

Zafer, Hamza Mahmood. 'Transformation in Early Muslim Prophetology: From Typology to Teleology in Narratives of Jonah and the Ninevites'. *Journal of Qur'anic Studies* 22.2 (2020): 1–32.

Zaman, Muhammad Qasim. *Religion and Politics Under the Early 'Abbāsids: The Emergence of the Proto-Sunnī Elite* Leiden: Brill, 1997.

Zellentin, Holger M. '*Aḥbār* and *Ruhbān*: Religious Leaders in the Qur'ān in Dialogue with Christian and Rabbinic Literature'. In *Qur'ānic Studies Today*, edited by Angelika Neuwirth and Michael A. Sells, 262–93. London: Routledge, 2016.

Zomeño, Amalia. 'The Stories in the Fatwas and the Fatwas in History'. In *Narratives of Truth in Islamic Law*, edited by Baudouin Dupret, Barbara Drieskens and Annelies Moors, 25–49. London: I. B. Tauris, 2008.

Zwemer, Samuel M. 'Hairs of the Prophet'. In *Ignace Goldziher Memorial Volume*, 2 vols, edited by Samuel Löwinger and Joseph Somogyi, 1:48–54. Budapest: Globus, 1948.

INDEX

Abān b. ʿUthmān b. ʿAffān, 184–6, 188, 190

al-ʿAbbās b. ʿAbd al-Muṭṭalib, 125, 188

ʿAbbāsids, 4, 16n, 64–5, 139, 163n, 167, 187–90, 195, 202, 223–4, 226–7

ʿAbd Allāh b. Salām, 48, 53

ʿAbd Allāh b. al-Thāmir, 99, 102–4

ʿAbd al-Malik b. Marwān, 72–6, 177n

Abraham, 47–9, 54–6, 58, 65, 67–8, 72, 75, 78, 87, 100, 107, 109, 110; *see also* Maqām Ibrāhīm

Abū al-ʿĀliya Rufayʿ b. Mihrān, 85–7, 90, 93, 94, 98

Abū Ayyūb al-Anṣārī, 166–70, 191

Abū Bakr b. ʿAbd Allāh b. Muḥammad b. Abī Sabra, 184

Abū Ghassān al-Kinānī, 41, 183, 184, 186, 187, 188

Abū Khalda Khālid b. Dīnār, 85, 94n

Abū Muslim, 224

Abū Qubays (mountain), 79

Abū ʿUbayda b. al-Jarrāḥ, 25

Abū Usāma Ḥammād b. Usāma, 197

ʿĀʾisha bt. Abī Bakr, 37, 39, 41, 110–11, 138, 147n, 175, 223

ʿAlī b. Abī Ṭālib, 29, 71, 125, 130, 146, 155–6, 161, 175n, 208

ʿAlī b. al-Ḥusayn Zayn al-ʿĀbidīn, 156

Anas b. Mālik, 62, 89–90, 98, 137n, 138n, 222, 224–5

Anastasius of Sinai, 31, 32

angels, 27n, 136, 144, 145, 154, 155, 157, 159

apocalypticism, 58, 73, 93–6, 127, 128, 142

  Day of Judgement, 73, 79, 118, 130, 136, 145, 149, 151, 155, 157

  Day of Resurrection, 29, 133–4, 149, 150, 157–8

Arab tribes
'Abs, 121–3
Khuzā'a, 66
Mudlij, 53, 55
Quraysh, 54, 107, 108–9, 110, 185
Zurayq, 99
Arabia and Arabian Peninsula, 24–6, 34–5, 100, 102, 150
'Arafat (mountain), 174, 177
archaeological evidence, 27, 37, 42–5; *see also* inscriptions
ascension
of God, 67–71
of prophets and holy people, 66–7, 74–6, 130–2, 134–5, 137, 140, 144–5, 160–1
asceticism, 170, 172, 207
'Aṭā' b. Abī Rabāḥ, 61, 136n, 178, 199, 205–6, 208
āthār
definitions and meanings, 7, 15–16, 28, 160, 173, 200
'following the Prophet's *āthār*', 172–6, 215–16
objects, 49, 55, 58, 78, 165, 192, 195
sites, 160–1, 165, 169, 174–5, 178, 181, 183n, 189–91, 195–6, 200–5, 211, 213, 218
al-Awzā'ī, 208
al-Azraqī, 179–80

Banū Ẓafar Mosque, 194–5
Baṣra, 85, 116–17, 138–9, 200, 205, 210
biblical texts, 29, 34, 57–9, 88n, 93–4, 100, 126n
Black Stone (al-Ḥajar al-Aswad) *see* Ka'ba
Brown, Peter, 30, 143, 144
al-Bukhārī, 16–18, 19, 162, 178, 180, 211, 212, 215–17, 224–6
Byzantium, Byzantines, 14, 31–2, 48, 50, 84

Christians, Christianity, 7, 8, 12, 14, 30, 40, 50–1, 65, 78, 118–19, 124, 134, 141–9, 170, 190, 219, 227
Christian texts, 15, 31–4, 49, 52, 59–60, 80–4, 86, 88–9, 91, 93, 96–8, 143–6
churches and shrines, 43–4, 111–12, 113, 119–20, 190
in Islamic texts, 3, 23–9, 34–9, 47–60, 95, 102–5, 203, 215
Companions of the Prophet (*aṣḥāb*), 1, 2–3, 25, 38, 42, 62, 67, 89, 123, 126, 127, 129–30, 152, 154, 166–9, 171–2, 175, 176, 177, 184, 185, 191, 193–4, 196, 197, 198–9, 222, 225, 227
conquests, Islamic, 28–9, 57–9, 80–6, 90, 93–6, 99, 114–17, 127, 177, 209

Damascus, 87n, 97, 111–13, 119–20, 135n, 137, 139, 220
Daniel (prophet), 80–96, 97, 98–9, 103, 104, 113–17
Dome of the Rock, 43, 72–5, 111, 150, 205n; *see also* Foundation Stone
du'ā' (invocation) *see* prayer

Egypt, 3, 96, 97, 136, 137
El-Hibri, Tayeb, 16

faḍā'il traditions, 137, 172, 174
al-Fākihī, 47–8, 65, 189, 192
al-Farazdaq, 224n
fitna, 94–5, 192, 194
Flood, Finbarr Barry, 182, 187
footprints *see* relics
Foundation Stone *see* Jerusalem

graves and tombs, 11
  prohibitions regarding, 37–8, 42, 82, 98
  as sources of sanctity, 96, 105–20, 144
  veneration of, 5–8, 12–14, 25–46, 82, 99, 111, 117, 135–7, 168, 170–2, 196–8
  visitation of *see* pilgrimage

ḥadīth, 8, 9, 11, 15–16
  on the Ka'ba, 110–11
  on Prophet Muḥammad's afterlife, 151–62
  on Prophet Muḥammad's prayer places, 177–84, 187, 189, 194–5
  on prophets' bodies, 1–6, 87–8, 92, 125, 130–3, 136–9, 147, 152
  regionalism of circulation, 135–41, 158–61, 196–206
  on veneration of tombs and relics, 18, 25–6, 28–9, 35–9, 42, 200–1
  'Three Mosques' *ḥadīth*, 206, 210–12
ḥadīth scholars and transmitters, 1, 2, 4, 6, 16–19, 24n, 36, 39, 40, 60–5, 73, 85, 92, 101, 105, 108, 110, 112–13, 116–17, 130, 137–8, 140, 147, 157–8, 163–4, 171–4, 178, 181, 184–92, 194, 196–8, 200, 202, 204–8, 211–17, 220, 222–3, 225, 227
ḥajj *see* pilgrimage
al-Ḥajjāj b. Yūsuf, 174
Hārūn al-Rashīd, 4, 188, 189–90
al-Ḥasan b. al-Ḥasan b. 'Alī b. Abī Ṭālib, 155–6
Ḥijāz, 24, 25, 38, 74, 96, 100, 102, 111, 121, 139–40, 161n, 169–202, 218
Ḥijr *see* Ka'ba
Hishām b. 'Abd al-Malik, 44
Hishām b. 'Urwa, 40n, 41n, 162n, 171
Holy Spirit (*al-rūḥ al-qudus*), 87–8
Hūd (prophet), 100–1, 106
al-Ḥudaybiyya, 191–3, 200, 203, 204, 206
al-Ḥusayn b. 'Alī b. Abī Ṭālib, 132, 138, 145, 161

Ibāḍī texts, 6, 67–8, 71–2
Ibn 'Abbās, 'Abd Allāh, 131, 154
Ibn Abī Fudayk, Muḥammad b. Ismā'īl, 164, 188, 198
Ibn Abī Yaḥyā, Ibrāhīm b. Muḥammad, 186, 200
Ibn 'Awn, 'Abd Allāh, 158, 191–2, 194, 200n
Ibn Baṭṭāl, 212–13
Ibn Ḥabīb, 'Abd al-Malik, 214
Ibn al-Ḥanafiyya, Muḥammad, 71–2, 75, 130
Ibn Ḥanbal, Aḥmad, 19, 61n, 214–15
Ibn Isḥāq, Muḥammad, 103, 109, 114, 126, 168n, 181
Ibn Jubayr, 65n
Ibn Jurayj, 24n, 178, 179, 192n, 200, 207, 209n
Ibn al-Kalbī, 99, 101
Ibn Mas'ūd, 'Abd Allāh, 67–8, 72, 154n

Ibn al-Musayyab, Saʿīd, 130, 133, 134–5, 147, 153–4, 164, 193, 194, 199–200, 207–8
Ibn Saʿd, Muḥammad, 127, 224
Ibn Sīrīn, Muḥammad, 200–1
Ibn Taymiyya, 82
Ibn ʿUmar, ʿAbd Allāh, 63, 68, 72, 170–9, 181–2, 184, 186, 189, 190, 191, 194, 196–9, 203, 205, 215, 216
Ibn Waḍḍāḥ, 192, 213
Ibn Zabāla, Muḥammad b. al-Ḥasan, 42, 163n, 186, 188, 195n
Ibn al-Zubayr, ʿAbd Allāh, 63, 74, 107–11, 168
iconoclasm, 5, 8, 31–2, 45, 46, 82, 98, 168, 194–5, 218–19
identity, 3, 4–11, 12n, 20, 23, 26–7, 31–6, 45–6, 51, 59, 63–5, 100, 202, 215
innovations (*bidaʿ*), 7, 192, 194, 218, 219
inscriptions
  in literary texts, 96–7, 99, 101–3, 112–13
  in material record, 119–20, 143, 150, 188
intercession
  of Christian and Jewish holy people, 148
  of Prophet Muḥammad, 124, 134, 148–62, 218
inventio (relic discovery), 52, 82–3, 96–99, 104, 105, 111–12, 119
Iraq, 85, 89–90, 118, 129n, 155, 158–61, 171, 198, 200–1, 204–6
Ishmael, 47, 56n, 99–100, 106–11, 145
isnād (chain of transmission), 10n, 39–42, 85, 89, 103, 108, 110, 112, 117, 129–32, 135–9, 157–60, 164, 167, 172–3, 184, 186, 188–200, 205, 213–14, 223

Jacob of Edessa, 33, 34
Jaʿfar al-Ṣādiq, 88, 131–2, 133, 134–5, 137, 147n, 159–61, 180, 199, 201, 214, 222
al-Jazūlī, Muḥammad b. Sulaymān, 221
Jerusalem, 43, 70–1, 72, 74–6, 89, 111, 150, 182, 205–14
  Foundation Stone, 67–76
  pilgrimage to, 74–5, 205–14
  Temple Mount, 67–8, 70–4
Jesus, 15, 27, 29, 32n, 43, 67, 89, 95, 103–4, 113, 123, 127
Jews, Judaism, 12, 23–31, 34–7, 39, 42, 46, 47–8, 50–60, 67–73, 76, 80, 82, 89, 92, 93, 95, 99, 104, 119, 124, 134, 141, 170, 203–4, 215, 219, 227
  rabbinic texts, 8–9, 30, 69–70, 86–7, 88, 91, 141, 144–5
  see also ʿAbd Allāh b. Salām; Kaʿb al-Aḥbār; Jerusalem
John the Baptist (Yaḥyā b. Zakariyyā), 111–13, 119–20

Kaʿb al-Aḥbār, 70–1, 71n, 73, 85, 93, 94, 103–4, 106, 136
Kaʿba, 41, 47, 64, 74–5, 106–11, 113, 117, 177–81
  Black Stone, 60, 79, 106
  Ḥaṭīm, 109

Ḥijr, 107–11, 145
Prophet Muḥammad's prayer space inside, 177–81, 187
Kathisma Church, 43–4
Kedar, 99–100
Khalek, Nancy, 14, 113
Khālid b. Sinān, 121–3
al-Khaṭṭābī, 211–12
al-Khayzurān, 188
Kūfa, 2, 85, 116–17, 118, 132n, 135, 137, 139, 145n, 187, 200, 210

late antiquity, late ancient studies, 6, 7, 8–9, 10, 12, 29n, 30–4, 48, 49–52, 60, 63n, 67, 77, 78, 82–91, 96–9, 111, 113, 116, 119–20, 124, 133, 140–8, 153, 169–70, 190, 208, 227
Layth b. Abī Sulaym, 61, 63

al-Mahdī (caliph), 64, 188, 224n, 226–7
Mālik b. Anas, 171, 173, 189, 210, 213, 214
al-Manṣūr, 16n, 163n, 187, 188, 223–4
Maqām Ibrāhīm, 47–67, 75–9, 80–1, 106, 168, 196, 202, 218, 226–7
Māriyya the Copt, 185; *see also* Mashrabat Umm Ibrāhīm
martyrs, martyrdom, 6, 15, 31, 50, 83, 88–9, 91, 96–7, 99, 102–4, 142–3, 152, 189, 201
of Uḥud, 5, 6, 184–5, 213–14
al-Maʿrūr b. Suwayd al-Asadī, 202–3, 204n
Marwān b. al-Ḥakam, 166–8, 169, 191
mashāhid (sites, shrines), 184–5, 187, 189, 201, 211
Mashrabat Umm Ibrāhīm, 184–5, 201
Mecca, 1–5, 24, 47–79, 105–11, 139, 145, 150, 157, 173–89, 206–12, 219
conquest of, 177, 209
Sacred Mosque (al-Masjid al-Ḥarām), 24, 206, 207, 211
Medina, 24, 55, 99–100, 135, 138–40, 157
pilgrimage to, 159–60, 171, 204–15
sacred sites in, 173–7, 181–204, 213–14
see also Prophet's Mosque
al-Minhāl b. ʿAmr, 154n, 223n
Moses, 28, 87, 97, 123, 126–7, 133, 136–7, 139, 145n, 147
Mount Sinai, 126, 205, 206
Muʿāwiya b. Abī Sufyān, 97, 118
Muḥammad al-Bāqir, 151, 208, 222
Muḥammad, the Prophet
birthplace of, 188, 189, 219
body of, 1–6, 16–19, 54–7, 78, 123–41, 146–9, 152–3, 162–5
death of, 1–6, 24–6, 28, 35, 37–9, 74–6, 123–9, 151–2
intercession by, 124, 134, 148–62, 218
places of prayer, 169–70, 173–95, 203–4, 212–14, 216, 218
relics of, 16–19, 42, 78, 198–200, 214–15, 217, 220–7
tomb of, 37–42, 124, 133–40, 145, 148–9, 153–72, 187, 191, 196–8, 215, 217, 218
Mujāhid b. Jabr, 49n, 60–1, 63, 79, 154n, 174
Munt, Harry, 38–9, 182
Muṣʿab b. ʿAbd Allāh al-Zubayrī, 173, 174, 199n

mushrikūn (associaters, polytheists, pagans), 25n, 35
al-Mutawakkil, 16n, 187

Nāfiʿ (client of Ibn ʿUmar), 173, 175, 177, 180n, 191, 193, 196
Najrān, 25, 102–4
North Africa (Ifrīqiyya), 96, 101
Nuʿaym b. Ḥammād, 94–5

paradise, 3, 67–71, 73, 74–6, 92, 124, 129–40, 142–8, 153, 155, 160–1, 164–5
patronage
  of buildings, 38–42, 44–5, 72, 74–6, 105–13, 176–91, 195, 215
  of scholars, 73n, 184–6, 189–90
pilgrimage
  Christian and Jewish sites and practices, 12, 30, 40, 43–5, 67, 78, 84, 118–20
  disputes about, 6, 26, 42, 74–5, 113, 117, 153–62, 168–71, 191–217
  to Dome of the Rock, 72, 74–5
  ḥajj, 48–9, 63, 64, 74–5, 174, 177–8, 183–5, 188, 189, 202, 206, 207, 208
  to 'places where the Prophet prayed', 172–217
  to tombs, 6, 14, 26, 40–2, 135–40, 153–62, 168, 170–2, 196–8
  ʿumra, 178, 206
  ziyāra, 117, 140, 206
'popular' practice, 7, 8, 42, 44, 62–3, 65, 140–1, 170, 189
prayer
  duʿā', 65, 149, 156, 198, 199, 219
  ṣalāt, 64, 177–81, 202–4, 182, 209
  reaching Prophet Muḥammad, 87, 152–62
  at tombs and relics, 38, 41–2, 61–5, 111, 120, 153–62, 166–219
Prophet's Mosque
  construction by Umayyads and ʿAbbāsids, 38–9, 41–2, 111, 162–4, 182–3, 187, 202
  minbar, 42, 198–200, 214–15, 217, 221, 227
  pilgrimage to, 206–7, 210–11
  Prophet Muḥammad's tomb, 38–42, 162–72, 187, 196–8

al-Qāḍī al-Nuʿmān, 201
Qatāda b. Diʿāma, 61–3, 194n
qibla, 41, 42, 49, 72, 75, 78, 196, 221
qiyāfa (physiognomy), 53–7, 58, 65–6
Qubā', 176–7, 181, 184–5, 201, 206, 213–14
Qur'ān, 24, 58, 63, 67–8, 73, 85, 92, 93, 101–3, 126n, 127, 185
  on Christians and Jews, 27, 119
  on intercession, 149
  on Maqām Ibrāhīm, 48, 61–2
  on martyrs, 142–3, 152
  on Prophet Muḥammad's mortality, 127–8
  on relics and tombs, 28
quṣṣāṣ (storytellers), 38n, 151, 154

relics
  contact relics, 18–19, 29, 31, 33, 40–1, 43, 44, 51, 64–5, 194–5, 198–200, 214–15, 220–7
  dust, 29, 33, 40–1

footprints, 29, 67–9, 75–8; *see also* Maqām Ibrāhīm
fragrance, 60, 72, 125, 146–7
liquids, 18–19, 31, 33, 43–4, 51, 64–5, 78
stones, 43–4, 47–79, 106, 181, 194–5; *see also* Maqām Ibrāhīm; Dome of the Rock
translation/transfer *see translatio*
see also āthār
rituals, ritualisation
and Islamic identity, 5–8, 17, 23, 36, 45–6, 51, 169, 202, 215, 219
Prophet Muḥammad's model, 17–18, 172–8, 180
at sites associated with Prophet Muḥammad, 173–81, 184–5, 189–217
supererogatory, 204, 209–10
at tombs, 28, 42–3, 117, 147–8, 159, 166–9, 170–1, 185, 189, 196–8, 213–15
with relics, 5–8, 18–19, 60–5, 72, 220–7
rukhṣa (concession), 207–10
Ruṣāfa, 43, 44–5, 101

Saḥnūn b. Saʿīd al-Tanūkhī, 210
ṣalāt (ritual prayer) *see* prayer
Ṣāliḥ b. Kaysān, 39
senses, sensory
smell, 60, 72, 125, 146, 147n, 176, 181
taste, 18–19, 40, 43–4, 64–5
touch, 5, 18–19, 42, 51, 58, 60–5, 119–20, 166, 168, 196–202, 214–15, 218–21, 226–7
al-Shāfiʿī, Muḥammad b. Idrīs, 210
al-Shaybānī, Muḥammad b. al-Ḥasan, 171
Shīʿa, 7–8, 118, 134, 135n, 140, 141, 148, 202
imams, 11, 88, 138, 161, 222
Ismāʿīlī texts, 201
Twelver/Imāmī texts, 29, 65–6, 71–2, 88, 130, 131–3, 134, 137–8, 145, 149, 151–2, 159–61, 167, 180, 199, 201, 214, 222
Zaydī texts, 130–1, 135, 139
Shoemaker, Stephen, 45, 129
sīra-maghāzī traditions, 54–7, 66n, 99, 103–5, 109, 124–9, 181, 186, 190, 209
al-Suddī, Ismāʿīl b. ʿAbd al-Raḥmān, 131–2n
al-Suddī, Muḥammad b. Marwān, 157, 161
Sufyān al-Thawrī, 130n, 154n, 156n, 200n, 204–5
Sufyān b. ʿUyayna, 2, 4, 35n, 155n, 205
Sulaymān b. ʿAbd al-Malik, 184–6, 187, 190
Sulaymān al-Aʿmash, 204n
sunna, 17, 173, 213, 223, 224
Sunnīs, 8, 16, 130, 134, 135n, 138–41, 148–9, 152, 158–61, 167, 171, 173, 191, 204–5, 215, 222
al-Sūs, 80, 84, 86, 95–6, 113–17
Syria, 28–9, 43–5, 71–2, 74–5, 87n, 96, 111–13, 118–20, 129n, 135, 137, 164–5, 208

Syriac sources
Cave of Treasures, 89
Disputation between a Muslim and a Monk of Bēt Ḥālē, 31, 32
Jacob of Edessa, 33, 34
Khūzistān Chronicle, 80–2, 84
Life of Peter the Iberian, 89
Life of Symeon Stylites, 146–7
Lives of the Prophets, 84n
Syriac Common Source, 223–4n
Szilágyi, Krisztina, 87n, 125n, 129, 132n, 163

al-Ṭabarī, ʿAlī b. Rabban, 57–9, 60, 94
al-Ṭabarī, Muḥammad b. Jarīr, 95, 98
Ṭāriq b. ʿAbd al-Raḥmān, 193
Ṭāwūs b. Kaysān, 61, 172, 206, 208
Thābit b. Aslam al-Bunānī, 103n, 138n, 139n, 222
Theophanes the Confessor, 31, 32, 223–4
Theophilus of Edessa, 223–4n
translatio (relic movement), 49–50, 52, 59, 81–2, 89, 114, 116–17
Tustar, 85–6, 90, 93, 96

ʿUbayd Allāh b. ʿAbd Allāh b. ʿUmar, 175
ʿUbayd Allāh b. ʿUmar b. Ḥafṣ, 171, 196
Uḥud, 5, 6, 184–5, 213, 214
ʿUmar b. ʿAbd al-ʿAzīz, 25, 38, 39n, 40n, 41, 42, 145, 162–5, 182–3, 184n, 187
ʿUmar b. al-Khaṭṭāb, 28–9, 85, 90, 92, 93, 98, 102–4, 114, 126–7, 128–9, 162–4, 170, 176, 191–2, 193–4, 202–5, 207, 212, 215
Umayyad Mosque (Damascus), 97, 111–13, 119–20
Umayyads, 4n, 38–42, 72–6, 107, 111–13, 118, 162–5, 167–8, 179, 182–7, 202, 224n
Umm Salama, 16, 18
ʿUrwa b. al-Zubayr, 40–1, 73–4, 163, 171
ʿUthmān b. ʿAffān, 127, 175, 185

Wakīʿ b. al-Jarrāḥ, 1–5, 205, 214
al-Walīd b. ʿAbd al-Malik, 38, 40n, 72, 111–13, 162, 179, 180, 182–4, 187
al-Wāqidī, 184, 189–90, 198n
Wheeler, Brannon, 77–8

Yaḥyā b. al-Ḥasan al-ʿAqīqī, 167n, 195n
Yemen, 96, 101–3

Zayn al-ʿĀbidīn *see* ʿAlī b. al-Ḥusayn Zayn al-ʿĀbidīn
ziyāra (visitation) *see* pilgrimage
al-Zubayr b. Bakkār, 88n, 184, 195n
al-Zuhrī, Ibn Shihāb, 24n, 37n, 129n, 223n